the next digital scholar

PRAISE FOR *THE NEXT DIGITAL SCHOLAR*

"This is a massively useful collection, including voices of English teachers, librarians, writing program and writing project directors, and English education faculty. Together, they synthesize educator-created professional standards with the Common Core to discuss practical ways of aligning the Common Core with good teaching. The *Next Digital Scholar* is the very next book I will recommend to colleagues and advanced methods students."
—Ken Lindblom, Director, English Teacher Education, Stony Brook University, and Past Editor, *English Journal* (2008–2013)

"*The Next Digital Scholar* is, indeed, a fresh and much needed approach to teaching with the CCSS: smart, practical, balanced, and well contextualized, presenting the best thinking and teaching practice of teachers, librarians, and administrators, K–college."
—Anne Herrington, Distinguished Professor of English Emerita, University of Massachusetts Amherst

"Every teacher of writing or ELA should use this book—with colleagues! It parses complexities of the CCSS and maps 21st-century research-based teaching practices that embrace students' digital practices inside and outside of school."
—Linda Hanson, Professor of English Emeritus and Former Director of the Indiana Writing Project

"Purdy and McClure provide an excellent resource for those wishing to engage with students' digital lives while maintaining the integrity of the Common Core Standards."
—Elizabeth Mary Hollis, Kennesaw State University

"*The Next Digital Scholar* offers thoughtful advice, critical research, and useful classroom examples for any educator wishing to meet and exceed the researching and writing requirements laid forth in the CCSS. The authors demonstrate the potential of digital literacies to engage students and teachers in more creative, meaningful, and authentic writing and research."
—Mark Dziedzic, Director, Greater Madison Writing Project

"When reading *The Next Digital Scholar*, I found myself regularly nodding my head in agreement. This book will help take many of the discussions I frequently have with school and public librarians to the next level."
—Linda W. Braun, Youth Services Manager, Seattle Public Library

"Here you will find university writing program administrators, Language Arts teachers, librarians, community literacy experts, and writing studies scholars in a rare and wonderful collaboration, exploring together how digital literacies might buttress the bridge between the Common Core and college-level writing and reading. As I read *The Next Digital Scholar*, I could almost hear the clank of hammers and grind of intellectual machinery as the contributors set about building something new."
—Bruce Ballenger, Professor of English, Boise State University, and Author, *The Curious Researcher*, *The Curious Writer*, and *The Curious Reader*

the next digital scholar

A Fresh Approach to the Common Core State Standards in Research and Writing

Edited by
James P. Purdy and Randall McClure

ASIST Monograph Series
Published on behalf of the
Association for Information Science and Technology by

Medford, New Jersey

First Printing, 2014

The Next Digital Scholar: A Fresh Approach to the Common Core State Standards in Research and Writing

Copyright © 2014 by the Association for Information Science and Technology

All rights reserved. No part of this book may be reproduced in any form or by any electronic or mechanical means, including information storage and retrieval systems, without permission in writing from the publisher, except by a reviewer, who may quote brief passages in a review. Published by Information Today, Inc., 143 Old Marlton Pike, Medford, New Jersey 08055.

Publisher's Note: The editors and publisher have taken care in the preparation of this book but make no expressed or implied warranty of any kind and assume no responsibility for errors or omissions. No liability is assumed for incidental or consequential damages in connection with or arising out of the use of the information or programs contained herein.

Many of the designations used by manufacturers and sellers to distinguish their products are claimed as trademarks. Where those designations appear in this book and Information Today, Inc. was aware of a trademark claim, the designations have been printed with initial capital letters.

Library of Congress Cataloging-in-Publication Data

The next digital scholar : a fresh approach to the common core state standards in research and writing / edited by James P. Purdy, Randall McClure.
   pages cm.
  Includes bibliographical references and index.
  ISBN 978-1-57387-495-3
  1. Language arts (Secondary)--Standards--United States. 2. Language arts (Higher)--United States. 3. Research--Methodology--United States. 4. Computer literacy--United States. 5. Electronic information resources--United States. I. McClure, Randall, editor of compilation. II. Purdy, James P., 1978- editor of compilation.
  LB1631.N45 2014
  428.0071'2--dc23

20140116871

President and CEO: Thomas H. Hogan, Sr.
Editor-in-Chief and Publisher: John B. Bryans
ASIST Monograph Series Editor: Gerald Benoît
Production Manager: Norma Neimeister
Managing Editor: Amy M. Reeve
Book Designer: Kara Mia Jalkowski
Cover Designer: Laura Hegyi

infotoday.com

Contents

Foreword xiii
    Pamela B. Childers

Acknowledgments xxiii

Introduction: The Common Core State Standards and
    the Next Digital Scholar 1
    James P. Purdy and Randall McClure

PART ONE: Trends in Digital Technology Use for Writing, Research, and Reading

Chapter 1: Ever Mindful of the Changes: What More We Know About Student Use of Emerging Technologies as They Move Closer to College and Career 21
    Randall McClure and James P. Purdy
    A Quick Look at the CCSS Through the
        Lens of the Digital 23
    Working Through It 24
    Responses to the "Problem" 30

Chapter 2: Learning From Digital Students and Teachers: Reimagining Writing Instruction and Assessment for the 21st Century 35
    Elizabeth Homan and Dawn Reed
    A Shifting Terrain: Digital Literacies in Today's Classrooms .. 35

The Competitive and the Collaborative in 21st-Century
      Writing Assessment 40
Writing Assessment, Digital Technologies, and the CCSS 46
Moving Forward in Our Digital Reality 59
Appendix: Hannah's Response to ACT Prompt
      About Bullying 66

PART TWO: Putting the Common Core State Standards Into Conversation With Other Standards

Chapter 3: Using Library Standards Assessment to Inform Common Core State Standards Instruction 71
Amanda Nichols Hess and Katie Greer

AASL and ACRL Standards 73
Assessing With Technology in the 21st-Century Classroom ... 74
Visions for the Future 99

Chapter 4: Using the Framework for Success in Postsecondary Writing to Foster Learning 107
Angela Clark-Oates, Allyson Boggess, and Duane Roen

The Framework in Use 109
A Framework for the CCSS 111
The CCSS and the Framework: A Dialogue 113
The Framework in the Writers' Studio 123
Habits of Mind Reflected in Digital Portfolios 127
Conclusion 136

Chapter 5: Participation and Collaboration in Digital Spaces: Connecting High School and College Writing Experiences 141
Rachel Bear, Heidi Estrem, James E. Fredricksen, and Dawn Shepherd

Participatory Culture and Literacy Classrooms 144
Collective Intelligence: Collaboration and Community in
      High School and College 147

Contents   vii

Networking: Source Use and Integration in High School
    and College 152
Negotiation: Rhetorical Flexibility in High School
    and College 157
Participatory Cultures and Literacy Classrooms 161
Appendix A: How Do Stories Matter?: Student-Led
    Lesson on Stories We Remember and Tell Assignment
    for Advanced Placement Literature and Composition 163
Appendix B: Using Google Presentations Informally in
    First-Year Writing 165
Appendix C: Advanced Placement Literature and
    Composition Multimodal Essay Assignment 166
Appendix D: Writing as Participation: Rhetorical Problem-
    Solving in a New Context Assignment 168

Chapter 6: College-(Writing) Ready: Aligning the Common Core State Standards With the WPA Outcomes for First-Year Composition 175
Clancy Ratliff

Shared Governance Theater: My Experience
    With the CCSS 177
Alignment of the WPA OS and CCSS for ELA
    (Grades 11–12, College and Career Readiness) 178
Similarities Between the WPA OS and CCSS 183
Genre in the WPA OS and CCSS 186
Critical Thinking and Writing in the WPA OS
    and the CCSS 189
Conclusion: The WPA OS and College-Level Writing 190

Chapter 7: Media Literacy Principles and the Common Core State Standards in English Language Arts Teacher Education 197
James Cercone and David L. Bruce

Media Literacy: A Way Forward 198
CCSS: Media Literacy and Historical Tensions
    Within ELA 199

A Next Digital Scholar Approach to Media Literacy and
    the CCSS 202
Conclusion 223

PART THREE: Classroom Assignments to Meet the Common Core State Standards

Chapter 8: Browsing With Intent: Digital Information Literacy and Distant Reading Practices 229
Laura J. Davies

Distant Reading, Close Reading, and the Common Core
    State Standards 231
Cultivating Digital Information Literacy 235
Browsing as Distant Reading 239
Patterns, Anomalies, and Surprises on the Search
    Results Page 243
Clouds, Links, and Tags: Other Information-Rich Avenues
    for Distant Reading 250
Suggestions for the Classroom 251
Conclusion 255

Chapter 9: Blogging as Public Writing: Meeting the Common Core State Standards Through Community-Centered Writing 259
Christina Saidy and Mark A. Hannah

Blogging in the Classroom 261
Public Writing, Blogging, and the CCSS 263
Learning as Partners 264
The Blogging Curriculum 266
Where to Begin 278
Conclusion 282

Chapter 10: Wherefore Art Thou Not Updating Thy Status?: Facebook, the Common Core State Standards, and the Power of Meaningful Work 285
R. Spencer Atkinson

Practical and Theoretical Context 285
Results of the Project 290
Meeting the CCSS 293
Implications for Future Practice 297

Chapter 11: Technology, the Common Core State Standards, and School Budgets: A Recipe for Necessary Innovation 303
Amanda Stearns-Pfeiffer
Curricular Shifts and Technology Demands 303
Websites and Weebly in the Classroom 307
Bye, Bye Index Cards. Hello, Storify! 314
Conclusion 321

PART FOUR: Curricular Initiatives to Meet the Common Core State Standards

Chapter 12: The Saving Our Stories Project: Pushing Beyond the Culturally Neutral Digital Literacies of the Common Core State Standards 325
Antero Garcia and Cindy O'Donnell-Allen
What's Missing in the CCSS? 327
The Saving Our Stories Project 331
Building Capacity Through Partnerships 336
Key Elements of the Framework 338
A Heuristic for Addressing Diverse Student Needs
   in the Age of the CCSS 347
Conclusion 349

Chapter 13: UnCommon Connections: How Building a Grass-Roots Curriculum Helped Reframe Common Core State Standards for Teachers and Students in a High-Needs Public High School 353
Stephanie West-Puckett and William P. Banks
Historicizing Old Connections 355
Imagining New Connections 357

Taking It Back to the Building 367
Project *Dis*Connect 372
Connectivity Not Portability 374
Reframing the CCSS: Making Networks Visible 375
Future Directions: Forging Uncommon Connections 378

Chapter 14: Multimedia Composers, Digital Curators: Examining the Common Core State Standards for Nonprint Texts Through the Digital Expository Writing Program.................................. 383
    Lisa Litterio
The Digital Expository Writing Program at Saint Rose 385
Remix Video Assignment: Rationale for Inclusion in a
    Writing Classroom 387
Teaching With Technology and Addressing Principles
    of Fair Use in the Age of Digital Freedom 389
Technical Proficiency 391
Fair Use Practices With Nonprint Texts 393
Integrating Multimedia Projects Into High School
    Classes: Research as Curation 396
Activities for Researchers as Curators 398
Conclusion: The Future of Classroom Writing 404
Appendix A: Remix Video Editing, Day 1 408
Appendix B: Prompts for Group Work on the
    Research Process 409
Appendix C: Analyzing Search Engines
    and Search Results 410

PART FIVE: Approaches to Teacher Training

Chapter 15: Preparing Pre-Service Writing Teachers to Enact the (Digital) Common Core State Standards in Secondary Writing Classrooms 415
    Christine Tulley
Using Action Research to Meet the CCSS Within the
    Writing Methods Course 420

Project Design 421
Outcomes 427
Caveats 429
Conclusions 432
Appendix: How Phases in Action Research Project
 Meet the CCSS 436

Chapter 16: From Do as We Say to Do as We (Digitally) Do: Modeling the Implementation of the Common Core State Standards 441

Tawnya Lubbes and Heidi Skurat Harris

Generation-D and the CCSS 443
Issues in Implementing the CCSS 445
The Need for Project-Based Professional Development 445
Three Models for Pre-Service and
 Professional Development 446
Conclusions and Implications for Implementation 459
Appendix A: What Is Project-Based Learning? 462
Appendix B: Types of Project-Based Learning 464
Appendix C: Project-Based Learning Checklist 464
Appendix D: Project-Based Learning Rubric 465

Chapter 17: Moving Beyond Transmission to Practice: Training Teachers to Be Digital Writers 467

Keri Franklin and Kathy Gibson

Aligning Our Institute With the CCSS and the Framework ... 468
Writing Prior to the Institute: The Setup 469
Recommendations for Planning Professional Development
 With the CCSS and the Framework in Mind 484
Conclusion 487

Conclusion: Teaching and Learning With the Common Core State Standards in the World of the Next Digital Scholar 491

James P. Purdy and Randall McClure

Afterword 497
Troy Hicks

About the Contributors 513

About the Editors 525

Index 527

Foreword

Pamela B. Childers

I have been involved in secondary education in public and independent schools all my professional life as an English and writing teacher, writing center and writing across the curriculum (WAC) director, teacher of teachers of writing, author, workshop facilitator, keynote presenter, and educational consultant. My perspective on *The Next Digital Scholar: A Fresh Approach to the Common Core State Standards in Research and Writing* edited by James P. Purdy and Randall McClure is based on my expertise in those areas. Like many of my fellow educators, I was born before digital technologies became part of teaching and learning. My undergraduate and graduate writing projects were completed first on a manual typewriter, then on an IBM Selectric (electric typewriter with an element that prevented keys from jamming), next on a PC with a dot matrix then daisy wheel printer, and finally on a MAC with a laser printer. For readers under 30, you may have to do a Google search to understand parts of that last sentence; however, even those born into digital technologies have seen major changes in teaching and learning with technology.

When I began teaching English in a high school in New Jersey in the late 1960s, not many secondary school faculty were involved in WAC, even though elementary school teachers had long taught most or all subjects in self-contained classrooms. Within one year, I had encouraged a history colleague to propose a team-taught class for at-risk incoming 9th graders at our high school. With the help of a supportive administrator, we began a program that grew until the team-taught course spanned all four grades with many of the best teachers volunteering to be part of teams. I mention this educational experience and others that follow to connect to what authors in this book describe.

Ten years later, I was invited by our superintendent to become part of an interdisciplinary team to participate in a WAC program at Rutgers University that formally began our school's WAC program and eventually our high school writing center (Farrell 1989) at Red Bank Regional High School (Little Silver, NJ). My strong belief in the early 1980s was that all of our students needed access to technology, not just those with the resources that afford them access. I even once referred to the writing center as Whitman's "great equalizer" because students of all academic abilities and socioeconomic backgrounds had access to collaboration; use of technology; feedback from peers; and special programs focusing on writing, research, and technology. At the same time, in the honors 11th-grade English class I taught, I was trying to take all of those ideas a step further by adding community service through students collaboratively researching and creating annotated bibliographies of American authors. We created annual booklets and made them available in the library for student use in research. Little did I know then that the technology of word processing would only be the beginning of advancements in research technology and ideas, such as those presented in Chapter 9 of this book, "Blogging as Public Writing: Meeting the Common Core State Standards Through Community-Centered Writing" by Christina Saidy and Mark A. Hannah.

By the time I moved to an independent boys' day/boarding school in Tennessee as an endowed chair of composition, computers were everywhere. The writing center I designed there held 15 Macintosh computers as part of a LAN and paired with access to three printers. Every student wanted to come in for word processing, and I used my personal AOL account with a telephone connection to help connect students in high school–college partnerships. For instance,

Sam Robinson at University of Saskatchewan had his secondary education majors partnering with students in our environmental science class. Students gave me their floppy disks with email responses, and I transferred the emails to my computer to send messages through my AOL account. Subject lines became very important as the students, after reading an essay by Aldo Leopold, discussed the main points of the essay and how they impacted their own issues with the environment. Robinson's students were learning how to respond to high school students' reading, writing, and thinking, while our students had a real audience away from the high school environment. As our technology advanced with internet service, so did our collaborative writing activities. Glenn Blaylock opened a website for our students to collaborate a few years later; his students at Stephen F. Austin State University suggested topics for essays based on a common reading and then responded to the high school students' final drafts. The interaction helped the secondary students prepare for writing in college, while Blaylock's students practiced responding to student writing. In this collection, Chapter 17, "Moving Beyond Transmission to Practice: Training Teachers to Be Digital Writers" by Keri Franklin and Kathy Gibson, provides more sophisticated teacher training suggestions suited for working with students transitioning to college and career in the digital age.

These early WAC and writing center collaborations (Farrell-Childers, Gere, and Young 1994) evolved into more sustainable cross-disciplinary (and cross-academic level) partnerships throughout the world in the 21st century, as teachers have become involved in such professional organizations as the National Writing Project, International Writing Centers Association, and International Writing Across the Curriculum Conference (Childers and Lowry 2012). And, through my instruction of a graduate course in the Teaching of Writing designed to prepare middle school and high school teachers, I have become acutely aware of how much more all of us can do with new technologies to improve the teaching and learning of reading, researching, and writing, even within the earliest grades. When I started teaching the graduate course at the beginning of this century, for example, I wanted to divide my students into small online research discussion forums as part of the course. The university was not sure how to equate that time, when I was part of all forums, with student-contact time, which now is an assumed part of many courses. For current and future teachers, Chapter 16, "From Do as We Say to Do as We (Digitally) Do: Modeling the Implementation of the Common Core State Standards" by Tawnya Lubbes and Heidi Skurat Harris, models how to merge technology skills and digital literacy in multiple ways. As I read through *The Next Digital Scholar*, I realized how far we have come with collaborations that help our students transition from high school to college and career, and how far ahead our future teachers and faculty colleagues are in their ability to apply technology to enhance writing and researching activities in their curricula. In this collection, readers will learn about high school teachers interacting with librarians for research, how supportive administrators are making a difference in teaching and learning at all academic levels, ways in which partnerships are developing around digital technologies between secondary and postsecondary educators, and how all constituencies are desiring to deal with the latest educational movements and how they impact what and how we teach as well as what and how students learn. Add into this mix the educational movement of the time, the Common Core State Standards (CCSS).

So much about the CCSS is hidden. *What are the Common Core State Standards?* and *How will they impact me?* are the questions students, faculty, administrators, and teacher educators are all asking. I hear college faculty saying, "I was on the committee to help create the assessment tool," while secondary educators and administrators are asking, "What assessment? We haven't even figured out how to fit all of these standards into our curriculum." And, more than that, school districts are wondering where they will get the funding to buy texts that are part of the recommended reading or equipment to meet the CCSS for integrating more technology into the curriculum as well as how they will train teachers to use it and how they will revise the curriculum to reflect its integration into research and writing. Finally, administrators are reaching for the latest texts that offer a quick fix or easy way to integrate the CCSS into their curriculum, as if most of the standards are not already part of existing curricula. So, why should faculty, administrators in schools, and teacher educators need something more?

The key problem for most teachers is not whether they can adapt their curriculum to the terminology of the CCSS but the mystique surrounding the assessment that follows. Teachers fear the unknown or rumored known and how it will affect the critical thinking, learning, and success of their students who will take the high stakes tests many believe are or will be attached to the CCSS, and what impact the results might have on their own evaluation as teachers and their future in the profession. When I conducted a survey of secondary English/Language Arts teachers and librarians (Childers 2013), I discovered what their particular needs were:

- Administrative leadership and support for school-wide professional development and hands-on time with computers and informational texts
- More computers for research and low-cost access to the internet
- More time to collaborate (cross-curricular work) and create new materials
- Smaller classes
- A technology expert and media specialist, and more support to implement technology expectations

I also asked what constraints prevented them from being as successful as they would like to be in meeting the CCSS in the areas of technology, research, and writing. Respondents said:

- Limited money (which impacts all the other limitations)
- Limited time and stress
- Limited professional development and communication across the curriculum
- Lack of strong administrators to support what they are doing
- Large classes
- Lack of reliable technology

Considering these survey responses from 30 states, one quickly understands the concerns of all involved. Some teachers mentioned teaching 7 out of 8 periods with class loads of 140–150 students per day, while others spoke of not enough funding for purchasing books required for the literature section of the CCSS and lack of enough advanced technology to implement the CCSS for all students. And some questioned who decides who gets the equipment and who doesn't. It has always been clear that some educators work around the system to ensure that all of their students receive the best possible education even with such constraints, and some students will learn to become tech savvy on their own. However, why should any teacher or student have to deal with socioeconomic issues that prevent successful teaching and learning? In this book, several authors offer suggestions to deal with such issues. For instance, in Chapter 13, "UnCommon Connections: How Building a Grass-Roots Curriculum Helped Reframe Common Core State Standards for Teachers and Students in a High-Needs Public High School," Stephanie West-Puckett and William P. Banks describe a writing project initiative partnership with a local "high needs" school. Their model can also be helpful to other schools with existing or possible future connections to sites of the National Writing Project.

The survey responses from teachers also made me question how some in and around education could see school librarians and media specialists as a luxury. Several teachers mentioned the potential elimination of these positions in their schools and districts, just when the CCSS so clearly emphasize media, especially digital technology, and research in all disciplines. In Chapter 3, "Using Library Standards Assessment to Inform Common Core State Standards Instruction," Amanda Nichols Hess and Katie Greer examine what teachers and administrators can apply from Library Standards Assessment, while in Chapter 5, "Participation and Collaboration in Digital Spaces: Connecting High School and College Writing Experiences," Rachel Bear, Heidi Estrem, James E. Fredricksen, and Dawn Shepherd offer strategies for engaging students in digital literacies to prepare them for college. Not only do these chapters demonstrate the increased value of librarians and media specialists in meeting the demands of the CCSS in the digital age, but also they offer extended partnerships that can make a difference.

Another question that came to mind is this: Where do school districts get funds to allow their students access to that which other schools already have? Chapter 11, "Technology, the Common Core State Standards, and School Budgets: A Recipe for Necessary Innovation" by Amanda Stearns-Pfeiffer, presents low-budget options for school districts faced with severe resource limitations to respond to the digital demands of the CCSS. A related question is this: How can our public schools be the great equalizers if the playing field is not a fair one? One survey respondent commented, for example, "Where is there time for student exploration, teacher creativity, fun? Don't get me wrong, I love CCSS, but I am not sure the vision of the standards are truly genuine." Perhaps Chapter 7, "Media Literacy Principles and the Common Core State Standards in English Language Arts Teacher Education" by James Cercone and David L. Bruce, answers this teacher's concern that focuses on "engaging students in meaningful literacy practices." So, the CCSS are not the problem as much as the lack of communication, understanding how students will be assessed on the CCSS, and when teachers can collaborate in preparing to meet the CCSS within the framework of where students are and where they need to be specifically with research, writing, and technology.

This book provides an invaluable resource for educators of all academic levels, but specifically secondary school teachers, administrators, and pre-service teachers (and their teachers), because it offers a unique approach quite different from texts that tell them how to teach to the CCSS. And, just as in McClure and Purdy's successful *The New Digital Scholar: Exploring and Enriching the Research and Writing Practices of NextGen Students* (2013), the contributors to this book present both sides of the standards debate as they explore the challenges of the CCSS for secondary educators and students. What makes the book unique is that it is not offering a "knee-jerk" reaction to the CCSS as the impetus for change in how we teach. Instead, its contributors are suggesting that educators and future teachers observe how digital scholars already research and use technology for reading and writing and use this understanding to guide how they teach reading and writing with technology. Often using Vygotsky's Zone of Proximal Development approach (1978), many authors consider what students know and how they already use technology for research to suggest ways that teachers may engage students to ask questions and discover what they don't know. For example, in Chapter 8, "Browsing with Intent: Digital Information Literacy and Distant Reading Practices," Laura J. Davies examines students' web browsing behaviors to cultivate more effective ways of choosing better sources for research writing.

Also, *The Next Digital Scholar* makes the necessary connections between secondary and university teaching of research and writing in this digital age to encourage more partnerships among educators within specific institutions and across academic levels. Having done research in the area of Writing Across the Curriculum (WAC) partnerships (Blumner and Childers 2011), I am aware of the importance of this collaborative effort in improving students' reading, writing, and thinking as well as preparing them for both postsecondary work and career. The last section of the book presents practical applications to improve teaching and learning on secondary and postsecondary levels through suggested faculty development opportunities and actual classroom lessons that include digital technologies as an integral part of the process. Authors help guide secondary school English/Language Arts teachers, administrators, librarians, and media specialists to redesign or adapt what and how they teach to the needs of their digital scholars in approaching the CCSS. Also, this section offers secondary education professors ideas to better prepare future teachers for their challenging new profession.

Although the collection focuses on ELA standards, the Literacy Standards for High School Social Studies, Science, and Technology also require competency in reading, researching, and writing in digital forms. Therefore, the chapters in this book clearly benefit not just English Language Arts educators, but those in other disciplines as well. If I were beginning my teaching career today—no matter whether as a teacher of English, science, mathematics, or history—I would want to use the ideas presented in *The Next Digital Scholar*. However, as a teacher and mentor of educators preparing students to successfully meet the CCSS in research and writing, *I know* I will be using this book.

References

Blumner, Jacob, and Pamela B. Childers. 2011. "Building Better Bridges: What Makes High School-College WAC Collaborations Work?" *WAC Journal* 21: 91–101. Accessed February 10, 2014. wac.colostate.edu/journal/vol22/blumner.pdf.

Childers, Pamela B. 2013. "How English/Language Arts Teachers Are Preparing to Meet Common Core State Standards." *Survey Monkey*. Accessed February 10, 2014. www.surveymonkey.com/s/R5HKYPF.

Childers, Pamela B., and Michael J. Lowry, eds. 2012. "Introduction to Writing Across the Curriculum in Secondary Schools" [Special issue on Writing Across the Secondary School Curriculum]. *Across the Disciplines* 9 (3). Accessed February 10, 2014. wac.colostate.edu/atd/second_educ/intro.cfm.

Farrell, Pamela B., ed. 1989. *The High School Writing Center: Establishing and Maintaining One*. Urbana, IL: National Council of Teachers of English. Reprint, Fort Collins, CO: WAC Clearinghouse, 2013. Accessed February 10, 2014. wac.colostate.edu/books/hswc.

Farrell-Childers, Pamela, Anne Ruggles Gere, and Art Young. 1994. *Programs and Practices: Writing Across the Secondary School Curriculum*. Portsmouth, NH: Heinemann. Reprint, Fort Collins, CO: WAC Clearinghouse, 2013. Accessed February 10, 2014. wac.colostate.edu/books/programs.

McClure, Randall, and James P. Purdy, eds. 2013. *The New Digital Scholar: Exploring and Enriching the Research and Writing Practices of NextGen Students*. Medford, NJ: Information Today, Inc.

Vygotsky, Lev S. 1978. *Mind in Society*. Cambridge, MA: Harvard University Press.

Acknowledgments

We are grateful to the contributors of this book for sharing their wisdom and for providing excellent models of strong commitment to improving research and writing instruction for future generations of students. John B. Bryans, Amy Reeve, Gerald Benoît, and Rob Colding of Information Today, Inc. were kind enough to support us in this follow-up project to *The New Digital Scholar*, and we appreciate their belief and enthusiasm. We thank Matthew Heilman and Lindsey Albracht for their stellar editorial assistance and proofreading. And we thank our students and colleagues, who continue to inspire our work and demonstrate what it means to make meaning in a digital world.

Jim thanks his wife Mary, parents James and Norma, and sister Amy for their unwavering love and support; Randall for his smarts and dedication; God for his opportunities and blessings; Duquesne University for the National Endowment for the Humanities grant to fund work on this project; and his past and present colleagues for their kindness. He also thanks Noah, his next digital scholar, for bringing him immeasurable joy and reminding him why all of this matters. He dedicates this book to the memory of his father.

Randall thanks his co-editor Jim for his patience and leadership; his colleagues at Miami University—especially LuMing Mao, Heidi McKee, and Jason Palmeri—for their understanding and the opportunity to work with some of the best students in the country; his family and friends for their unwavering support; his Lord for His mercy and blessing; and his wife Christine and his children Connor, Aislinn, Rowen, and Flynn for reminding him why he writes and why he lives.

INTRODUCTION

The Common Core State Standards and the Next Digital Scholar

James P. Purdy and Randall McClure

The Common Core State Standards (CCSS) have created quite a stir in the educational community. As readers of this volume may likely know, the CCSS are a set of learning outcomes published in 2010 for K–12 schools. The CCSS are designed to enhance students' "college and career readiness" across a range of subjects, including English Language Arts (ELA), and to afford standardization and easier comparison of student performance across different states (Council of Chief State School Officers [CCSSO] and the National Governors Association [NGA] 2010).[1] At the time of this writing, the CCSS have been adopted by more than 40 states, Washington, DC, and four U.S. territories ("In the States" 2014). As a result, they are poised to have a significant impact on American elementary, middle, and secondary education as well as postsecondary training of K–12 teachers. Further, this wide adoption of the CCSS has left many teachers, librarians, instructional designers, and administrators searching for a response.

Our argument in this collection is that librarians, ELA teachers, curriculum designers, writing studies scholars, and writing program administrators at presecondary, secondary, and postsecondary levels need to collaborate in responding to the demands within the CCSS. We are certainly not the first in calling for increased collaboration between librarians, teachers, and curriculum designers, and we are encouraged by what we see as a swell in the recent literature that grounds collaboration between curriculum experts and library science professionals in the attempt not only to understand and educate the new (and next) digital scholar, but also to understand and educate the teacher faced with the new (and next) digital scholar. From collaborative inquiry projects (McClure and Clink 2009) to co-teaching initiatives (Cullen, Gaskell, Garson, and McGowan 2009), from integrated information literacy and writing programs (Holliday and Fagerheim 2006; Peele, Keith, and Seely 2013) to new approaches to teacher education (McClure 2014), we believe that we are bearing witness to changes inside education that we see as a collective and positive response to the ways in which students are collaborating in digital spaces. We believe collaboration here is crucial; therefore, this collection seeks to act out this renewed commitment to partnerships by bringing together contributions from across the diverse educational community.

While the CCSS have been widely adopted, it is clear that teachers, librarians, and curriculum designers, and the school districts within which they work, are not fully prepared to help students achieve the CCSS, particularly given the increased emphasis on digital literacy. Take, for example, the following comment from fourth-grade teacher Franki Sibberson, whose post "Digital Writing: The First Six Weeks of School" to her popular blog *A Year of Reading* has been picked up by several prominent news feeds, including the feed from the National Council of Teachers of English (NCTE):

> [S]o much of life as a digital writer is in the behaviors and stances we have as writers, the expectation for participation, for changing our thinking, for conversation. I know this

about myself as a writer but I have struggled with making this work for kids. (Sibberson 2012)

Sibberson's literacy concern for connecting the researching and writing behaviors that occur in digital environments with her students is a concern at the heart of the CCSS, which emphasize the need for K–12 students to demonstrate competency with reading, researching, and writing in digital spaces. This concern is real, not just for teachers and students working in traditional classrooms, but also for those in online venues. In the 2011–2012 academic year, for example, close to 150,000 K–12 students in Florida participated at least part time in the Florida Virtual School program, enrolling in more than 300,000 half-credit courses, a pace that nearly doubles enrollment since the 2008–2009 academic year (Florida Virtual School 2012a, 2012b).

Sibberson's literacy concern has been echoed by those at the top of the K–12 pyramid as well, such as Dennis M. Walcott, Chancellor of New York City Schools. Walcott announced that, with the "rollout of tougher [CCSS] and the need to get students better prepared for college and careers," his district is teaming up with more than 30 major school districts—including Chicago and Washington, DC— to pressure the publishing industry to provide them with materials to meet the CCSS (Fertig 2012). Through what the chancellors are collectively calling the "Publishers' Criteria," they have announced that they will "reject any textbooks or other instructional materials that aren't aligned with the Common Core's more demanding … literacy standards."

These examples of popular press coverage of the CCSS show that teachers are struggling with the CCSS related to digital literacy, that (at least some of) their school districts recognize the lack of resources to support their teachers, and that those districts see the need for—and are calling for—resources to help. Moreover, in his essay on the importance of the CCSS, Richard R. Schramm (2012) affirms that the "rigorous and sophisticated instruction called for by the new standards will, in many cases, require considerable teacher training." That is where this book seeks to intervene. In this collection, practicing ELA teachers, university English faculty, librarians, and National Writing Project (NWP) administrators offer theoretically informed practical suggestions for helping librarians and ELA teachers achieve and their districts assess—as well as university administrators and faculty best prepare the next generation of teachers for—the CCSS focused on digital literacy and reading, researching, and writing.

A number of sources already offer lesson plans for meeting the CCSS for ELA, working from the CCSS to students (e.g., Giouroukakis and Connolly 2012; Heard 2013; Ryan and Frazee 2012).[2] While these sources do productive work, providing concrete activities and assignments for teachers, we might argue they approach working with the standards backward, starting with the CCSS document rather than with student and teacher practices. This volume takes a different approach, working largely from students and technologies to the CCSS, letting students' information behaviors drive the discussion rather than vice versa. Understanding and accounting for what students do online and how they do it brings the CCSS into focus, rather than using the CCSS to bring students' research-writing behaviors into line (or perhaps into submission). Extant research already shows the curriculum and pedagogy of submission doesn't work (e.g., Freire 1970; McClaren 1988). Remember when students were told not to use Google or Wikipedia as research tools?

In ways similar to the response by some educators to the advancements in digital technologies and the literacy practices and information behaviors that have resulted from their use by students in and out of the classroom, the CCSS and their adoption have been surrounded by controversy. Much of this controversy centers on concerns over the stipulated balance of 70 percent nonfiction and 30 percent fiction in reading assignments across subject areas (CCSSO and NGA 2010, 5, footnote 1; Jago 2013; Layton 2012; Ravitch 2013), the economic motivations of the CCSS (Cuban 2010; Flanagan 2011; Ravitch 2013; Zhao 2013), and the CCSS' connection to and support of standardization and/or standardized testing (Cody 2012; Fuller 2011; Matthews 2012; Toppo 2012; Zhao 2010). We recognize that the CCSS, like any national educational standards or outcomes system, are imperfect.

This collection neither wholly endorses nor decries the CCSS. Instead, we and our contributors focus on implications of the CCSS and practical responses to them. Ken Kay and Bob Lenz (2013) point out in their *Education Week* commentary on the CCSS what they see as two paths in response to the CCSS: one path that approaches the CCSS as yet another set of standards that teachers must "map their curricula [to] in a compliance-driven exercise" and another path that takes time to consider what possibilities for productive change the CCSS can bring so that they can "serve as a unique transformational opportunity for our nation's teaching and learning systems." While arguably idealistic, we and the contributors to *The Next Digital Scholar* attempt to follow this second path. We seek to move beyond the hand-wringing that characterizes much of the response to the CCSS in the popular press and blogosphere and instead offer theoretically rich practical responses from professionals who recognize the realities of the CCSS.

This collection's approach does not mean that we are blind to the limits and potential problems of the CCSS. In fact, many of the contributors effectively address these flaws, particularly regarding the CCSS' culturally neutral stance, limited notion of genre, and acontextual treatment of technology. However, we are interested in moving toward action and response. We are focused on what we as teachers, librarians, instructional designers, administrators, and researchers can do given the reality of the CCSS.

Indeed, despite their shortcomings, we find some aspects of the CCSS heartening. For instance, the presence of both digital information literacy and writing in digital environments across the K–12 level outcomes outlined in the CCSS supports a notion of writing as technological and situated, a vision long embraced by information science professionals and writing studies and education scholars, including new literacy studies, postprocess theory, and cultural historical activity theorists. The authors of the CCSS describe the desired student attribute of digital information literacy as the ability to "use technology and digital media strategically and capably" (CCSSO and NGA 2010, 7). Proficiency in gathering, synthesizing, and evaluating digital resources as well as composing with them in digital spaces are integral to the CCSS. At least five of the 10 Anchor Standards for Writing (CCSSO and NGA 2010, standards 5, 6, 7, 8, 9, 10), for example, address the role of reading, researching, and/or writing in digital environments. This orientation is at least partly consistent with the recently published Framework for Success in Postsecondary Writing (Framework), developed collaboratively by the Council of Writing Program Administrators (CWPA), NCTE, and NWP (2011), and the similarities between the CCSS and Framework are addressed by several contributors to this collection. In a sense, then, the CCSS offer standards that show some theoretical consistency with prevailing thinking in ELA.

Moreover, the CCSS' "integrated model of literacy" situates the processes of reading, writing, speaking, listening, and language use as inextricably connected with one another and with activities of researching and media/technology use across the disciplines (CCSSO and NGA 2010, 4). The CCSS, then, seek to enact what writing across the curriculum/writing in the disciplines and research and information skills movements have sought to do: emphasize the crucial role of research-writing in learning and knowledge production in all subject areas, not just writing or ELA classes. As Patricia Dadonna (2013) puts it, in summarizing comments from Bonnie Hain, senior advisor for ELA and literacy for the Partnership for Assessment of Readiness for College and Careers (PARCC), "The [CCSS] were created to improve students' ability to translate information and communicate through writing across disciplines—a skill needed for careers beyond college and technical school."

While some teachers may be understandably uncomfortable with the seemingly careerist orientation of the CCSS, the CCSS offer a counterbalance to the STEM push that has characterized much popular media coverage of secondary and postsecondary education (Megan 2013; Tilsley 2013). The CCSS, of course, cover math as well, but particularly noteworthy is that the non-math standards document is written for "English Language Arts & Literacy in History/Social Studies, *Science, and Technical Subjects*" (our emphasis; CCSSO and NGA 2010).

In the CCSS, literacy—grounded in digital literacy practices—is central to humanities fields *as well* as science and technology fields. We see this model of literacy as an opportunity to emphasize and showcase to colleagues across education and to the larger public the tremendous importance of attention to digital literacy practices and the significant value of the work of ELA teachers, librarians, and administrators in developing them.

To that end, Part One of *The Next Digital Scholar* looks at trends in student and teacher digital literacy practices. Randall McClure and James P. Purdy begin in Chapter 1, "Ever Mindful of the Changes: What More We Know About Student Use of Emerging Technologies as They Move Closer to College and Career," by synthesizing findings from several recent studies on computer, media, and web use of students and the impact of this use on students' information behaviors as well as their research, reading, and writing practices. After briefly analyzing how the CCSS acknowledge the digital, they review studies from the Pew Internet & American Life Project, National Literacy Trust (U.K.), and the National Center on Education and the Economy that report teachers' perceptions of students' practices do not always match students' perceptions of their own practices, including their use of and reliance on search engines and mobile technologies. They explain how *The Next Digital Scholar* "widen[s] the lens" offered in their previous edited collection, *The New Digital Scholar* (2013), to elementary and secondary students in order to continue their effort to explore how writing teachers, librarians, instructional designers, and administrators can make productive pedagogical and curricular decisions for NextGen students based on empirical studies of students' digital behavior, students' online literacy practices and proficiencies, instructor expertise, and strategic partnerships, rather than misperception and fear (of students, standards, and/or technologies). In Chapter 2,

"Learning From Digital Students and Teachers: Reimagining Writing Instruction and Assessment for the 21st Century," Elizabeth Homan and Dawn Reed continue this approach of understanding the CCSS by first looking at the practices of those who read, write, and research in digital spaces. By describing the work of one student, Hannah, and two high school ELA teachers, they show that the digital practices of students and teachers in today's schools provide insight into how digital technologies can be used to better understand student writing. They express concern at how trends in writing assessment, particularly approaches by standardized test developers like PARCC and Smarter Balanced Assessment Consortium (SBAC) and trends in student and teacher digital technology use are incompatible. The authors argue that automated assessment tools threaten the role of authentic digital writing in literacy instruction, which the CCSS call for, and suggest that teachers in local contexts are able to glean more from attending to the multimodal, interactive textual creations of students like Hannah.

To understand the broader landscape in which the CCSS intervene, Part Two puts the CCSS into conversation with other pertinent standards, outcomes, and disciplinary statements. In Chapter 3, "Using Library Standards Assessment to Inform Common Core State Standards Instruction," librarians Amanda Nichols Hess and Katie Greer continue the discussion of assessment begun by Homan and Reed, focusing on what insight library standards can provide for our understanding, assessment, and implementation of the CCSS. They analyze the CCSS through the lens of the American Association of School Librarians' Standards for the 21st Century Learner and the Association of College and Research Libraries' Information Literacy Competency Standards for Higher Education and conclude that "linking and blending these standards" can help students not only achieve the CCSS College and Career Readiness Anchor Standards, but also prepare them to be digital scholars who are literate in the multiple venues of their secondary and postsecondary lives. In Chapter 4, "Using the Framework for Success in Postsecondary Writing to Foster Learning," Angela Clark-Oates, Allyson Boggess, and Duane

Roen draw attention to another organizational outcomes document, NCTE's Framework. They outline how first-year writing students' use of Google Sites to construct an electronic portfolio in the Writers' Studio at Arizona State University illustrates the eight habits of mind in the Framework, which correspond indirectly with several of the Anchor Standards for Writing in the CCSS. The authors argue for the value of putting the Framework and CCSS into conversation and affirm that this connection can be used as a lens for interpreting and implementing the CCSS for grades 6–12. Like Clark-Oates, Boggess, and Roen, Rachel Bear, Heidi Estrem, James E. Fredricksen, and Dawn Shepherd put the CCSS into conversation with the Framework. In Chapter 5, "Participation and Collaboration in Digital Spaces: Connecting High School and College Writing Experiences," they apply not only the Framework, but also media scholar Henry Jenkins's ideas for literacy instruction to "connect these educational contexts to a conception of the hope and possibility in online cultures" in order to show "curricular connections" and "instructional gaps" between public secondary ELA classrooms and university first-year writing courses.

To consider how the CCSS fulfill their goal of making students "college ready," Chapter 6, "College-(Writing) Ready: Aligning the Common Core State Standards With the WPA Outcomes for First-Year Composition," explores ways in which another relevant document, the CWPA's Outcomes Statement for First-Year Composition, aligns with the CCSS for ELA grades 11–12. Director of First-Year Writing at the University of Louisiana at Lafayette, Clancy Ratliff argues that while there is overlap between the WPA Outcomes and the CCSS, there are important differences regarding context and genre, with the CCSS offering a limited view of genre in the ELA classroom. She concludes by explaining what she sees as a "valuable challenge offered by the CCSS to writing classrooms at the high school and college level: to distinguish civic goals from academic goals through a focus on genre." Chapter 7, which finishes Part Two, "Media Literacy Principles and the Common Core State Standards in English Language Arts Teacher Education" further addresses how principles of media literacy help us better understand the CCSS. James Cercone and David L. Bruce put the disciplines of media studies and ELA into conversation, exploring how media literacy standards can inform instruction in the CCSS. In particular, they address how media literacy principles "provide English teachers ... a theoretical base from which to address the demands of the CCSS while at the same time engaging students in meaningful literacy practices." Taken together, the chapters in Part Two remind us that the CCSS do not work in isolation but rather as part of a larger framework of texts that seek to shape and inform how we approach and understand literacy instruction in the digital age.

Part Three brings the conversation about the CCSS to the classroom, presenting assignments that ELA teachers can use (and have used) to meet particular standards in the CCSS. To follow the approach laid out in Part One, chapters in this section ground their assignment suggestions in student practices with digital technologies. To begin the section, Laura J. Davies, in Chapter 8, "Browsing With Intent: Digital Information Literacy and Distant Reading Practices," explores students' web browsing behaviors and how, rather than providing evidence of detached disengagement that thwarts achievement of the CCSS, they can serve as a precursor to distant reading, a practice she argues can cultivate the ability to choose better sources for academic research-writing projects. This chapter offers assignments that capitalize on this digital reading practice of students, including analyses of search results from different search engines and databases. In Chapter 9, "Blogging as Public Writing: Meeting the Common Core State Standards Through Community-Centered Writing," Christina Saidy and Mark A. Hannah turn to another student practice, public writing using blogs, and how this approach can be used to meet the CCSS. They discuss a ninth-grade curricular unit that arose from a secondary school-university partnership and include assignments where students use blogs to produce, publish, and update writing about public issues. Saidy and Hannah argue that such public writing positions students as "advocates in a variety of public spaces, including schools, communities, and workplaces." High school ELA teacher R. Spencer Atkinson, in Chapter 10, "Wherefore

Art Thou Not Updating Thy Status?: Facebook, the Common Core State Standards, and the Power of Meaningful Work," explores another common student digital writing practice: writing for social networking sites. Throughout this chapter, Atkinson addresses how to leverage students' proclivity for social networking sites like Facebook and shares an assignment utilizing Facebook to help students meet the CCSS. Atkinson analyzes two student responses to the assignment, which asked them to create Facebook profiles for characters in *Romeo and Juliet*, in order to illustrate how Facebook helped ninth-grade English students develop critical thinking and metacognition skills. The final chapter in Part Three considers the economic realities of preparing the digitally literate students called for in the CCSS. In particular, Chapter 11, "Technology, the Common Core State Standards, and School Budgets: A Recipe for Necessary Innovation" addresses the challenges these realities pose for less affluent school districts. To assist in overcoming these challenges, Amanda Stearns-Pfeiffer overviews several free web-based writing and researching tool options and offers specific suggestions for how teachers and librarians can use them.

Part Four looks beyond the individual classroom to offer a variety of curricular initiatives to meet the CCSS. To begin the section, Antero Garcia and Cindy O'Donnell-Allen, university faculty and former high school ELA teachers, explain the Saving Our Stories (SOS) Project, a summer digital-storytelling program for elementary school English Language Learners, as a means to achieve the CCSS while valuing cultural difference. Chapter 12, "The Saving Our Stories Project: Pushing Beyond the Culturally Neutral Digital Literacies of the Common Core State Standards," provides a critical analysis of the CCSS' culturally neutral approach to digital tools. In making this analysis and sharing the SOS Project, Garcia and O'Donnell-Allen argue that "[c]ulturally proactive teaching requires identifying salient social issues, underrepresented histories, and opportunities for digital and physical exploration within a school's community." In Chapter 13, "UnCommon Connections: How Building a Grass-Roots Curriculum Helped Reframe Common Core State Standards for Teachers and Students in a High-Needs Public High School," Stephanie West-Puckett and William P. Banks take up the approach offered in Part One of looking first at students' (and teachers') existing practices in considering ways in which to teach and design curricula to achieve the CCSS. They review an initiative of the Tar River Writing Project to redesign writing curricula at a local "high needs" high school in order to meet the CCSS—particularly by focusing on participatory learning. West-Puckett and Banks provide useful practical advice for how to implement a teacher-centered professional learning program to support a teacher-designed digital writing curriculum. In Chapter 14, "Multimedia Composers, Digital Curators: Examining the Common Core State Standards for Nonprint Texts Through the Digital Expository Writing Program," Lisa Litterio offers an additional curricular initiative—this one focused on the CCSS' call for more multimodal and nonprint textual products. Litterio provides a case study of the Digital Expository Writing Program at the College of Saint Rose and how the program uses digital technologies to teach students to produce multimodal texts. Litterio argues for teaching the digital research process as curation and explains two specific example assignments—a remix video and a multimodal final project—that illustrate this approach.

The final portion of the collection, Part Five, offers approaches to teacher training, considering how future teachers can learn to enact the classroom and curricular approaches presented in Parts Three and Four with the awareness of student practice and multiple interconnected ELA standards and outcomes addressed in Parts One and Two. Part Five opens with Christine Tulley's model for how university instructors can teach pre-service ELA teachers to provide instruction that meets the CCSS. Chapter 15, "Preparing Pre-Service Writing Teachers to Enact the (Digital) Common Core State Standards in Secondary Writing Classrooms," explores how a curriculum that asks pre-service teachers to conduct and publish action research with digital technologies can prepare them to assess students' achievement of the CCSS. Noting how "writing teachers are caught in a cycle of having less time to devote to writing instruction while being held more accountable for how students write in ways that often work against students' out of class literacies," Tulley suggests pre-service teachers get practice themselves using digital technologies to meet the elements in the CCSS Anchor Standards for Writing related to digital literacy.

After explaining ways in which the language of the CCSS begins to bridge the gap between students' technological skills and their need for digital literacy, Tawnya Lubbes and Heidi Skurat Harris advance two models for pre-service teaching and faculty professional development that provide project-based learning experiences designed to merge technology skills and digital literacy. In Chapter 16, "From Do as We Say to Do as We (Digitally) Do: Modeling the Implementation of the Common Core State Standards," the authors affirm that pre-service teacher training (and experienced faculty professional development programs) should provide opportunities for project-based learning. Like Tulley, the authors stress that pre-service teachers should be asked to use digital technologies to complete assignments that meet the CCSS regarding digital literacy. Specifically, Lubbes and Harris suggest pre-service teachers work with Web 2.0 technologies to design "inquiry-based projects" that require using digital technologies "to gather, assess, and implement" digital sources and "to produce, publish, and update" textual products, skills articulated in the CCSS. Part Five closes with Chapter 17, "Moving Beyond Transmission to Practice: Training Teachers to Be Digital Writers." By discussing a digital writing institute taught for K-University teachers, Keri Franklin, a university professor and director of the local site of the NWP, and Kathy Gibson, a middle school and high school teacher, argue that we need to encourage teachers to write digitally themselves. This final chapter echoes the call of both Tulley and Lubbes and Harris for pre-service teachers to gain experience using the digital technologies their students will be using (and already use). It provides assignment ideas and suggestions for teacher and librarian training to prepare the next generation of instructors to help students achieve the learning goals outlined in the CCSS.

Our hope is that this collection, with an eye toward the practices of the next digital scholar and the realities of the CCSS, will assist the multiple constituencies grappling with these new standards, particularly those standards related to digital research, reading, and writing. The CCSS remind us of the skills—and, perhaps more importantly, the approach to literacy—that the next digital scholar will need to negotiate his or her college and career life. We believe that ELA teachers and librarians, with the flexibility to implement the CCSS in ways that allow them to capitalize on their experience and expertise, are uniquely positioned to work together to help students succeed in attaining the outcomes outlined in the CCSS document.

Endnotes

1. Included with the ELA standards are Literacy standards in "History/Social Studies, Science, and Technical Subjects" (CCSSO and NGA 2010, 1). This collection focuses on the ELA standards.
2. ASCD, Common Core, NCTE, and Teacher's Life all have book series devoted to the CCSS.

References

Cody, Anthony. 2012. "The Common Core: The Technocrats Re-Engineer Learning." *Education Week*, April 27. Accessed February 14, 2014. blogs.edweek.org/teachers/living-in-dialogue/2012/04/the_common_core_the_technocrat.html.

Council of Chief State School Officers (CCSSO) and the National Governors Association (NGA). 2010. *Common Core State Standards for English Language Arts & Literacy in History/Social Studies, Science, and Technical Subjects*. Washington, DC: National Governors Association Center for Best Practices, Council of Chief State School Officers. Accessed August 16, 2012. www.corestandards.org/assets/CCSSI_ELA%20Standards.pdf

Council of Writing Program Administrators, National Council of Teachers of English, and National Writing Program. 2011. *Framework for Success in Postsecondary Writing*. Accessed February 10, 2014. wpacouncil.org/files/framework-for-success-postsecondary-writing.pdf.

Cuban, Larry. 2010. "Common Core Standards: Hardly an Evidence-Based Policy." *Larry Cuban on School Reform and Classroom Practice*, July 25. Accessed February

10, 2014. larrycuban.wordpress.com/2010/07/25/common-core-standards-hardly-an-evidence-based-policy.

Cullen, Ann, Millicent Gaskell, Deborah Garson, and Eileen McGowan. 2009. "Co-Teaching: Why Two Heads Are Better than One." *SLA Conference Proceedings*, June 15. Accessed February 10, 2014. bf.sla.org/wp-content/uploads/2009_cullen.pdf.

Dadonna, Patricia. 2013. "Writing Across the K12 Curriculum: Common Core Mandates for Success." *District Administration Magazine*, January 11. Accessed February 10, 2014. www.districtadministration.com/article/writing-across-k12-curriculum.

Fertig, Beth. 2012. "School Districts Team Up to Demand Better Textbooks." *New York Times*, June 28. Accessed February 10. 2014. www.nytimes.com/schoolbook/2012/06/28/school-districts-team-up-to-demand-better-textbooks.

Flanagan, Nancy. 2011. "The Common Core: Policy Triumph or Commercial Bonanza?" *Education Week*, January 12. Accessed February 10, 2014. blogs.edweek.org/teachers/teacher_in_a_strange_land/2011/01/the_common_core_policy_triumph_or_commercial_bonanza.html.

Florida Virtual School. 2012a. "2011–2012 Part-Time Enrollment Summary." *FLVS.net*, June 30. Accessed February 10, 2014. www.flvs.net/areas/aboutus/Documents/EnrollmentSummary.pdf.

———. 2012b. "FLVS Semester Completion History." June 30. Accessed February 10, 2014. www.flvs.net/areas/aboutus/Documents/FLVS%20Completions%20History%202011-2012.pdf.

Freire, Paulo. 1970. *Pedagogy of the Oppressed*. Trans. Myra Bergman Ramos. New York: Continuum.

Fuller, Bruce. 2011. "Understandable, But Wrong" (opinion). *New York Times*, January 25. Accessed February 10, 2014. www.nytimes.com/roomfordebate/2010/7/21/who-will-benefit-from-national-education-standards/hold-schools-accountable-but-dont-standardize-learning?src=tp.

Giouroukakis, Vicky, and Maureen Connolly. 2012. *Getting to the Core of English Language Arts, Grades 6–12: How to Meet the Common Core State Standards With Lessons From the Classroom*. Thousand Oaks, CA: Corwin.

Heard, Georgia. 2013. *Poetry Lessons to Meet the Common Core State Standards: Exemplar Poems With Engaging Lessons and Response Activities That Help Students Read, Understand, and Appreciate Poetry*. New York: Scholastic.

Holliday, Wendy, and Britt A. Fagerheim. 2006. "Integrating Information Literacy With a Sequenced English Composition Curriculum." *portal: Libraries and the Academy* 6 (2): 169–184.

"In the States." 2014. *Common Core State Standards Initiative*. Accessed March 25, 2014. www.corestandards.org/in-the-states.

Jago, Carol. 2013. "What English Classes Should Look Like in Common Core Era." *Washington Post*, January 10. Accessed February 10, 2014. www.washingtonpost.com/blogs/answer-sheet/wp/2013/01/10/what-english-classes-should-look-like-in-common-core-era.

Kay, Ken, and Bob Lenz. 2013. "Commentary: Which Path for the Common Core?" *Education Week*, March 22. Accessed February 10, 2014. www.edweek.org/ew/articles/2013/03/22/26kay.h32.html.

Layton, Lyndsey. 2012. "Common Core Sparks War Over Words." *Washington Post*, December 6. Accessed February 10, 2014. articles.washingtonpost.com/2012-12-02/local/35584536_1_informational-text-middle-school-teacher-english-teachers.

Matthews, Jay. 2012. "Why Common Core Standards Will Fail." *Washington Post*, February 23. Accessed February 10, 2014. www.washingtonpost.com/blogs/class-struggle/post/why-common-core-standards-will-fail/2012/02/23/gIQATLgbUR_blog.html.

McClaren, Peter L. 1988. "Culture or Canon? Critical Pedagogy and the Politics of Literacy." *Harvard Educational Review*, 58 (2): 213–235.

McClure, Randall. 2014. "It's Not 2.0 Late: What Late Adopters Need to Know About Teaching Research Skills to Writers of Multimodal Texts." *The Writing Instructor*. Accessed March 23, 2014. www.writinginstructor.com/currentmoment-mcclure.

McClure, Randall, and Kellian Clink. 2009. "How Do You Know That? An Investigation of Student Research Practices in the Digital Age." *portal: Libraries and the Academy*, 9 (1): 115–132.

McClure, Randall, and James P. Purdy, eds. 2013. *The New Digital Scholar: Exploring and Enriching the Research and Writing Practices of NextGen Students*. Medford, NJ: Information Today, Inc.

Megan, Kathleen. 2013. "Malloy Wants to Invest $1.5 Billion in UConn Sciences, Technology." *Hartford Courant*, January 30. Accessed February 10, 2014. www.courant.com/community/mansfield/hc-uconn-engineering-school-0131-20130130,0,4906946.story.

Peele, Thomas, Melissa Keith, and Sara Seely. 2013. "Teaching and Assessing Research Strategies in the Digital Age: Collaboration Is the Key." In *The New Digital Scholar: Exploring and Enriching the Research and Writing Practices of NextGen Students*, edited by Randall McClure and James P. Purdy, 313–330. Medford, NJ: Information Today, Inc.

Ravitch, Diane. 2013. "Why I Cannot Support the Common Core Standards." *Diane Ravitch's Blog*, February 26. Accessed February 10, 2014. dianeravitch.net/2013/02/26/why-i-cannot-support-the-common-core-standards.

Ryan, Susan, and Dana Frazee. 2012. *Common Core Standards for High School English Language Arts: A Quick-Start Guide*. Ed. John Kendall. Alexandria, VA: ACSD.

Schramm, Richard R. 2012. "Strengthening the Core." *Inside Higher Ed*, September 18. Accessed February 10, 2014. www.insidehighered.com/views/2012/09/18/essay-importance-common-core-standards.

Sibberson, Franki. 2012. "Digital Writing: The First Six Weeks of School." *A Year of Reading: Two Teachers Who Read. A Lot*, August 7. Accessed February 10, 2014. readingyear.blogspot.com/2012/08/digital-writing-first-six-weeks-of.html.

Tilsley, Alexandra. 2013. "Finding More STEM Students." *Inside Higher Ed*, February 1. Accessed February 10, 2014. www.insidehighered.com/news/2013/02/01/connecticut-and-texas-aim-grow-stem-enrollment-take-different-approaches.

Toppo, Greg. 2012. "Common Core Standards Drive Wedge in Education Circles." *USAToday*, May 1. Accessed February 10, 2014. usatoday30.usatoday.com/news/education/story/2012-04-28/common-core-education/54583192/1?csp=34news.

Zhao, Yong. 2010. "Sesame vs. Watermelon: What Is Missing in the National Standard Debate." *Education in the Age of Globalization*, January 19. Accessed February 10, 2014. zhaolearning.com/2010/01/19/sesame-vs-watermelon-what-is-missing-in-the-national-standard-debate.

———. 2013. "Five Questions to Ask About the Common Core." *Education in the Age of Globalization*, January 2. Accessed February 10, 2014. zhaolearning.com/2013/01/02/five-questions-to-ask-about-the-common-core.

PART ONE

Trends in Digital Technology Use for Writing, Research, and Reading

CHAPTER 1

Ever Mindful of the Changes
What More We Know About Student Use of Emerging Technologies as They Move Closer to College and Career

Randall McClure and James P. Purdy

In the opening section of our last volume, *The New Digital Scholar: Exploring and Enriching the Research and Writing Practices of NextGen Students*, we and our contributors highlighted the changing practices in technology and media use as well as those in information behavior of students entering our college writing classrooms. We offered this overview of the new digital scholar to confront what many have viewed as the research-writing "problem" in our colleges and universities caused by the information explosion brought on by advances in digital technologies. This overview served to "focus attention on the sometimes daunting challenge we are faced with when students enter our college writing classrooms, the challenge to help them become academic researchers in the digital information age. This challenge is intensified by the amount and variety of writing, reading, and researching activity students engage in on the web, and by the information behaviors students have developed as a result of such activity" (McClure 2013, 19–20). Along with our contributors, we then responded in *The New Digital Scholar* to the research writing "problem" in college writing classrooms in a variety of ways. We first, through historical analyses, case studies, teacher and student surveys, and other mechanisms, tried to make sense of and to define the problem. We then took it to task, often leveraging the same technologies and behaviors some researchers have cited as the root of the so-called problem. Here in this new book, however, we have a different exigency—the Common Core State Standards (CCSS).

In this book, *The Next Digital Scholar: A Fresh Approach to the Common Core State Standards in Research and Writing*, we widen the lens offered in *The New Digital Scholar* to elementary and secondary students in the U.S., with particular attention to students in secondary English Language Arts (ELA) classrooms. We do this, in large part, to help K–12 administrators, curriculum designers, librarians, and ELA teachers respond to the demands of the recent near nationwide adoption of the CCSS. We believe this book will help those working to meet and assess the CCSS by considering how digital technologies have shaped the ways in which students locate, evaluate, and use information, especially in their reading and writing, and how these technologies can be leveraged to better prepare students for college and career.

Instead of relying on our years of experience as an administrator of several college writing programs and director of several university writing centers, respectively, we (Randall and James, respectively) in this chapter turn to national reports and published studies from the U.S. and U.K. on the information behavior, technology use, media use, and research-writing practices of NextGen students to present a picture of today's student. It is difficult to make this picture clear, as what it means to be digitally literate today is increasing complex. This definition "continually shifts in its complexities as new technologies surface, and these tools enable people to shape texts as much as these texts shape [them]" (Albers 2013, 44). While digital tools, and the behaviors that students develop while using them, come at us as educators at a blistering pace, we have found that study after study from national research centers, such as the Pew Internet & American Life Project and the Kaiser Family Foundation, and university programs known for their work with digital technologies and learning, such as the Center for Research on Writing in Digital Environments at Michigan State University and the Global Information Industry Center at University of California, San Diego, make one point crystal clear: The computer is the gateway to the information universe for today's students, and the web is their primary information interface (McClure 2013, 23).

Before offering a more detailed analysis of the findings from several reports on technology use and information behavior, however, we first offer here our take on the CCSS, focusing on the standards for ELA in grades 6–12, in terms of how the CCSS acknowledge the digital. We then turn, as we did in the opening of *The New Digital Scholar*, to recent national reports and published studies on the technology uses, and research and writing habits of tweens and teens. By more closely connecting the CCSS with the digital, we hope to offer our readers help in understanding the impact of digital technologies on the information behaviors of students and in responding in proactive ways to these behaviors within their curricula as they strive to meet and assess the CCSS.

By helping our readers better understand the information behaviors and technology uses of the next digital scholar, our goal is to provide a stronger framework within which teachers and librarians can prepare students to be college and career ready.

A Quick Look at the CCSS Through the Lens of the Digital

As we discuss in the Introduction, our purpose in this book is to assist teachers, librarians, curriculum designers, and others engaged in teaching ELA or reading, researching, and writing across the K–12 experience to meet the demands of the CCSS when working with students increasingly influenced by the digital. We acknowledge that some significant critiques have been levied against the CCSS, but we remain steadfast in our belief that opportunities exist within the CCSS to bring curricula into the digital age and meet students, as the expression goes, "where they are." It is true that many of the Anchor Standards in language and literacy are print-centric, holdovers from an approach to education that may be poorly suited for students born into a digital world exploding with social technologies and information portals. However, we see opportunities in those standards to recognize the presence and value of multimedia, digital tools and resources, and online collaboration.

As we note in the Introduction, five of the 10 Anchor Standards for Writing connect to the digital. In fact, the strongest statement in the CCSS for digital teaching and learning is found in Anchor Standard for Writing 6, one of three standards for the "Production and Distribution of Writing": Students should be able to "[u]se technology, including the internet, to produce and publish writing and to interact and collaborate with others" (Council of Chief State School Officers [CCSSO] and the National Governors Association [NGA] 2010a). For those who criticize the CCSS for limitations related to print-centric texts, we see tremendous opportunity here for digital textual production. Combine this with four of the other Anchor Standards in ELA that focus on research, and we read the standards as giving attention to researching and writing in the digital age. With at least one reference to digital sources or digital media in three of the four areas of ELA—reading, writing, and speaking and listening—and similar references in the standards for writing in other disciplines, the standards signify a need to understand and educate the next digital scholar.

Working Through It

While many in and out of education circles view the CCSS primarily as a new problem (or as the recurring problem of externally imposed standards on our public education system), we wish to view them as a set of opportunities to bring digital technologies and the corresponding behaviors of students using (and innovating) with these technologies to bear on an educational system that has remained largely print-centric, dated, and disconnected from today's students. We acknowledge that many pointed critiques of the CCSS exist in the literature of education and are at times accurate, but we opt to see the CCSS as the authors[1] of a 2013 report from the National Center on Education and the Economy do, as part of a "serious discussion of what it might take to make sure that our students leave high school college and career ready" (2013, 1). We believe that understanding the technological skills and information behaviors of the next digital scholar is a critical component of this dialogue.

Take, for example, the views offered by students on the types of literacy skills they believe valuable to the future of work. In the 2013 study *Young People's Views on Literacy Skills and Employment* conducted by the National Literacy Trust (U.K.), researchers Christina Clark and Susie Formby present the results of a survey of young people's perceptions of traditional and technological literacies and their value in the workplace of the future, a literacy venue that the authors of the CCSS return to time and time again beginning in their mission statement: "The standards are designed to be robust and relevant to the real world, reflecting the knowledge and skills that our young people need for success in college and careers. With American students fully prepared for the future, our communities will be best positioned to compete successfully in the global economy" (CCSSO and NGA, 2010b). In their survey of more than 35,000 teen and tween students in the U.K., a country with an unemployment rate of higher than 20 percent for the generation attempting to enter the workforce in 2012, Clark and Formby conclude that "we [those of us in education] know very little of how young people construct their identities as employees" and their "perceptions of the (literacy) skills that they will need in order to compete within and succeed in the workplace" (2013, 3). For example, Clark and Formby were clearly surprised that, while nearly all (88.3 percent) students responded that good communication skills were necessary to get a good job, "four in 10 children and young people do not appear to see the link between writing skills and their job prospects" (5).

The fact that many young people do not see strong writing skills as important to their career, and for that matter college, may not surprise many of the readers of this chapter. And it certainly is an assumption of the authors of the CCSS, who identify the Anchor Standards for Writing across the K–12 educational experience. What may not have received the appropriate amount of attention in the CCSS, including within the Anchor Standards for Writing, is the impact and role of digital technologies on college and career success. Clark and Formby drive this point home when they write that "young people are also now joining the workforce with technological knowledge that is often far beyond that of the generation before them at a time when the workplace is becoming increasingly technology-driven" (7). This "generation before them"—authors of the CCSS, assessment experts, current K–12 teachers, administrators, curriculum designers, and even teacher-educators—must find ways to leverage students' technological knowledge to improve their college and career preparation, which includes students' ability to read, research, and write digital texts.

We and our contributors believe attention to preparation for living, learning, and working in an increasingly digital world is critical for a variety of reasons. For example, while it is somewhat comforting to know that researchers like Clark and Formby (2013) believe that today's students are coming to the world of work with technological knowledge, it is clear that they will need it to manage the information load they will certainly encounter. In *How Much Information? 2010 Report on Enterprise Server Information*, researchers James E. Short, Roger E. Bohn, and Chaitanya Baru of the Global Information Industry Center at the University of California, San Diego comment that "[b]usinesses today are awash with information and the data used to create it. Daily, managers are confronted with growing information volumes far greater than can possibly be consumed" (2011, 8). The researchers base this claim on their study of the amount of information processed on servers worldwide, with a volume in 2008 equal to 3 terabytes of information per worker per year, or 12 gigabytes per worker per day. This amount is roughly equivalent to 2 hours of high definition video or 12 million pages of text per worker per day (9).

Another reason has to do with how students today are interacting with information through their digital devices. While it likely will not surprise most readers of this chapter that recent studies suggest more and more young people are reading on digital devices rather than holding traditional texts, they might not realize just how significant of a generational shift has occurred and just how much digital technologies are impacting students' interaction with information. The Pew Internet & American Life Project report *Teens and Technology 2013*, for example, highlights a national survey of more than 800 teens in which authors find that "[o]ne in four teens are 'cell-mostly' internet users, who say they *mostly go online using their phone* and not using some other device such as a desktop or laptop computer" (Madden et al. 2013, 2; emphasis in original). Another set of Pew researchers, in fact, claim that more than 70 percent of students today use their phones to complete school assignments (Purcell, Buchanan, and Friedrich 2013, 4), and a 2013 study from the U.K. finds that the only type of text that has increased in readership among young people over the past few years is the ebook, which has seen twice as many young people (11.9 percent) reading this type of text since 2010 (5.6 percent) (Clark 2013, 12). Clark and Formby (2013) present similar findings in their report when they note that 64 percent of students read on a mobile phone, 70 percent on a tablet, and 38 percent on a gaming console, leading the researchers to conclude that "young people are technology-savvy, using it not only to communicate and to stay connected but also as part of their wider literacy lives. This savviness ... should be harnessed accordingly" (8). We see the approaches and responses to the CCSS offered by contributors to the collection as one way of harnessing this savviness.

The contributors to this book do not consider the full impact of this emerging "mobile generation"[2] and the ways in which internet-ready mobile technologies could be integrated into the ELA curriculum, as doing so is far beyond the current version and vision of the CCSS;[3] however, contributors do attempt to harness students' technological literacies, pairing them with the CCSS Anchor Standards for Reading and for Writing. In doing so, the contributors are not just bringing the CCSS into the digital age but also helping those working with the standards to prepare their students to be more college and career ready. Even as our contributors try to pair the CCSS with the realities of living in the digital age, it is clear that further steps will need to be taken as the technology uses and information behaviors of the next digital scholar become more fully understood. As Madden and colleagues (2013) note, "In many ways, teens represent the leading edge of mobile connectivity" (3). The authors rightly conclude that the technology uses of today's students "often signal future changes" to the adult world (3), a world of work that is increasingly digital.

Another reason has to do with students themselves, as their college and career aspirations along with their perceptions of their literacy skills and needs to be career ready appear to be out of step with the perceptions of employers and those often charged with preparing them to transition from requisite to vocational education. While a 2013 Nielsen poll of more than 29,000 internet users in 58 countries around the globe found that more than 70 percent believed receiving a higher education degree is important to both better employment and higher income (3), a 2012 survey conducted by the Confederation of British Industry, the leading organization on employment and labor in the U.K., found that 35 percent of employers were dissatisfied with the English literacy and 30 percent with the math skills of high school graduates (Macey 2013, 3). Researchers in two recent empirical studies—one in math and the other in English—in the U.S. examining what skills are needed to be successful in community college (the site of most vocational education in the U.S.) similarly conclude that "a large fraction of high school graduates cannot now do the work required of them in the first year of the typical community college program ... these studies show [us] that our [K–12] schools do not teach what their students need, while demanding of them what they don't need; furthermore, the skills that we do teach and that the students do need, we teach ineffectively" (National Center on Education and the Economy 2013, 2).

The studies, conducted by the National Center on Education and the Economy, investigated the level of literacy needed to be successful in typical first-year courses in math and English at community colleges. In their study on English language skills, the researchers collected materials—student assignments and tests—from community colleges in seven U.S. states to analyze the reading and writing skills needed for success in the first-year writing course (4). Their results signal that many secondary students are not receiving the ELA preparation that they need in high school, at least according to those who educate them in the beginning stages of their postsecondary careers. This finding suggests that secondary and postsecondary educators, administrators, and information science professionals must have more and better conversations about the learning needs of students.

The perspective of teachers on the influence of digital technologies—and the access to information they facilitate—on young people's writing, reading, and researching habits and skills is just as telling. In the first of a three-part report published by the Pew Internet & American Life Project, *How Teens Do Research in the Digital World*, Kristen Purcell and colleagues discuss the results of a survey of more than 2,000 Advanced Placement (AP) and National Writing Project (NWP) teachers asked to respond to the ways in which the rise in digital technologies and materials have affected the work of students. In what the researchers term the "information-saturated digital lives of teens," they see in the survey results that teachers' top priority working with next digital scholars is teaching them how to locate, evaluate, and use quality information (2012, 2). As we have reported elsewhere,[4] the influence of search engines and social technologies on students' research, reading, and writing habits is profound. The Pew researchers report that more than half of teachers responding to the survey say that students are "very likely" to use Google, Wikipedia, and YouTube in a typical research-writing assignment, with nearly all respondents (94 percent) noting students' affinity for Google. These results signal that the next digital scholar engages in research, writing, and reading behaviors from a different foundation than many of us who teach them and devise standards documents for them. It is imperative, therefore, that we seek to come to a better understanding of what students do and how they see the digital information landscape when we endeavor to prepare students to be "college and career ready."

Responses to the "Problem"

Despite the inclination of many to see students' heavy use of search engines and social technologies as the cause of the research-writing "problem," a topic we discuss at length in *The New Digital Scholar*, Purcell, Judy Buchanan, and Linda Friedrich argue differently, claiming that "the concerns actually reflect a slow response from parents and educators to shape their own expectations and students' learning environments in a way that better reflects the world today's students live in" (2013, 7). Teachers themselves see students' heavy reliance on digital technologies and social media as a mixed bag. More than half of teacher respondents in Purcell, Buchanan, and Friedrich's study find their students quite savvy in using these technologies to locate information. Where students seem to falter is evaluating and using it: 71 percent have difficulty recognizing bias, 61 percent struggle with identifying quality, and 59 percent fail to see a need for synthesis. In fact, the largest concern teachers have is students' apparent lack of patience and determination when researching, with 77 percent of teachers reporting this concern, leading more than 90 percent of teachers to agree that "content focusing on digital literacy *must be* incorporated into every school's curriculum" (Purcell, Buchanan, and Friedrich 2013, 6–7, emphasis in original). While the CCSS are an imperfect initiative to accomplish this goal, they do represent an important opportunity to begin to achieve this end.

Whereas teachers routinely have a mixed response to students' digital research behavior, they usually have a more positive view of students' digital writing behavior. They see digital technologies as facilitating the teaching and learning of writing. In particular, teachers see the influence of digital tools in students' understanding, investment, and engagement with audience, genre, personal expression and creativity, collaborative writing, and the writing process (Purcell, Buchanan, and Friedrich 2013, 2). Purcell, Buchanan, and Friedrich find that more than half of the teachers in their survey believe students have above average ability in organizing writing, understanding diverse perspectives, and using an appropriate tone for their audience. We acknowledge that the teachers surveyed for this Pew report are by their role as AP teachers and NWP participants not only invested in their own professional development but also working with advanced students. We assume that a survey representing a broader audience across the K–12 experience would likely yield less impressive results. Still, this report suggests that teachers are seeing some benefit to students' writing from their experiences with digital technologies.

What the report also suggests, however, and what a broader sample would likely reinforce, is the struggle that students have blending researching, reading, and writing. More than two-thirds of teachers report that students do not navigate well fair use and copyright in writing. Nor do they read and digest long or complicated texts well. More than half of teachers report students do not appropriately cite or reference source material in their writing (Purcell, Buchanan, and Friedrich 2013, 4). While most teachers spend class time discussing these issues with students, they regularly note "how easy it is for students to copy and paste others' work into their own and how difficult it often is to determine the actual source of much of the content they find online" (5). As trainers of new writing teachers and writing consultants, we include in this volume a section on teacher preparation (see Part Five, "Approaches to Teacher Training") precisely to help new ELA teachers respond to the CCSS in ways that better prepare students for this work. While we are concerned with students' information behaviors and how these behaviors manifest themselves in student writing, we are encouraged by the innovative ways in which teachers and librarians across the country, like those collected in this book, are responding in step with advancements in digital technologies. Indeed, we have no choice if we are to take seriously the charge of the CCSS and what studies like those referenced in this chapter reveal.

Endnotes

1. Members of the English Panel include names recognizable to writing studies specialists, including George Hillocks and Howard Tinberg.
2. Christina Clark in a separate 2012 study of 21,000 students ages 8–16 in the U.K. for the National Literacy Trust found that close to nine out of 10 (88.6 percent) had their own mobile phone. It seems that the mobile phone is almost as common as the pencil in classrooms today.
3. We recognize, as critics of the CCSS have pointed out, that the Anchor Standards for Reading and for Writing maintain an overall print-centric approach to ELA; however, they also acknowledge, more so than previous national standards, the role of—and provide standards specific to—digital technologies. While we would argue that the CCSS could (and should) go further, we see this inclusion as a productive gesture.
4. See Purdy's "Wikipedia Is Good for You!?" (2010) and "Scholarliness as Other" (2013) and McClure's "Googlepedia: Turning Information Behaviors into Research Skills" (2011).

References

Albers, Peggy. 2013. "Understanding Digital and Media Texts in the Common Core." In *Closer Readings of the Common Core: Asking Big Questions About the English/Language Arts Standards*, edited by Patrick Shannon, 43–52. Portsmouth, NH: Heinemann.

Clark, Christina. 2012. *Young People's Writing in 2011*. National Literacy Trust (U.K.). Accessed February 10, 2014. www.literacytrust.org.uk/assets/0001/3536/Young_people_s_writing_in_2011-final.pdf.

———. 2013. *Children's and Young People's Reading in 2012*. National Literacy Trust (U.K.). Accessed February 10, 2014. www.literacytrust.org.uk/assets/0001/8829/Young_people_s_reading_2012_-_Final.pdf.

Clark, Christina, and Susie Formby. 2013. *Young People's Views on Literacy Skills and Employment*. National Literacy Trust (U.K.). Accessed February 10, 2014. www.literacytrust.org.uk/assets/0001/7767/Young_people_and_employment.pdf.

Council of Chief State School Officers and the National Governors Association. 2010a. *Common Core State Standards for English Language Arts & Literacy in History/Social Studies, Science, and Technical Subjects*. Washington, DC: National Governors Association Center for Best Practices, Council of Chief State School Officers.

Accessed February 10, 2014. www.corestandards.org/assets/CCSSI_ELA%20 Standards.pdf.

———. 2010b. "Mission Statement." *Common Core State Standards Initiative.* Accessed February 10, 2014. www.corestandards.org.

Macey, Emma. 2013. *Employers' Views of Youth Literacy and Employability.* National Literacy Trust (U.K.). Accessed February 10, 2014. www.literacytrust.org.uk/assets/0001/7766/Employer_perspective.pdf.

Madden, Mary, Amanda Lenhart, Maeve Duggan, Sandra Cortesi, and Urs Gasser. 2013. *Teens and Technology 2013.* Pew Internet & American Life Project. Accessed February 10, 2014. www.pewinternet.org/~/media/Files/Reports/2013/PIP_TeensandTechnology2013.pdf.

McClure, Randall. 2011. "Googlepedia: Turning Information Behaviors into Research Skills." In *Writing Spaces: Readings on Writing*, Volume 2, edited by Charles Lowe and Pavel Zemliansky. Anderson, SC: Parlor Press.

———. 2013. "Min(d)ing the Gap: Research on the Information Behaviors of NextGen Students." In *The New Digital Scholar: Exploring and Enriching the Research and Writing Behaviors of NextGen Students*, edited by Randall McClure and James P. Purdy, 19–40. Medford, NJ: Information Today, Inc.

McClure, Randall, and James P. Purdy. 2013. *The New Digital Scholar: Exploring and Enriching the Research and Writing Practices of NextGen Students.* Medford, NJ: Information Today, Inc.

National Center on Education and the Economy. 2013. *What Does It Really Mean to Be College and Work Ready? The Mathematics and English Literacy Required of First Year Community College Students.* Accessed February 10, 2014. www.ncee.org/college-and-work-ready.

Nielsen Company. 2013. *A Gateway to a Better Life: Education Aspirations Around the World.* New York: Nielsen. Accessed February 10, 2014. www.nielsen.com/content/dam/corporate/us/en/reports-downloads/2013%20Reports/Nielsen-Global-Education-Aspirations-September-2013.pdf.

Purcell, Kristen, Judy Buchanan, and Linda Friedrich. 2013. *The Impact of Digital Tools on Student Writing and How Writing Is Taught in Schools.* Washington, DC: Pew Internet & American Life Project. Accessed February 10, 2014. pewinternet.org/reports/2013/teachers-technology-and-writing.

Purcell, Kristen, Lee Rainie, Alan Heaps, Judy Buchanan, Linda Friedrich, Amanda Jacklin, Clara Chen, and Kathryn Zickuhr. 2012. *How Teens Do Research in the Digital World.* Washington, DC: Pew Internet & American Life Project. Accessed February 10, 2014. pewinternet.org/reports/2012/student-research.

Purdy, James P. 2010. "Wikipedia Is Good for You!?" In *Writing Spaces: Readings on Writing*, Volume 1, edited by Charles Lowe and Pavel Zemliansky. Anderson, SC: Parlor Press.

———. 2013. "Scholarliness as Other: How Students Explain Their Research-Writing Behaviors." In *The New Digital Scholar: Exploring and Enriching the Research and

Writing Practices of NextGen Students, edited by Randall McClure and James P. Purdy, 133–159. Medford, NJ: Information Today, Inc.

Short, James E., Roger E. Bohn, and Chaitanya Baru. 2011. *How Much Information? 2010 Report on Enterprise Server Information*. San Diego: Global Information Industry Center.

CHAPTER 2

Learning From Digital Students and Teachers
Reimagining Writing Instruction and Assessment for the 21st Century

Elizabeth Homan and Dawn Reed

A Shifting Terrain: Digital Literacies in Today's Classrooms

Hannah[1] walks into class ready for the new school year. A typical high school student who texts every day, Hannah types her papers on her phone then emails them to herself, takes pictures of notes from the board to use later on, and feels more confident when her cell phone is nearby, ready to capture her latest thought via text, Twitter, or other social media. Hannah embraces these common technology uses in her everyday life, which led to a smooth experience using online forums for class discussions. Hannah is ready to jump right in and share her work in collaborative spaces, discussing texts in online spaces and creating multimedia compositions. She is ready to enhance her 21st-century literacy skills and to learn alongside her teachers, as they together explore blogging for a real world audience.

Students come to our classes with skills for using technologies from their everyday lives, but merging these skills with the "school context" isn't always seamless. Sometimes teachers fear learning something new at the same time as their students. In other cases, professional development and support for teachers to learn digital technologies isn't readily available. The never-ending time crunch is also a constant nemesis for teachers. Districts are not sure how to design policies for web safety; some block students from websites and track technologies students and teachers are using for purposes of "catching" them off task, while others allow full access to online spaces and trust students and teachers alike to practice "web smarts" in school. Students, too, sometimes struggle when they are taken out of their technological comfort zones or when they aren't sure how their multimedia work will be assessed by teachers. Students may worry about losing a digital composition, failing to effectively save or post a composition, or posting their writing for an online audience that includes their teenage peers. And, despite the popular belief that students are constantly connected like Hannah, some simply resist digital assignments or aren't interested in engaging with new online writing spaces. Moreover, some students do not come to our classes with skill sets such as Hannah's and need to learn the technology basics.

Dawn Reed is a high school English teacher at Okemos High School (OHS), in Okemos, Michigan, and co-director of the Red Cedar Writing Project at Michigan State University. She works with Hannah and students like her every day, making decisions about how, when, and where to best use digital technologies to meet their curricular goals. Elizabeth Homan, a doctoral candidate at the University of Michigan and a former middle and high school English Language Arts (ELA) teacher, has spent time with Reed and her co-workers, learning how their decisions about digital technology use revolve around social, structural, and material factors in the classroom. This collaborative research has led us to question how some digital environments enable or constrain particular types of assessment, and what digital technologies bring to (or detract from) the assessment and evaluation of student writing.

Despite the common obstacles facing students like Hannah and teachers like Reed, communication in digital spaces is an essential component of learning and student preparation for college and career readiness. As the Common Core State Standards (CCSS) emphasize, "The skills and understandings students are expected to demonstrate have wide applicability outside the classroom or workplace," and students today must be able to "habitually perform the critical reading necessary to pick carefully through the staggering amount of information available today in print and digitally" (Council of Chief State School Officers [CCSSO] and the National Governors Association [NGA] 2010, 3). Educators, therefore, must prompt students to carefully consider their audiences and purposes for their writing as well as assist them in the reading and information gathering process that makes writing work. They must prepare students for online environments so that students can become conscientious and critical users of online spaces.

Regardless of where the students and teachers fall on the spectrum of knowledge and use of digital literacies, the reality is that digital technologies have changed the way we communicate and interact with the world.

As Sara Kajder (2010), digital writing scholar, secondary ELA teacher, and former professor of English education notes, 21st-century students come to teachers with multiple literacies that are "social, active, and connective" in nature (7), regardless of which technologies they find familiar or foreign. Kajder describes students whose digital literacies vary across platforms and devices. For example, an aspiring photographer who used Flickr branched out to begin blogging on WordPress.com, and a student collaborated with his peers to take an oral history assignment to a new level with podcasting. We have seen similarly diverse literacy practices come to our classrooms and have witnessed teachers and students working together to reimagine writing instruction and, by extension, writing assessment.

Like their students, teachers and librarians also engage with digital technologies in their lives inside and outside of school, and the span of their experiences varies as well. Educators are putting digital technologies to work in their teaching and personal lives in ways as diverse and complex as those of the adolescents who populate their classrooms. In a survey Homan recently conducted in one Midwestern high school, 46 percent of teachers reported using smart phones and tablets in their teaching, and 60 percent reported using video or photo sharing sites like Flickr or YouTube at least occasionally in lessons. Many teachers who integrated these resources into their curricula felt it was important for students to learn how to use these digital technologies critically and effectively. Teachers also cited collaboration, communication between parents and students, and the need to create engaging and relevant lessons as reasons for integrating digital technologies into their curricula.

Many teachers, echoing what Kajder notes is a move toward the use of digital technologies as social tools, argue that digital technologies transform the ways in which they interact and communicate with students and parents. For example, Sarah Zerwin (2011), a high school ELA teacher in Boulder, Colorado, maintains an active class website where she not only posts upcoming assignments, notes from class, and links to her own reading blog, but also links to her class Twitter handle and Facebook page. Using Google Drive and other Google apps, Zerwin is able to extend the reach of her classroom, communicating with students as they revise essays from home or as they post videos or other resources to the class Facebook page or in their own online spaces.

Other teachers, such as Laura Sauer, a high school ELA teacher in Okemos, Michigan, use digital technologies in their private lives as they maintain their own blogs and write columns for popular online news sources. For example, Sauer writes as a featured education and parenting contributor for Yahoo! (2013). Teachers like Sauer use digital writing spaces as a means to hone their own craft of writing and to inform their communities and colleagues or to reflect on their teaching; sometimes, these teachers prepare to lead students in their own adventures with digital technologies such as blogs, challenging them to seek out audiences for their own work.

Educators are also using digital technologies to expand the reach of their professional and personal networks. Zerwin, for example, is using her blogging life to extend her professional network and learning opportunities. Her blog, *The Paper Graders*, which she co-authors with her colleagues Jay Stott and Paul Bursiek, discusses issues related to the teaching of English, and many of her posts reflect on the role of online technologies in the interactive and collaborative ELA classroom. For example, in a blog post from September 11, 2011, Zerwin writes:

> As my students worked (and by "worked" I mean that some were working madly writing with pen or pencil on paper in their writer's notebooks and some were on the computers adding to the collective poem), I had the collective poem Google Doc projected on the big screen from my computer. Some of my students and I watched the poem erupt on the screen, totally transfixed by what was going on. A Google Doc with several people editing it at once looks kind of like Harry Potter's Marauder's Map.

This kind of collaborative composing and group workshopping is commonplace in Sauer's and Zerwin's classes, where students have the ability to share their writing with one another instantaneously and even co-produce texts. This collaborative approach to writing instruction is not a surprise, considering the role of collaborative and network-driven writing in Sauer's and Zerwin's work as teachers within and beyond their classrooms. Teachers' own experiences engaging with authentic audiences help foster rich conversation and reflection with students and colleagues about the role of digital technologies for today's writers. Sauer's and Zerwin's blogging and digital networking outside the classroom enable them to reflect on their teaching experiences, share ideas with other educators, and find new resources for their ELA curricula. Yet, as teachers like Sauer and Zerwin work to include collaborative digital spaces in their teaching lives, current assessment pressures motivate instructional practices that make little room for such writing experiences in today's ELA classrooms—creating an ever-widening gap between writers' realities and the world of writing assessment.

In this chapter, we will first explore how digital writing environments and assessment settings provide different contexts for writing for today's students—contexts that we believe should be questioned and critically examined for their potential to encourage or discourage particular types of writing instruction. We will then describe how one student, Hannah, engages with digital spaces to improve her writing and how Hannah's *digital writing* is very different from the *digitally aided assessment* students like Hannah might soon encounter on standardized tests designed around the CCSS. Finally, we will argue that though the CCSS may offer new ways for educators to think about 21st-century writing, particular approaches to assessment may discourage the very instructional approaches—like those employed by Reed, Sauer, and Zerwin—that are required if we wish to enhance students' digital awareness and literacies and meet the demands of the CCSS.

The Competitive and the Collaborative in 21st-Century Writing Assessment

Despite the shifting literacy practices of students and teachers that we have just described, writing assessment has, in large part, failed to respond to these changes. As we've noted here, many teachers are changing how they assess writing at the local level to reflect the literacy experiences of 21st-century students. However, on district, corporate, and national levels, writing assessment looks much the same as it did three decades ago. The Smarter Balanced Assessment Consortium (SBAC) and Partnership for Assessment of Readiness for College and Careers (PARCC) are developing tests that will include digital components, to be implemented as early as 2015 (with field tests in 2014). As these tests are being developed to assess achievement of the CCSS, various factors are still in question: How will the writing process be represented on these assessments compared to former assessments? How will computerized and human scoring play a role in these assessments?

What are the implications of the answers to these questions for students taking the test and for teachers in the classroom?

While change may be around the corner, trends in writing assessment over the past few decades set a grim precedent. Students still sit down to write essays with pencil and paper on the ACT and SAT, restricted by time, space, medium, and prompt. Their writing is still scored by "normed" readers who have no information about the students' backgrounds, contexts, or experiences. And student revision practices are limited to quick proofreading—if time allows—at the end of a timed testing session. The two testing consortia, SBAC and PARCC, have promised to use online technologies in their national tests; however, these shifts do not necessarily reflect the shift in writing *practices* that we see when we look at writers like Hannah. For example, PARCC's (2014b) literacy component promises to engage students in three "literacy tasks" that require both reading and writing: a literary analysis task, a narrative task, and a research simulation task (for more information, visit parcconline.org/samples/ELA). PARCC's description of the research simulation task is as follows:

> Students will analyze an informational topic presented through several articles or multimedia stimuli, the first text being an anchor text that introduces the topic. Students will engage with the texts by answering a series of questions and synthesizing information from multiple sources in order to write two analytic essays.

Though perhaps students will be encouraged to engage with and analyze texts in an environment that more closely mimics how students today conduct research (e.g., by searching online or synthesizing sources from diverse spaces and genres), this task and others like it still serve to engage students with prompts that are, as we argue here, more driven by competition and isolation than by comprehensive revision and collaboration. Authentic writing often requires collaborative writing—even in work and college settings that are simultaneously competitive. The CCSS recognize and call for this sort of collaborative writing to happen in classrooms; for example, ELA writing standards for 11th and 12th grade state that students should be able to "use technology, including the internet, to produce, publish, and update individual *or shared* writing products *in response to ongoing feedback*" (our emphasis; CCSSO and NGA 2010, W.11–12.6).

In Table 2.1, we examine the composition task from PARCC alongside the digital practices in which students are actively engaged outside (and occasionally inside) of school, and the contrast is easy to see.

Hannah and her peers at OHS regularly use digital technologies to share calendars and make appointments with peers to work on projects; compose poems collaboratively in their creative writing classes; swap drafts with their journalism student editor; and communicate with teachers via email, chat, and even Facebook. However, the writing situations designed to judge their writing abilities are isolated, require students to write in only one mode (verbal), revolve around pre-determined texts and topics that students may or may not find interesting or relevant, and are void of interaction, conversation, or collaboration. Even if students are practicing synthesis (as in the previous example from PARCC), and even if they are engaging texts in a digital format, this does not necessarily mean they are engaging in 21st-century literacies.

Given the CCSS' focus on "college and career readiness" and our concerns about how students' "readiness" is or should be assessed, we turned to leading scholars in writing studies in order to ascertain what skills high school writers might need to develop before entering college. The Framework for Success in Postsecondary Writing (Framework) developed by the Council of Writing Program Administrators (Council of Writing Program Administrators, National Council of Teachers of English, and National Writing Program 2011) in collaboration with other leading professional organizations notes that students need to develop flexible writing processes, including regular revision and feedback from peers and teachers; particular habits of mind, such as metacognition and curiosity; and experiences with critical analysis to be successful after high school. These writing practices are reflected in the left half of our table and are uniquely supported by digital

Table 2.1   Digital vs. Standardized Composition

Characteristics of Digital Composition Opportunities	Characteristics of Standardized Writing Assessments
Interactivity: Social network platforms allow for diverse and overlapping networks, where students develop relationships with other writers and readers who share interests or concerns.	**Isolation:** The writing task involves no interaction with or even knowledge about the reader and no chance for a relationship with the reader.
Revision: Blog posts, wikis, and work in Google Drive can be revisited and revised indefinitely, allowing for constant reworking and representation of ideas. The CCSS identify this requirement (see W.9–12.6).	**Time Constraints:** Though students are encouraged to "review" their work, comprehensive revision is impossible under given time constraints.
Collaboration: Google Drive, Google Hangouts, Skype, social networks (e.g., Spruz, Ning), wikis, and blogs allow for co-authorship and collaborative composing.	**Competition:** Students are not allowed to get ideas from others or collaborate in any way as they compose, and in many cases, their writing will be judged against the ideas of others.
Multimodality: Movie making, blogging, and digital storytelling blend film clips, images, and audio compositions for new rhetorical situations. Visual literacy and the role of copyright are also key issues writers need to consider for this work.	**Unimodality:** Students are limited to verbal expression only in a rhetorical situation that does not mimic what students will encounter in their lives outside of school with authentic audiences and purposes for their writing.
Intellectually Conversational: Students locate, evaluate, and reference online resources. Moreover, this work has expanded to students' participatory culture of research, in which they too contribute to sources, such as through use of Wikipedia.	**Conversationally Void:** Students must form responses to prompts that often would benefit from careful reading and research to inform the writer about the topic. While writing in class may challenge students to inform themselves about the topic and enter a conversation about a text that has already occurred, isolated writing does not allow for this.
Purpose-Driven Navigation: Students must purposefully navigate digital spaces to learn and think as they gain new skills and increase their knowledge. Students must distinguish between sources from diverse genres and writers and synthesize these sources to develop complex arguments.	**Pre-Determined Texts and Topics:** As in the PARCC example, students are given a topic and a number of sources to synthesize instead of being allowed to define a purpose, select sources, and define an audience for their work. Students do not show how they are able to navigate and find sources, but instead they are given texts with which they need to interact.

environments that offer students the "ability to analyze and act on understandings of audiences, purposes, and contexts in creating and comprehending texts" in various media (6). The authors of the Framework and other scholars argue, and we agree, that students need to experience entering existing conversations through inquiry driven by students' own curiosity.

Additionally, in *Because Digital Writing Matters*, the National Writing Project (NWP 2010) offers a "condensed list of traits and actions" that characterizes digitally literate citizens in today's classrooms (100). This list includes, among many other things, the ability to communicate in rhetorical contexts, engage in self-evaluation, remix and repurpose digital texts, and engage in responsible use of media in digital composing. The CCSS address some of these expectations, noting that students need to write with their audiences in mind and in response to social interactions about writing (for example, see CCSSO and NGA 2010, W.9–12.4 and W.9–12.10). Today's large-scale assessments, as they are now conceived and implemented, do not assess the criteria laid out by the Framework, by NWP's exhaustive list of the traits of digital citizens, or by the very standards they purport to assess: the CCSS.

These large-scale assessments are able to address *some* of the requirements of the CCSS, which define genres such as "personal narratives," "informative/explanatory texts," and "arguments," and lay out the requirements for each type of writing (for example, see CCSSO and NGA 2010, W.8.1–3). However, they are unable to assess a critical component recognized by the CCSS, which requires that students engage with writing in collaborative environments, seeking the social assistance of their peers and teachers as they work to revise their writing. For example, the eighth-grade standards for writing include two standards that current large-scale assessments are incapable of assessing. These include one writing standard that requires students to seek "guidance and support from peers and adults," in order to "develop and strengthen writing as needed by planning, revising, editing, rewriting, or trying a new approach, focusing on how well purpose and audience have been addressed" (CCSSO and NGA 2010, W.8.5), and another that requires students to specifically use online environments for collaboration and interaction (CCSSO and NGA 2010, W.8.6). Standards such as these require assessments that can evaluate whether students are able to write and revise collaboratively and constructively over longer periods of time than a single testing session.

As Anne Herrington, Kevin Hodgson, and Charles Moran (2009) note, digital writing and electronic texts "challenge our basic notion of written texts as linear, verbal, single-authored texts," yet the texts students are required to produce in many assessment environments are just that: linear, verbal, and single-authored. They argue that these assessment trends make trouble for teachers who want to reinvent writing assessment to meet the existing literacy needs of students and teachers as well as those standards that call for interactive, collaborative composing:

> At the same time that new forms of writing—and thus literacy—are emerging in our culture and in our classrooms, forces of assessment and standardization exert a counter-pressure, asking us to prepare students to produce conventional, formulaic print texts in scripted ways. (2)

This mismatch between what happens in digital writing environments and what happens during writing assessment is further perpetuated by companies that wish to capitalize on teachers who are trying to prepare students for tests such as the SAT, ACT, or future national tests. As Troy Hicks and colleagues (2014) discuss in their wiki, "School TM: Teacher Decision-Making in the Era of the (For-Profit) Corporate Classroom," many companies are more than willing to capitalize on the testing movement, advertising—as Pearson Education does—that their textbook authors "helped develop the Common Core" (Pearson 2013). Specifically, publishing and testing companies have begun creating automated essay assessment technologies—computerized systems that will "score" student writing, without the need for a human reader. These systems make use of online technologies but do not engage students in "digital writing" in ways that are interactive or promote thoughtful revision. Instead, these systems move linear, verbal, single-authored "school genres" of writing, such as the persuasive essay, into an online program that calculates scores based on mechanics, vocabulary, and sentence structure.

This is not *digital writing*, but *digitally aided writing assessment*. It does not reimagine or redesign writing assessment for the 21st century, but instead it uses digital technologies to engage in assessment practices that remain unchanged at their core.

Three companies are currently leading others in the development and distribution of automated essay assessment systems. These include Vantage Learning, whose MY Access! program has been gaining in popularity in recent years; the Educational Testing Service (ETS), whose

E-Rater and Critique technologies have been applied to multiple products, including Criterion, which is marketed to secondary educators and school districts; and Pearson, who developed its Intelligent Essay Assessor to market as an element of textbook packages (Warschauer and Ware 2006). Systems like MY Access! and Criterion are designed to take the place of individualized teacher feedback on drafts in local, specific classroom settings; teachers dictate which prompt students respond to, the "genres" in which students are writing, and the number of "revisions" students are able to submit. These technologies, which do not take into account the possibilities of digital writing spaces such as blogs, wikis, or document collaboration, adhere to a dated conception of genre that perpetuates an isolated, linear view of writing.

It is unclear at the moment how technologies such as E-Rater will play a role in national assessments currently being designed by SBAC and PARCC. PARCC, however, has created an Automated Scoring Technical Working Group, which, according to its website, is tasked with "advising on issues related to the automated scoring of student writing" (PARCC 2014a). SBAC has similarly promised to use computer adaptive testing techniques in its scoring of student short responses and has teamed with ETS (SBAC 2012b). Thus, it is reasonable to predict that these technologies will play roles in future national assessments. However, this role appears to be limited to online test-taking and online scoring, *not* online writer collaboration and interaction, which the CCSS specifically call for and which, perhaps more importantly, scholars have argued is the direction professional and academic writing are headed in the 21st century.

Writing Assessment, Digital Technologies, and the CCSS

Allow us to return to Hannah, whose writing and composing experiences in her English classes have, over the past few years, enabled us to see the limitations of some forms of writing assessment in the digital age. Here, we will describe one project of Hannah's and contrast it with her writing in response to an ACT-style prompt. In the following section, we will discuss how Hannah's composing process in the two situations differed, from both her perspective as a writer and from our perspectives as English teachers.

Hannah's Digital Composition

Hannah has been afforded opportunities to engage in writing on demand for standardized tests, including the development of essays that take positions on predetermined issues in provided prompts. Hannah has also been involved in various projects designed to help her consider real audiences and purposes and to engage her with multiple media. In her junior year, Hannah participated in discussion forums for her American Literature class through her online academic course network on Spruz, an online social network developed for community networking that allows students to engage in forum discussions, share links, upload presentation materials, and more. Several classes at OHS connect students through online spaces such as this one—some paid for by the district or through grants the teachers write themselves (such as Spruz), others that are free online (such as Google Groups).

American Literature courses at OHS are connected in one academic network across three teachers and five sections, comprising an audience of 180 students and three teachers. In American Literature, Hannah wrote her own "This I Believe" essay and created a podcast of her work focusing on revision through the use of audio and vocal delivery of a message. She then posted her work on the American Literature academic network to share with peers in her class and across classes. These practices were commonplace in her American Literature classroom, so that by the time she was given the assignment "This I Wish to Change"—a research project focused on social awareness or action—Hannah was familiar with many of the affordances of digital composition. Hannah decided to research bullying. Her work culminated in a presentation for her peers and her own selected audience of the high school principal. She designed her project around self-motivated goals to promote awareness for students and her school administrators and requested a school-wide conversation about bullying the following year. Hannah even volunteered to present to the student body, sharing her goals and challenging her peers to take a stand against bullying. The following school year, in her Expository Writing class, Hannah revisited this topic in further research, reimagining her own understanding of bullying among teens using recent cases of bullying in her community and across the nation.

Hannah developed both a research paper and a repurposed presentation for her peers, each designed to relay similarly powerful messages. For her presentation, Hannah created her first video documentary, which focused on an interview she conducted with a student in her class who faced serious bullying that led her to change schools. Hannah wrote and directed a short film to show her class an "insider's perspective" of bullying's consequences. As Hannah explained, to understand the negative impact of bullying one needs to witness firsthand the experiences of a person who is or has been bullied. Hannah's bullying project and its many iterations illustrate how today's students are ready to engage in the possibilities digital composition offers. It demonstrates the development of student thinking over the course of not just one isolated piece of writing, but multiple projects over multiple school years. Moreover, in accordance with the characteristics outlined in Table 2.1, her documentary work demonstrates the following qualities.

Interactivity

The CCSS call for students to produce compositions that respond to rhetorical situations, taking into consideration audience, purpose, and other contextual elements of the writing situation (CCSSO and NGA 2010, W.11, 12.4–6). Hannah's piece meets these requirements, because it was designed with her peer/administrator audience in mind and focused on Hannah's desire to entertain and inform her peers about the severe consequences of bullying. Hannah's piece not only required peer interaction (through interviews and the production of a film), but also allowed Hannah to speak to an audience beyond just her teacher. Moreover, although Hannah's film is not currently posted online, it could be published and reach an even wider audience. This is a piece of audience interaction that Hannah continues to debate, despite the fact that she has completed the class. In this way, this writing experience is one that remains interactive even after the course has ended.

Revision

Through the pairing of print and digital technologies, Hannah's compositions and critical thinking were extensively revised, developed, and honed based on new research, which the CCSS call for in multiple standards (for example, see CCSSO and NGA 2010, W.11–12.2, W.11–12.5). Moreover, Hannah reimagined her work through a repurposed presentation. Her assignment was to extend her thinking about the topic beyond one rhetorical situation and for different audiences. She needed to provide a new purpose for her research, in which she would inform an audience (her class and ideally a larger audience of her choice) about her topic. Her presentation needed to be designed with persuasive use of visual, auditory, or other digital media. She was also instructed to pay attention and give careful thought to engaging her audience. With that in mind, Hannah revised not only her print text, but also take-after-take of her interviews and film, requiring her to reimagine and repurpose her content for multiple media and multiple audiences.

Collaboration

From working in Google Drive on her research paper to texting ideas to her "actors" and interviewees about her film production, the entire process of Hannah's research was one in which collaboration and peer response moved her writing and thinking forward. Her work in digital spaces spilled into the classroom during small group discussions and conversations where students huddled around a keyboard. She was coached by peers and her writing instructor to further her thinking. This collaboration echoes writing production as noted in ELA and Literacy standards, specifically W.11–12.5 and W.11–12.6.

Multimodality

Considerations of film angles, soundtrack options, and video (re)mixes were all part of the multimodal analysis Hannah needed to create her film. She also needed to thank and cite her interviewees and actors as well as cite material she mixed into the film, including music clips and additional film clips she used from YouTube. Through crediting her sources, interviewees, and actors, Hannah participated in interactive and important considerations for multimodal composition, which included addressing proper copyright information associated with such publication. Unfortunately, the CCSS do not always acknowledge the importance of composition in multiple modes, yet some standards call for students to be aware of the affordances and limitations of resources and information presented in various digital and material sources (for example, see CCSSO and NGA 2010, W.11–12.6, W.11–12.9).

Intellectually Conversational

A major component of the writing process is publication, and this is reflected in the CCSS for writing (CCSSO and NGA 2010, W.11–12.6). In her research assignment, Hannah challenged herself to enter intellectual conversations about bullying and to add something new to the conversation through her research paper and project—and conversations can only be entered publicly through publication. To meet this goal, Hannah engaged in primary research through interviews while also evaluating current films and other secondary sources online for credibility and potential bias. To fully enter the intellectual conversation about bullying, Hannah will need to put herself "out there" by sharing her work with a larger audience. Therefore, Hannah is considering the ultimate challenge of sharing her work in an online space for the purpose of intellectual conversation, which means reception of not only praise for her work, but also critical response.

Purpose-Driven Navigation

Hannah selected her topic for research based on her own interests, and she decided how to approach the repurposed presentation by considering both genre and audience. Hannah chose to work with film production for the first time in her repurposed bullying project. Through her integration of her own film with video clips from YouTube, she wove together and remixed texts to create her own unique argument about bullying and how to address it. Her choice to create a documentary to reach her audience provided the opportunity for Hannah not only to highlight her understanding of writing for an audience, but also to merge her thinking into different genres in order to create complex arguments. The CCSS call for students to do the kinds of purpose-driven, audience-aware composition that Hannah does here, but, as any English teacher can tell you, such compositions are strongest when they demonstrate the rhetorical awareness Hannah's project shows (CCSSO and NGA 2010, W.11–12.4).

Hannah also recognized that the evaluation for her work was based on her purposeful thinking and on how she extended her research paper to another rhetorical situation. For her repurposed research presentation, she was instructed to provide a new purpose for her research, reaching a different audience through different media. With these guidelines in mind, Hannah knew she needed to think carefully about purpose and audience, and ultimately, her work was evaluated on how she executed her plan to share her writing with others for the purpose of informing her audience about the impact of bullying. This type of an assignment and the assessment echo the CCSS' call to produce and distribute writing as well as to research and build knowledge and to offer a range of writing experiences. ELA and Literacy standards (CCSSO and NGA 2010, W.11–12.4, 11–12.5, 11–12.6) suggest that writing with audience and purpose in mind and embracing writing as a process are the skills needed for students to be college and career ready. Hannah employed these skills in her documentary work.

Hannah's Standardized Writing

As excited as we are about Hannah's rich digital work, we wondered what Hannah's work in the context of a standardized test would reveal. We asked her to respond to the following ACT style prompt (which we created for this exercise):

> Across the United States, schools are working to address the issue of bullying. Some believe bullying is a major issue in America's schools that needs attention and should be

addressed by schools. Others believe that bullying is a major issue in America's schools that needs attention and should be addressed by parents. Others believe that bullying is not a major issue in America's schools and that media coverage is blowing the topic out of proportion. In your opinion, is bullying an issue that should be addressed?

As is common in ACT tests, the prompt concludes "In your essay, take a position on this question. You may write about either of the points of view given, or you may present a different point of view on this question. Use specific reasons and examples to support your position" (ACT, Inc. 2014). Hannah responded to this question with paper and pencil in a 30-minute time frame. Hannah's writing is included in the appendix at the end of this chapter.

Based on her writing and the juxtaposition of this 30-minute timed writing as compared to her research paper and documentary work, we noted the following about Hannah's work in this (admittedly fabricated) writing situation.

Isolation

This writing selection cannot be considered from an interactive stance because the piece was written in one 30-minute time slot for what she perceived as an outside, unknown audience. ACT scoring offers a standard list of comments that could be assigned to a text besides just the score. Those comments, however, are generic. While some may argue that this is an interactive experience based on the use of these generic generated responses, Hannah would receive no more than her score and a comment based on the corresponding number for that comment, which is designed to respond to any type of writing submitted on the ACT. Despite these audience complications, Hannah recognized this lack of audience and interaction, as evidenced in the title of her piece, "ACT Writing."

Time Constraints

We gave Hannah 30 minutes to write the entire essay. While she did add in a few details on lines and in the margins after she wrote her two-page response, no planning was done to map out her ideas, her writing showed little revision, and she took the entire 30 minutes to write. When we asked Hannah to reflect on her experience with this writing, she noted her lack of time, saying "standardized test taking is still very hard for me because I feel I am being pressured and crunched on time which can cause me to not do my best." Though tests like the ACT provide space for students to plan their writing (and even encourage students to do so in the directions), many students may feel that they cannot afford to "waste time" planning or proofreading, which sends a message that writing happens on the fly, with no revision necessary.

Competition

Though Hannah certainly was not competing with any of her classmates in this situation, writing in standardized testing situations may make some students feel as though they are in competition with one another as they strive to get the best scores in order to be competitive for positions in the best universities. Because standardized tests ask thousands of students to respond to a single prompt, evaluators naturally compare student writing during scoring. Instead of working together to construct texts around shared goals, students in situations like Hannah's write in an effort to "stand out" amongst their peers. At times this can be a motivator for students. However, for some students, including Hannah, this stress may lead to a piece of writing that does not showcase their writing skills. For her research paper and repurposed documentary, Hannah employed various forms of persuasion, and she was especially drawn to the powerful influence of stories, as she used them to engage her audience and make bullying awareness a heartfelt issue—a mode of persuasion not encouraged in most standardized test prompts. Further, writing to an unknown audience deprives Hannah of a rhetorical situation and target audience, and thus of a sense of urgency and purpose for her writing. In this context, Hannah did not engage as richly in thinking about the rhetorical awareness of audience and purpose, partly because they were void, but also because of the time and pressure of standardized testing situations.

Unimodality

Hannah, who most often writes on a digital device, was given an option to respond to this ACT writing prompt on a computer or with pencil and paper. Despite the fact that writing on a computer (or her phone) was her usual preference, because we called it "ACT writing," she opted for paper and pencil. A few months after she wrote for this prompt, we asked her why she made this choice. Her response indicates recognition of a testing situation as well as the concept that the restraints of the writing situation limit her ability to truly express herself because she has more ideas than she feels she can effectively organize. She said:

> When you shared with me that I could write my paper on the computer, I decided to use paper and pencil to be in the reality aspect of what it would be like when I wrote it because that's what I would have to do on the standardized test. For other papers I wanted to use my phone, tablet or a laptop because I knew that's what I was going to have to do and wanted to have a jump start to the writing.

This response from Hannah further suggests her awareness of writing situations that impact her approaches to writing. Though future students may be able to type their ACT essays, they will not be able to use social media or document collaboration to share ideas or receive feedback from peers.

Conversationally Void

This writing task did not engage Hannah in a conversation with others. Hannah understood the conversation to be isolated from other intellectual conversations. Though she has entered intellectual conversations about bullying while working on components of her evolving project, she did not integrate these conversations in her essay nor did she reference what she has learned about bullying through research. True, Hannah could have cited sources she already knew from her research; however, despite the work Hannah had done on her research paper and documentary, she neglected to engage in an intellectual conversation about bullying (a topic she was equipped to discuss at a high level). This could be partly because of time restraints, but may also be because Hannah did not recognize this as a conversational form of writing or as a form of writing that required her to synthesize multiple sources.

Pre-Determined Texts and Topics

For this prompt, Hannah was given a topic that she has a lot of interest in and that she was knowledgeable about given her extensive research. Yet despite Hannah's efforts, interests, and research knowledge, she lacked the passion that she brought to the topic when truly considering the needs of her audience. When asked to reflect on her writing after she completed the ACT essay, she mentioned that she felt there "were a lot of gaps in this piece of writing, so it's more of a drafty piece for me where if I spent enough time and effort there would be more details and thoughts." Her reflection here shows her recognition that she could build in more information for an intellectual conversation. However, when we asked her what she meant by "gaps," she noted specific content she would have included, such as "reasons people fall into bullying" and "what leads them to bully others." Despite her intrinsic interest in this topic, time constraints limited her ability to produce the kind of text she wants to and can produce.

Beyond Hannah's observations, we were curious how an automated assessment system would "read" Hannah's writing. We explored the free website Paper Rater (paperrater.com), where we entered Hannah's writing for a score from the machine grader, similar to the work of Herrington and Moran (2001). Paper Rater's technology "combines the power of natural language processing (NLP), artificial intelligence (AI), machine learning, information retrieval (IR), computational linguistics, data mining, and advanced pattern matching (APM)" (Paper Rater 2010). These algorithms are similar to those marketed by ETS, Pearson, and Vantage Learning, all of whom use natural language processing techniques to design their algorithms (however, because those algorithms and programs are proprietary, we were not able to access or analyze them for this example).

The first scores that Paper Rater gave us in response to Hannah's essay were grammar and spelling scores. Word choice was the next factor in the report, in which Hannah's writing received a "Bad Phrase Score," which examines the degree to which Hannah uses "bad phrases" in her writing. This score assured us (and Hannah) that her score was "within an acceptable range, which shows that you have a solid grasp on which phrases to avoid in your writing." However, which phrases Hannah successfully avoided were not listed in the feedback. Writing style was scored through a focus on "transitional words." Hannah's writing received the following feedback: "Good job! Your usage of transitional phrases is within an acceptable range!" Hannah's writing also received a "Vocabulary Score" of 49 with the comment "This paper could benefit from greater usage of vocabulary words. Although your vocabulary score is within the average range for most writers, boosting it above 60 will help your paper stand out." Ultimately, Hannah's paper was auto-graded as follows: "Grade: 81% a B based on college grading scale."

Despite the rhetorical skills Hannah demonstrated through her work with extensive research, revision, and multimodal composition in her research paper and documentary, this ACT writing sample was one that we would not grade as a B in a college course, especially if we considered global concerns of idea development and argument support. As Hannah's teachers, we hoped her writing would further engage existing conversations about bullying and that her argument would develop over the course of the essay, instead of jumping as it does from self-esteem to self-absorption to punishment. Spelling, grammar, and style, while relevant, hardly seem to be the top concerns in an essay meant to assess students' argument development and critical thinking.

After Hannah wrote this piece, we asked her about her own strengths and weaknesses in her response to the ACT-style prompt. Hannah told us she believed she had well-rounded ideas but that she thought her "sentence flow" was a weakness. She also noted that she would have gone in more depth if she had more time. We also asked Hannah to score her own writing. She gave herself a 4.5/10 (a score much lower than Paper Rater). After Hannah shared her initial reactions, we showed Hannah the results from Paper Rater. Hannah shared her reaction:

> I looked at the results from the machine and I'm pretty shocked at what I recieved [*sic*]. I do agree about the use of vocabulary. I could have used a better word choice, but that comes from being timed and having to put together a paragraph to a page in a certain amount of time without really thinking about how you're going to start your paper, paragraphs, sentences and have a good conclusion to wrap it altogether [*sic*].

Though Hannah did agree with concepts noted in the scoring of her essay, such as the vocabulary comment, her shock further echoes our reaction to the grade received. She said "The shock about the machine scoring would be the score I recieved [*sic*]. I gave good information and thought it out as best as I could with the time I had, but didn't feel I did as good as what the machine said."

Our—and Hannah's—Reflections

After comparing Hannah's writing experiences with our impressions and her auto-assessed results, we wanted to know how she would compare multimodal composition and standardized writing. In her documentary project, Hannah immediately responded to her desire to address the needs of her audience. Hannah argues that "visual is more efficient for your audience because they are going to understand the message they are trying to get across rather than in a 30 minute" writing session. Hannah also spoke about the need to map ideas out visually as part of her writing process. We asked her, "How do you view your process as a writer when you are involved in multimedia composition?" She noted that she brainstormed to start, and her process of brainstorming focused on a visual map of her ideas:

> The way that I brainstorm it, isn't like through writing it down, it's through like making a diagram on a PowerPoint or on a Word document [...]. So, all my ideas are in a web or a list or something like that so, when I go to ACT for the prompt area and I have to do the 30 minutes, I kinda struggle because I'm visual and it's easier for me to see things and I feel like I don't have enough time to make a full length web or list with all my ideas that I have.

She noted that she appreciates when she can map out her ideas in a web format or an outline in a visual space, such as in Microsoft PowerPoint. Recognizing the value of feedback, Hannah praised collaboration and feedback on writing that doesn't have constraints like those established in a timed writing. She also lauded the opportunity to make her work visual whenever possible.

We asked Hannah about her voice as a writer within these two writing contexts: "What about voice? How do you understand your voice as a writer in multimedia compositions or standardized testing?" Hannah replied:

> When I'm doing visuals for like PowerPoint or my [film] or anything like that, I feel like I have more power, because I know what I'm trying to say, and I know what I'm trying to get across. I can improvise if I need to stop it. I can talk about something really quick. [In] the ACT I'm not able to clarify or explain something, because it's written down, and there is no way of contacting me when you do that.

So we asked Hannah, "Is it because it's timed and you have more time to think it out?" She replied, "I think it helps when I think it out more." When comparing her work on her research paper and repurposed presentation, however, she commented that she felt like her work in standardized testing was "not giving her full potential" based on the constraints of the writing prompt and setting. She notes, "I feel like when you do the ACT writing it is less interactive, because you're not able to explain yourself to the readers who are reading it and you don't really know who your audience is going to be, which can make it hard." Students like Hannah understand that standardized testing situations are not reflective of real-life writing situations, nor do they enable writing experiences that may best reflect today's college and career settings.

Moving Forward in Our Digital Reality

In a 2011 article that analyzed and reported on various writing assessment technologies, Colleen Vojak and colleagues argue that "many of these programs largely neglect the potential that technology has to offer in terms of our three foundational understandings of writing: that it is a socially situated practice; that it is a functionally and formally diverse activity; and that it is increasingly multimodal" (108). The authors note that many technologies made *specifically for* writing assessment mimic the forms of writing students will find on standardized tests, and they are marketed as such, proclaiming that the use of these technologies will raise student test scores in writing. The problem is not with the technology, they argue, but lies in the use of digital technologies to "reinforce old practices" (108), such as those Hannah encountered as she responded to a bullying prompt instead of imagining and speaking to an existing audience and developing a purpose-driven argument for that audience.

What we have learned from students like Hannah and from other teachers like Reed, Sauer, and Zerwin is not new. Writing studies scholars long ago acknowledged that writing is best when it is authentic and purpose-driven, and offers multiple opportunities for collaboration and revision. Today, however, our ability to encourage collaboration and revision is enabled by technologies that, in Sauer's words, "change writing instruction entirely." Google Drive allows teachers to view revision histories, making the process of revision "more fluid," as Sauer said in an interview conducted by Homan.[2] Free blogging sites like Edublogs, Blogger, and WordPress.com make it easy for students to share their writing with authentic audiences students can both identify and target. iMovie, Movie Maker, and digital voice recorders make it easy for teachers and students to engage in multimodal composition that brings together audio, images, video, and text.

The CCSS point in some promising directions. They encourage teachers to engage students with the rhetorical context of their writing by considering audience and purpose and revising regularly and comprehensively. It remains to be seen how national assessments will respond to these shifts in standards, but it will be difficult to impossible for national tests to assess students' ability to effectively engage in interactive and collaborative writing processes. Recent trends concern us because, as Bill Cope and colleagues (2011) note, today's computing practices are social and interpersonal, not isolated and independent. Though students certainly need to be able to show what they have learned through their writing, 21st-century literacies challenge policymakers and test developers to acknowledge the role of formative assessment for today's students and tomorrow's digital scholars. Cope and his colleagues go so far as to imagine a future dominated by these formative assessments:

> The shifts we are experiencing today [...] offer enormous opportunities for the reform of assessment. We imagine a time in the not-too-distant future when there is no practical distinction between formative and summative assessment. [...] If and when this day arrives, there will be no need for the problematic end-of-program, high-stakes, or accountability-defining tests that we have today. Formative assessment will be pervasive—a repertoire of modes of machine-assisted social intelligence that provides continuous feedback to learners in a rapidly responsive manner and with sufficient substantive feedback. (91)

This vision for a future dominated by formative assessment and meaningful, collaborative social interactions around the multimodal texts students produce is an enticing one. However, college placement tests like the SAT and ACT and the national assessments being designed by SBAC and PARCC are realities for today's teachers, who need to prepare students to be high achievers, however one chooses to define "achievement." To that end, we see some promising trends in the CCSS and in what we currently know about the future national assessments. We are concerned, however, about gaps that we believe need to be addressed before we can move forward into our new digital reality.

In the writing section of the CCSS for high school, it is clear that students should be able to "use technology, including the internet, to produce, publish, and update individual or shared writing products, taking advantage of technology's capacity to link to other information and to display information flexibly and dynamically" before the end of 10th grade (CCSSO and NGA 2010, W.9–10.6). This standard and others like it encourage teachers to take advantage of digital texts' capabilities to hyperlink to other sources, to enable collaboration with writers across time and space, and to regularly revise and reimagine one's writing for new audiences—all components of the digital literacies many students already enact in other spaces. Another standard requires that students be able to "make strategic use of digital media (e.g., textual, graphical, audio, visual, and interactive elements) in presentations to enhance understanding of findings, reasoning, and evidence and to add interest" (CCSSO and NGA 2010, SL.9–10.5). Hannah illustrated mastery of both of these goals in the many manifestations of her project on bullying. These standards offer many and varied opportunities for assessment, including (but not limited to) co-authored or individually authored student blogs; co-authored class wikis on student-generated topics; and digital storytelling or other video editing projects, such as annotated photo sharing.

Further promise lies in potential attempts by PARCC to integrate digital texts into writing assessment prompts such as the "research simulation tasks." PARCC may also incorporate a speaking and listening nonsummative component to their benchmark testing which will require students "to integrate and evaluate information from multimedia sources" (PARCC 2014c). Similarly, SBAC (2012a) pilot items take advantage of computer technologies by allowing students to view and respond to multimodal texts. These shifts acknowledge *some* of the changing reading and text consumption practices and expectations of today's student population.

However, the sample items we could find for the yet-to-be-implemented SBAC and PARCC national tests were unable to capture the digital *composing* practices of today's ELA classroom teachers and students. Though students may be asked on new national assessments to engage with multimodal texts, they will not, it appears, be asked to compose multimodally or collaboratively. And even if this component were integrated into these standardized assessments, it would be impossible for these tasks to imitate the classroom interactions and assignments that are so motivating for students like Hannah. The very contextual cues that were integral to these students' success cannot be mimicked on a standardized assessment that will be scored by an unknown audience or, worse, a machine. Though the CCSS seem to encourage integration of online digital technologies into the curriculum, assessments may not be able to respond to these calls for change, because they inherently separate the writer from his or her audience, purpose, and topic.

Further complicating any potential reforms of writing assessment—small-scale or large-scale—is the rising popularity of automated assessment systems such as the open-access system we used to "grade" Hannah's ACT essay. These technologies may make assessing writing more "efficient," but as many scholars have noted, they completely negate the many human elements of writing that comprise meaningful writing experiences in both digital and nondigital spaces (Cope et al. 2011; Herrington and Moran 2001; Rothermel 2006). These technologies also promote writing that is very distinct from the *digital writing* we describe in this chapter. This is instead *digitally aided assessment of writing* that threatens, with its promises to streamline grading and make testing more efficient, to make impossible reforms that incorporate the collaborative, interactive, and multimodal forms of writing that we see our students bringing to the classroom. Indeed, as we have shown in our description of Hannah's distinct engagements with writing about bullying, an approach that engages students in *digital writing* instead of *digitally aided assessment* requires significant support from teachers and peers, engagement with authentic audiences close to students' experiences, and the opportunity to consistently and frequently revise. Assessment in the digital age, then, requires an acknowledgement of the local, immediate, and social nature of writing.

We would like to acknowledge that the skills measured by standardized assessments—current and future—are not entirely inapplicable to the tasks students will be required to perform in college or career settings. Students certainly need to engage in somewhat independent development of complex arguments in order to succeed in the college writing classroom, and engaging students in independent writing tasks in both formative and summative assessments remains an integral component of any literacy curriculum. However, there are many ways in which the "independent" writing students do in school is collaborative and interactive, even if it is not multimodal or "born digital." As the classrooms and digital practices of Reed, Sauer, and Zerwin illustrate, even linear essays or poems can be places for productive interactions surrounding writing, and in the classroom setting, writing and ideas can be revised, reframed, or repurposed based on students' interactions with one another. Digital spaces are making these sorts of interactions around student texts easier to facilitate for teachers who in the past would have needed to do quite a lot of paper-shuffling in order to effectively implement student writing groups.

It is our hope that in the coming years policymakers and educators alike will explore the possibilities for frequent student–student interaction, student–teacher conferencing, and formative assessment enabled by online technologies. Some groups, such as the NWP (2013) and its collaborators on the online Digital Is, are already doing this work, making digital conversations visible, offering recommendations, and developing frameworks such as the Multimodal Assessment Project's Framework, which helps educators and administrators think about what participatory digital writing assessment might look like. The project leaders note that many rubrics, though relevant for some elements of digital composition, often do not address the multifaceted and interactive nature of digital compositions like digital stories or other projects, such as Hannah's, that mix media. We hope developers of writing assessments at local, district, and national levels will look to the work being done by the NWP and its affiliates to see how professional educators are adapting their curricula to meet the needs of 21st-century students.

It is also our hope that "writing" will come to mean more than essay-writing in summative assessments, and that those who design standardized tests will consider the role of technologies other than automated essay assessment tools in their design and implementation of summative assessments. Standards like the CCSS, however, cannot change assessments. Changes like these, which are beyond the scope of this chapter and even this book, will require some major cultural shifts—shifts in how districts conceive of the role of digital technologies in the writing classroom, how teacher knowledge is valued and integrated into the development of writing assessments, and how student interaction and collaboration is integrated into the learning process.

We further encourage researchers, policymakers, and administrators to remember that teachers are not prehistoric in their approaches to writing instruction; rather, as we have discussed, teachers are embracing the "new" writing as the way to communicate and think in the world today. Teachers share their classroom spaces with students like Hannah, who carry multimodal and interpersonal literacies into the classroom with them every day. They use digital spaces to their own personal and professional ends, leveraging the possibilities of our hyper-networked digital world. Perhaps, then, the best place to start as we reimagine writing assessment for the 21st century is in the classroom, alongside those students and teachers who are already in the process of transforming how, why, where, and for whom they write.

Endnotes

1. Hannah has given us permission to use her real first name.
2. Laura Sauer, interview with Elizabeth Homan, February 6, 2013, Okemos High School, Okemos, MI.

References

ACT, Inc. 2014. "Sample Essays." Accessed February 10, 2014. www.actstudent.org/writing/sample.

Cope, Bill, Mary Kalantzis, Sarah McCarthey, Colleen Vojak, and Sonia Kline. 2011. "Technology-Mediated Writing Assessments: Principles and Processes." *Computers and Composition* 28 (2): 79–96.

Council of Chief State School Officers and the National Governors Association. 2010. *Common Core State Standards for English Language Arts and Literacy in History/Social Studies, Science, and Technical Subjects*. Washington, DC: National Governors Association Center for Best Practices, Council of Chief State School Officers. Accessed February 10, 2014. www.corestandards.org/assets/CCSSI_ELA%20Standards.pdf.

Council of Writing Program Administrators, National Council of Teachers of English, and National Writing Project. 2011. *Framework for Success in Postsecondary Writing*. Accessed February 10, 2014. wpacouncil.org/files/framework-for-success-post secondary-writing.pdf.

Educational Testing Service. 2006. "Criterion Topics 10th Grade." Accessed February 10, 2014. www.ets.org/Media/Products/Criterion/topics/topics-10thgrade.htm.

Herrington, Anne, Kevin Hodgson, and Charles Moran. 2009. *Teaching the New Writing: Technology, Change, and Assessment in the 21st-Century Classroom*. New York: Teachers College Press.

Herrington, Anne, and Charles Moran. 2001. "What Happens When Machines Read Our Students' Writing?" *College English* 63 (4): 480–499.

Hicks, Troy, Jory Brass, Allen Webb, Robert Rozema, and Linda Cristensen. 2014. "School TM: Teacher Decision-Making in the Era of the (For-Profit) Corporate Classroom." Accessed February 10, 2014. schooltm.wikispaces.com/Welcome.

Kajder, Sara B. 2010. *Adolescents and Digital Literacies: Learning Alongside Our Students*. Urbana, IL: National Council of Teachers of English.

National Writing Project. 2013. "The NWP Multimodal Assessment Project." *Digital Is.* Accessed February 14, 2014. digitalis.nwp.org/resource/1577.

National Writing Project with Danielle Nicole DeVoss, Elyse Eidman-Aadahl, and Troy Hicks. 2010. *Because Digital Writing Matters: Improving Student Writing in Online and Multimedia Environments*. San Francisco: Jossey-Bass.

Paper Rater. 2010. Accessed February 10, 2014. www.paperrater.com.

Partnership for Assessment of Readiness for College and Careers. 2014a. "Automated Scoring Technical Writing Group." Accessed February 10, 2014. www.parcconline.org/automated-scoring-twg.

———. 2014b. "Grade 10 ELA/Literacy: Performance-Based Component." Accessed February 10, 2014. www.parcconline.org/samples/english-language-artsliteracy/grade-10-elaliteracy.

———. 2014c. "High School Assessment System." Accessed February 10, 2014. www.parcconline.org/high-school.

Pearson Education. 2013. "Reading/Language Arts." Accessed February 14, 2014. www.pearsonschool.com/index.cfm?locator=PSZu64.

Rothermel, Beth Ann. 2006. "Automated Writing Instruction: Computer-Assisted or Computer-Driven Pedagogies?" In *Machine Scoring of Student Essays: Truth and Consequences*, edited by Patricia Freitag Ericsson and Richard Haswell, 199–210. Logan, UT: Utah State University Press.

Sauer, Laura. 2013. "3 Reasons Romney Is Wrong About Class Size." *Yahoo! News*, June 12. Accessed February 10, 2014. news.yahoo.com/3-reasons-romney-wrong-class-size-132400190.html.

Smarter Balanced Assessment Consortium. 2012a. "Sample Items and Performance Tasks." Accessed February 10, 2014. www.smarterbalanced.org/sample-items-and-performance-tasks.

———. 2012b. "Smarter Balanced Assessment Consortium: English Language Arts/Literacy Item Specification." Accessed February 10, 2014. www.smarterbalanced.org/smarter-balanced-assessments.

Vojak, Colleen, Sonia Kline, Bill Cope, Sarah McCarthey, and Mary Kalantzis. 2011. "New Spaces and Old Places: An Analysis of Writing Assessment Software." *Computers and Composition* 28 (2): 97–111.

Warschauer, Mark, and Paige Ware. 2006. "Automated Writing Evaluation: Defining the Classroom Research Agenda." *Language Teaching Research* 10(2): 157–180.

Zerwin, Sarah. 2011. "Google Docs Fun." September 20. *The Paper Graders*. Accessed February 10, 2014, thepapergraders.org/?p=136.

Appendix: Hannah's Response to ACT Prompt About Bullying

Schools in America do have a bullying problem that needs to continue to be looked at. There are thousands of children & teenagers who have died over a year's worth of time from bullying. A change needs to be made. Bullying in schools causes lots of stress on a victim who is being bullied with distraction from learning, feeling lonely which can lead to depression & if the bullying progresses it can lead to suicidal thoughts, not having very many friends and potentially a group, gang, clique of people/students could begin to bully one person.

Why does bullying happen?

There are a lot of students/teenagers who may have a *lower* self-esteem. This causes them to talk "down" on other peers. This can be caused by poor home life style, not feeling like they fit in to the groups, cliques or gangs, because they may not be "good", "smart", "measure up" to the groups, cliques, or gangs standards. They may also want attention, but don't know how to get it besides getting in trouble. With having groups, cliques & gangs in schools or "higher" class it can cause those who don't feel good about themselves to feel worse about themselves because they don't fit in or no one offers to reach out a helping hand or offer to become friends with someone who looks lonely.

This being said shows that people are more obsessed about themselves and their life rather than saving someone who may be on the route to ending their life because they feel invisible, lonely, not accepted, not smart, or lower than someone else.

In today's society we focus more on ourself rather than what's going on around us. We don't see the severity of an issue until we pay the consequences of losing a life; that's when people start to feel bad or are mourning—when it's too late to save the life that passed.

In American schools we really struggle with staying consistent in the punishments, messages and ideas we have to make the school environment a healthy and safe places to be. The consequences that have been assigned I don't think are severe enough to keep people from starting to hurt and tear someone apart. We as a nation need to come together and make higher punishments, bullying is a severe issue that really needs to be taken care of. Majority of deaths come from suicide in the bullying topic.

Bullying is not a joke and the consequences/punishments shouldn't be either.

PART TWO

Putting the Common Core State Standards Into Conversation With Other Standards

CHAPTER 3

Using Library Standards Assessment to Inform Common Core State Standards Instruction

Amanda Nichols Hess and Katie Greer

The Common Core State Standards (CCSS) represent a concerted effort to unify the direction of American K–12 education. That nearly all states have adopted these learning guidelines signifies a shift toward a common level of knowledge and educational expectations for future generations. The CCSS, however, are not the only national set of learning standards for 21st-century digital learners. Examining standards in like documents, and how they deal with skills and competencies similar to what the CCSS address, can help teachers and librarians identify concrete ways to implement and assess the CCSS in their classrooms.

The American Association of School Librarians' (AASL) Standards for the 21st Century Learner (2007) and the Association of College and Research Libraries' (ACRL) Information Literacy Competency Standards for Higher Education (2000) focus on students' ability to gather, synthesize, and evaluate information, and these competencies link directly to the CCSS' emphasis on digital information literacy.

Further, library standards have been used in both K–12 and higher education to design and assess curricula related to digital literacy; therefore, they offer a lens through which educators invested in the CCSS can see how the information literacy skills of finding, evaluating, and using digital information have been taught and assessed in recent years. As such, the environments in which library standards have been implemented and assessed provide excellent venues for considering how digital information literacy practices can inform CCSS implementation.

The CCSS represent technology as a skill rather than as a separate set of competencies. Technological skill and knowledge is named in the Anchor Standards, as students who are college and career ready "use technology and digital media strategically and capably" (Council of Chief State School Officers [CCSSO] and National Governors Association [NGA] 2010, 7); how students can demonstrate this capability is woven throughout the Reading, Writing, Speaking, Listening, and Language content areas. The integration of technology gives teachers and school librarians the opportunity to blend the CCSS with the Standards for the 21st Century Learner while using a diverse technology toolkit to help students learn. By linking these standards, students can achieve the college and career readiness Anchor Standards of the CCSS and be equipped for the Information Literacy Competency Standards for Higher Education of the ACRL they will encounter in postsecondary life.

Before examining how information literacy skills have been taught and assessed, this chapter will consider the origins of the library standards to offer readers a better sense of their history. After providing this history, we walk through each step in the information literacy cycle, identify digital technologies that librarians and teachers can use to teach that step, and provide an "assessment in action" section that gives an example of an assignment using one or more of these technologies. Table 3.1 at the end of this chapter includes technology tools discussed (and additional resources that serve similar purposes) and URLs for each resource, and aligns the tools to information literacy standards.

AASL and ACRL Standards

The AASL has provided learning standards and benchmarks for its practitioners in library and information science since the publication of *School Libraries for Today and Tomorrow* in 1945. This first set of national school library standards gave school librarians guidelines and structure for their teaching. While this publication focused on differentiating between school librarians and public librarians, more recent iterations—*Standards for School Library Programs* (AASL 1960), *Standards for School Media Programs* (Joint Committee of the AASL and the Department of Audiovisual Instruction of the National Education Association 1969), *Media Programs: District and School* (AASL and Association for Educational Communications and Technology [AECT] 1975), and *Information Power: Guidelines for School Library Media Programs* and *Information Power: Building Partnerships for Learning* (AASL and AECT 1988, 1998)—have chosen to collectively address the growing availability of rich informational resources and new, educationally significant technology developments. *Information Power* aimed to help students become skillful consumers and producers of information, grouping nine standards of student learning and performance around three categories: information literacy, independent learning, and social responsibility (AASL and AECT 1998). From these categories, the ACRL developed Information Literacy Competency Standards for Higher Education.

Published in 2000, the Information Literacy Competency Standards for Higher Education quickly became, and has remained, the benchmark for planning and assessing information literacy in institutions of higher learning. The committee responsible for the document built upon Information Power's standards, bridging to what was being done in K–12 education by providing a college-level information literacy assessment map. Five standards, with accompanying performance indicators and assessment outcomes, outline the skill set information-literate students should have at the conclusion of their collegiate careers. The standards address the core principles of identifying, accessing, evaluating, and using information fluently and ethically (ACRL 2000).

Since the development of the ACRL standards, and in recognition of the changing nature of information literacy learning (particularly in technology use and digital resources), the AASL revised and expanded its standards to include the digital, visual, textual, and technological literacies now crucial for student success. Standards for the 21st Century Learner (2007), the AASL's most recent standards iteration, addresses students' skills, dispositions in action, responsibilities, and self-assessment indicators as related to their ability to inquire, think critically, and gain knowledge; to draw conclusions, make informed decisions, apply knowledge to new situations, and create new knowledge; to share knowledge and participate ethically and productively as members of our democratic society; and to pursue personal growth.

Assessing With Technology in the 21st-Century Classroom

The release of the CCSS postdates Standards for the 21st Century Learner, and the AASL connected its standards to the new curricular guidelines. Noting that integrating school library standards with the CCSS gave students "the opportunity to be well-prepared as life-long learners facing the challenges of college and careers," the AASL (2010) identified the school librarian's role in co-teaching "tasks that integrate key critical thinking skills, technology and information literacy skills with subject area content" with classroom teachers. It is from this position that we consider how library instruction, either in a secondary school or higher education institution, inform CCSS implementation and assessment.

To best consider the different skills needed for digital learning, we will address information literacy in five distinct stages (Figure 3.1):

1. Determining information needs
2. Accessing information
3. Evaluating information
4. Using information
5. Ethically considering information use and access

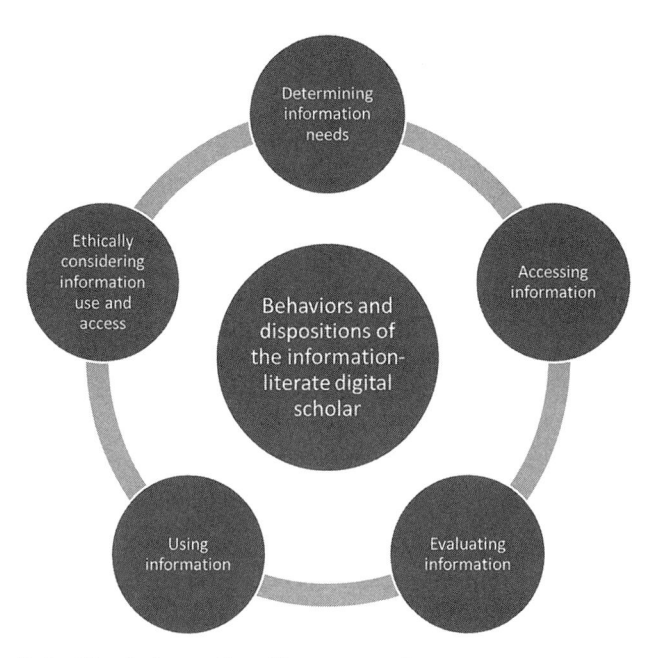

Figure 3.1 The information literacy cycle

Part of a broader cycle, these five stages require unique information literacy knowledge and skills while also reflecting the CCSS' digital literacies. Technology is a key component in each information literacy stage, and this chapter will suggest a variety of tools teachers can use to help students understand these concepts while illustrating just a few in detail. For a more detailed discussion on technology integration and the CCSS, see Chapter 11 by Amanda Stearns-Pfeiffer in this book.

Determining Information Needs

The cycle of the literate student's information seeking begins by determining their information need, as represented in Figure 3.2. In the CCSS, this step is a part of how students "conduct short as well as more sustained research projects to answer a question (including a self-generated question) or solve a problem; narrow or broaden the inquiry when appropriate" (CCSSO and NGA 2010, W.9–10.7 and W.11–12.7). These standards directly connect to the AASL and ACRL

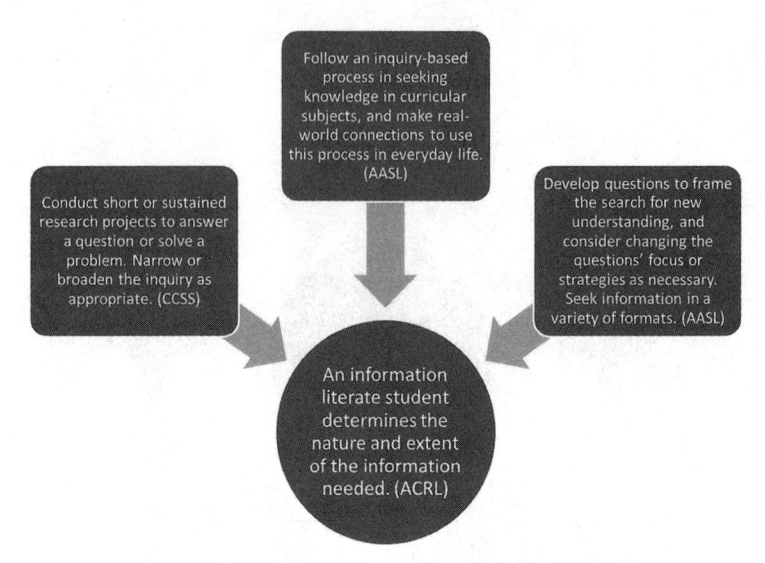

Figure 3.2 Determining information need represents the first step in a student's information-seeking process

standards that address how students determine their information need and nature of their search. The AASL standards (2007) state that students should "follow an inquiry-based process in seeking knowledge in curricular subjects, and make the real-world connection for using this process in [their] own life" (4). This involves developing and refining "a range of questions to frame the search for new understanding," demonstrating "adaptability by changing the inquiry focus, questions, resources, or strategies when necessary," and seeking "information … in a variety of formats" (4, 7). Similarly, the ACRL standards begin with the cogent expression of an information need, noting that an "information literate student determines the nature and extent of the information needed" (8).

Two learning tools and assessment techniques that school and academic librarians have used at this first stage cycle are concept mapping and think-pair-share exercises. These activities help students form their research question and identify keywords for finding information on their topic. These strategies can also be used to learn and develop the skills and dispositions identified in the CCSS.

Concept Mapping

The process of mind or concept mapping has long been acknowledged as a useful tool for initial "pre-research" inquiry, as well as a strategy for refining or altering one's research questions (Markham, Mintzes, and Jones 1994; Novak 2010; Schick 1991; Sherrat and Schlaback 1990). This learning activity is certainly familiar to English Language Arts (ELA) teachers, and it is an essential tool to visualize brainstorming and connect ideas. However, as students venture increasingly into the digital realms and use technology to represent their learning, librarians and ELA teachers must consider how concept mapping can be represented and fostered in technology-rich ways.

Many technology tools exist to facilitate the concept-mapping process and make it an electronically collaborative endeavor. Traditional software- or subscription-based tools such as Inspiration (inspiration.com) and Webspiration (mywebspiration.com) help students map their thinking. Online concept-mapping tools allow students to see others' thinking, share their own thoughts, and receive feedback from others on their own work. There are free tools available online, including Text2MindMap (text2mindmap.com) and DebateGraph (debategraph.org), that represent information in a traditional concept or mind map format. Other more social tools exist that can accomplish the same end. Students may already be familiar with Web 2.0 tools that generate word clouds and other visual concept representations. By bringing these tools into the classroom, teachers and librarians can initialize the research and writing process as a structured activity, either independently or in groups. Other options for concept mapping include those that engage deeper visual literacies. Prezi (prezi.com) and Mindomo (mindomo.com), for instance, allow for more creative expression; with these resources, students are able to include images, video clips, or external files to support and develop their initial ideas. Finished products using any of these tools can be graded to provide qualitative assessment of a student's invention process. This formative assessment can provide direction and assistance in adjusting ideas early in a student's research and writing process.

Assessment in Action

At Oakland University, a concept map assessment was conducted as part of information literacy instruction in Studio Art classes. Students began with a thesis question or rough idea and then used Prezi to draw out the main keywords and possible related concepts through mapping. In this instructional situation, Prezi proved to be an ideal tool because it allowed art students to integrate images and even videos into their concept maps. They could draw visual representations including their own photography or material from one of the library's art databases. Students submitted rough draft concept maps outlining their artistic research needs to the library faculty member; based on the students' Prezi concept maps, the faculty member then provided guidance on further ideas for exploration as well as recommended library resources (Figure 3.3). Such an activity could be easily transferred into an ELA classroom for a variety of learning topics, particularly with support of a school librarian.

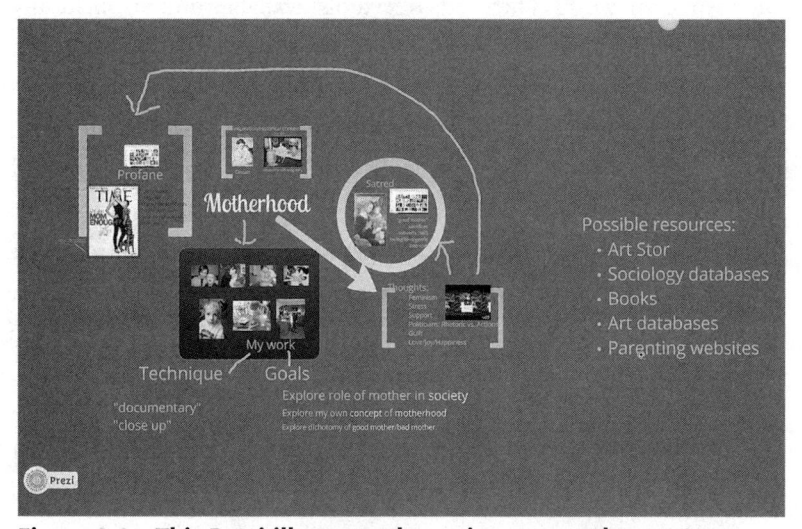

Figure 3.3 This Prezi illustrates the various research avenues a learner can explore for the topic of *motherhood and art* and demonstrates the defining of a research question

Think-Pair-Share Brainstorming

Another brainstorming strategy familiar to teachers is think-pair-share (Lyman 1981; King 1993; Kagan 1994). This active learning technique can be used effectively to foster class discussion, opinion sharing, and idea generation, but it can also be used to further a student's understanding of his or her research topic and push his or her information seeking further. Digital tools such as Padlet (formerly Wallwisher; padlet.com), Pinterest (pinterest.com), and Learnist (learni.st) as well as wikis and blogs and other reflective writing technologies may serve the same purpose, allowing students to structure their terms and test them out while also soliciting feedback from their peers. These types of activities provide for excellent self- and peer-assessment, as students can immediately assess the effectiveness of their chosen keywords and adjust their information queries accordingly (Burkett 2011; Byrne 2010; Naslund and Giustini 2008).

Assessment in Action

A think-pair-share activity done in collaboration with an eighth-grade ELA class and the school media specialist at Clarkston Junior High School asked students to use Padlet (called Wallwisher at the time) to engage in discussion around ideas and information. This simple tool allowed them to respond both to the teacher's prompt and to their peers' thinking in short, yet meaningful, ways. And, importantly, Padlet allowed the teacher to moderate comments *before* they were published, so only appropriate contributions made it onto the class wall. In such a way, teachers can assess students' understanding of keyword searching and help them develop a comprehensive and well-rounded search strategy with synonyms and like phrases. They can also determine students' comfort with and ability to use technology for research and writing activities.

Connecting to College and Career Readiness

Both concept mapping and think-pair-share exercises make the process of determining an information need more concrete, for they require students to apply, discuss, write, and visualize their own research directions. At the same time, these activities also open the door for students to understand others' assertions and arguments. In accomplishing these objectives, students meet the CCSS Anchor Standards for Reading in learning to "analyze the structure of texts, including how specific sentences, paragraphs, and larger portions of the text (e.g., a section, chapter, scene, or stanza) relate to each other and the whole," and "delineate and evaluate the argument and specific claims in a text, including the validity of the reasoning as well as the relevance and sufficiency of the evidence" (CCSSO and NGA 2010, Anchor Standards for Reading 3 and 8). The process of outlining or mapping another's arguments, and participating in collaborative discussion around a topic or issue, gives students a chance to reflect upon a reading, analyze the content, and ensure that main ideas are understood. Furthermore, these skills prepare students for information seeking after high school.

Accessing Information

The second stage in the information literacy learning cycle deals with access. Once students have determined their information need, they need to search for, find, and retrieve the information related to their search, as illustrated in Figure 3.4.

Access in the CCSS is addressed as students' skills to "integrate multiple sources of information presented in diverse media or formats (e.g., visually, quantitatively, orally) evaluating the credibility and accuracy of each source" and "integrate and evaluate multiple sources of information presented in different media or formats (e.g., visually, quantitatively) as well as in words in order to address a question or solve a problem" (CCSSO and NGA 2010, SL.9–10.2 and RI.11–12.7). Similarly, ACRL (2000) standards note that the "information literate student accesses needed information effectively and efficiently" (9), while AASL (2007) standards call on librarians to teach students to "find, evaluate, and select appropriate sources to answer questions" (4). These standards, and their respective performance indicators, deal with constructing and implementing effective search strategies to find the best sources and then choosing and retrieving the most appropriate

```
                    ┌─────────────────┐
                    │ Integrate and evaluate │
                    │ multiple sources of    │   ┌─────────────────┐
                    │ information presented  │   │ Find, evaluate, and │
                    │ in different media or  │   │ select appropriate  │
                    │ formats to address a   │   │ sources to answer   │
                    │ question or solve a    │   │ questions. (AASL)   │
                    │ problem. (CCSS)        │   └─────────────────┘
                    └─────────────────┘
```

┌─────────────────┐   ┌─────────────────┐
│ Integrate multiple │   │ Demonstrate mastery of │
│ sources of information │   │ technology tools for   │
│ presented in diverse │   An information   │ accessing information, │
│ media or formats,   │   literate student   │ including using social │
│ evaluating the   │   accesses needed   │ networks to gather and │
│ credibility and accuracy │ information   │ share information.   │
│ of each source. (CCSS) │ effectively and   │ (AASL)   │
└─────────────────┘   efficiently. (ACRL)   └─────────────────┘

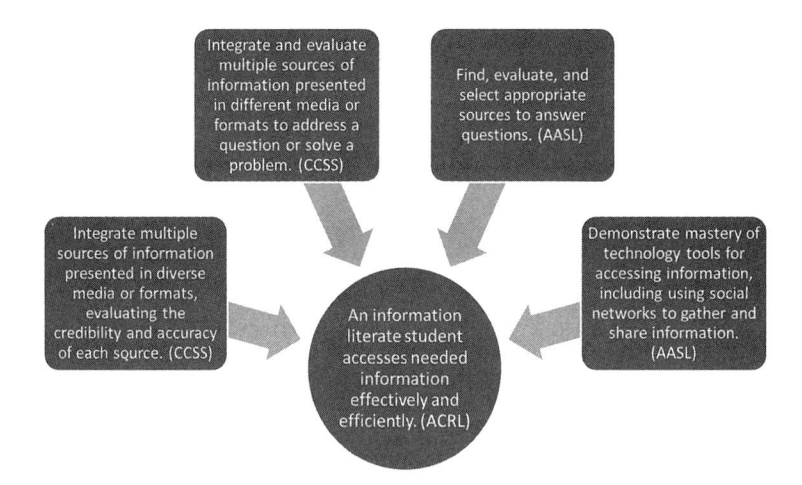

Figure 3.4 The process of accessing information occurs after a student has determined his or her area of inquiry or information needs

source of information (whether a subscription database, a website, a book, or other media). This step involves students demonstrating their "mastery of technology tools for accessing information and pursuing inquiry" and may ask students to "use social networks and information tools to gather and share information" (4, 7). Information pathfinders and online quizzes have been used to teach these skills in library instruction; these activities can be easily transferred to the secondary ELA classroom.

Information Pathfinders

To effectively choose sources from which to access information, students must be aware of the options available and understand how they are used. In their personal lives or in their academic research, students often begin an information-seeking process with Wikipedia or Google, and such tools can help develop students' thinking about a question, idea, or topic (Head and Eisenberg 2009; McClure 2011; Purdy 2009). However, getting students beyond these understanding-gathering tools and into the meaty world of databases and scholarly information—and making these resources as simple and uncomplicated as possible (Purdy 2012)—is a skill that needs to be taught and practiced. Information pathfinders can simplify these resources and push students' information seeking further since they give students broader access to information and ask them to assess these resources.

Pathfinders can provide lists of both written and printed research resources for students. However, using digital tools can transform the learning resource. A web-hosted pathfinder or resource page allows students to access the information immediately and continue their learning anytime, anywhere. Pathfinders also aid students' integration of "multiple sources of information ... in order to address a question or solve a problem" (R.11–12.7) which classroom teachers can use to achieve the CCSS' aim of students "read[ing] and comprehend[ing] complex ... information texts independently and proficiently" by the end of high school (Anchor Standard for Reading 10). Teachers wishing to employ this learning tool have a variety of digital options at their disposal: a school web design platform or a wiki that provides a free and simple interface on which they can design and build a skeleton of research resources could be used. From there, the ELA teacher, the school librarian, or even the students in the course can build and identify informational resources available (Koechlin and Zwan 2008; Kuntz 2003; O'Sullivan and Scott 2000).

Assessment in Action

To illustrate how pathfinders can be implemented, we offer one instance of how they have been used at the secondary level. For U.S. history research on World War II, the school librarian at Clarkston Junior High School created a shared online learning guide in Wikispaces, a wiki creation site, as shown in Figure 3.5. This tool was dynamic and flexible, and students and other teachers could add information or comments as they accessed the provided resources or found new related research. If so interested, the teachers involved could assess students' ability to access and evaluate the information they shared with their classmates, specifically through students' brief description of *why* they shared a resource in the wiki. Secondary ELA teachers can consider using such a

Using Library Standards Assessment 83

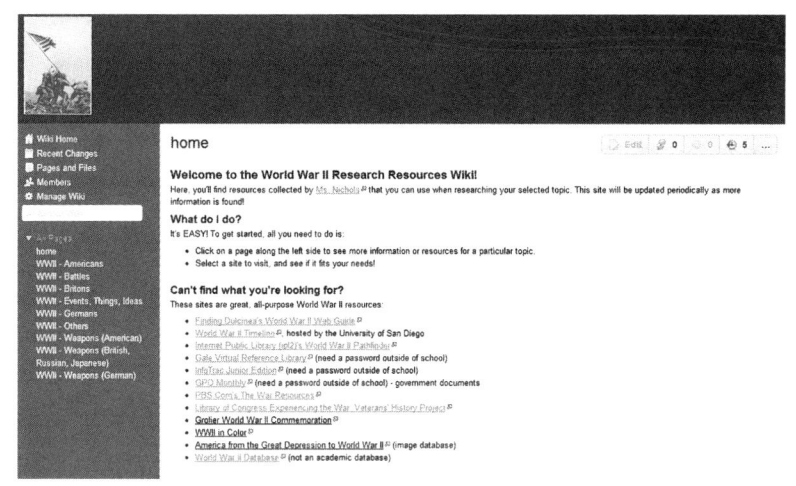

Figure 3.5 In this pathfinder, the school librarian and classroom teachers can help students access appropriate research resources

digital pathfinder as a skeleton for nonfiction research projects, or even to scaffold students' understanding of a text. When reading *The Great Gatsby*, for instance, a teacher could create a basic pathfinder with links to relevant information about Long Island, the Jazz Age, Prohibition, and other topics, and, as students found additional resources, they could add them to this informational repository and build collective knowledge.

Online Quizzes

Once discussions regarding access have occurred, formal assessment tools can determine and measure students' growth in assessing information. Tests as assessment tools have been widely used in information literacy instruction, with more and more online components being created to track student progress (Mulherrin and Abdul-Hamid 2009). Learning management systems such as Moodle (moodle.org) with built-in data storage and analysis tools provide tools for online tests, but web-based tools such as Google Forms (go to google.com/drive/apps.html and click on Forms), Survey Monkey (surveymonkey.com), and Microsoft Access databases could also serve this purpose.

Assessment in Action

Oakland University Library uses an online quiz administered during the first-year writing course to determine students' ability to access information appropriately. Students receive instruction in keyword searching strategies and database use, and then complete an online course component designed within Moodle, the university's course management system. The online portion of the course includes a final exam that students must pass in order to earn library credit for their writing course; the questions include assessment of students' keyword strategies and approaches to accessing information. The student response data is stored and can be accessed by library faculty to assess learning outcomes and track whether changes need to be made. This data can also be shared with teachers to further improve or supplement instruction. Such a learning experience can be duplicated in the ELA classroom within a course management system or free online survey tool such as those mentioned previously.

Connecting to College and Career Readiness

These learning activities and assessment techniques help prepare students for life after high school. Broadly, they are part of the CCSS' aim to teach students to "conduct short as well as more sustained research projects based on focused questions, demonstrating understanding of the subject under investigation" and "gather relevant information from multiple print and digital sources, assess the credibility and accuracy of each source" (CCSSO and NGA 2010, Anchor Standards for Writing 7 and 8). Specifically, information pathfinders and resource evaluations help students "evaluate a speaker's point of view, reasoning, and use of evidence and rhetoric," while online quizzes help students "evaluate information presented in diverse media and formats" (Anchor Standard for Writing 3). Through the use of technology tools integrated into these processes, students are equipped to become digital scholars.

Evaluating Information

The third stage in the information-seeking cycle involves evaluating information. In this stage, students interpret and consider the information accessed for their research topic or question, as shown in Figure 3.6.

The CCSS consider evaluation by asking students to "gather relevant information from multiple authoritative print and digital sources" and assess "the strengths and limitations of each source in terms of the task, purpose, and audience" or "the usefulness of each source in answering the research question" (W.9–10.8 and W.11–12.8). Similarly, the AASL (2007) standards state that students should learn to "evaluate information found in selected sources on the basis of accuracy, validity, appropriateness for needs, importance, and social and cultural context," that they need to "make sense of information gathered from diverse sources by identifying misconceptions, main and supporting ideas, conflicting information, and point of view or bias," and that they must "monitor

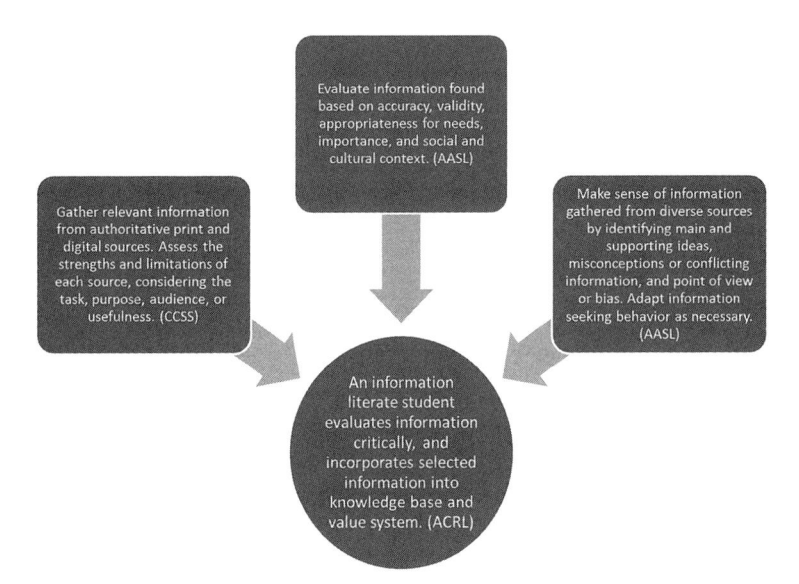

Figure 3.6 Evaluating information is the crucial third step in the information-seeking process, as it asks students to make their own determinations of whether information retrieved is valid to their research question

[their] own information-seeking processes for effectiveness and progress, and adapt as necessary" (4, 6). The ACRL (2000) standards also require that an "information literate student evaluates information and its sources critically and incorporates selected information into his or her knowledge base and value system" (11). In library instruction, these standards have been addressed and assessed through research journals and resource/website evaluations. In the classroom, such strategies can be used to meet the CCSS.

Research Process Journals

Research journals or research logs give educators insight into students' information-seeking behavior and can function as a formative evaluation tool. More than a bibliography, these documents represent an account of a student's research process and can provide a glimpse into their information literacy strengths and struggles. A research journal or log details the "step-by-step ... moves [a student] made to find their sources" and helps to ensure that "students are using multiple research platforms" (Peele and Phipps 2007). These can be paper-and-pencil assignments, but digital technology can make the process more engaging for the next digital scholar. Collaboration tools including Google Docs (go to google.com/drive/apps.html and click on Docs), Dropbox (dropbox.com), and Microsoft Office 365 allow students and teachers to participate in a dialogue around the research evaluation process. Other students, collaborating teachers, or school librarians can also offer their thoughts and see others' thinking made visible.

Another technology tool that could be used to a similar end in the classroom is a blog, where students can post regularly on their information findings. This tool allows teachers and students to offer probing, insightful, or meaningful questions. Both the student and the teacher can view the progression of the work, thinking, and the evaluation process at the end of the unit or semester. Blogs also situate the student's thinking in the public discourse around academic ideas and learning (Harris 2006; Lamb and Johnson 2006).

Alternately, the research journal can be approached as a visual object. Instead of creating a citation list with comments, a tool like

VoiceThread (voicethread.com) allows a creator to share images, presentation slides, or videos related to the research need then comment on it with drawings, voiceovers, or text. Others can participate in this dialogue in the same ways, and students can learn from new and diverse perspectives on presenting research (Sprankle 2009).

Assessment in Action

Oakland University librarians have used research journals to generate individualized feedback on student projects. During subject-focused class sessions, students received an overview of library resources in their major area as well as guidance on locating books in the catalog or other discovery tool. They then individually located examples of several different types of resources—books, scholarly articles, and images—that related to their research. From this research, they submitted a research journal, including citation information for each item, where and how it was located, and why the item was useful to their project. Figure 3.7 shows the journal structure for the assignment. These entries provided multiple levels of assessment for the teacher, with glimpses into the student's keyword strategies, choice of and ability to efficiently use resources to access information, and evaluation of information. The research journals were created in Google Drive or word processing software, and then shared with the teacher, who commented directly on the files for students to see.

Resource and Website Evaluation

Resource and website evaluation skills are critical components of school librarians' instruction on information evaluation skills, and they provide a means by which students' knowledge and ability to evaluate that information can be assessed (Kral 2007; Kuiper, Volman, and Terwel 2005; Schrock 2014). Such activities connect directly to the CCSS' aims of teaching students to "assess the strengths and limitations of each source in terms of the task, purpose, and audience" (CCSSO and NGA 2010, W.11–12.8). Technology tools are essential to teaching and assessing these evaluative skills. Students must *use* technology to access online information; in fact, some websites exist solely for the

> **SA 381 – Advanced Photography**
>
> **Research Journal Assignment**
>
> Using what you learned during the library session today, locate at least six sources of interest and create a research journal entry for each source. Please include at least one book, one scholarly journal article, one news article, one website, and one Artstor image.
>
> Each entry should include:
>
> o   The source citation information, using Chicago style.
>
> o   Indicate how you located this item: library catalog search, database search, or browsing.
>
> o   A sentence or two summarizing the item: What is the book or article about? What is the image? If using a book, feel free to focus on a particular section that pertain to your interests.
>
> o   After summarizing the source, write a paragraph evaluating it using the guidelines in the "Evaluating Sources" handout on your course page. If the source is an image, evaluate the quality of composition, light, etc.
>
> o   After summarizing and evaluating the source, add a final paragraph detailing how the item fits into your artistic goals and interests. How is this relevant, or how do you hope to use the information for your future projects?
>
> The citations should be organized alphabetically, by author's last name.

Figure 3.7 These structured guidelines for a research journal ask students to consider and evaluate their own information-seeking behaviors as well as the resources they use

purpose of helping to teach students evaluative skills (see, for instance, the Pacific Northwest Tree Octopus or Feline Reactions to Bearded Men websites),[1] and these may serve as good starting points. However, students may think that such exercises are silly or irrelevant.

In lieu of these resources, teachers might consider using information online that students frequently use: a school page, a local newspaper, or even a Wikipedia entry. From there, students can evaluate content based on the central tenets of website evaluation: accuracy, authority, objectivity, currency, and coverage. To then assess students' ability to evaluate websites, technology tools including blogs, online journals, or online forms can be used. Each of these tools enables educators to determine a student's knowledge level in terms of evaluation, and what additional support, scaffolding, or further information students need to advance their knowledge and meet standards.

Academic libraries have used such practices to help students determine author bias and distinguish scholarly and popular sources of information. In academic library instructional sessions, informal class discussions can provide a vehicle for this assessment. Increasingly, though, library faculty are embedded in online courses and are able to take advantage of online discussion forums within the learning management system to facilitate a conversation about how students are evaluating information. Such environments have the advantage of allowing students to discuss with their peers the relevance, authority, and perceived usefulness of information and get feedback from each other. This discussion could be recreated through a social networking or course management site.

Assessment in Action

An information evaluation assessment strategy librarians have employed effectively at Oakland University is to ask students to work in pairs or small groups to use and evaluate a subject database and then present their findings to their peers by demonstrating the resource to the entire class. The student groups receive a worksheet (which teachers can provide digitally through an online form or webpage) that guides them through questions to ask as they conduct searches in the database, including those on audience, content, and general usability and usefulness (Burkhardt and McDonald 2010). The teacher can decide upon the resources for evaluation prior to class, based on the research projects the students are working on and what resources may be new to students. These resources may include highly specialized databases, ebook collections, or authoritative websites (e.g., government publications) that will provide support for their needs. The students' presentations of their findings to their peers allow for the teacher to assess how effectively students are using the resource, correct any misinformation about structure and features, suggest search term refinements, and provide further guidance.

Connecting to College and Career Readiness

As students critically examine the content and intended goals of information sources, and reflect on the sources for research journals or online resource evaluations, they put into practice the skill of assessing "how point of view or purpose shapes the content and style of a text" (CCSSO and NGA 2010, Anchor Standard for Reading 6). Furthermore, these evaluation skills ensure students "integrate and evaluate content presented in diverse formats and media, including visually and quantitatively, as well as in words" (Anchor Standard for Reading 7). When teachers and librarians consider the range of majors and future employment today's students will pursue, the ability to critically evaluate information is essential. Consider the *Project Information Literacy Research Report* findings that employers place "a high premium on graduates' abilities for ... identifying the best solution for all the information they had gathered" (Head 2012, 3). Teaching students to consider, process, check, and make value judgments about the information they find helps prepare them for a diverse array of future employment environments.

Using Information

The fourth step of the information-seeking cycle involves information use (Figure 3.8). While determining, accessing, and evaluating information are important to information literacy, using information is the stage that has the most concrete implications for students' lives. Through synthesizing information, they have determined their need, accessed appropriately through multiple means of investigation, and evaluated for appropriateness and validity; students should be able to tangibly demonstrate learning in meaningful ways.

The CCSS ask students to "use technology, including the internet, to produce, publish, and update individual or shared writing products," which relates to information use, both in terms of students "taking advantage of technology's capacity to link to other information and to display information flexibly and dynamically" and when considering how to use "ongoing feedback, including new arguments or information" (CCSSO and NGA 2010, W.9–10.6 and W.11–12.6). The AASL (2007) learning standards directly link to these goals, stating that the 21st-century information literate student will "use technology and other information tools to analyze and organize information" and will "use the writing process, media and visual literacy, and technology skills

Using Library Standards Assessment 91

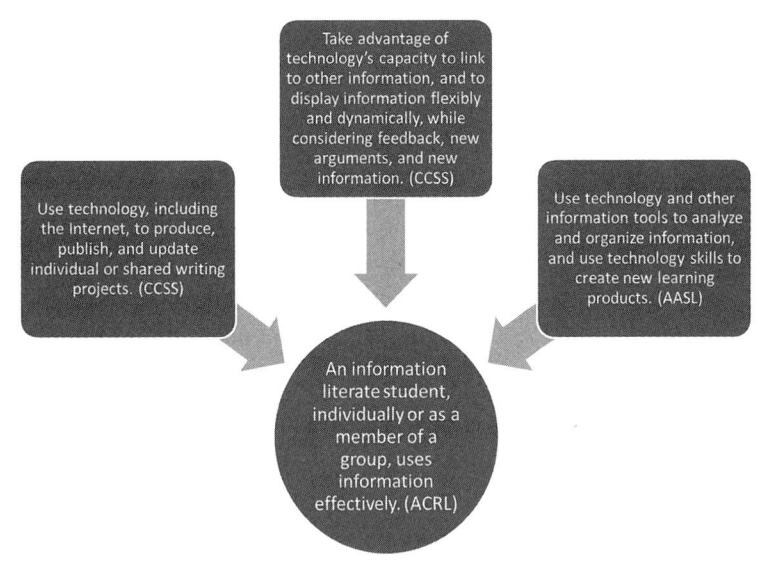

Figure 3.8 Using information, the fourth step in the information-seeking process, represents the critical point where students must take the information found and transform it into a representation of their knowledge and understanding

[Diagram contents:
- Take advantage of technology's capacity to link to other information, and to display information flexibly and dynamically, while considering feedback, new arguments, and new information. (CCSS)
- Use technology, including the Internet, to produce, publish, and update individual or shared writing projects. (CCSS)
- Use technology and other information tools to analyze and organize information, and use technology skills to create new learning products. (AASL)
- An information literate student, individually or as a member of a group, uses information effectively. (ACRL)]

to create products that express new understandings" (5). Similarly, the ACRL (2000) standards require that an "information literate student, individually or as a member of a group, uses information effectively to accomplish a specific purpose" (13). Because these standards represent a culmination of the previous information-seeking stages, assessment strategies often center on significant projects: online collaborative learning projects through Web 2.0 tools or social media resources, or online portfolios composed of digitally rich learning products.

Social and Collaborative Tools

A variety of social and collaborative tools allow students to connect the information they carefully accessed and evaluated with broader learning communities. When using these tools to demonstrate learning, students can see connections, correlations, and real-world implications of their information. Wikis are tools that present a social and collaborative learning opportunity where students can make their process of determining, accessing, and evaluating information visible. A wiki's design, which is built around collaboration, fosters group work in synthesizing information. A wiki provides an opportunity for students to create new, meaningful, communal knowledge rather than work in silos (Hamilton 2012; Lundin 2008). Other social and collaborative tools that students can use to make meaning and demonstrate their use of information include Google Docs' shared file interface or VoiceThread, which allows students to use technology tools "to analyze and organize information" and "to create products that express new understandings" through audio and visual means (AASL 2007, 5).

Assessment in Action

In a classroom-school library collaborative lesson at Wylie E. Groves High School, 11th-grade ELA students used VoiceThread in groups to illustrate how they learned about a global issue or problem. They used images and video to demonstrate their information-seeking process and then pushed their learning further by synthesizing this information with their own opinions about how to best solve the problem. Their classroom teacher, school librarian, and fellow students all engaged in a dialogue around each of these global issues and commented on students' learning, thinking, understanding, and synthesizing within each VoiceThread. This learning project became a powerful way to consider global issues through the students' eyes.

Digital Portfolio Tools

An electronic version of the traditional hard copy compilation of a student's work, digital portfolios can store meaningful artifacts of learning, which students can use throughout their educational careers. Digital portfolios offer students the opportunity to create digitally rich learning projects and illustrate a specific instance where technology can be used to infuse the research paper with 21st-century digital literacies. While formulating and writing an extended research paper is an important academic skill, more digitally rich representations of learning offer students the opportunity to transform information with tools that relate to 21st-century skills and dispositions. This may mean creating a video or podcast with tools that offer real-world learning and a connection to resources students will encounter in post-secondary life (Cambridge, Cambridge, and Yancey 2009).

The act of grouping and sorting their texts can help students reflect on their own learning process and allow others to see the progression of students' work. Such learning projects offer students the opportunity to "[take] advantage of technology's capacity to link to other information and to display information flexibly and dynamically" by allowing them to represent how they use, and have used, information in a variety of ways (CCSSO and NGA 2010, W.9–10.6).

Digital portfolios can be created with a variety of resources. Free web design tools, such as Google Sites (sites.google.com), Weebly (education.weebly.com), Wix (wix.com), or WordPress (wordpress.com or wordpress.com/classrooms), are ideal for this type of project, but digital portfolios can also be created using proprietary software and housed on school servers, which give educational entities a greater measure of control. Such projects give students hands-on experience in crafting their own digital identity, and in creating this online persona, they can learn about maintaining control of the information they share—or choose not to share—with others.

Assessment in Action

As a part of a collaborative ELA unit, a secondary school librarian worked with students to create digital portfolios in Google Sites. Each student created and maintained his or her own page and shared it with the classroom teacher and librarian for review (see a sample in Figure 3.9). Students used these portfolios as a repository for the digitally rich learning projects they created throughout the course of classroom units or projects, and they also worked to make these digital portfolios appropriate for viewers outside of the classroom (e.g., parents, future employers). As these portfolios developed over the course of a term, they became a tool students and the classroom teacher used to share and discuss students' work at parent–teacher conferences. In doing so, the portfolios presented a meaningful representation of student

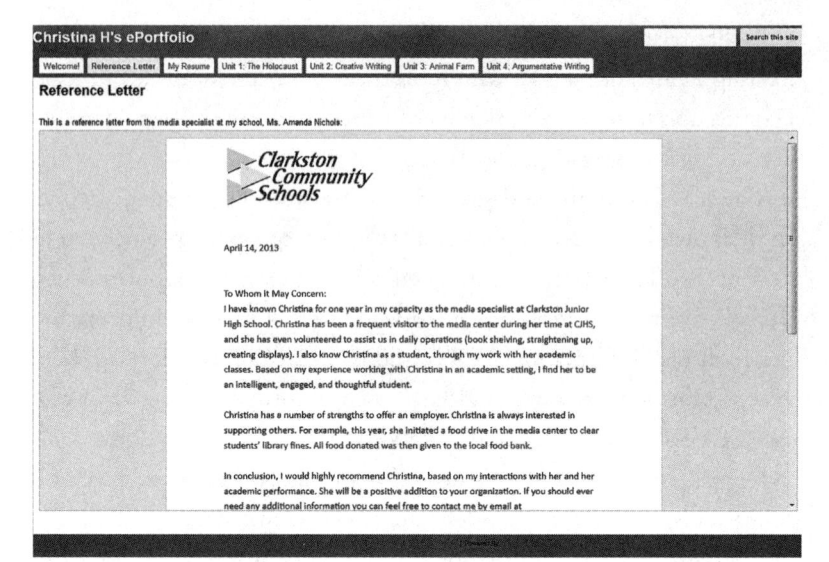

Figure 3.9 This sample digital portfolio illustrates the features a student can employ to show and share his or her work from a course, a school year, or an academic career

learning to parents and later to administrators. In this case, digital portfolios illustrated how students used information and how their use of information had grown, changed, shifted, and was shaped over the course of a project and a class. This assignment could be expanded to an examination of a student's growth throughout a grade level or an educational career (Purcell 2011; Scharf et al. 2007).

Connecting to College and Career Readiness

Digital portfolios with digitally rich learning products and the social and collaborative tools that demonstrate students' use of information highlight how students "integrate and evaluate content presented in diverse formats and media" (CCSSO and NGA 2010, Anchor Standards for Reading 7). Furthermore, they ask students to "use technology, including the internet, to produce and publish writing" (Anchor Standards for Reading 6), and "make strategic use of digital media ... to express information and enhance understanding" (Anchor Standards for Reading 5). Portfolios initially created in secondary schools can continue to be developed at the college or university level, where students are increasingly encouraged to create online learning artifacts. Such projects then not only satisfy graduation requirements but also provide a showpiece of a student's exemplary work for potential employers.

Ethically Considering Information Access and Use

Underlying each information-seeking area, however, are the ethical responsibilities and considerations students must learn and demonstrate to be well-rounded, information literate digital scholars. The final stage of the cycle, then, involves the ethical access and use of information (Figure 3.10).

The CCSS assert that students should conduct and present research while "avoiding plagiarism and overreliance on any one source and following a standard format for citation" (CCSSO and NGA 2010, W.9–10.8 and W.11–2.8), and both the AASL and the ACRL standards identify the ethical considerations as a foundation on which future information-seeking behavior can be built. The AASL (2007) standards require that students "use information and technology ethically and

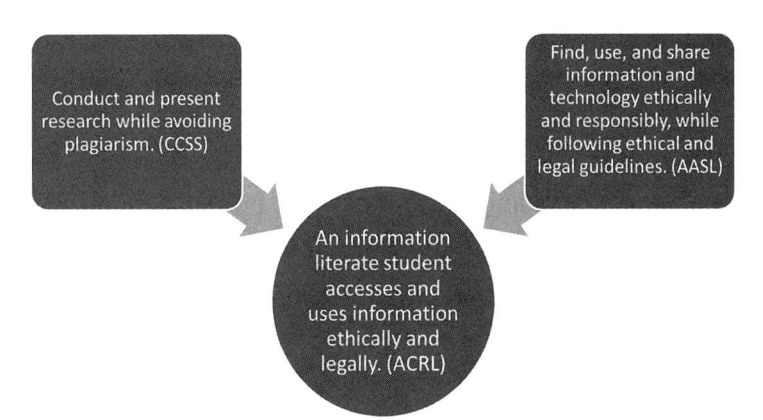

Figure 3.10 Underlying all previous information-seeking steps, students' understanding of ethical practices and use of information is a critical skill they must master to be effective digital scholars

responsibly" (6). This involves students following the "ethical and legal guidelines in gathering and using information" (4); of particular relevance to teachers of the next digital scholar, these ethics include "safe ... behaviors in personal electronic communication in interaction" (7). Academic libraries are increasingly responsible for educating students about the ethics of information, including teaching students about plagiarism, copyright, and responsible information access and sharing. Teachers and librarians then must teach to the standard that an "information literate student understands many of the economic, legal, and social issues surrounding the use of information and accesses and uses information ethically and legally" (ACRL 2000, 14). This expectation specifically links to school and academic libraries' work in teaching and assessing ethical information literacy behaviors with citation tools, plagiarism instruction, and online tutorials and quizzes.

Citation Management Tools

Citation management tools can help to encourage the ethical use of information. Such tools can be used for instruction and assessing student knowledge and understanding. Citation generators abound; not only can these tools assist students with learning the laborious process of proper citation methods, but also they can help students organize sources. By providing students with examples of citations for online or print research, images, or other informational works, students can begin to understand what citation entails. In addition, the frequency of errors from these tools provides ample fodder for a discussion on how a correct citation should appear and why it is dangerous to rely fully on computer-generated shortcuts.

Assessment in Action

Research assignments provide opportunities to assess students' use of citation tools because many of the available options offer sharing capabilities. RefWorks (refworks.com), the tool used at Oakland University, has a RefShare feature available that allows users to create folders that may be accessed and edited by others. CiteULike (citeulike.org) is another, more social citation tool teachers and students can use to collaborate and develop ethical behaviors. This resource, along with Diigo (diigo.com), follows the logic of folksonomies and offers students the opportunity to share collected research with others. CiteULike's tagging feature allows users to see what words or authors are most or least frequently used. Through exposure to peers' examples, this feature can help students expand or better focus their research. This feature also helps teachers determine whether a student or group of students is on the right track with an assignment (Grenhow 2009; Yorke-Barber, Ghiculescu, and Possin 2009).

Online Tutorials

Online learning objects such as demonstration videos and interactive lessons allow students to learn about and consider ethical uses of information. Videos created with free screencasting tools, including Screencast-o-matic (screencast-o-matic.com), Jing (techsmith.com/jing.html), Screencastle (screencastle.com), or Screenr (screenr.com), can help "flip the classroom" and take content instruction into the online realm. More robust proprietary tools are also available in Adobe Captivate (adobe.com/products/captivate.html) or TechSmith's Camtasia Studio (techsmith.com/camtasia.html). By sharing these resources online, teachers can frame class periods as a time to practice and explore, rather than an opportunity to "sit and get." Students can then practice building ethical information.

Assessment in Action

Oakland University's librarians created a short online course on avoiding plagiarism that included not only a final exam, but also provided opportunities for students to answer questions with feedback throughout the course, and a place for them to practice the crucial skill of paraphrasing (Figure 3.11). Housed within Moodle with the final exam recorded into a Microsoft Access database, the course allowed for multiple levels of assessment, as students were able to receive immediate feedback as they worked through the material and faculty were able to access the results of students' paraphrasing practice and final exam (Greer et al. 2012). Such a course unit could be replicated as a unit or

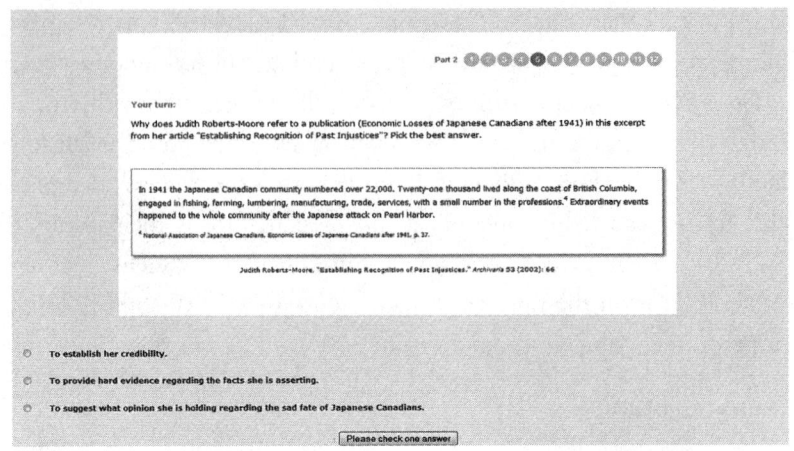

Figure 3.11 Oakland University's Plagiarism Tutorial provides librarians and instructors a structured and scaffolded means to teach students about ethical uses of information, and then to assess students' understanding

learning module in a secondary classroom and presents a collaborative opportunity for the teacher and school librarian to work together to achieve both CCSS and AASL learning standards.

Connecting to College and Career Readiness

Teaching students ethical information literacy behaviors prepares them for the rigorous academic research of a college career and the appropriate use of information in whatever career they choose. Citation tools require students to consider how they "draw evidence from literary or informational texts to support analysis, reflection, and research," while also illustrating their ability to accurately and ethically "gather relevant information from multiple print and digital sources … and integrate the information while avoiding plagiarism" (CCSSO and NGA 2010, Anchor Standards for Writing 9, 8), an essential skill for any learner advancing into postsecondary education, where the ramifications of plagiarism and academic dishonesty are well-known. However, as cases of inappropriate attribution and plagiarism have become more prevalent in many working environments (e.g., Jayson Blair of the *New York*

Times, or James Frey's *A Million Little Pieces*), knowing how to properly cite and credit others' work has also become an essential skill for any student seeking a job in the 21st century.

Visions for the Future

How the AASL and ACRL standards have been taught and assessed provides a vision for how the CCSS can be implemented in today's classrooms. The technology used and recommended throughout the information-seeking cycle present viable resources for teaching students to "use technology and digital media strategically and capably" (CCSSO and NGA 2010, 7). However, they may not exist in the classrooms of tomorrow. In fact, these tools may be replaced with options altogether new and innovative. In considering how to best equip the next digital scholar, the future of K–12 technology should be considered, too—and there are several shifts on the horizon that could affect how learning happens (for further prognostications, see Walker et al. 2011).

At a very basic level, learning environments are increasingly virtual, and thereby increasingly personal. Loertscher and Koechlin's (2012) "virtual learning commons," in which a whole school is digitally engaged in a learning community, is not far off. And as learning communities develop online, students' own learning may become increasingly individualized. This development will certainly change the types of technology used to teach students how to determine, access, evaluate, and use information in ethical ways, such as adaptive tests or targeted online learning assessments. These may come in massive online open courses, the MOOCs that are shaking higher education's long-settled paradigms; they may simply take the form of assessments that move beyond Google-able questions into deeper, more authentic learning quests. Whatever the tools, such virtual learning environments and dynamic learning objects can help achieve the true aims of the CCSS, AASL, and ACRL standards, creating the next generation of digital scholars.

Table 3.1 Digital Tools for Each Information Literacy Stage

Information Literacy Stage	Assessment Strategy	Tool	URL
Determining information need	Concept mapping	Inspiration	inspiration.com
		Webspiration	mywebspiration.com
		Text2MindMap	text2mindmap.com
		DebateGraph	debategraph.org
		Prezi	prezi.com
		Mindomo	mindomo.com
	Think-pair-share	Padlet	padlet.com
		Pinterest	pinterest.com
		Learnist	learni.st
		Wikis (e.g., Wikispaces)	wikispaces.com
		Blogs (e.g., Blogger, Edublogs)	blogger.com, edublogs.org
Accessing information	Information pathfinders	Wikis (e.g., Wikispaces)	wikispaces.com
		Google Sites	sites.google.com
		School-provided web creation tools	Contact your school or district's technology department for specific resources available
	Online quizzes	Google Forms	Located within drive.google.com
		Survey Monkey	surveymonkey.com
		Course management systems (e.g., Blackboard, Moodle)	blackboard.com, moodle.com
Evaluating information	Research process journals	Google Forms	Located within drive.google.com
		Google Docs	Located within drive.google.com
		Blogs (e.g., Blogger, Edublogs)	blogger.com, edublogs.org
		Dropbox	dropbox.com
		VoiceThread	voicethread.com
	Website and resource evaluation	Sample websites for evaluation (Pacific Northwest Tree Octopus, Feline Reactions to Bearded Men, Kathy Schrock's Sites to Use for Demonstrating Critical Evaluation)	zapatopi.net/treeoctopus, improbable.com/airchives/classical/cat/cat.html, schrockguide.net/critical-evaluation.html
		Wikipedia	wikipedia.org
		Blogs (e.g., Blogger, Edublogs)	blogger.com, edublogs.org
		Google Forms	Located within drive.google.com
		Survey Monkey	surveymonkey.com

Table 3.1 (cont.)

Information Literacy Stage	Assessment Strategy	Tool	URL
Using information	Social and collaborative tools	Wikis (e.g., Wikispaces)	wikispaces.com
		VoiceThread	voicethread.com
		Google Drive	drive.google.com
		Podcast/video creation tools (e.g., Audacity for podcasting, Animoto for videos, Photo Peach for photo slide shows)	audacity.sourceforge.net, animoto.com, photopeach.com
	Digital Portfolios	Google Sites	sites.google.com
		Weebly for education	education.weebly.com
		Wix	wix.com
		WordPress	wordpress.com or wordpress.com/classrooms
		Proprietary web design software	Contact your school or district's technology department for specific resources available
Ethically considering information use and access	Citation management tools	RefWorks	refworks.com
		CiteULike	citeulike.org
		Diigo	diigo.com
		EasyBib	easybib.com
		NoodleTools	noodletools.com
		Son of Citation Machine	citationmachine.net
	Online tutorials	Screencast-o-matic	screencast-o-matic.com
		Jing	techsmith.com/jing.html
		Screencastle	screencastle.com
		Screenr	screenr.com
		Adobe Captivate	adobe.com/products/captivate.html
		Camtasia Studio	techsmith.com/camtasia.html

Endnote

1. These amusing internet hoax sites may be found (as of May 2013) at zapatopi.net/treeoctopus and improbable.com/airchives/classical/cat/cat.html, respectively.

References

American Association of School Librarians. 1945. *School Libraries for Today and Tomorrow: Functions and Standards.* Chicago: American Library Association.

———. 1960. *Standards for School Library Programs.* Chicago: American Library Association.

———. 2007. *Standards for the 21st Century Learner.* Chicago: American Library Association.

———. 2009. *Standards for the 21st Century Learner in Action.* Chicago: American Library Association.

———. 2010. "Position Statement on the Common Core College- and Career-Readiness Standards." Accessed February 10, 2014. www.ala.org/aasl/aaslissues/positionstatements/collegecareerstandards.

American Association of School Librarians and Association for Educational Communications and Technology. 1975. *Media Programs: District and School.* Chicago: American Library Association.

———. 1988. *Information Power: Guidelines for School Library Media Programs.* Chicago: American Library Association.

———. 1998. *Information Power: Building Partnerships for Learning.* Chicago: American Library Association.

Association of College and Research Libraries. 2000. *Information Literacy Competency Standards for Higher Education.* Chicago: American Library Association.

Burkett, Rebecca. 2011. "Inquiry and Assessment Using Web 2.0 Tools." *School Library Monthly* 28 (1): 21–24.

Burkhardt, Joanna M., and Mary C. McDonald. 2010. "Exercise 39: Database Discovery Project." In *Teaching Information Literacy: 50 Standards-Based Exercises for College Students,* 2nd edition, edited by Joanna M. Burkhardt and Mary C. McDonald, 77–78. Chicago: American Library Association.

Byrne, Richard. 2010. "Stick It: Use Online Sticky Notes to Answer Student Questions and Get Feedback." *School Library Journal* 56 (10): 13.

Cambridge, Darren, Barbara Cambridge, and Kathleen Yancey, eds. 2009. *Electronic Portfolios 2.0.* Sterling, VA: Stylus Publishing.

Council of Chief State School Officers and National Governors Association. 2010. *Common Core State Standards for English Language Arts and Literacy in History/Social Studies, Science, and Technical Subjects.* Washington, DC: National Governors Association Center for Best Practices, Council of Chief State School Officers. Accessed February 10, 2014. www.corestandards.org/assets/CCSSI_ELA%20Standards.pdf.

Greer, Katie, Stephanie Swanberg, Mariela Hristova, Anne T. Switzer, Dominique Daniel, and Sherry Wynn Perdue. 2012. "Beyond the Web Tutorial: Development and Implementation of an Online, Self-Directed Academic Integrity Course at Oakland University." *Journal of Academic Librarianship* 38 (9): 251–258.

Grenhow, Christine. 2009. "Social Scholarship: Applying Social Networking Technologies to Research Practices." *Knowledge Quest* 37 (4): 42–47.

Hamilton, Buffy J. 2012. "Embedded Librarianship in a High School Library: Cultivating Student Participatory Literacy and Personal Learning Environments." *Library Technology Reports* 48 (2): 21–26.

Harris, Christopher. 2006. "School Library 2.0." *School Library Journal* 52 (5): 50–53.

Head, Alison J. 2012. "Learning Curve: How College Graduates Solve Information Problems Once They Join the Workplace." *Project Information Literacy Research Report*. Accessed February 10, 2014. projectinfolit.org/pdfs/PIL_fall2012_work placeStudy_FullReport.pdf.

Head, Alison J., and Michael B. Eisenberg. 2009. "Lessons Learned: How College Students Seek Information in the Digital Age." *Project Information Literacy Research Report*. Accessed February 10, 2014. projectinfolit.org/pdfs/PIL_Fall2009_finalv_YR1_12_2009v2.pdf.

Joint Committee of the American Association of School Librarians and the Department of Audiovisual Instruction of the National Education Association. 1969. *Standards for School Media Programs*. Chicago: American Library Association.

Kagan, Spencer. 1994. *Cooperative Learning*. San Juan Capistrano: Kagan Cooperative Learning.

King, Allison. 1993. "From Sage on the Stage to Guide on the Side." *College Teaching* 41 (1): 30–35.

Koechlin, Carol, and Sandy Zwan. 2008. "Everyone Wins: Differentiation in the School Library." *Teacher Librarian* 35 (5): 8.

Kral, Steve. 2007. "The Necessity of Website Evaluation." *School Library Monthly* 23 (7): 12–15.

Kuiper, Els, Monique Volman, and Jan Terwel. 2005. "The Web as an Information Resource in K–12 Education: Strategies for Supporting Students in Searching and Processing Information." *Review of Educational Research* 75 (3): 285–328.

Kuntz, Kelli. 2003. "Pathfinders: Helping Students Find Paths to Information." *Multimedia Schools* 10 (3): 12–15.

Lamb, Annette, and Larry Johnson. 2006. "Blogs and Blogging, Part II." *School Library Monthly*, 22 (9): 40–44.

Loertscher, David V., and Carol Koechlin. 2012. "The Virtual Learning Commons and School Improvement." *Teacher Librarian* 39 (6): 20.

Lundin, Rebecca Wilson. 2008. "Teaching With Wikis: Toward a Networked Pedagogy." *Computers and Composition* 25 (4): 432–448.

Lyman, Frank T. 1981. "The Responsive Classroom Discussion: The Inclusion of All Students." In *Mainstreaming Digest*, edited by Audrey Springs Anderson, 109–113. College Park, MD: University of Maryland Press.

Markham, Kimberly M., Joel J. Mintzes, and Gail M. Jones. 1994. "The Concept Map as a Research and Evaluation Tool: Further Evidence of Validity." *Journal of Research in Science Teaching* 31 (1): 91–101.

McClure, Randall. 2011. "Googlepedia: Turning Information Behaviors into Research Skills." In *Writing Spaces: Readings on Writing*, Volume 2, edited by Charles Lowe and Pavel Zemliansky, 221–241. Anderson, SC: Parlor Press. Accessed February 10, 2014. writingspaces.org/sites/default/files/mcclure--googlepedia.pdf.

Mulherrin, Elizabeth A., and Husein Abdul-Hamid. 2009. "The Evolution of a Testing Tool for Measuring Undergraduate Information Literacy Skills in the Online Environment." *Communications in Information Literacy* 3 (2): 204–215.

Naslund, Jo-Anne, and Dean Giustini. 2008. "Towards School Library 2.0: An Introduction to Social Software Tools for Teacher Librarians." *School Libraries Worldwide* 14 (2): 55–67.

Novak, Joseph Donald. 2010. *Learning, Creating, and Using Knowledge: Concept Maps as Facilitative Tools in Schools and Corporations*. 2nd ed. New York: Routledge.

O'Sullivan, Michael K., and Thomas J. Scott. 2000. "Pathfinders Go Online." *Library Journal NetConnect* Summer (supplement): 40–42.

Peele, Tom, and Glenda Phipps. 2007. "Research Instruction at the Point of Need: Information Literacy and Online Tutorials." *Computers and Composition Online*. Accessed February 10, 2014. www.bgsu.edu/departments/english/cconline/PeeleandPhipps.

Purcell, Melissa. 2011. "Digital Portfolios: A Valuable Teaching Tool." *School Library Monthly* 27 (6): 21–22.

Purdy, James P. 2009. "When the Tenets of Composition Go Public: A Study of Writing in Wikipedia." *College Composition and Communication* 61(2), W351–W373. Accessed February 10, 2014. www.ncte.org/library/NCTEFiles/Resources/Journals/CCC/0612-dec09/CCC0612When.pdf.

———. 2012. "Why First-Year College Students Select Online Research Resources as Their Favorite." *First Monday* 17 (9). Accessed February 10, 2014. www.firstmonday.org/htbin/cgiwrap/bin/ojs/index.php/fm/rt/printerFriendly/4088/3289.

Scharf, Davida, Norbert Elliot, Heather A. Huey, Vladimir Briller, and Kamal Joshi. 2007. "Direct Assessment of Information Literacy Using Writing Portfolios." *Journal of Academic Librarianship* 33 (4): 462–477.

Schick, Carla J. 1991. *The Use of Concept Mapping to Evaluate the Effects of Both Bibliographic Instruction and Discipline-Based Art Education on the Library Skills of Elementary Art Teachers*. ERIC document [ED 352981].

Schrock, Kathy. 2014. "Critical Evaluation of Information." *Kathy Schrock's Guide to Everything*. Accessed February 10, 2014. www.schrockguide.net/critical-evaluation.html.

Sherrat, Christine S., and Martin L. Schlaback. 1990. "The Applications of Concept Mapping in Reference and Information Services." *Reference Quarterly* 30 (1): 60–69.

Sprankle, Bob. 2009. "VoiceThread." *School Talk* 15 (4): 1.

Walker, Janice R., Kristine L. Blair, Douglas Eyman, Bill Hart-Davidson, Mike McLeod, Jeff Grabill, et al. 2011. "Computers and Composition 20/20: A Conversation Piece, or What Some Very Smart People Have to Say About the Future." *Computers and Composition* 28 (4): 327–346.

Yorke-Barber, Phil, Cristina Ghiculescu, and Gisela Possin. 2009. "RefWorks in Three Steps: Undergraduate Team Bibliographies." *Issues in Science and Technology Librarianship* 58. Accessed February 10, 2014. www.istl.org/09-summer/article4.html.

CHAPTER 4

Using the Framework for Success in Postsecondary Writing to Foster Learning

Angela Clark-Oates, Allyson Boggess, and Duane Roen

Authors' Note: We obtained institution review board approval for using students' course materials.

In response to the Common Core State Standards (CCSS), the Council of Writing Program Administrators (CWPA), the National Council of Teachers of English (NCTE), and the National Writing Project (NWP) collaborated to draft, revise, and endorse the Framework for Success in Postsecondary Writing (Framework), published in 2011. These organizations banded together to develop the Framework because, although the CCSS writers may have consulted teachers, our conversations with leaders of these organizations suggest that there is little evidence that they consulted relevant professional organizations when drafting the CCSS document.

The Framework was built on the foundation established in the WPA Outcomes Statement for First-Year Composition authored by the CWPA in the late 1990s and augmented 8 years later (CWPA

2008). The WPA Outcomes Statement describes five areas of learning outcomes for students in first-year writing courses and other courses, including:

- Rhetorical Knowledge
- Critical Thinking, Reading, and Writing
- Processes
- Knowledge of Conventions
- Composing in Electronic Environments

As Edward White (2005) notes in "The Origins of the Outcomes Statement," these are outcomes, not standards, methods, or materials. This is an important distinction. Although the WPA Outcomes Statement offers outcomes that reflect what scholars in the field of English studies consider important for students as they learn to write more effectively in the academic, professional, civic, and personal arenas of life, there are many ways to help students achieve that learning. Sherry Rankins-Robertson (2013) underscores this principle: "To help students meet those expectations, though, we bear a responsibility to produce assignments that are informed by, and that articulate with, the desired learning outcomes of a course, a program, and/or an institution" (58).

Although the WPA Outcomes Statement has been instrumental in shaping writing courses across the U.S. and in institutions in other countries, the Framework extends the discussion by advocating for eight habits of mind, briefly defined as follows:

- Curiosity: The desire to know more about the world
- Openness: The willingness to consider new ways of being and thinking in the world
- Engagement: A sense of investment and involvement in learning
- Creativity: The ability to use novel approaches for generating, investigating, and representing ideas
- Persistence: The ability to sustain interest in and attention to short- and long-term projects

- Responsibility: The ability to take ownership of one's actions and understand the consequences of those actions for oneself and others

- Flexibility: The ability to adapt to situations, expectations, or demands

- Metacognition: The ability to reflect on one's own thinking as well as on the individual and cultural processes used to structure knowledge

Since 2011, many secondary and postsecondary writing teachers have used the Framework to guide their instruction because they recognize that the eight habits of mind can help students become more effective learners, thinkers, readers, and writers. As we have discussed the eight habits of mind with colleagues across the country, we have come to appreciate that the habits can apply more broadly to learning in other courses and to success in life more generally. These habits can help people succeed in the academic realm of life as well as in the professional, civic, and personal realms.

Working from this point, we first argue in this chapter that the Framework should be used as a lens for understanding and integrating the CCSS in English Language Arts (ELA) classrooms. We then provide evidence for understanding the Framework. To do this, we highlight how the Writers' Studio, an online first-year composition program at Arizona State University, uses the Framework to guide curriculum and teaching practices. After illustrating how the Framework informs a writing curriculum, we construct a dialogue between the Framework and the CCSS. Finally, we discuss the implications of using the Framework to influence the implementation of the CCSS for teachers and librarians.

The Framework in Use

As Peggy O'Neill and colleagues (2012) note, the Framework reflects the "belief that writing instruction is an activity shared by K–16 teachers" (520). In articulating this shared responsibility, they call teachers and researchers in postsecondary institutions to a discussion about the CCSS, which is especially relevant, as they note, when we acknowledge the impact the CCSS will have on students' writing experiences before they get to college (522). To address this shared ethos with K–12 educators and to answer O'Neill and her colleagues' call, we present our curriculum and practices in the Writers' Studio as a lens for interpreting the CCSS for Writing in grades 6–12. In particular, we focus on our use of the Framework because we understand the burden teachers and students in K–12 settings face as they prepare, once again, to be evaluated on their ability to articulate teaching and learning in the language of state standards, an ever changing process driven by competition, testing, and efficiency (Rush and Scherff 2012). By describing our first-year composition courses as a tool to support teachers in grades six through 12, we critique the CCSS and advocate for an implementation that is filtered through a lens constructed by practitioners and scholars in the field of writing studies.

We argue that the curriculum in the Writers' Studio with its focus on multimodal assignments, rhetorical knowledge, and engagement with research can also impact the work of librarians as they conceptualize how to engage and support students and teachers through the implementation of the CCSS. In this way, our chapter also views the role of librarians as integral to how the CCSS will be realized in the classroom (Gewertz 2012), especially given that librarians are prepared as both teachers and information specialists (Hill 2011). Therefore, we argue that librarians are uniquely positioned to engage with teachers to imagine the critical possibilities of using the Framework because, like Bundy (1999), we view librarians as more than harbingers of information literacy; we view them as change agents.

To demonstrate some of the ways in which the Framework is shaping practice in the field, we point to Asao Inoue's work at Fresno State University, where Inoue has developed a program called Self-Paced Online Tutorial (SPOT). As noted in the SPOT materials: "[T]he eight habits of mind [...] guide the outcomes, process, and expectations of the SPOT experience" (Inoue 2013). Participating students have 6 months to work through writing units specific to their academic and professional interests. Once the tutorial is complete, students have the opportunity to demonstrate significant evidence of their learning by submitting a portfolio of their work as a method for fulfilling California State University's Upper Division Writing Requirement. Students must develop, engage with, and utilize the eight habits of mind in order to be successful as self-directed learners. Moreover, it has been our experience through our work in redesigning first-year writing courses at our own institution and working with colleagues on redesigns at their institutions that the habits of mind serve as a powerful tool for articulating programmatic goals and outcomes. Such habits of mind can also be traced back to the work of educators such as John Dewey. For example, in his influential book *How We Think* (1933), Dewey describes the importance of specific habits of mind: "open-mindedness" (30), "whole-heartedness" (31), "responsibility" (32), and "curiosity" (36–40).

This universality of the habits of mind—with its roots in a humanist approach to teaching and learning and its implication for 21st-century literacy practices—makes it a relevant complement to the CCSS.

A Framework for the CCSS

In Chapter 6 of this volume, Clancy Ratliff articulates the alignment of the WPA Outcomes Statement, which is included in the Framework, and the CCSS for ELA for grades 11 and 12. Through her development of a side-by-side comparison chart, Ratliff concludes that the marked differences between the two documents became visible, reminding us of the importance of using one as a lens for understanding the other. And we would argue that these differences are predicated on the fact that, unlike the CCSS, the WPA Outcomes Statement emerged from the research and practice of scholars, teachers in K–12 classrooms, teacher educators, and faculty in the field of English studies. This historical and philosophical influence is equally important when discussing how the Framework can influence the implementation of the CCSS in ways that honor the best practices of K–16 writing teachers in our field.

Through our experiences with faculty and students in the Writers' Studio, we advocate for the use of the Framework because it provides a nonstandardized approach to standardization, meaning that it provides a language for teachers to emphasize what Robert Yagelski (2011) calls in his address to the Conference on English Education "the humanness of schooling and the capacity of writing to help us live our lives more fully and mindfully and to seek well-being." Although the Framework has been critiqued for its elusiveness (Summerfield and Anderson 2012), this feature makes it a professional complement to the CCSS because the Framework leaves room for imagining, treats teachers as intellectuals, and demonstrates—through its articulation of the habits of mind—an understanding that creativity and scholarship should undergird any writing curriculum. Echoing this, Bruce McComiskey (2012) writes, "Although I initially found the Framework puzzling, as I have continued to think about the document and how it might function in my own local context, I have begun, more recently, to value the Framework, not as a guide to secondary or postsecondary writing instruction, but as a bridge between the CCSS and the CWPA Outcomes Statement" (538). Accordingly, our purpose, then, is to show how writing curricula—assignments, assessment tools, and projects—can be modified by teachers in grades 6–12 to support the implementation of the CCSS.

In the CCSS, the Council of Chief State School Officers (CCSSO) and the National Governors Association (NGA) (2010) argue that for students to build a strong foundation for college and career, they must be given opportunities to "learn to use writing as a way of offering and supporting opinions, demonstrating understanding of the subjects they are studying, and conveying real and imagined experiences and events" (18). In a similar manner, the authors of the Framework write, "At its essence, the Framework suggests that writing activities and assignments should be designed with genuine purposes and audiences in mind (from teachers and other students to community groups, local or national officials, commercial interests, students' friends and relatives, and other potential readers) in order to foster flexibility and rhetorical versatility" (CWPA, NCTE, and NWP 2011, 3).

Although echoes of the Framework can be heard in the CCSS, the CCSS seem more focused on school-based literacy practices, whereas the Framework broadens its definition, seeking to support students' in-school and out-of-school literacy practices. In this way, we begin to understand why it is so important to use multiple documents when building a writing curriculum and pedagogy. The alternative is for K–12 teachers to feel compelled to rely solely on the CCSS, using it as the only "guiding document and framing for classroom teaching, ignoring the social and cultural influences of teaching and learning" (Scherff and Rush 2013, 110). In advocating for the use of the Framework as a tool for designing curriculum that "illustrates the expectations of college students' digital writing and researching behaviors," we are aware of the difficult task of articulating college readiness, but we share Carol Severino's belief that the Framework helps to demystify what happens in writing: "Communicating even more explicitly and honestly the social and emotional skills, the language skills, and the knowledge of controversies that enable survival in composition and college will uncover other key requisite abilities and address the differences in backgrounds and skill levels of students from differently resourced high schools" (2012, 536).

The CCSS and the Framework: A Dialogue

In this section, we want to be explicit about how teachers, librarians, and students can use the Framework to engage with the CCSS in ways that foster the habits of mind listed earlier in this chapter. Like Lisa Scherff and Leslie Rush (2013), our goal is to highlight how "educators have agency to help all students work toward powerful literacy education" (104). To do this, we focus on the College and Career Readiness Anchor (CCRA) standards because doing so allows us to focus less on standards for specific grade levels and more on the standards that anchor all grade levels, broadening our audience to include all educators in grades 6–12.

Although our goal is to describe similarities between the two documents and to invoke the habits of mind where the documents diverge, it is important first to note a stylistic difference. The CCRA standards are written as commands, in imperative form without accompanying rationales, whereas the Framework is written as a process of experiences with a description of consequences. This stylistic difference is not merely a difference of convention. The CCRA standards focus on the products of learning; the Framework focuses on mental habits that can lead to effective products. Philip Eubanks (2011) explains, "If we want to think more carefully about who writers are, what writing is, and how writing affects our lives, we should pay attention to our figurative language and thought" (13). And when we consider the figurative language of each document—the global competition alluded to in the CCSS and the literate citizenry in the Framework—we may find ourselves constructing a binary between the two. Instead, what we want to do in this chapter is to construct a dialogical encounter, to support teachers and librarians as they use their intellect and expertise to design their curriculum in the space that exists between the two. In doing so, we endeavor to help teachers remember that "we do not teach writing effectively if we try to make all students and all writing the same. ... There is no single kind of person to teach, no one reason to write, no one message to deliver, no one way to write, no single standard of good writing" (Murray 2004, 5).

CCRA Standards: Text Types and Purposes

The first three Anchor Standards for Writing address text types and purposes: (1) "Write arguments to support claims in an analysis of substantive topics or texts using valid reasoning and relevant and sufficient evidence"; (2) "Write informative/explanatory texts to examine and convey complex ideas and information clearly and accurately through the effective selection, organization, and analysis of content"; and (3) "Write narratives to develop real or imagined experiences or events using effective technique, well-chosen details and well-structured event sequences" (CCSSO and NGA 2010, 18). All three of these standards echo what the Framework categorizes as critical thinking:

Writers use critical writing and reading to develop and represent the processes and products of their critical thinking. For example, writers may be asked to write about familiar or unfamiliar texts, examining assumptions about the texts held by different audiences. Through critical writing and reading, writers think through ideas, problems, and issues; identify and challenge assumptions; and explore multiple ways of understanding. This is important in college as writers are asked to move past obvious or surface-level interpretations and use writing to make sense of and respond to written, visual, verbal, and other texts that they encounter. (CWPA, NCTE, and NWP 2011, 7)

Although the Anchor Standards deem the argument, the expository, and the narrative as critical to college and career readiness, teachers and librarians must design curricula that do more than provide contrived assignments, which, in our experience, often fail to connect with students. Instead, they "must offer the best assignment … to stimulate our students' creativity and willingness to learn what we teach" (White 1995, 1–2). In this space between an articulated standard and the mind of a student, a teacher and librarian have a moment to connect with students' curiosities. To engage students in the task of writing arguments, making claims through analysis, synthesizing complex texts, and crafting entertaining narratives, teachers should build opportunities for students to pursue their own curiosity. If we ignore this habit of mind, we force our ethos as educators into a small box that is only relevant—if we are lucky—in a school building or a classroom.

Developing a student's curiosity is equally important if we want students to persist in their research, taking time to find "relevant and sufficient" evidence, an arduous task for a novice writer and researcher. In the Writers' Studio, we ask students to pursue issues that are meaningful to them in their personal, academic, or professional lives. Although we assign a generic purpose for their writing, we ask students to explore, select, and analyze topics, using a reflective process by considering the following questions: What content should I use? Why should I use this content? How should I organize the content? Why should I organize the content this way? Moreover, while students clearly see writing narratives about imagined experiences as an act of *creativity*, writing about lived experience can also be highly creative. Even in autobiographical writing, students have opportunities to narrate events and craft descriptive details in novel ways. We offer this approach as a model for how other teachers and librarians can apply the CCSS while still allowing for creativity.

CCRA Standards: Production and Distribution of Texts

Like the Framework, the CCSS are also concerned with the rhetorical decisions and the writing processes that inform the production and distribution of a text. The CCSS addresses these concerns in the next three Anchor Standards for Writing: (4) "Produce clear and coherent writing in which the development, organization, and style are appropriate to task, purpose, and audience"; (5) "Develop and strengthen writing as needed by planning, revising, editing, rewriting, or trying a new approach"; (6) "Use technology, including the internet, to produce and publish writing and to interact and collaborate with others" (CCSSO and NGA 2010, 18). The fourth standard relates to what the Framework describes as rhetorical knowledge:

> Rhetorical knowledge is the basis of good writing. By developing rhetorical knowledge, writers can adapt to different purposes, audiences, and contexts. Study of and practice with basic rhetorical concepts such as purpose, audience, context, and conventions are important as writers learn to compose a variety of texts for different disciplines and purposes. For example, a writer might draft one version of a text with one audience in mind, then revise the text to meet the needs and expectations of a different audience. (CWPA, NCTE, and NWP 2011, 6)

When students make decisions about such features of their texts, they reflect on their practices as writers. Such metacognition is essential for any writer who is trying to do something with, for, or to readers. When students are asked to reflect deeply on their learning, teachers are giving themselves an opportunity to witness an evaluative claim about what a student sees, feels, and understands as they engage in the messy and complex task of learning. In the Writers' Studio, we begin our courses by asking students two simple questions: What do you already know about rhetoric? How would you describe your writing process? In this way, the premise of our course honors the different knowledge the students bring with them. It is easy to read a document like the CCSS or the Framework and interpret teaching as a linear process in which the end goal is to have every student end up in the same place, using the same methods, and producing the same artifacts. This is why using the habits of mind, which are ways of being instead of ways of acting, is so important when thinking about the relationship between the CCSS and the Framework.

When metacognition is an embedded practice of a curriculum, each unit, each topic covered, and each project crafted begins with one simple question: What do you already know? And the benefits of this guiding question—a question that acts more like a principle in the Writers' Studio curriculum—emerge later when teachers ask students to be intentional about their rhetorical choices. In the Writers' Studio, we ask students to describe their audience, articulate their purpose for writing, and explain the reason for choosing a genre, and because we have built our teacher–student relationship on the idea that the students' knowledge matters, they are more apt to reflect on and share their rhetorical decisions. It does not benefit the student to view metacognition, a process of being, as a futile school activity. Of course, we expect informed reflection with ample evidence for support. Moreover, we honor the practice of metacognition by ensuring that each student engages with others during the reflection process. In this way, we are encouraging a writing practice that is also based on openness. To be open to suggestions of others, to commit to a lifelong practice of revision, to take risks by trying new approaches (not just in school), one must view these ubiquitous acts of writing as being inescapably linked to metacognition. When writers plan, revise, edit, and rewrite, they are engaged in metacognition. They are responding to the following questions: What am I doing? Why?

Accordingly, the Framework stresses the importance of writing processes, but, unlike the CCSS, it explicitly emphasizes flexibility:

> Writing processes are not linear. Successful writers use different processes that vary over time and depend on the particular task. For example, a writer may research a topic before drafting, then after receiving feedback conduct additional research as part of revising. Writers learn to move back and forth through different stages of writing, adapting those stages to the situation. This ability to employ flexible writing processes is important as students encounter different types of writing tasks that require them to work through the various stages independently to produce final, polished texts. (CWPA, NCTE, NWP 2011, 8)

In the Writers' Studio, we provide students with a variety of ways to engage in the writing process. First, for each project, we ask students to be intentional about their invention work, practicing strategies like clustering, freewriting, brainstorming, and listing. In short, we ask students to try on invention work by moving those ephemeral thoughts of an unarticulated idea to paper. We understand that these strategies might not work for every student, but our intention is to give students tools they can carry with them, tools for getting started, and tools for persisting. We also strive to foster persistence by asking students to seek feedback from a variety of sources: peers, graduate and undergraduate writing fellows, reference librarians, and staff members in the writing center. And, of course, we want them to participate with their teachers in one-on-one conferences.

In short, our goal is to guide students as they are asked to be responsive to the reviewer. We accomplish this by having them complete an audience analysis of their work in progress. By engaging the student with an audience analysis tool, we ask the students to submit responses to the reviewer for the following questions: What is the purpose of your piece and what need is it fulfilling for your audience? Who is your audience? What do you know about them? What is their level of expertise? Their cultural perspectives? Their education? From where do you write and to where are you writing? What is your medium? Our students struggle to engage with an audience analysis tool because school writing for most of them has been relegated to one audience member—the classroom teacher. Although the teacher evaluates the project in the Writers' Studio, she does not evaluate it from the perspective of an audience member. Instead, she evaluates it as an informed reader. And because the student must negotiate the needs of an audience beyond the informed reader position of her teacher, she has to be flexible with her own intentions and purpose for writing.

Using digital technologies also requires flexibility. The CCSS, like the Framework, recognizes that effective writers know when to use a particular digital technology to meet the needs of a particular audience for a particular purpose. The Framework expands the idea of technology in the following way:

> All forms of writing involve technologies, whether pen and paper, word processor, video recorder, or webpage. Research attests to the extensive writing that students produce electronically; composing in or outside of school, students and instructors can build on these experiences. As electronic technologies continue to spread and evolve, writers (and teachers) need to be thoughtful, effective users who are able to adapt to changing electronic environments. For example, a writer might be asked to write a traditional essay, compose a webpage or video, and design a print brochure all based on similar information. While many students have opportunities to practice composing in electronic environments, explicit and intentional instruction focusing on the use and implications of writing and reading using electronic technologies will contribute to students' abilities to use them effectively. (CWPA, NCTE, and NWP 2011, 10)

The Framework's expanded notion of technology helps to foster openness in students, many of whom, like teachers, conceptualize technology too narrowly. When we bring the CCSS into a dialogue with the Framework around this issue of technology, we open up possibilities for students to reflect on their use of technology, asking how digital technology enhances rhetorical choices. In the Writers' Studio, we challenge students' assumptions about technology by asking them to craft both multimodal projects and traditional academic essays. To engage fully in both types of projects, the students must use a variety of technological resources including Audacity (audacity.sourceforge.net), iMovie (apple.com/mac/imovie), word processing programs, Google Sites (sites.google.com), and many others. We also give the students access to a variety of multimodal examples, and in this way, they begin to craft criteria they can use when developing their own projects (CWPA, NCTE, and NWP 2011, 10). We also ask them to use a variety of technologies for gathering evidence, from traditional searches in our library databases to primary research in the form of an interview (for details on library standards, see Chapter 3 by Amanda Nichols Hess and Katie Greer in this volume).

By using technology for a variety of purposes, we are expanding students' interactions with it, which can help them become more effective users of technology when writing. Moreover, we are fostering the habit of persistence. Our course is predicated on the belief that technology can fail, so we want students to do more than live with this inevitable consequence. We want them to use their resources to solve problems. In our course shells, we have detailed instructions for trouble-shooting technology issues, from chatting with a librarian online to contacting tech support.

As technology begins to undergird every practice of schooling—from the federal standards that guide educational practices to the local practices of teachers and students—we include our students in a rich discussion, where they are not "left to negotiate the space between the print and online spaces on their own" (Callaway 2013, 276). Our students need more than a declaration of the importance of technology;

they need class time that allows them to explore "the interrelation of writer, writing technology, and self-formation, and that recognizes and encourages the multiple literacies that students bring with them" (282–283). The chapters in this book form a collective effort in this regard.

CCRA Standards: Research to Build and Present Knowledge

The CCSS articulate goals for researching in the following three Anchor Standards for Writing: (7) "Conduct short as well as more sustained research projects based on focused questions, demonstrating understanding of the subject under investigation"; (8) "Gather relevant information from multiple print and digital sources, assess the credibility and accuracy of each source, and integrate the information while avoiding plagiarism"; and (9) "Draw evidence from literary or informational texts to support analysis, reflection, and research" (CCSSO and NGA 2010, 18). In the Writers' Studio, we too, following the Framework, believe in the importance of conducting research, evaluating sources, and using evidence in ways that honor the source without canceling out the student-writer's ideas and voice.

One way to accomplish this is to allow time for reflection because metacognition is crucial for writers as they determine the relevance, accuracy, and credibility of a source. Moreover, metacognition is essential for determining what counts as supporting evidence for a particular audience, purpose, and occasion. In implementing the CCSS, teachers must build assignments that have the potential to "reverse students' preconception that research means collecting other people's opinions and patching them together with a bit of rhetorical glue" (White 1995, 20).

In the Writers' Studio, we focus on scaffolding students' research experiences. We are explicit with our instruction about steps in the research process, asking students to share as they engage in the process. This allows the teachers to informally assess the student's analysis and evaluation of the source. We also encourage students to be open to listening to unlikely sources (e.g., their peers). Although many of our students are novice academic writers, they bring a wealth of professional and personal experiences with them into our classrooms.

We deny a space for the habits of mind when we present the research process as a lock-step linear method where following a tangent is detrimental to project. Rankins-Robertson (2013) writes about her own practice, "I want my students to break away from the 'box checking' to which they are accustomed and have minimal concern for including font size or the number of mandatory sources" (69).

If we foster responsibility in our students, allowing them to research and write as a response to their own curiosities, it will be much more difficult than assigning the topic, choosing a sufficient but arbitrary amount of sources for them to use, and evaluating the students on how well they followed the style guide assigned, yet it will be, at the same time, much more rewarding for the student and the teacher.

CCRA Standards: Range of Writing

The CCSS want students to "write routinely over extended time frames (time for research, reflection, and revision) and shorter time frames (a single sitting or a day or two) for a range of tasks, purposes, and audiences" (Anchor Standard for Writing 10; CCSSO and NGA 2010, 18). Although students often write relatively short pieces in secondary and post-secondary classes, some writing can require more persistence and sustained engagement than some students have experienced in other academic settings. To help students realize that they are capable of persistent engagement, teachers can ask students about what they do when no one is telling them what to do.

Posing such a question can reveal that many students have devoted substantial time and effort to activities that interest them. Dennis Gioia (1987), in his article on student engagement in the classroom, asserts that "*Participation* connotes involvement, sharing, and simply taking part, all desirable attributes especially for the social dimensions of a class. *Contribution*, on the other hand, connotes not only social, but also intellectual involvement and sharing of knowledge and knowledge construction" (16, emphasis in original). Helping students value their current forms of persistence and engagement is an important first step (see Chapter 1 by Randall McClure and James P. Purdy in this volume for more discussion of students' current forms of persistence in the area of technology and media use). And helping students deepen this level of engagement is another step forward.

The Framework in the Writers' Studio

When teachers choose to foster environments where students are supported to make informed rhetorical choices, explore their curiosities, engage in processes that foster responsible creativity and persistent responsibility, and are given quiet moments to reflect on their learning in ways that demand openness, they embrace what Murray (2004) calls "learning to allow learning" (1). Yet, in an era of standardization, teachers might be overwhelmed by and resistant to the idea of learning another framework outside of the CCSS. To lessen this anxiety, we provide rich examples to illustrate the influence of the Framework in the Writers' Studio.

As mentioned at the beginning of the chapter, the Writers' Studio in the School of Letters and Sciences at Arizona State University is an alternative, online version of a first-year writing course. We offer the standard two-semester course sequence as English 101 and 102, as well as English 105, an accelerated one-semester course, and for each course, students have a choice of enrolling in either a 15-week or 7.5-week version. Because our courses are online, students also learn by engaging with a variety of instructional modes: text, videos, slide presentations, and an electronic textbook. This gives students a chance to analyze and critique a variety of media, contributing to their understanding of how technology can both help and hinder the communication of ideas. When our students are crafting the three required writing projects and building a digital writing portfolio, we ask them to engage deeply with both the WPA Outcomes Statement and the Framework's eight habits of mind. In this way, we provide students with a language for participation in our academic discourse communities and offer them the language and the space to "try-on" this talk. And like our first-year writing students, we believe that students in grades 6–12 ELA classrooms could also benefit from a similar practice because the language within these two documents provides a rich frame for learning academic discourse, the same kind of discourse being assessed in the CCSS.

Moreover, we also encourage our faculty—through professional development—to use the language from both the WPA Outcomes and the Framework when giving feedback on any formal or informal assignment. And because we use a writing workshop model in the Writers' Studio, the students have many opportunities to receive feedback that echoes the language and the goals of these two documents. Each student is required to complete a minimum of three drafts before submitting a project for a final evaluation from the teacher. If the teacher indicates that a writing project is satisfactory, the student adds it to her portfolio. Once the portfolio is deemed satisfactory, the student has completed the course. We like to think of the Writers' Studio as a digital space where students have "freedom to learn by doing in a setting relatively low in risk, with access to coaches who initiate students into the 'traditions of the calling' and help them, by 'the right kind of telling' to see on their own behalf and in their own way what they most need to see" (Schön 1991, 17).

The capstone project for the first-year writing course requires students to use Google Sites to design digital portfolios. Google Sites is easy for students to use, and it allows them to share their work with whomever they wish. In their portfolios, students demonstrate what they have learned about rhetoric, genre, medium, style, and other choices that writers make, reflecting on their rhetorical actions, the impact of these actions, and how they might revise their actions in the future.

As students work with digital technologies, we witness the eight habits of mind at work in meaningful ways. Students at varying levels of digital literacy and rhetorical awareness are challenged to use these spaces to demonstrate evidence of their learning. In this practice, students learn to be open to the experience of acquiring new technologies and flexible when figuring out which digital tools work best for them. When they persist, students discover and reap the benefits of pushing through the anxiety of learning new rhetorical and digital tools.

Ultimately, students reflect on how they have developed and strengthened the eight habits; often, they have acquired these habits of mind through the very process of constructing the digital portfolio. To the student, the act becomes a dynamic learning opportunity to share the growth of the (writer-researcher) self.

Because the CCSS stress student growth across the writing standards and across several grade levels, it is vital for teachers to engage students in a practice of self-evaluation, one that can be documented in formal, informal, and cumulative writing projects. To do this, we advocate for using digital portfolios, which are similar to those we ask students to create in the Writers' Studio. In this way, students can document, self-reflect, and receive teacher-driven assessments each year, and carry their writing with them, using it to "demonstrate increasing sophistication in all aspects of language use, from vocabulary and syntax to the development and organization of ideas, and … address increasingly demanding content and sources" (CCSSO and NGA 2010, 19, 42).

Although portfolios may seem like a recent innovation in writing classrooms, James Moffett and Betty Jane Wagner advocated for the use of portfolios in the 1970s. In their influential *Student-Centered Language Arts and Reading, K–13* (1976), they argue for portfolios by noting, "You should judge a student's writing by generalizing as many instances of it as you can have access to" (421). They also argue that "only by continual self-evaluation can practice make perfect and that language arts methods consist mostly of human feedback systems" (418). Although self-evaluation is most apparent in students' course portfolios, it is woven into other activities in the Writers' Studio course. For example, when students craft the three writing projects for the course, they respond to the following questions:

- Who is my audience for this project?
- What is my purpose in this project?
- What genre will help me accomplish my goal in this project?
- What medium will help me accomplish my goal?

- What discourse conventions—macro and micro—will help me accomplish my goal?
- How can my peers help me as I work on this project?
- How can I help my peers as they work on their projects?

Moreover, this digital portfolio could be conceptualized as not only a practice for reflection on writing like the one we have constructed in the Writers' Studio, but also a genre analysis and reading reflection archive for the complex texts students will be asked to read and create. By housing the writing and the reading in one digital portfolio, teachers construct an opportunity to approach reading and writing from an inquiry perspective. Katie Wood Ray (2006) argues:

> When teachers immerse students in reading and studying the kind of writing they want them to do, they are actually teaching at two levels. They teach students about the particular genre or writing issue that is the focus of the study, but they also teach students to use a habit of mind that experienced writers engage in all the time. (242)

In our writing program, the curriculum emphasizes the importance of studying a genre before attempting to craft it. Therefore, in reimagining the digital portfolio in a way that is reflective of the CCSS, we suggest that grades 6–12 teachers also construct opportunities to invite their teacher-librarians to participate in finding relevant texts for students and helping students archive these texts (Hill 2011). White (1995) delineates the strengths and weaknesses of portfolios, but he concludes, "[P]ortfolios disallow the too easy reduction of assessment to tests and to test scores for the sorting of students. ... If portfolios do become the standard method of evaluating writing, we will be assured that writing itself remains valued, taught, and delightfully unpredictable" (163). Using portfolios as an assessment tool for the CCSS allows students to articulate their learning in a relevant and meaningful context (for further ideas on assessment, please see Chapter 2 by Elizabeth Homan and Dawn Reed in this volume).

In the Writers' Studio, when students construct their digital course portfolios, they essentially make the following case: "In light of the learning outcomes and the eight habits of mind, here is what I have learned in the course. Further, here is evidence that I have learned what I claim to have learned." The evidence consists of diverse artifacts: excerpts from course writing projects, transcripts or recordings of peer-review sessions, and even transcripts of conversations in other settings (e.g., home, workplace, recreational sites). Although we are interested in the learning outcomes that students have achieved, we are less interested in where they developed a piece of knowledge or a particular skill. Most important is that they have developed it somewhere—either in the course or outside the course.

Early in a 7.5- or 15-week term like that of the Writers' Studio, students bring these artifacts together as a rough collage, which is then woven into a narrative account of their learning. After the first project cycle, the evidence-gathering process for such a course can feel disorienting, but students quickly begin to see how the accumulation of evidence leads to a richer classroom experience. They also gain a greater appreciation for the depth and breadth of the skills and knowledge that they are developing in the course. They come to understand Kathleen Blake Yancey's observation that "we learn to understand ourselves through explaining ourselves to others" (1998, 11).

The digital portfolio is a space where students can record rich metacognitive moments, and it is a space where teachers can witness students' learning. Learning to write for a variety of purposes and audiences in a variety of genres happens over time; writing cannot be assessed by one test on one day. Portfolios allow teachers to see learning happen over time while simultaneously providing opportunities for students to synthesize their learning across genres.

Habits of Mind Reflected in Digital Portfolios

One way to ensure that student portfolios are supporting the outcomes of the CCSS is to ask students to organize the portfolio by genre. In this way, students can record artifacts from their inquiry work into a new genre, upload mentor texts that will support the writing of texts in a particular genre, archive drafts of their own attempts, and post their reflections of the entire learning process.

Aram Kabodian (2013), in his article for NWP's *Digital Is* website, writes about his integration of digital writing portfolios in his seventh-grade classroom. Like in the Writers' Studio, Kabodian uses the Framework to help him articulate his goals for the students. He also discusses his structured approach to teaching students to manage their portfolio. Finally, he shares the connection between digital writing portfolios and the CCSS, which asks students to "use technology" (Anchor Standard for Writing 6) and "write routinely over extended periods of time" (Anchor Standard for Writing 10; CCSSO and NGA 2010, 18).

Moreover, writing portfolios can be used as an authentic assessment tool of the CCSS. Portfolios provide students with opportunities to participate in the assessment of their learning and allow for an assessment of their writing over time. Portfolios also give teachers, regardless of grade level, an opportunity to provide rich and timely feedback during the process of writing and learning to write. To illustrate this point, we next discuss the eight habits of mind and provide excerpts from student reflections curated from digital portfolios in the Writers' Studio.

Curiosity

The first of the eight habits of mind described in the Framework—curiosity—manifested itself in a number of ways for students in the Writers' Studio. Students used multimodal assignments to articulate their desire to learn more about the world. By interacting with one another, students were able to observe the diverse approaches used by their classmates to complete the assignments. And finally, students were introduced to new technologies that enabled them to compose and collect evidence of their learning. Google Sites provided students an array of options for designing the look and feel of their portfolios. Students were also able to view their classmates' portfolios in order to read and explore additional approaches. In using a digital platform where face-to-face interaction rarely occurred, the visiting, viewing, and reviewing of peer portfolios became a way for students to get to know their peers and their peers' learning. Students could interact on discussion boards by offering ideas in response to a prompt or question, and they could experience a peer's collective work in progress.

Openness

The Framework defines openness as "the willingness to consider new ways of being and thinking in the world" (CWPA, NCTE, and NWP 2011, 4). Without accepting new experiences and perspectives, the opportunity to learn and expand one's thinking is lost: "Students cannot learn to think critically until they can, as least momentarily, set aside their own visions of truth and reflect on alternatives" (Meyers 1986, 27). Of course, openness is crucial when students craft arguments or propose solutions to problems. In arguments, writers and readers need to be open to others' perspectives. We encourage students to use a Rogerian approach[1] to considering others' perspectives, an approach marked by common goals, mutual respect, and consensus building (Rogers 1961).

The development of openness in the Writers' Studio serves to prepare students for learning across disciplines. It is crucial to the process of discovering new personal interests, potential career paths, and the world in which they live. Among other things, students need to be open to how discourse is constructed in their chosen fields. This is no small feat, for, as Richard Light (2001) notes in his influential study of students' success in college, "[a] surprising number of graduates describe learning how to use evidence to resolve controversies in their field, whatever their field, as a breakthrough idea" (122).

In the following reflection, Abigail[2] notes how she cultivated openness by exploring multimodal writing in the Writers' Studio:

> At first I was very skeptical about incorporating all the new information into my work but I knew that change wouldn't hurt me, it would only help me. One major change was using mediums for my projects. In past English courses, my

fellow classmates and I were only asked to write traditional formal essays. When Professor Boggess explained using a medium, I was sort of nervous. So many questions were going in and out of my mind. What if I pick the wrong medium? What if I couldn't do it? Once I sat down and began my first project using a journal-like medium, I was very excited to see the end results of my project. This idea of using a medium has been the most interesting change in my writing.

This student's ability to overcome her skepticism and work with new technologies illustrates the importance of openness. It reveals a growing confidence in her work and in herself.

Engagement

The Framework defines engagement as "a sense of investment and involvement in learning" (CWPA, NCTE, and NWP 2011, 4). Engagement inside the Writers' Studio required presence and active commitment to the course material and to peers. The following statement by Charlie shows how his use of technology ensured further engagement with class materials:

> Every step of the way we students are engaged to use good writerly habits and critical thinking to complete the various writing assignments and projects. I was engaged in discourse with my fellow students in the peer review process as well as being engaged in the discussion board posting and responding. Working in tandem with a tutor or writing fellow kept me engaged by all the constructive criticism I got and put to use through the revision process of my writing.

As Charlie's quote illustrates, not only did students have the opportunity to strengthen interpersonal skills through interactions on discussion boards, peer review, and emails to writing fellows and teachers, but also they learned about writing with a purpose by envisioning a specific audience. Relationships were developed and passions were discovered through engagement. Of course, we hope that our students retain these skills to become lifelong learners.

Creativity

In the Writers' Studio courses, most of the major writing assignments were multimodal. Students were required to work with a genre and medium other than the traditional academic essay. Students' decisions on genre and medium depended on how they defined their specific audience. It was common to hear from students how they were initially intimidated by multimodal assignments. It was equally common to hear at the end of the course how much students grew because they were expected to step outside their comfort zones. Alfonso's reflection illustrates how he grew by using creativity in the Writers' Studio:

> Creativity allows writers to explore new methods and tactics for representing their ideas and gives their audience an opportunity to connect with them in new and more effective ways. While choices in genre and medium can help dictate the creative approach to a project, creativity doesn't stop there. Creativity goes hand in hand with openness and gives the writer an opportunity to harvest information in different and exciting ways.

Alfonso's reference to openness in conjunction with creativity makes sense: If our students are not open-minded to the possibilities of writing, then how can they allow themselves to explore their full creative potentials?

Persistence

Persistence in writing requires a return to the page: the notebook where the first sketches of a brainstorm are done, perhaps the blank field of a word processing screen or blog page. Writing requires sustained attention. In the Writers' Studio, we emphasized the importance of sustained attention through the feedback cycle. Students with the tendency to procrastinate on assignments found it difficult to put off writing in this course because the process was divided into multiple mental operations, from invention to the final polished version. In a 7.5-week course in which work is due almost every day, students must engage with the current project regularly or risk falling behind. These thoughts from Alfonso affirm the significance of persistence as an asset to the writing student:

> Persistence is the habit of keeping your eye on the prize and understanding that the investment in time and energy will pay off dividends at the conclusion of your effort. It's the voice inside that tells you not to give up. Persistence doesn't mean burnout, but it gives the writer fortitude to continue, even if that means stepping away from your project for a while. It is the persistence that brings you back to complete the task or project.

In the Writers' Studio when students get stuck on a certain aspect of the project cycle, they are encouraged to ask for help, which is another example of persistence. The Writers' Lounge, a discussion board set up specifically in all Writers' Studio courses to foster a space for students to ask questions, provided the primary venue of additional support. Teachers, writing fellows, and class members all contributed to this space. It was not uncommon to find students answering a fellow student's questions in the Writers' Lounge. There was a spirit of common purpose and a genuine desire to help one another achieve learning goals. Of course, teachers and writing fellows were available to answer questions via email, but the Writers' Lounge was preferable, given the larger audience and therefore quicker response time. Another venue of support was the writing center, which provides assistance to students both on-campus and online.[3] Ultimately, the writing center and the writing fellow components allowed the Writers' Studio to foster persistence in our students. Beyond these specific mechanisms of support, however, the most important takeaway for teachers and librarians implementing the CCSS is the sustainable idea that persistence happens with the support of others.

Ultimately, we wish every student the determination to do the hard work of learning in our courses. When a student remains open to trying alternative approaches when the first attempts fall flat, that persistence will carry her through the challenges. In the words of Alfonso, "I found myself stymied early on in the project, because of some bad choices I made in getting started. My persistence kept me coming back for more, until I was able to find my groove and move forward towards the end. If writers' block is a sin, then persistence is the virtue that counteracts it!"

Responsibility

Responsibility presented a new challenge for some of the first-year college students in the Writers' Studio. These students came from diverse walks of life—some had professional experience before returning to school, while others were fresh out of secondary school. Regardless of prior work or life experience, all students were charged with new responsibilities in the Writers' Studio classroom: responsibility to the self in terms of completing the work of the course and for the act of learning; responsibility to others through full participation on discussion boards and in the feedback cycle; and responsibility to the work itself through the dedication of time and attention. Learning in an online course requires high levels of responsibility and discipline. In a 7.5-week course, students needed to engage with course material every day, and for some students this daily regimen presented a major challenge, despite the routines that were common to their experiences in the typical ELA classroom.

Writing is a commitment, even a scary endeavor for some students. By developing a strong sense of responsibility over the course of the term, they recognize the value of their personal investment in the practice. Some students already have a deeply rooted sense of responsibility derived from previous personal or work experience. By arriving together in the online space of the class, students have opportunities to strengthen their sense of responsibility to themselves, to the work, and to others. Alfonso's reflection on his work shows this recognition:

> When you are working in a collaborative environment such as a classroom, on-campus, or online, you have an obligation to your peers and classmates. The obligation is providing constructive feedback by staying engaged and thinking critically [about] their material and how your feedback contributes to their success as well as your own. This feedback and collaboration requires employment of all the habits of mind that we have learned about this year. I met this obligation with responsibility in mind, understanding that my success was no more or less important than that of my classmates.

Without student participation in the Writers' Studio, the feedback cycle would be incomplete, and the learning experience for all would be diminished. Students are accountable for following through on their commitments to review each other's work. However, peer review in the virtual classroom is a new experience for many students, so it is sometimes easy to forget that the human being on the other side of the computer screen is asking, "What do you think of my work?" As many students have never participated in peer review before, teachers need to provide the necessary scaffolding for students to succeed in fulfilling their responsibility to their classmates. When students make the connection between offering rich, detailed feedback to peers and receiving a greater understanding of the project itself, the process becomes an invaluable tool.

Flexibility

When the unexpected happens—a peer forgets to complete peer review, a server goes down, a computer crashes—students need to be flexible in their approaches to learning to be successful. This is especially relevant in the digital learning environment. Students sometimes enter the college writing classroom with minimal experience developing writing flexibility as defined in the Framework: "the ability to adapt to situations, expectations, or demands" (CWPA, NCTE, and NWP 2011, 5).

It is our responsibility to encourage students to develop flexibility as writers by asking them to design texts that vary along the following dimensions: audience, purpose, occasion, topic, genre, and medium. Although flexibility is important in a writing classroom, it becomes essential when students venture out into other classrooms as well as the professional, civic, and personal arenas of life.

We need to prepare our students for audiences that may range from supportive to hostile; purposes that cover Britton and colleagues' spectrum of expressive, transactional, and poetic (1975); genres that vary from formal academic essays to corporate memos to tweets; and settings that include the academic, professional, civic, and personal.

Chad, a nontraditional student, illustrates this habit of mind in his reflection on his flexibility in adapting to his rhetorical situation in the Writers' Studio:

> I feel that, through the course of this class, I became much more flexible as a writer due to the different conditions I worked through and mediums I wrote in. I came to the belief and understanding that good writing is flexible to a number of situations, as I mentioned above, which are continually changing as technology, and the means with which we communicate, evolves.

This reflection shows that Chad understood that "[a] major goal of schooling is to prepare students for flexible adaptation to new problems and settings" (Bransford, Brown, and Cocking 2001, 77).

Metacognition

In the Framework, metacognition, the last of the eight habits of mind, is defined as "the ability to reflect on one's own thinking as well as on the individual and cultural processes used to structure knowledge" (CWPA, NCTE, and NWP 2011, 5). This habit of mind was an indispensable element of the Writers' Studio, and we argue that it should receive substantial attention in any course, whether the focus is writing, literacy more generally, or any other subject matter.

Dewey (1933) writes about the importance of reflective thinking, which he defines as *"Active, persistent, and careful consideration of any belief or supposed form of knowledge in light of the grounds that support it and the further conclusions to which it tends"* (9, emphasis in original). He suggests that such reflective thinking emphasizes the importance of evidence. In the Writers' Studio, students examined evidence of their own learning—evidence gleaned from their experience in the course and in other settings (e.g., high school classes, library research, digital spaces, other college courses, the workplace, social situations)—as they constructed their course portfolios. As students reflected on their literate practices, they not only gained greater appreciation of what they learned, but they also developed a stronger sense of what they still need to learn about rhetoric, critical thinking and reading, composing processes, conventions, and composing in digital environments. Students also reflected on how they developed habits of mind in the course and how those habits will help them succeed in college and in life more generally.

Conclusion

In this chapter we have examined the CCSS from a critical yet constructive position, viewing them through the lens of the Framework, offering suggestions for what role the CCSS might play in writing pedagogy and assessment in K–16 settings, and articulating what role teachers and librarians might play as they implement the standards and support students as students strive to meet them. The Framework was crafted as an intentional response to the CCSS, and it should be used intentionally by K–12 educators and librarians to frame the CCSS' implementation. In this way, theories and practices endorsed by years of educational research will inform how these standards impact students and their learning. Moreover, the Framework provides eight habits of mind that should be developed in ELA classrooms, habits that can act as touchstones for curriculum building, assessment, and outcomes.

We encourage teachers and librarians to approach the CCSS as agents, and as agents, they can use the Framework to construct a critical dialogue with the CCSS, one that lessens the possibility of crafting a disconnected curriculum for the sake of a test. A critical and sustained dialogue with the CCSS can also reveal the limitations of implementing any standard and "disrupt any attempt to position the CCSS as the sole actor in creating a high-quality educational experience for all students" (Scherff and Rush 2013, 112).

In a keynote address at the Language and Literacy conference at Arizona State University in 2013, Yetta Goodman and Kathy Short argued that we inevitably turn standardized tests into verbs because verbs tell stories. Their assertion begs us to ask the following question: Who is the storyteller? We understand that K–16 teachers and librarians are astute surfers of the standardization wave, but this should not imply passivity. Instead, we all should work together actively to ensure that students at all levels have opportunities to achieve meaningful learning outcomes and to develop habits of mind that will serve them well in and out of school. Advocating for this type of learning promises teachers, librarians, and students that they have the potential to be their own storytellers.

Endnotes

1. Rogerian rhetoric is based on the work of psychologist Carl Rogers, who was well known for focusing on healthy relationships. In Rogerian rhetoric, as Maxine Hairston (1976) notes, participants "scrupulously avoid evaluative language" and "listen to each other with understanding and acceptance" (373).
2. Pseudonyms are used to protect the identity of the students.
3. Although many middle schools and high schools do not have writing centers on their campuses, there is a growing practice of building writing centers in these spaces (Childers, Fels, and Jordan 2004; Fels and Wells 2011). Teachers and librarians can work together to build this learning support practice, but even if a writing center is not a viable option at a school, teachers and librarians can build a pedagogy of writing and researching that constructs opportunities for what Muriel Harris (1995) calls an introduction of a "middle person" to the educational setting (27). It is this idea of a middle person that can support teachers and librarians as they foster persistence in their students.

References

Bransford, John D., Ann L. Brown, and Rodney R. Cocking, eds. 2001. *How People Learn: Brain, Mind, Experience, and School*. Expanded edition. Washington, DC: National Academy Press.

Britton, James N., Tony Burgess, Nancy Martin, Alex McLeod, and Harold Rosen. 1975. *The Development of Writing Abilities (11–18)*. London: Macmillan.

Bundy, Alan. 1999. "Challenging Technolust: The Educational Responsibility of Librarians." *Proceedings of the International Association of Scientific and Technological University Libraries Conference*. Accessed February 10, 2014. docs.lib.purdue.edu/iatul/1999/papers/7.

Callaway, Michael. 2013. "What Role Should Technology Play." In *The WPA Outcomes Statement: A Decade Later*, edited by Nicholas N. Behm, Gregory R. Glau, Deborah H. Holdstein, Duane Roen, and Edward M. White, 271–284. Anderson, SC: Parlor Press.

Childers, Pamela, Dawn Fels, and Jeanette Jordan. 2004. "The Secondary School Writing Center: A Place to Build Confident, Competent Writers." *Praxis* 2. Accessed February 10, 2014. emil.uwc.utexas.edu/praxis/?q=node/91.

Council of Chief State School Officers and National Governors Association. 2010. *Common Core State Standards for English Language Arts and Literacy in History/Social Studies, Science, and Technical Subjects*. Washington, DC: National Governors Association Center for Best Practices, Council of Chief State School Officers. Accessed February 10, 2014. www.corestandards.org/assets/CCSSI_ELA%20Standards.pdf.

Council of Writing Program Administrators. 2008. *WPA Outcomes Statement for First-Year Composition*. Accessed February 10, 2014. wpacouncil.org/positions/outcomes.html.

Council of Writing Program Administrators, National Council of Teachers of English, and National Writing Project. 2011. *Framework for Success in Postsecondary Writing*. Accessed February 10, 2014. wpacouncil.org/files/framework-for-success-postsecondary-writing.pdf.

Dewey, John. 1933. *How We Think: A Restatement of the Relation of Reflective Thinking to the Educative Process*. Boston: D.C. Heath.

Eubanks, Philip. 2011. *Metaphor and Writing Figurative Thought in the Discourse of Written Communication*. New York: Cambridge University Press.

Fels, Dawn, and Jennifer Wells, eds. 2011. *The Successful High School Writing Center*. New York: Teachers College Press.

Gewertz, Catherine. 2012. "Common Core Thrusts Librarians into Leadership Roles." *Education Week* 32 (3): 18–19.

Gioia, Dennis. 1987. "Contribution! Not Participation in the OB Classroom." *Journal of Management Education* 11 (4): 15–20.

Goodman, Yetta, and Kathy Short. "The Role of Story in a World of Tests and Standards." Keynote address at the 43rd annual Language and Literacy Conference, Arizona State University, Tempe, Arizona, February 8, 2013.

Hairston, Maxine. 1976. "Carl Rogers's Alternative to Traditional Rhetoric." *College Composition and Communication* 27 (6): 373–377.

Harris, Muriel. 1995. "Talking in the Middle: Why Writers Need Writing Tutors." *College English* 57 (1): 27–42.

Hill, Rebecca. 2011. "Common Core Curriculum and Complex Texts." *Teacher Librarian* 38 (3): 42–46.

Inoue, Asao. 2013. Self-Paced Online Tutorial (SPOT). Division of Continuing and Global Education. Fresno State University. Accessed February 10, 2014. www.fresnostate.edu/cge/writing/index.html.

Kabodian, Aram. 2013. "Reflecting on the Move to Digital Writing Portfolios." *Digital Is*. National Writing Project. Accessed February 10, 2014. digitalis.nwp.org/resource/5015.

Light, Richard J. 2001. *Making the Most of College: Students Speak Their Minds*. Cambridge, MA: Harvard University Press.

McComiskey, Bruce. 2012. "Bridging the Divide: The (Puzzling) Framework and the Transition from K–12 to College Writing Instruction." *College English* 74 (6): 537–540.

Meyers, Chet. 1986. *Teaching Students to Think Critically: A Guide to Faculty in All Disciplines*. San Francisco: Jossey-Bass.

Moffett, James, and Betty Jane Wagner. 1976. *Student-Centered Language Arts and Reading, K–13*. 2nd edition. Boston: Houghton Mifflin Company.

Murray, Donald M. 2004. *A Writer Teaches Writing*. Revised 2nd edition. Boston: Thompson-Heinle.

O'Neill, Peggy, Linda Adler-Kassner, Cathy Fleischer, and Anne-Marie Hall. 2012. "Creating the Framework or Success in Postsecondary Writing." *College English* 74 (6): 520–524.

Rankins-Robertson, Sherry. 2013. "The Outcomes Statement as Support for Teacher Creativity: Applying the WPA OS to Develop Assignments." In *The WPA Outcomes Statement: A Decade Later*, edited by Nicholas N. Behm, Gregory R. Glau, Deborah H. Holdstein, Duane Roen, and Edward M. White, 58–70. Anderson, SC: Parlor Press.

Ray, Katie Wood. 2006. "Exploring Inquiry as a Teaching Stance in the Writer's Workshop." *Language Arts* 83 (3): 238–247.

Rogers, Carl R. 1961. *On Becoming a Person: A Therapist's View of Psychotherapy*. Boston: Houghton Mifflin.

Rush, Leslie S., and Lisa Scherff. 2012. "Opening the Conversation: NCLB 10 Years Later." *English Education* 44 (2): 91–101.

Scherff, Lisa, and Leslie S. Rush. 2013. "Opening the Conversation: The Common Core and Effective Literacy Education." *English Education* 45 (2): 99–114.

Schön, Donald A. 1991. *Educating the Reflective Practitioner: Toward a New Design for Teaching and Learning in the Professions.* San Francisco: Jossey-Bass Publishers.

Severino, Carol. 2012. "The Problems of Articulation: Uncovering More of the Composition Classroom." *College English* 74 (6): 533–536.

Summerfield, Judith, and Philip M. Anderson. 2012. "A Framework Adrift." *College English* 74 (6): 544–547.

White, Edward M. 1995. *Assigning, Responding, Evaluating: A Writing Teacher's Guide.* New York: St. Martin's Press.

———. 2005. "The Origins of the Outcomes Statement." In *The Outcomes Book: Debate and Consensus After the WPA Outcomes Statement*, edited by Susanmarie Harrington, Keith Rhodes, Ruth Overman Fischer, and Rita Malenczyk, 3–7. Logan, UT: Utah State University Press.

Yagelski, Robert. 2011. "Writing as Praxis." *English Education* 44 (2): 188–204.

Yancey, Kathleen Blake. 1998. *Reflection in the Writing Classroom.* Logan, UT: Utah State University Press.

CHAPTER 5

Participation and Collaboration in Digital Spaces
Connecting High School and College Writing Experiences

Rachel Bear, Heidi Estrem, James E. Fredricksen, and Dawn Shepherd

As literacy educators, we're particularly mindful of two different and current conversations about digital literacies that directly inform our experiences in the classroom. The first conversation stems from the development and initial implementation of the Common Core State Standards (CCSS) for high school instruction (Council of Chief State School Officers [CCSSO] and National Governors Association [NGA] 2010) and the work informing the Framework for Success in Postsecondary Writing (Framework), a statement that outlines expectations for incoming college students (Council of Writing Program Administrators [CWPA], National Council of Teachers of English [NCTE], and the National Writing Project [NWP] 2011). These documents directly affect our curricular decisions in a host of ways.

The second conversation that informs our experiences in the classroom is a larger cultural conversation about the implications of digital literacy practices and opportunities. Together, these twin conversations highlight the unsettled, ever-shifting landscape in which the authors of this chapter (Rachel Bear, a high school English teacher; Heidi Estrem and Dawn Shepherd, college professors and writing program administrators; and James E. Fredricksen, a college English education professor) work.

In particular, we focus on how digital literacy practices are developed, enhanced, and supported in two specific settings: one high school English classroom and several classes within a college first-year writing program. Our goal is to consider how our pedagogical decisions in these two different contexts might helpfully echo each other, providing opportunities for richer professional conversations and continued productive learning for students. To deepen our analysis, we explore how the CCSS and Framework inform our teaching while sometimes rendering invisible the kinds of digital literacies our students embody and that we describe in this chapter.

The CCSS are usefully described in this volume's introduction; the Framework is delineated in Chapter 4. Readers of this book might be less familiar with the Framework, a document that evolved out of a critical collaboration between leading professional organizations (NCTE, CWPA, and NWP) engaged with writing instruction at the postsecondary level. Leaders from these organizations developed a framework statement that seeks to describe both the "habits of mind" and the literacy-based "skills and experiences" that are "critical for college success" (CWPA, NCTE, and NWP 2011, 1). The eight habits of mind are curiosity, openness, engagement, creativity, persistence, responsibility, flexibility, and metacognition; the skills and experiences include rhetorical knowledge, critical thinking, writing processes, knowledge of conventions, and the ability to compose in multiple environments (1). Together, the CCSS and the Framework provide two important external maps, one of high school curriculum and one of entering college-level expectations, that capture an important perspective on the current national context within which literacy education occurs. Their purpose is to provide clear points of entry into curricula for a variety of stakeholders. Our goal, then, is to locate how practices that support rhetorical digital literacy might best be supported within very specific, localized practices and through these macro-lens documents.

The intersections of these various contexts—in particular, the classroom and these standards-like documents—can make for a difficult landscape for teachers of writers to navigate. However, all of us are members of a larger "participatory" culture that digital work makes possible. This third factor—a proposal for 21st-century literacy education by media scholar Henry Jenkins and colleagues—helps connect these educational contexts to a conception of the hope and possibility in online cultures. We use Jenkins's *Confronting the Challenges of Participatory Culture: Media Education for the 21st Century* (2006) because he describes elements of a culture based on participation that we try to promote in our classrooms. Moreover, we believe his concepts aid us in helping to step back from our immediate contexts so that we might identify the challenges and gaps we often feel, but can't quite name, in our day-to-day work. Although Jenkins locates participatory cultures as sites *beyond* "institutions" such as schools, our experiences demonstrate that the classroom can, in fact, embody and promote many aspects of participatory culture. As we aim to demonstrate here, the classroom often offers unique opportunities for students to engage with and experience many features of a "participatory" online culture within a specific community of learners.

In this chapter, we first describe Jenkins's vision of participatory culture. We then use three selected terms from his definition—*collective intelligence*, *networking*, and *negotiation*—as especially powerful lenses to help enrich our understandings of rhetorical digital education. Using examples from high school and college classrooms, we draw from the CCSS and the Framework to explore the connections (or lack thereof) between participatory culture and the implications of these two documents for classroom practice. In doing so, we hope readers will be able to imagine new possibilities for digital literacies while also gaining a more complex understanding of the possibilities and challenges of working in classrooms that are already a part of a participatory culture.

Participatory Culture and Literacy Classrooms

In *Confronting the Challenges of Participatory Culture*, Jenkins offers three faulty assumptions embedded in a "laissez faire approach" to media literacy. First, Jenkins describes the *participation gap*, or the assumption that all young people have even and equitable access to technologies. Second, the *transparency problem* is the assumption that students actively engage with and reflect on their encounters with media. Third, the *ethics challenge* is the assumption that adolescents can cultivate ethical standards in isolation (2006, 12). This kind of approach, also echoed in the culturally held stereotype that students are digital natives who take to new technologies effortlessly and willingly, expects students to acquire the competencies necessary for meaningful engagement with new media without training and support from educators or other adults. (For more on the controversy surrounding the term *digital natives*, see Prensky [2001] and Bennett, Maton, and Kervin [2008]. In this volume, see Chapter 16 by Tawnya Lubbes and Heidi Skurat Harris. Also see Chapter 7 in this volume by James Cercone and David L. Bruce, which discusses media literacy as a lens for understanding the CCSS).

Jenkins advocates for an approach to digital literacy that includes training not only in critical engagement with digital information, but also production of digital texts. He argues, "[T]he core goals of the media literacy movement should be helping young people to acquire the skills and competencies they need to meaningfully participate in the culture around them" (2006, 12). For Jenkins, participatory culture is "the emergence of a cultural context that supports widespread participation in the production and distribution of media" (6). Contemporary participatory culture includes these traits (7):

- *Low barriers* for making artistic or civic contributions
- *Strong support* for creating and sharing

- *Informal mentorship* in which experts assist novices with their work
- A feeling among all participants that what they do *matters*
- And a feeling that they are *socially connected* to one another

In addition to these five traits, the degree to which individuals contribute in a participatory culture matters less than the fact that members feel free to participate within that culture. Considering new media literacies as a matter of cultural participation, rather than technological expertise, allows us to situate writers and technologies within larger systems. This *ecological approach* includes "thinking about the interrelationship among all of these different communication technologies, the cultural communities that grow up around them, and the activities they support" (Jenkins 2006, 8).

Jenkins describes a kind of culture we hope to create in our classrooms of writers; in high school and college, we want our students to make contributions, to feel and to provide support for one another, to learn from more experienced writers, to write about topics and in different modes and media that matter to them and to others, and to feel connected to other members of the classroom community. As a new media scholar, Jenkins writes about young people participating in communities within and outside classrooms, which allows him to highlight participatory practices rather than concentrate on individual performances. This broader focus helps us understand literacy and learners in our classrooms. For example, when Jenkins writes that "all youth need to learn if they are going to be equal participants in the world of tomorrow" (2006, 21), we can begin to imagine a classroom community in which students participate in one another's growth as writers. This, in turn, can help us and our students understand literacies "as ways of interacting within a larger community, and not simply an individualized skill to be used for personal expression" (20). Creating and sustaining a participatory culture in our classrooms of writers is difficult, challenging, and exciting, especially during a time with dynamic conversations that fuel changes in our teaching contexts. However, by imagining classroom spaces as yet another "cultural community"—one with the affordances of participatory culture, even if mediated through the institutional setting—we can facilitate learning and empower students with important skills required for contemporary professional and civic engagement.

Participatory culture requires a unique set of capacities, and Jenkins identifies eleven key competencies for contemporary media literacy (4):

- Play
- Performance
- Simulation
- Appropriation
- Multitasking
- Distributed cognition
- Judgment
- Transmedia navigation
- Collective intelligence
- Networking
- Negotiation

Some of these competencies share a common spirit with important concepts in the fields of writing studies and English education. For example, Jenkins defines play as "the capacity to experiment with one's surroundings as a form of problem-solving" and emphasizes the significance of engagement, as opposed to fun" (4–5). Likewise, one central component of most writing classes is a focus on the writing process, including drafting and revising, that allows students to experiment, explore, engage with ideas, and problem solve. All of these skills are valuable for writers and writing, and we cannot adequately account for all in the space of one chapter. We have chosen to highlight three skills—collective intelligence, networking, and negotiation—because we have focused on them in our teaching and because they are especially illuminating when applied to English Language Arts (ELA) and first-year writing pedagogies.

Collective Intelligence: Collaboration and Community in High School and College

Drawing on Pierre Levy, Jenkins defines *collective intelligence* as a capacity for cooperative knowledge production that allows people to come together, share what they know, and work toward a united objective. Capitalizing on computer network capabilities, individuals can participate in collaborations where "everyone knows something, nobody knows everything, and what any one person knows can be tapped by the group as a whole" (Jenkins 2006, 39). Levy is especially interested in the political and civic implications of collective intelligence, such as empowering citizens to organize for political action. Wikipedia—in which users work together to research, write, edit, and connect online encyclopedia entries—serves as a familiar example of collective intelligence at work. Jenkins offers potential collective intelligence class projects, including a student-created guide to local government that brings together officials' contact information, reports, policies, discussions of local issues, and so on (43).

Just as digital spaces can increase opportunities for the benefits of collective intelligence to accrue, literacy classrooms can offer multiple opportunities for collaborative, collective work. In high school English and college first-year writing classrooms, collaboration (e.g., group work, peer review, and even pedagogical commonplaces like "think-pair-share") is nearly a given. *Collaboration* is described in several places in the CCSS and points to how high school students could and should interact with others. However, re-thinking this term through understanding it as a form of collective intelligence helps us unsettle and enrich this kind of classroom practice.

As we see in Table 5.1, these frameworks usefully overlap with one another: Jenkins's hopeful vision of collective intelligence imagines a space where "problem-solving [is] an exercise in teamwork" (2006, 40). The CCSS and the Framework approach this kind of purposeful collaboration in different ways. The CCSS see collaboration as a joint enterprise to help individuals make a point or to develop their own perceptions. For instance, the CCSS want students to build on others'

Table 5.1 Jenkins's Idea of Collective Intelligence Compared to the CCSS and Framework

Confronting the Challenges of Participatory Culture (Jenkins et al. 2006)	CCSS (CCSSO and NGA 2010)	Framework (CWPA, NCTE, and NWP 2011)
Collective Intelligence: The ability to pool knowledge and compare notes with others toward a common goal	Anchor Standard for Speaking and Listening #1 for 6–12: "Prepare for and participate effectively in a range of conversations and collaborations with diverse partners, building on others' ideas and expressing their own clearly and persuasively" (48) Anchor Standard for Writing #6 for 6–12: "Use technology, including the internet, to produce and publish writing and to interact and collaborate with others" (41) Anchor Standard for Writing #7 for 6–12: "Conduct short as well as more sustained research projects based on focused questions, demonstrating knowledge of the subject under investigation" (41) Anchor Standard for Writing #8 for 6–12: "Gather relevant information from multiple print and digital sources, assess the credibility and accuracy of each source, and integrate the information while avoiding plagiarism" (41)	*Openness:* "The willingness to consider new ways of being and thinking in the world. ... Openness is fostered when writers are encouraged to: • Examine their own perspectives to find connections with the perspectives of others • Practice different ways of gathering, investigating, developing, and presenting information" (4) *Engagement:* "A sense of investment and involvement in learning. ... Engagement is fostered when writers are encouraged to: • Make connections between their own ideas and those of others • Find meanings new to them or build on existing meanings as a result of new connections • Act upon the new knowledge that they have discovered" (4) *Responsibility:* "The ability to take ownership of one's actions and understand the consequences of those actions for oneself and others. ... Responsibility is fostered when writers are encouraged to" • Recognize their own role in learning • Act on the understanding that learning is shared among the writer and others—students, instructors, and the institution, as well as those engaged in the questions and/or fields in which the writer is interested • Engage and incorporate the ideas of others, giving credit to those ideas by using appropriate attribution" (5)

ideas in conversations and to use technology to collaborate with others. When it comes to research, the CCSS also call for students to gather information from many types of sources and integrate that information in a final product, but doesn't necessarily require that the information be shared with the group as a whole. The CCSS *seem* to see collaboration as a desirable practice for individuals; however, the implicit benefit is that the collaboration with others enables individual production.

Less clear is what the CCSS see as benefits for the entire group. That is, unlike Jenkins, the CCSS do not address how collaboration shapes the group or the community as a whole, which is something that educators who work with groups of all kinds must consider.

Similarly, the Framework describes *a* learner—a learner who embodies the eight habits of mind outlined in the Framework and will, in turn, be well situated for participatory culture. However, this vision of a learner is one who might "find connections" between her ideas and those of others and "engage and incorporate" the ideas of others. The document does state that "learning is shared," which usefully points back to Jenkins's vision of collective, generative knowledge production. Overall, though, the location for the learning is within the individual.

Collective Intelligence in a High School English Classroom Context

Over several years of experimentation with wikis in the classroom, Bear, a high school ELA teacher, has seen how and why wikis are particularly useful in helping students experience and navigate participatory culture. A wiki is only sustainable, in our opinion, through collective intelligence. In order to effectively use wikis, Bear sets up a situation where students have a common goal and a reason for pooling knowledge, a presentation project where students research a story that is often referenced in literature and pop culture, and then present the information to their classmates and share the information on a wiki. This is a relatively short research project (Anchor Standard for Writing 7; CCSSO and NGA 2010, 18), but one that gives students an opportunity to gather and integrate "information from multiple print and digital sources" (Anchor Standard for Writing 8; CCSSO and NGA 2010, 18) with the goal of "demonstrating understanding of the subject under investigation" (Anchor Standard for Writing 7; CCSSO and NGA 2010, 18). By making presentations available to all class periods, the wiki provides an opportunity for students to reach an audience of more than 120 students and to think about revising content for a different "task, purpose, and audience" (Anchor Standard for Writing 4; CCSSO and NGA 2010, 18).

Bear emphasizes the importance of making decisions based on a different task, purpose, and audience, and the fact that students are accountable to their peers for what they produce. The idea is to set up a situation focused on collaboration and teamwork, as Jenkins puts it, "how the workplace is structured—around ad-hoc configurations of employees, brought together because their diverse skills and knowledge are needed to confront a specific challenge, then dispersed into different clusters of workers when new needs arise" (2006, 41). Once students start working on their wikis in their groups, they quickly began negotiating how to meet a specific challenge, creating the document for their peers to view, understand, and, perhaps most importantly, use.

During one wiki project, Bear saw much evidence of collective intelligence (see Appendix A at the end of this chapter for the complete assignment). Groups who were not ready to tackle an entirely new digital space collaboratively composed a document or a slideshow to upload to the wiki. These students learned "to work and play in [this] knowledge culture" and "to think of problem-solving as an exercise in teamwork" (Jenkins 2006, 40). The same was true for groups who embraced the challenge of creating a wiki, something none of them had done before; they embedded videos, images, and songs to their pages; hyperlinked to other websites; and composed simultaneously, adding new ideas as they developed. Some students were interested in visuals and films and brought their knowledge to the table. Other students conducted research while still others employed their skills to embed video clips. During the composing process, some groups accessed other groups' sites from across class periods to get ideas for how to make their own pages better. Although a new opportunity for these traditionally "autonomous problem solvers," Bear was amazed at how easily students joined this "collective intelligence community [which encouraged] work as a group" (Jenkins 2006, 41).

Collective Intelligence in a First-Year Writing Context

As we note in Bear's experience, digital work is challenging and even results in productive failure for students and educators. At Boise State University, the first-year writing curriculum of Estrem and Shepherd takes up many of the same practices that Bear employs in her ELA classroom. Like many educators working within institutions, they too have kept the focus on individual students because of assessment demands. However, many informal activities within the writing classroom have helped provide students with brief, informal, low-stakes experiences as a member of a team working within a collective, unstable knowledge community.

The first-year writing curriculum at Boise State coheres around shared outcomes. For example, the English 101 curriculum focuses on exploring and analyzing writing as a subject while experiencing (and reflecting on) writing as an activity. Informal and formal writing assignments generally engage students in thinking carefully about their writing experiences and those of others as they work to build their own theory of writing, analyze and contribute to ongoing intellectual conversations, analyze discourse communities, and engage in rhetorical problem-solving in a new context.

The first-year writing instructors at Boise State, like Rachel, intuitively understand the pedagogical power of collaborative online work. To develop more intentional opportunities for experiencing ways to build collective intelligence within the classroom, they have encouraged the use of digital tools, and more and more instructors have used seemingly simple Google apps in ways that engage students in "pool[ing] observations and work[ing] through interpretations with others studying the same problems" (Jenkins 2006, 42). They have seen how low-stakes engagements in spaces that encourage collective intelligence can occur even within the physical classroom space.

Jessica Ewing, a teaching assistant (TA) in the first-year writing program, experiments alongside her students with Google apps. As a strategy to foster interaction and brainstorming, she implements in-class, informal Google presentations that in some ways push back against the very genre expectations themselves, using a *presentation* tool as an *inventive* space. In teams, students generate a slide about a particular course reading (see Appendix B at the end of this chapter for an explanation of this activity). During one recent class, Ewing used an incredibly challenging article that requires students to think about professional writing and community-specific vocabulary. Ewing's students expressed discomfort with the reading, but after demonstrating how they could all collaborate on their slides, she encouraged them to read and re-read, to work on their slides, to see what others were sharing, and to check in verbally as needed. Students were engrossed in their work, moving quickly between online composing, in-person discussions, and immediate revisions to their collaborative slide presentations. This teamwork approach, then, became an exercise in problem-solving on the fly. It wasn't just an act of collaboration; it was an experience that demonstrated how their perspectives could shift and change as they added, refined, and deepened their understanding of a difficult reading through this form of online composing.

Networking: Source Use and Integration in High School and College

Within participatory culture, *networking* is "the ability to search for, synthesize, and disseminate information" (Jenkins 2006, 49). Jenkins points out that contemporary students regularly use web applications that rely on social information sharing and knowledge production. Search engines, online retailers, and streaming media services use a combination of user-generated content (e.g., reviews) and aggregated data about users to make suggestions. For example, Amazon recommends products to customers based on items they have previously viewed or purchased—and items previously viewed or purchased by other, similar users. Customers can then further filter their options by reading user-created reviews. In such a data-rich, networked world, it's no longer enough to imagine an individual scholar working independently. Instead, as Jenkins describes, a "resourceful student" is "one who is able to successfully navigate an already abundant and continually changing world of information" (49).

As Table 5.2 demonstrates, these statements all ascribe some degree of value to the ability to navigate information through research. In both high school English and college first-year writing classrooms, deepening

Table 5.2 Jenkins's Idea of Networking Compared to the CCSS and Framework

Confronting the Challenges of Participatory Culture (Jenkins et al. 2006)	CCSS (CCSSO and NGA 2010)	Framework (CWPA, NCTE, and NWP 2011)
Networking: The ability to search for, synthesize, and disseminate information (49)	Anchor Standard for Writing #2 for 6–12: "Write informative/explanatory texts to examine and convey complex ideas and information clearly and accurately through the effective selection, organization, and analysis of content" (35) Anchor Standard for Writing #8 for 6–12: "Gather relevant information from multiple print and digital sources, assess the credibility and accuracy of each source, and integrate the information while avoiding plagiarism" (41) Anchor Standard for Reading #7 for 6–12: "Integrate and evaluate content presented in diverse media and formats and media, including visually and quantitatively, as well as in words" (35) Anchor Standard for Speaking and Listening #5 for 6–12" "Make strategic use of digital media and visual displays of data to express information and enhance understanding of presentations" (48)	*Curiosity:* "The desire to know more about the world. ... Curiosity is fostered when writers are encouraged to: • Use inquiry as a process to develop questions relevant for authentic audiences within a variety of disciplines • Seek relevant authoritative information and recognize the meaning and value of that information • Conduct research using methods for investigating questions appropriate to the discipline • Communicate their findings in writing to multiple audiences inside and outside school using discipline-appropriate conventions" (4) *Openness:* "The willingness to consider new ways of being and thinking in the world. ... Openness is fostered when writers are encouraged to: • Examine their own perspectives to find connections with the perspectives of others • Practice different ways of gathering, investigating, developing, and presenting information • Listen to and reflect on the ideas and responses of others—both peers and instructors—to their writing *Creativity:* "The ability to use novel approaches for generating, investigating, and representing ideas. ... Creativity is fostered when writers are encouraged to: • Take risks by exploring questions, topics, and ideas that are new to them • Use methods that are new to them to investigate questions, topics, and ideas" (4–5)

students' flexibility as researchers is a key goal. Successful writers grow to understand these concepts:

1. "Information" is not static.
2. The "information" landscape is not flat—that is, there are quite different values, contexts, and purposes for publications that might appear similar when read, for example, on a screen.
3. They need not just to consume "information" but to interpret, analyze, and reshape it.

These are highly context-specific strategies that writers accumulate over time and space. Or, in Jenkins's words, students must be able to "identify which group is most aware of relevant resources and choose a search system matched to the appropriate criteria ... networking involves the ability to navigate across different social communities" (2006, 50). It's not only about identifying sources; it's also about "a process of synthesis, during which multiple resources are combined to produce new knowledge" (50). Students, then, need to understand "how to sample and distill multiple, independent perspectives" (51).

This process of synthesis and knowledge production is something the CCSS expect of students. For example, the CCSS ask students to "convey complex ideas and information clearly and accurately (Anchor Standard for Writing 2; CCSSO and NGA 2010, 18), to "gather relevant information from multiple print and digital sources" (Anchor Standard for Writing 8; CCSSO and NGA 2010, 18), to "integrate and evaluate content presented in diverse media and formats" (Anchor Standard for Reading 7; CCSSO and NGA 2010, 10), and to "make strategic use of digital media and visual displays of data to express information and enhance understanding of presentations" (Anchor Standard for Speaking and Listening 5; CCSSO and NGA 2010, 22). Situated behind each of these individual standards is an overarching emphasis for students to take into account the task, purpose, and audience during rhetorical occasions, whether the student is a writer, reader, speaker, or listener during those moments. The implication for us as teachers and librarians is clear: We must teach students to be able to navigate rhetorical situations independently and strategically. That is, context matters. By this, we mean that networking is not a skill that is practiced in isolation; instead, it is a practice that relies on being able to read situations in which writers, readers, speakers, and listeners participate.

Networking practices are also present in the Framework; the habits of mind section of the Framework speaks to the intellectual dexterity and rhetorical flexibility that 21st-century literacies demand. The description of learners who are curious, open, creative, and persistent describes the kind of student who is able to search for, analyze, and interact with others' ideas. The Framework also imagines "information" as something relatively static, something that writers "seek … gather, investigate, develop, and present" (CWPA, NCTE, and NWP 2011, 4). Similar to Jenkins's point that networking is a process of synthesis and knowledge production, the Framework describes how engagement is fostered through students' work to "find meanings new to them or build on existing meanings as a result of new connections; and act upon the new knowledge that they have discovered" (4). Networking, then, might occur within a literacy classroom in a variety of ways; it might mean how to navigate search engines, how to make informed rhetorical decisions about source use and accessibility, and how to integrate those ideas within one's own in a meaningful way (see Table 5.2).

Networking in a High School English Classroom Context

Bear recently integrated a multimodal project into her senior high school English course (see Appendix C at the end of this chapter for the complete assignment). Students used their wikis as a platform for composing and sharing different modes of writing (e.g., visual text, videos, hyperlinks, written words) to explore a topic. Since wikis provide a situation in which students can view the work of their peers *as they are composing*, Bear's students were able to use the in-progress work of others to inform their own multimodal projects. Understanding that their work is being shared during and after writing was a huge motivator for Bear's students to create something that fits the specific purpose of the writing task—and to understand *audience* differently than they might have before. This understanding points to the notion that networking is a process in which students need to see and discuss the choices they and their peers make as they are searching for, synthesizing, and sharing the material they shape into texts for audiences. That is, networking is not something that is done in isolation; it involves choices based on purpose and audience. When students like Bear's can see and discuss those choices in real-time, then they can see networking of knowledge and networking of practices in tandem. Moreover, such transparency about process can assist not only individual writers, but also communities of writers.

Networking in a First-Year Writing Context

One feature of Estrem and Shepherd's first-year writing curriculum is their commitment to engaging students with academic inquiry in new and different ways; the "abundance" of resources is both a challenge and an opportunity for writers new to college. Networking is a rhetorical act, one where students need to learn a lot: how to find sources, how to synthesize them, how to consider when, how, and why to use them. Just as multimodal projects are employed in Bear's high school classes, many first-year writing instructors use digital projects with relatively accessible points of entry for student writers to gain experience with how information develops within networks—and how to assess, synthesize, and respond to that information.

For an English 101 unit, the TA Ewing uses an approach that gives her students immediate experience with networked information. Throughout the semester, Ewing's students regularly share ideas and negotiate understandings of what writing really *is* through collaborative Google presentations, docs, and site pages. This consistent, ongoing informal work prepares her students well for their final project—a collaborative, dynamic online map that identifies locations of writing on campus (see Appendix D at the end of this chapter for the complete assignment). For example, many student groups created SlideRocket slideshows depicting the writing practices of a discourse community they had studied. Then they linked those slideshows to an interactive Google map, which allowed readers (initially within their class and later beyond) to toggle through various writing contexts within a particular location. Recently, as students read and re-read one another's work, they shifted and revised their embedded presentations, integrating sources and adapting to ongoing in-process feedback as needed. Their first-year writing classroom became a space for trying out new digital tools, reflecting on how they affected a community of peers, and integrating evidence thoughtfully and purposefully. They networked information and ideas within a classroom reflecting many features of participatory culture: ongoing exchanges, constant purposeful play and revision, and immediate audience.

Negotiation: Rhetorical Flexibility in High School and College

The concept of negotiation highlights the competencies necessary for navigating networked and globalized contexts. Jenkins defines *negotiation* as "the ability to travel across diverse communities, discerning and respecting multiple perspectives, and grasping and following alternative sets of norms" (2006, 52). He notes that online spaces, such as social networking sites, allow not only connections based on shared interests and values, but also exclusions based on difference. For this reason, Jenkins calls for fostering digital literacies that enable students to interact decorously in new environments. He presses educators to build on activities that address cultural awareness and sensitivity—such as reading and discussing work from other cultures or analyzing portrayals of gender, race, and religion in popular media—with those that empower them to participate within these "diverse communities." Such participation requires the capacity to negotiate "between dissenting perspectives" and "through diverse communities" (53). Jenkins recommends having students observe or contribute to online spaces (e.g., Wikipedia) that include deliberating among users with multiple perspectives and backgrounds or discussing cultural norms (e.g., what it means to be a good parent) with students in other countries (54–55).

Both the CCSS and the Framework recognize the value in the ability to negotiate diverse contexts and situations (see Table 5.3). This kind of meta-awareness about what one is doing is an "active, dynamic process,"

Table 5.3 Jenkins's Idea of Negotiation Compared to the CCSS and Framework

Confronting the Challenges of Participatory Culture (Jenkins et al. 2006)	CCSS (CCSSO and NGA 2010)	Framework (CWPA, NCTE, and NWP 2011)
Negotiation: The ability to travel across diverse communities, discerning and respecting multiple perspectives, and grasping and following alternative norms (52)	Anchor Standard for Speaking and Listening #1 for 6–12: "Prepare for and participate effectively in a range of conversations and collaborations with diverse partners, building on others' ideas, and expressing their own clearly and persuasively" (48) Anchor Standard for Language #3 for 6–12: "Apply knowledge of language to understand how language functions in different contexts, to make effective choices for meaning or style, and to comprehend more fully when reading or listening" (51) Anchor Standard for Speaking and Listening #2 for 6–12: "Integrate and evaluate information presented in diverse media and formats, including visually, quantitatively, and orally" (48) Anchor Standard for Reading #6 for 6–12: "Assess how point of view or purpose shapes the content and style of a text" (35)	Flexibility: "The ability to adapt to situations, expectations, or demands" (4) Metacognition: "The ability to reflect on one's own thinking as well as on the individual and cultural processes used to structure knowledge" (5) Critical thinking: "The ability to analyze a situation or text and make thoughtful decisions based on that analysis, through writing, reading, and research" (7)

and engaging in this process increases the opportunities for the transfer of learning from one situation to the next (Bransford 2000, 53). In other words, students in literacy classes both *do* things and *reflect* on them. In the CCSS, students need to be able to work on "collaborations with diverse partners," to use "diverse media," and to understand how "point of view or purpose shapes ... a text" (Anchor Standards for Speaking and Listening 1 and 2; CCSSO and NGA 2010, 48, 35). As writers, students are expected to engage with divergent perspectives and then shape their writing in response to audience expectations. Similarly, the Framework emphasizes flexibility, adaptiveness, and metacognition. It describes writers who are able to adapt and respond to a variety of rhetorical choices, "reflect on the choices they made," and "reflect on one's own thinking" (CWPA, NCTE, and NWP 2011, 4).

Negotiation in a High School English Classroom Context

Secondary teachers often have concerns about whom students will meet in the virtual world and how to ensure that they are respectful of other students in online collaborations. Jenkins points out that "cyber communities often bring together groups that would have no direct contact in the physical world" (2006, 52), but dealing with this problem is not so different from teaching a group of 15-year-olds to have a respectful, academic conversation about a political topic or a work of literature. The answer to concerns about respect in digital platforms is the same as the answer to concerns about other peer interactions: Students need to be *taught* (through modeling, reflection, and evaluation) the skills necessary for "understanding multiple perspectives, respecting and even embracing diversity of views, understanding a variety of social norms and negotiating between conflicting opinions" (2006, 53).

One strategy Bear uses for teaching these skills is to simulate online discussions in the classroom before setting students free to practice in digital spaces. For example, an in-class discussion activity with sticky notes added to posters around the room can simulate the kind of online post-and-comment exchanges that writers negotiate. After in-class work, students can then write entries on individual blogs and comment on one another's posts. Bear has found that understanding the scarcity of reader attention is a huge motivator for students to create posts that look appealing and are easy to read. In addition, Bear's classes review blogs in class and discuss strengths and areas for improvement. This creates a culture of openness about proper etiquette for online discussions and strategies for setting up "a deliberative process in the classroom that encourages collaboration and discussion across different positions" (Jenkins 2006, 55). The key to ensuring students have the skill of negotiation (and can demonstrate the related CCSS) is to keep in mind that this must be taught just as we teach the other necessary skills more explicitly outlined in the CCSS.

Negotiation in a First-Year Writing Context

Like Bear, Estrem and Shepherd also view negotiation both as something that needs to be taught and as something for which literacy classrooms have particularly rich opportunities. They are especially appreciative of Bear's activities described earlier, as they demonstrate how "digital" and "online" work can occur in low-tech settings. They too make use of posters, sticky notes, and "commenting" in many classroom activities. Instead of sharing examples along those lines, they would like to build on Bear's activity descriptions and consider how to foster knowledge *transfer*, how to help students like Bear's find their bearings and negotiate new rhetorical contexts when they come to college. Skilled negotiators will, they believe, have better opportunities for understanding learning in different contexts as they move from high school to college, from first-year writing to disciplinary contexts, from disciplines to the workplace and the community.

Like Jenkins, Estrem and Shepherd are interested in providing an environment where students learn to negotiate across communities, particularly rhetorical contexts and situations. Digital learning experiences give students multiple opportunities to experience different rhetorical contexts—and then to critically analyze and reassess their work within those contexts. Digital platforms make abstract concepts about writing—in particular, *audience* and *context*—differently visible, and thus afford an opportunity to unsettle students' sometimes-rigid definitions of writing.

One strategy to help foreground audience is facilitated through the use of Google Docs (go to drive.google.com and click on Docs*)*. For example, students write and share their writing within a classroom group on Google Docs, adding their own questions and comments about their evolving text—and inviting others to do the same. Much like Bear describes, Estrem, Fredricksen, and Shepherd too see students who begin to understand audience differently when they must repeatedly make decisions about how to address audience needs and questions. This kind of commenting is easily replicated in a low-tech classroom and gives students a different way to understand audience since the audience is in the room with them. (For further discussion on how economically strapped schools are meeting the CCSS, see Chapter 11 by Amanda Stearns-Pfeiffer in this volume). Writers can respond to comments and can—either immediately or over days and weeks—rethink and revise. The text becomes an act of connection, an opportunity to communicate, and a means through which a writer must revise if she is to be heard. Like Bear describes, "commenting" has become a common digital practice, and learning how to imagine an audience and respond to it is a 21st-century negotiation skill that literacy classrooms can foster.

Participatory Cultures and Literacy Classrooms

In this chapter, we have worked to explore the possibilities for participatory culture within classroom contexts, and Jenkins's vision has helped us enrich the CCSS and the Framework by giving us a way to see the gaps and connections between our contexts and by providing a new lens for understanding our students' experiences in learning to write, particularly in digital environments. Our aim has been to use the notion of participatory culture to enrich our understanding of teaching. At the same time, we have shared experiences from our own teaching contexts to better comprehend the challenges, nuances, and tensions of working with writers under a framework that centers on learning within participatory culture.

This collection's goal is, in part, to support teachers' and librarians' implementation of strategies related to the CCSS. Working with the CCSS is deeply important and can bring layers of productive change to the classroom. Simultaneously, a focus on "college and career readiness" can diminish the importance of preparing students for civic engagement, just as a reliance on individual assessment can limit opportunities to develop truly collaborative social skills required in participatory culture. Indeed, the CCSS and the Framework emphasize individual *performance* while Jenkins emphasizes individual *participation*. However, this distinction sheds light on the silences in our driving documents and opens up the opportunity for us to reframe how we think about working and writing together.

Finally, the contexts in which we teach matter a great deal to us. That is, our contexts shape what we think is possible and desirable for our students; they shape our vision of professional practice. When we have students collaborate, for instance, they have to negotiate what things mean (e.g., what a task means, what content means, what audiences expect, and so on). The same is true when teachers collaborate; we have to navigate and negotiate a whole host of communities we participate in, and documents like the CCSS and the Framework become sites where that negotiation of meaning is made visible. Much of what we've discussed from our literacy classrooms has been rooted in understanding writing as a conversation, and this chapter is a conversation starter rather than a last word. As we bring together the CCSS, the Framework, and *Confronting the Challenges of Participatory Culture*, we see a chance to refocus our attention on ideals that we honor, such as collaboration and civic engagement, that are fostered overtly in digital spaces.

References

Bennett, Sue, Karl Maton, and Lisa Kervin. 2008. "The 'Digital Natives' Debate: A Critical Review of the Evidence." *British Journal of Educational Technology* 39 (5): 775–786.

Bransford, John. 2000. *How People Learn: Brain, Mind, Experience, and School.* National Research Council Committees on Developments in the Science of Learning and Learning Research and Educational Practices. Washington, DC: National Academy Press.

Council of Chief State School Officers and National Governors Association. 2010. *Common Core State Standards for English Language Arts and Literacy in History/Social Studies, Science, and Technical Subjects.* Washington, DC: National Governors Association Center for Best Practices, Council of Chief State School Officers. Accessed February 10, 2014. www.corestandards.org/assets/CCSSI_ELA%20Standards.pdf.

Council of Writing Program Administrators, National Council of Teachers of English, and National Writing Project. 2011. *Framework for Success in Postsecondary Writing.* Accessed February 10, 2014. wpacouncil.org/files/framework-for-success-postsecondary-writing.pdf.

Jenkins, Henry with Katie Clinton, Ravi Purushotma, Alice J. Robison, and Margaret Weigel. 2006. *Confronting the Challenges of Participatory Culture: Media Education for the 21st Century.* Chicago: MacArthur Foundation. Accessed February 10, 2014. digitallearning.macfound.org/atf/cf/%7B7E45C7E0-A3E0-4B89-AC9C-E807E-1B0AE4E%7D/JENKINS_WHITE_PAPER.PDF.

Prensky, Marc. 2001. "Digital Natives, Digital Immigrants." *On The Horizon* 9 (5): 1–6.

Appendix A: How Do Stories Matter?: Student-Led Lesson on Stories We Remember and Tell Assignment for Advanced Placement Literature and Composition

Purpose

The purpose of this assignment is for students to research and present a character, object, event, place or plot line, or story that is often alluded to in literature in order to help all students have a better understanding of these elements to identify and analyze them when they appear.

Assignment

Each group will choose one item from the list I have compiled. It will be your job to research this item and teach it to the rest of the class in a way that is meaningful. You will also need to create an electronic document with the information to be posted to the wikispace. Finally, you will turn in a hard copy MLA formatted Works Consulted Page (it's just like a works cited page only it includes all the sources you consulted in creating your presentation and documents). You are encouraged to use Dropbox to create these parts of the assignment to ensure a balanced workload.

Requirements

Both parts of the assignment (presentation and post to wiki) should include:

- Definition/explanation of the story (background, heritage, chronology, summary, etc.)
- Exploration of how the story functions within a specific text (a direct passage and explanation of its significance)
- "Tip-Offs"—for the allusion or its presence in the work
- Examples of the story in mythology, fairy tales, pop culture, music, contemporary literature, etc.

Basically, your presentation and other documents should address what it is, where we can find it, how we know when we come across it and why it matters.

The Different Parts
Presentation

You will have 8 to 10 minutes to "teach" your story to the class. I do not consider standing up and reading PowerPoint slides to be teaching. Think about the effective ways in which you learn new concepts and draw from that experience to teach your peers. Of course it is acceptable to have information on PowerPoint slides and to use slides to guide your lesson, but find an engaging and meaningful way to share the information you have found. All group members should be involved in the presentation in some way. You will have access to the computer, smartboard, document camera, and whiteboard in your presentation. Please test all technology prior to the day of presentations. Consider what is typically done in class presentations and avoid doing that so we are not overwhelmed by repetition during presentations.

Some ideas: guided small/large group discussion; creation of visual representations; sharing and discussing videos, commercials, ads, songs, etc.; games, dramatization, etc.

Wiki Document

Each group will be expected to create an electronic document to post to the provided page on the wikispace. This document should be designed so that students from the other class periods can access it and get the information you have found. Your audience is different (individuals reading the information on a computer rather than receiving a presentation) so this document should not be exactly the same thing you share in class. You have a number of options for the format of this document, but remember that your purpose here is the same as the presentation: to teach the other Advanced Placement (AP) Literature and Composition students about your story. The title of this document should be the name(s) of your story followed by the names of your group members. Your audience is other AP students who need this information. Consider how you can most effectively share it with them. Some ideas: interactive PowerPoint, web page, multimodal essay, wiki page.

MLA-Formatted Works Consulted Page

You must submit an MLA-formatted Works Consulted Page to me on the day of your presentation. This document should include *all* the sources you consulted in the process of planning your presentation and wiki document. Google *Owl Purdue* for a great site that will help you with this task.

Appendix B: Using Google Presentations Informally in First-Year Writing

Process

1. Before the class session, Jessica creates one Google presentation and shares it with the class. It includes blank slides for students to use during class.

2. Before class, students are put into groups.

3. In class, students sit with their group and have one assigned slide per group.

4. Depending on the reading, each group has a prompt or activity. For example, Jessica has used this approach for informal work, from having students deliberately apply reading strategies they'd generated as a class to a particular text to brainstorming ideas around a particular topic.

5. Students then work individually on computers but near each other. This way, they are talking and writing and revising at the same time. Throughout this work time, slides evolve and change quickly; students often experiment with formatting and even write questions to each other within the slide.

6. Then, students present their findings to the class (see, for example, Figure 5.1).

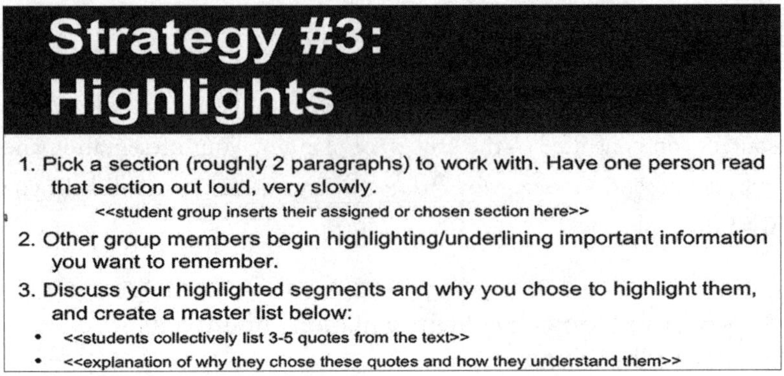

Strategy #3: Highlights

1. Pick a section (roughly 2 paragraphs) to work with. Have one person read that section out loud, very slowly.
   - <<student group inserts their assigned or chosen section here>>
2. Other group members begin highlighting/underlining important information you want to remember.
3. Discuss your highlighted segments and why you chose to highlight them, and create a master list below:
   - <<students collectively list 3-5 quotes from the text>>
   - <<explanation of why they chose these quotes and how they understand them>>

Figure 5.1 Example of a student-generated slide

Appendix C: Advanced Placement Literature and Composition Multimodal Essay Assignment

Essential Question

Whose Story Gets Told?

Sub-Questions

How Can We Listen to Silenced Voices? To What Extent Are Our Views of the World Shaped *for* Us Through Story?

Objective

Synthesize examples from literature, information from research and ideas from another student relating in some way to the question "Whose Story Gets Told?" by composing a collaborative multimodal essay.

What Is a Multimodal* Essay?

An essay that blends multiple modes.

What Is a Mode?

Mode can be conceived of in many ways. On the most basic level a mode is "how something is done or how it happens" (Princeton University).

Other Definitions and Examples of Modes
(from a variety of sources)

1. Modes of Discourse = descriptive, narrative, imaginative, persuasive, expository.

2. Mode = a particular form, variety, or manner.

3. According to The Writers Web, *A List of Important Literary Terms*, the term "mode" can be described in the following way: "An unspecific critical term usually identifying a broad but identifiable literary method, mood, or manner that is not tied exclusively to a particular form or genre. [Some] examples are the satiric mode, the ironic, the comic, the pastoral, and the didactic." (CB)

4. Other ways to think about mode: letters, journal entries, poems, images, graphs, music, audio recordings, videos, blogs, podcasts, mind-mapping, etc.

Requirements

1. Create a collaborative composition with another AP Lit Student. You are encouraged to use the wikispace to compose and present this composition, but it is not required. You may choose to turn in a hard copy if you wish.

2. Composition must address the essential question or a sub-question (or a question you create that relates to the topic) in some way.

3. Include ALL of the following *blended* in a composition:
   - original words and ideas from each partner
   - passages from *Things Fall Apart* or *Heart of Darkness*
   - researched information from a credible, reliable source (use databases!)
   - visuals—original creation, photographs, art, video, graphs or tables, mind-map, etc.
   - an MLA formatted Works Cited Page for *all* sources

4. Include *at least* two "modes" from the list below *blended* in the composition:

   - images
   - music
   - audio recording
   - interview
   - graph
   - mind map
   - symbolic representation
   - newspaper article
   - original letters or journal entries written
   - from the perspective of a character
   - researched information
   - maps
   - comic strip
   - storyboard
   - advertisements
   - Wordle
   - another mode you identify

Appendix D: Writing as Participation: Rhetorical Problem-Solving in a New Context Assignment

Overview

In Unit 3, you observed and studied the writing that occurs in particular contexts, considering such aspects as genre, communication, and audience. You explored and analyzed these written conversations and then developed a lengthier, more thorough and thoughtful essay on one textography. Now, in Unit 4, you have the opportunity to repurpose your Unit 3 Project for a specific identified audience in a *nonprint medium* of your choice. Your culminating project will depend upon focused writing, detailed analysis, and critical, rhetorical decision making. I am opening the door wide on this unit project: You all have creative control—and I'm excited to see what you come up with—but I will have to first approve your project and then evaluate how well you meet your own goals.

You'll be required to propose your project, to complete a progress update, and to reflect on the process. These three brief assignments will be required for all students, but the individual Unit 4 projects will, I imagine, be quite different. The work in this fast-paced unit asks you to plan, revise, and reflect; to be creative and take risks; and to explore how writing can be represented through different methodologies and modes. You will need to further develop your meta-awareness of your own writing at each stage in order to successfully complete this task.

Your creative contributions to Unit 4 will be presented in digital map form: We will work as a class to develop a Google MyMap that illustrates the writing you've studied at BSU. Mapping your projects in various ways will (re)present all of your hard work, reinforce the notion that writing takes place in a community, foster peer-to-peer collaboration, and create an opportunity for further academic success (more on that later).

Readings
(From custom reader)
Scott McCloud, From "Understanding Genres"
Anne Frances Wysocki, "The Multiple Media of Texts: How Onscreen and Paper Texts Incorporate Words, Images, and Other Media"

Reading Responses
There will be one reading response for this unit, and you may use either/both of the above readings. You'll continue to post your responses to your Reading Journal sub-page off of your personal student page. The rules from Units 1–3 still apply: You have until the start of class (10:30 AM) to post a brief response to the day's reading assignment, you should include a proper MLA citation for the reading as the post's title, and

you should spend at least 150 words *thinking with* the reading. Ask questions, summarize, quote parts that you found confusing or particularly interesting—really get in there and try to make sense of it. These journal entries count toward your participation grade (I will not be evaluating them, but I will sometimes add comments to your page), and I will occasionally use them to trigger class discussions.

In Unit 2, we engaged with challenging reading materials and strengthened our reading strategies in order to become active, critical readers. I expect your reading journals to reflect the strategies we covered in class and through our readings. As always, I encourage you to employ a specific strategy or two as you navigate these texts. You should also make clear connections between the assigned readings and the observations you've made—as well as the texts you've encountered—through your Explorations.

All Explorations must follow MLA conventions and be at least 2 pages in length, typed in Google Docs, shared with me (give me editing privileges), and uploaded to your Assignments page, within a "Unit 4" folder.

Proposal

After we do some brainstorming in class, you'll want to focus on what, exactly, you hope to accomplish by repurposing Unit 3's culminating project. You'll need to identify an audience and to describe the final outcome, as well as which methods will be used to reach that goal. So, you need to propose a Unit 4 Project by addressing the following:

- Clearly state what you think your specific focus will be as a one-sentence statement or question.

- Describe your project—what it will look like, which non-print medium you'll work with, what type of product will best capture your focus.

- Identify your specific, chosen audience for this piece.

- Explain your purpose—why you're writing for this audience, as well as the intended effect.

- List your materials, programs, apps, etc.

- Create a brief timeline, setting yourself small goals for specific steps and dates.
- Brainstorm solutions to any possible difficulties.

Essentially, you need to convince me that this is a viable option—that this project (whatever it may be) is doable and appropriate. Don't worry; I'm easy to convince.

Progress Update

About halfway through the unit, I'll want to know how you're doing. Use this exploration to update me on your work. Please respond to the following prompts:

- What have you accomplished so far and when? Are you following your timeline well?
- What rhetorical decisions have you made? How have you revised your project since the proposal?
- What difficulties did you encounter, and how did you handle them?
- What have you done really well? What are you excited about?
- What more needs to be done, and how will you do it?
- Do you have any questions or concerns?

Reflection

This exploration will be an extended cover letter—or a really extended writer's memo—in which you look back on the work you completed leading up to the final Unit 4 project. Please be thorough and specific, and please answer the following (but feel free to add more thoughts):

- What went really well for you in Unit 4? What are you most proud of? What were some of your best moments in the writing process?
- What did you struggle with? Which difficulties did you face, and were they expected or unexpected? How did you handle them? How did you learn from them?

- What more would you like to do? To write? To know? If you had more time to spend with this project, how would you further revise it? What more would you like to accomplish?

Unit 4 Writing Project

In addition to the three brief assignments described here, each of you will submit a culminating project in a non-print medium of your choice. How you create this project will depend on what it is, and the requirements for this project will depend on your proposal. I will be evaluating your three explorations in relation to your final project, in order to ensure fairness in the midst of creative chaos (everyone will be required to write the same three texts, but the final projects will vary greatly); this means that, basically, I'm evaluating the process more than the product. We will work on a rubric together.

I expect you to take risks, to have fun, and to do a lot of thinking. By the end of the unit, you will have three explorations in your Unit 4 folder on your Assignments page, and you will have submitted/shared/presented your culminating project on our Google MyMap. Your Unit 4 project should be clearly focused and should represent your Unit 3 project somehow; it should utilize the tools of your chosen medium; and it should reflect the plans and revisions that occurred throughout these two weeks. We will spend nearly all of our class time on creating this project; every class day will be a workshop day—workshopping in a community of writers means providing feedback and support and sharing ideas. I expect you to use this time wisely and purposefully.

Course Outcomes

- **Writerly Choices/Rhetorical Awareness:** Producing writing with a clear focus, purpose, and point
- **Meta-Awareness Of Rhetorical Choices:** Articulating rhetorical choices; illustrating your awareness of your relationship to your subject and the context surrounding these choices

- **Processes:** Understanding that writing takes place through recurring processes of invention, revision, editing, and reflection; and in a community of resources and support

Week 11 Unit 4 Schedule

Date	What's Due	What We're Doing in Class
Tuesday Nov. 6	McCloud, "Understanding Genres" Wysocki, "The Multiple Media of Texts [...]" Journal entry	Student Success Stories Exploration 3.1 Proposal Workshop
Thursday Nov. 8		Workshop
Sunday, Nov. 11: Exp. 4.2 Progress Update is due by the end of the day (11:59 PM)		

Week 12 Unit 4 Schedule

Date	What's Due	What We're Doing in Class
Tuesday Nov. 13	Nathan, "Academically Speaking..."	Workshop
Thursday Nov. 15	Complete and final Unit 4 Project	Exp 4.3 Reflection Other activities TBD, pending identification of culminating projects

CHAPTER 6

College-(Writing) Ready
Aligning the Common Core State Standards With the WPA Outcomes for First-Year Composition

Clancy Ratliff

For the last 7 years, I have been a writing program administrator. During that time, I have become more involved with secondary English Language Arts (ELA) education than I ever expected to be, through mandated expansion of our university's dual enrollment offerings and service on College of Education committees. Because I now work at the junction between high school and college, I have served for the last 2 years as our university's de facto English Education professor. In this role, I have become acquainted with the Common Core State Standards (CCSS). I approach the CCSS as someone whose background in pedagogical theory has come from writing studies and who is encountering a new discourse from the field of education and educational assessment: indicators, descriptors, alignments, grade-level expectations (GLEs), anchor standards, and so on.

As part of my expanded role in the university, I was recently tasked with aligning the Louisiana Department of Education's teacher evaluation rubric with standards from the National Council of Teachers of

English (NCTE). An alignment, in this sense, is essentially a mash-up of one rubric with another, a review of both rubrics to see which standards from each rubric can be linked together. During this time, I also served on our university's Campus Leadership Team for the Partnership for the Assessment of Readiness for College and Careers (PARCC) and worked with the CCSS in that capacity, so I decided to take my recent experience with standards alignment and apply it to a different pair of outcomes statements: the Writing Program Administrators Outcomes Statement (WPA OS) for First-Year Composition (Council of Writing Program Administrators [CWPA] 2008) and the CCSS for writing for grades 11–12 (Council of Chief State School Officers [CSSO] and National Governors Association [NGA] 2010).

Why align the WPA OS and the CCSS? I was interested in testing the CCSS, which are oriented toward college and career readiness, with the WPA OS, the set of outcomes most closely representing consensus among scholars in writing studies on the issue of what students need to know about writing. In this chapter, I first explain my involvement in PARCC and its implementation of the CCSS. Then I reveal my alignment of the CCSS and the WPA OS and analyze the similarities between the lists, both of which prioritize audience and purpose, and both of which put sentence-level writing proficiency in its proper perspective, as subordinate to larger discursive features of a text. I analyze the differences between the CCSS and WPA OS as well. Two differences, in particular, have special implications for the teaching of writing at the secondary level: 1) the treatment of genres, and 2) the treatment of critical pedagogy. I end by explaining what I see as a valuable challenge offered by the CCSS to writing classrooms at the high school and college level: to distinguish civic goals from academic goals through a focus on genre.

Shared Governance Theater: My Experience With the CCSS

In July 2011, I received an email from the dean of my university's College of Education asking me to join our university's Campus Leadership Team in its work to "review the new national standards for ELA and math." I would soon learn about PARCC and Louisiana's role as a governing state.[1] I agreed to join the team, which resulted in four encounters so far with PARCC and the CCSS.

The first two encounters were overviews of the CCSS and PARCC. One was a webinar in July 2011, which was an orientation introducing us to PARCC, with a description of Louisiana's problems (low graduation rates and high need for remediation in college), but curiously lacking a logical link for how the CCSS would improve conditions in Louisiana, except to say that the CCSS would be more challenging and rigorous. The slides explained that ELA would be taught in collaboration with teachers in other subject areas, and they showed the adjustment of the grade-level designations of some works of literature, most notably Shakespeare's *Macbeth*, which will go from a 12th-grade level to a ninth- or 10th-grade level. The slides also explained the timeline for implementation in Louisiana. The other orientation session was a statewide meeting in September 2011, which included presentations by members of Achieve, an organization consisting of government and industry leaders facilitating the transition to the CCSS.

The third experience with PARCC was a meeting of the Campus Leadership Team in April 2012 seeking to identify up to 20 core competencies required for college-level English. The leader of the team submitted the document to the Louisiana Board of Regents' PARCC liaison. The document we were asked to create had two columns, one asking for "[e]ssential core competencies that should be measured on a PARCC assessment that would indicate that a high school student has a 75 percent likelihood of achieving a C or better (50 percent chance of a B or better) without need for remediation in a college-level credit-bearing English I course." The right column asked for "[e]vidence that could be found on a PARCC assessment that would indicate that a high school student exhibits the core competencies at the necessary proficiency level for success." Throughout this document, our team wrote about the importance of portfolio assessment and referred to habits of mind in the Framework for Success in Postsecondary Writing, which is discussed in Chapters 4 and 5 in this volume. It was disappointing, though not surprising, when we later received a report titled "Statewide English Critical Competencies Identified by PARCC Campus Leadership Teams," which seemed to be a compiled list based on the competencies that all the Louisiana universities sent, and our team's competencies were not included in any way that I could recognize.

The most recent experience I've had with the CCSS was a 2-day Louisiana Department of Education CCSS training workshop in October 2012. The workshop, run by a state Department of Education official, was essentially an explanation of the changes ahead for K–12 schools and for teacher preparation on higher education's end. The work of our Campus Leadership Team, even though the professors on it have been collegial and engaged, has been frustrating. However, it has prompted me to pay much more attention to the overlaps and gaps between K–12 and college-level writing pedagogy. Those overlaps and gaps have been the source of quite a bit of confusion and frustration for many years among educators at both the high school and college level.[2] Without that experience, I wouldn't have been motivated to align the CCSS with the WPA OS.

Alignment of the WPA OS and CCSS for ELA (Grades 11–12, College and Career Readiness)

In Table 6.1, I illustrate the similarities and differences among the CCSS and the WPA OS. The CWPA adopted the WPA OS in 2000 after a long process of discussion with over 100 writing teachers (Yancey 2002, 379). Another section of outcomes related to technology was added in 2008.

Table 6.1 is a mash-up of—loosely speaking—one list with another. I looked carefully at both documents and paired up list items that seemed the most similar to me. Another person looking at both documents might have produced a different alignment. To give a sense of my reasoning, an example is the alignment of the WPA OS' "Develop knowledge of genre conventions ranging from structure and paragraphing to tone and mechanics" with the CCSS' W.11–12.2d, "Use precise language, domain-specific vocabulary, and techniques such as metaphor, simile, and analogy to manage the complexity of the topic." I paired these two list items because they both deal with rhetorical choices at the word choice and sentence level. These two statements are not identical, of course; the WPA OS specifically names "genre conventions," and the CCSS name "metaphor, simile, and analogy." Still, with the focus on "genre conventions" and "tone and mechanics" in the WPA OS item and "precise language" and "domain-specific vocabulary" in the CCSS, I thought the resemblance was enough for an alignment. Most of the remainder of this chapter will be a more macro-level analysis and comparison of these two lists.

I should clarify at the outset that I'm comparing outcomes with standards. The CCSS are explicitly presented as standards, while the creators of the WPA OS have been quick to say that their list consists of outcomes, which are different from standards: "Outcomes are goals that can be met on many levels, depending on local conditions (students, teachers, curriculum, etc.); standards are points at which those outcomes can be measured" (Behm et al. 2012, ix–x). In Chapter 4 of this volume, Angela Clark-Oates, Allyson Boggess, and Duane Roen further explain the difference between outcomes and standards. In Table 6.1, I have aligned the CCSS *to the* WPA OS, clearly favoring the latter. I chose to organize the table this way because I wanted to put the CCSS into a schema that was familiar to me and that was representative of college-level writing pedagogy. The CCSS are designed for college and career readiness, so I wanted to test them against real college-level standards. The outcomes in the WPA OS appear in their original order, whereas the corresponding CCSS are out of order (first W.11–12.4, then W.11–12.1b, then W.11–12.1d, and so forth). I am using the categories in the WPA OS: Rhetorical Knowledge; Critical Thinking, Reading, and Writing; Processes; Knowledge of Conventions; and Composing in Electronic Environments. The CCSS are grouped in a different set of categories: Text Types and Purposes; Production and Distribution of Writing; Research to Build and Present Knowledge; and Range of Writing.

Table 6.1 Similarities and Differences Between the CCSS and WPA OS

	WPA OS (CWPA 2008)	CCSS (CSSO and NGA 2010)
Rhetorical Knowledge	Focus on a purpose.	Produce clear and coherent writing in which the development, organization, and style are appropriate to task, purpose, and audience. (W.11–12.4)
	Respond to the needs of different audiences.	Develop claim(s) and counterclaims fairly and thoroughly, supplying the most relevant evidence for each while pointing out the strengths and limitations of both in a manner that anticipates the audience's knowledge level, concerns, values, and possible biases. (W.11–12.1b)
	Respond appropriately to different kinds of rhetorical situations.	
	Use conventions of format and structure appropriate to the rhetorical situation.	Establish and maintain a formal style and objective tone while attending to the norms and conventions of the discipline in which they are writing. (W.11–12.1d)
	Adopt appropriate voice, tone, and level of formality.	
	Understand how genres shape reading and writing	
	Write in several genres.	
Critical Thinking, Reading, and Writing	Use writing and reading for inquiry, learning, thinking, and communicating.	Conduct short as well as more sustained research projects to answer a question (including a self-generated question) or solve a problem; narrow or broaden the inquiry when appropriate; synthesize multiple sources on the subject, demonstrating understanding of the subject under investigation. (W.11–12.7)
	Understand a writing assignment as a series of tasks, including finding, evaluating, analyzing, and synthesizing appropriate primary and secondary sources.	Gather relevant information from multiple authoritative print and digital sources, using advanced searches effectively; assess the strengths and limitations of each source in terms of the task, purpose, and audience; integrate information into the text selectively to maintain the flow of ideas, avoiding plagiarism and overreliance on any one source and following a standard format for citation. (W.11–12.8)
	Integrate their own ideas with those of others.	
	Understand the relationships among language, knowledge, and power.	

Table 6.1 (*cont.*)

	WPA OS (CWPA 2008)	CCSS (CSSO and NGA 2010)
Processes	Be aware that it usually takes multiple drafts to create and complete a successful text.	Develop and strengthen writing as needed by planning, revising, editing, rewriting, or trying a new approach, focusing on addressing what is most significant for a specific purpose and audience. (W.11–12.5)
	Develop flexible strategies for generating, revising, editing, and proofreading.	
	Understand writing as an open process that permits writers to use later invention and re-thinking to revise their work.	
	Understand the collaborative and social aspects of writing processes.	Use technology, including the internet, to produce, publish, and update individual or shared writing products in response to ongoing feedback, including new arguments or information. (W.11–12.6)
	Learn to critique their own and others' works.	
	Learn to balance the advantages of relying on others with the responsibility of doing their part.	
	Use a variety of technologies to address a range of audiences.	
Knowledge of Conventions	Learn common formats for different kinds of texts.	
	Develop knowledge of genre conventions ranging from structure and paragraphing to tone and mechanics.	Use precise language, domain-specific vocabulary, and techniques such as metaphor, simile, and analogy to manage the complexity of the topic. Use appropriate and varied transitions and syntax to link the major sections of the text, create cohesion, and clarify the relationships among complex ideas and concepts. (W.11–12.2d)
	Practice appropriate means of documenting their work.	
	Control such surface features as syntax, grammar, punctuation, and spelling.	Use words, phrases, and clauses as well as varied syntax to link the major sections of the text, create cohesion, and clarify the relationships between claim(s) and reasons, between reasons and evidence, and between claim(s) and counterclaims. (W.11–12.1c)

Table 6.1 (cont.)

	WPA OS (CWPA 2008)	CCSS (CSSO and NGA 2010)
Composing in Electronic Environments	Use electronic environments for drafting, reviewing, revising, editing, and sharing texts.	Use technology, including the internet, to produce, publish, and update individual or shared writing products in response to ongoing feedback, including new arguments or information. (W.11–12.6)
	Locate, evaluate, organize, and use research material collected from electronic sources, including scholarly library databases, other official databases (e.g., federal government databases), and informal electronic networks and internet sources.	Write informative/explanatory texts to examine and convey complex ideas, concepts, and information clearly and accurately through the effective selection, organization, and analysis of content. (W.11–12.2)
	Understand and exploit the differences in the rhetorical strategies and in the affordances available for both print and electronic composing processes and texts.	

CCSS With No Clear Counterpart in the WPA OS
Introduce precise, knowledgeable claim(s), establish the significance of the claim(s), distinguish the claim(s) from alternate or opposing claims, and create an organization that logically sequences claim(s), counterclaims, reasons, and evidence. (W.11–12.1a)
Provide a concluding statement or section that follows from and supports the argument presented. (W.11–12.1e)
Introduce a topic; organize complex ideas, concepts, and information so that each new element builds on that which precedes it to create a unified whole; include formatting (e.g., headings), graphics (e.g., figures, tables), and multimedia when useful to aiding comprehension. (W.11–12.2a)
Provide a concluding statement or section that follows from and supports the information or explanation presented (e.g., articulating implications or the significance of the topic). (W.11–12.2f)
Write narratives to develop real or imagined experiences or events using effective technique, well-chosen details, and well-structured event sequences. (W.11–12.3)
Engage and orient the reader by setting out a problem, situation, or observation and its significance, establishing one or multiple point(s) of view, and introducing a narrator and/or characters; create a smooth progression of experiences or events. (W.11–12.3a)
Use narrative techniques, such as dialogue, pacing, description, reflection, and multiple plot lines, to develop experiences, events, and/or characters. (W.11–12.3b)
Use a variety of techniques to sequence events so that they build on one another to create a coherent whole and build toward a particular tone and outcome (e.g., a sense of mystery, suspense, growth, or resolution). (W.11–12.3c)
Use precise words and phrases, telling details, and sensory language to convey a vivid picture of the experiences, events, setting, and/or characters. (W.11–12.3d)
Provide a conclusion that follows from and reflects on what is experienced, observed, or resolved over the course of the narrative. (W.11–12.3e)
Write routinely over extended time frames (time for research, reflection, and revision) and shorter time frames (a single sitting or a day or two) for a range of tasks, purposes (W.11–12.10)
Write arguments to support claims in an analysis of substantive topics or texts, using valid reasoning and relevant and sufficient evidence. (W.11–12.1)

Similarities Between the WPA OS and CCSS

To be sure, some similarities between the WPA OS and CCSS are evident. The CCSS do acknowledge the need for thinking about purpose and audience. Together, purpose and audience are addressed in three of the CCSS and audience alone in another. Standard W.11–12.4 casts organization and style in terms of audience and purpose, asking students to "Produce clear and coherent writing in which the development, organization, and style are appropriate to task, purpose, and audience." This is a step in the right direction; writing studies scholars have problematized the notion that there is a universally recognized idea of "well organized" and one of "disorganized." Adding "development" to this standard suggests to me that academic audiences are in mind, which helps a bit to explain mysterious rules students encounter regarding page length ("this research paper has to be six to eight pages long"), as academic audiences expect thorough development. Standard W.11–12.1b states that students need to "Develop claim(s) and counterclaims fairly and thoroughly, supplying the most relevant evidence for each while pointing out the strengths and limitations of both in a manner that anticipates the audience's knowledge level, concerns, values, and possible biases." Again, both teachers and students are directed to approach writing assignments rhetorically, with the audience in mind, and not in a way that simply gestures superficially, but that specifically refers to the audience's "knowledge level, concerns, values, and possible biases." This is an analytical approach to audience.

This focus on audience is sustained in W.11–12.5, which combines attention to writing process and rhetorical strategy when it states that students should "Develop and strengthen writing as needed by planning, revising, editing, rewriting, or trying a new approach, focusing on addressing what is most significant for a specific purpose and audience." Even W.11–12.8, the standard that has to do with research, addresses purpose and audience, prompting students to "assess the strengths and limitations of each source in terms of the task, purpose, and audience." If the CCSS help K–12 administrators to prioritize purpose and audience over results of standardized tests, it would be to students' benefit and would, in the process, likely help them be better prepared for college and career.

Standard W.11–12.7 directs students to engage in "short as well as more sustained research projects to answer a question (including a self-generated question) or solve a problem; narrow or broaden the inquiry when appropriate; synthesize multiple sources on the subject, demonstrating understanding of the subject under investigation." I mention this standard because of its focus on inquiry. At least three popular college writing textbooks—Bruce Ballenger's *The Curious Researcher* (2011a) and *The Curious Writer* (2011b), and John Ramage, John Bean, and June Johnson's *Writing Arguments* (2012)—have lengthy sections on approaching writing and research as inquiry, in a manner similar to how the standard does: starting with a research question rather than a predetermined claim (or "thesis statement").

Research techniques are emphasized in both the WPA OS and the CCSS, but not in quite the same way. The CCSS highlight "the effective selection, organization, and analysis of content" (W.11–12.2). They expect students to: "Gather relevant information from multiple authoritative print and digital sources, using advanced searches effectively" and "assess the strengths and limitations of each source in terms of the task, purpose, and audience" (W.11–12.8). The WPA OS states that students should be able to: "Understand a writing assignment as a series of tasks, including finding, evaluating, analyzing, and synthesizing appropriate primary and secondary sources." In an even closer resemblance, the WPA OS expects students to: "Integrate their own ideas with those of others," while the CCSS state that students should "integrate information into the text selectively to maintain the flow of ideas," adding that this involves "avoiding plagiarism and overreliance on any one source and following a standard format for citation" (W.11–12.8). Still, the WPA OS seems to recognize librarians' role in the research process more explicitly than the CCSS; the WPA OS expects students to: "Locate, evaluate, organize, and use research material collected from electronic sources, including scholarly library databases; other official databases (e.g., federal government databases); and informal electronic networks and internet sources." Again, the CCSS are already fairly well aligned with our existing document explaining the outcomes of college-level writing courses, but I maintain that effective implementation of the particular research-related standards, W.11–12.2 and especially W.11–12.8, depends on sufficient state and district funding for school libraries and librarian positions.

The CCSS also show the important role of reader response, in keeping with the other standards about purpose and audience. Standard W.11–12.6 requires students to use digital technology to "produce, publish, and update individual or shared writing products in response to ongoing feedback." This standard suggests that feedback would be substantive, looking beyond sentence-level writing issues. Moreover, because the CCSS place responsibility for writing pedagogy in the hands of not only ELA teachers but also teachers of other subjects, such as history and science, this standard would suggest that feedback would address content in multiple subjects, perhaps a writing-to-learn model.

Like any set of writing standards, though, the CCSS do deal with sentence-level errors. Even the WPA OS does. But the CCSS situate sentence-level writing issues within the larger context of the writing project. Standard W.11–12.2d explains that students must "Use precise language, domain-specific vocabulary, and techniques such as metaphor, simile, and analogy to manage the complexity of the topic." This standard dispels the idea that "good writing" is correct writing; command of the language is joined with "the complexity of the topic." Standard W.11–12.1c keeps with the interdependence of sentence-level proficiency and overall rhetorical fluency: "Use words, phrases, and clauses as well as varied syntax to link the major sections of the text, create cohesion, and clarify the relationships between claim(s) and reasons, between reasons and evidence, and between claim(s) and counterclaims." These standards reveal a thoughtful view of sentence-level writing proficiency as geared toward meaning-making and communication with an audience rather than correctness without a purpose. The CCSS as a whole would seem to discourage formulaic shortcuts in the teaching of writing: the old five-paragraph essay structure (5PE) as well as the MEAL (Main idea, Evidence, Analysis, Link) plan for constructing paragraphs. The CCSS force teachers, students, and parents to attend to many other qualities of a piece of writing beneath the surface features of sentence-level correctness.

Genre in the WPA OS and CCSS

I would argue that the most consequential difference between the CCSS and WPA OS is the treatment of genre. Genre, as a codified response to a recurring rhetorical situation, is an important conceptual tool for writers to understand and use. Understanding genre helps students to become rhetorically aware writers who can shift from one situation to another and one discourse community to another, transferring and applying knowledge about writing from one context to another. The CCSS and WPA OS both seem to be striving for higher-order thinking and knowledge transfer, but the CCSS make no mention of the term *genre*. Instead, they follow the outdated model of "the modes of discourse": exposition, description, narration, and argument (EDNA). The modes of discourse, typically shortened to "the modes," was a classification system for the teaching of writing that became popular in the mid-1890s. For approximately the next 50 years, "the modes" was the way most assignments in writing courses were sequenced and designed: a narrative essay, a descriptive essay, an expository essay, and a persuasive essay, sometimes in a different order. In an aptly titled 1981 article, "The Rise and Fall of the Modes of Discourse," Robert Connors writes that the modes "became popular and stayed popular because they fit into the abstract, mechanical nature of writing instruction at the time, and they diminished in importance as other, more vital, ideas about writing appeared in the 1930s and after" (453). These more vital ideas include a focus on prewriting, process, rhetorical invention, and genre. Connors continues:

> The weakness of the modes of discourse as a practical tool in the writing class was that they did not really help students to learn to write. When we look closely at the nature

of modal distinctions, it is not hard to see why: The modes classify and emphasize the product of writing, having almost nothing to do with the purpose for which the writer sat down, pen in hand. (454)

In other words, although we still see some outposts of modes teaching in college-level writing pedagogy, "the modes" have been largely discredited as a pedagogical approach, course design, and assignment sequence. Connors reflects on the long history of "the modes":

> Our discipline has been long in knuckling from its eyes the sleep of the nineteenth and early twentieth centuries, and the real lesson of the modes is that we need always be on guard against systems that seem convenient to teachers but that ignore the way writing is actually done. (455)

Most college writing teachers would recognize that "the modes" do not exist in isolation in any real genre, such as a grant proposal, which might blend narrative, argument, exposition, and description, and that treating "the modes" in isolation reduces writing to nothing but a classroom exercise done for a grade, with no real transferability to other classes or writing situations outside of school. Still, Connors notes that, "[s]tripped of their theoretical validity and much of their practical usefulness, the modes cling to a shadowy half-life in the attic of composition legends" (453). We see these vestiges in the CCSS, well into the 2010s.

The CCSS for writing are divided into "arguments," "informative/explanatory texts," and "narratives," with specific outcomes for each mode. The way the CCSS for writing are classified concerns me that "the modes" will make a resurgence, as publishers pump out books of lesson plans and other teaching resources aligned to the CCSS. Such a move would reverse the progress writing teachers have made in providing more sophisticated treatment of genre.

Unlike the CCSS, the WPA OS explicitly names genre awareness as a goal in college-level writing pedagogy, suggesting that students be able to, by the end of first-year writing, to "[u]nderstand how genres shape reading and writing" and "[w]rite in several genres." These genres include texts like proposals, letters to the editor, op-eds, abstracts, recommendation letters, minutes of meetings, and so forth, which call to mind the situations that student writers will address in college and career as well as allow them a better sense of audience and purpose. Contexts are also emphasized more in the WPA OS, whereas school (academic) writing is assumed to be the major or only context in the CCSS. The WPA OS offers the outcome that student writers should be able to "[r]espond appropriately to different kinds of rhetorical situations," yet there isn't any language in the CCSS that captures this outcome. The same is true with the WPA OS outcome, which reads that students should be able to "[u]nderstand and exploit the differences in the rhetorical strategies and in the affordances available for both print and electronic composing processes and texts." Ironically, for an initiative so focused on college and career readiness, the authors of the CCSS appear not to have examined existing standards for college-level writing expressed in the WPA OS, informed by theory and research on rhetoric and writing instruction.

Several scholars in writing studies have expressed concerns about the CCSS, most notably Kristine Johnson, who in a February 2013 *College Composition and Communication* article connects "the modes" approach to the highly technical and decontextualized standards relating to writing introductions and conclusions (instead of recognizing that a "good" introduction or conclusion varies according to the purpose, genre, and audience), and "using words such as consequently and specifically to link opinion and reasons" (520). Johnson adds:

> Writing in the [CCSS] is limited to two modes, and this narrowing effect is further pronounced because the standards are based on spiraling—returning to the same skills at increasing levels of complexity—rather than instructional coverage. Spiraling certainly scaffolds knowledge and reinforces skills, but in the Common Core standards, it further

constrains the types of writing and purposes for writing students' experience. (520)

By "two modes," Johnson refers to informational (expository) and argumentative texts, but even though the narrative category raises the number to three modes, the point stands: Context and genre are not emphasized in the CCSS; instead, the focus is on severely outdated, disconnected modes.

Critical Thinking and Writing in the WPA OS and the CCSS

The WPA OS contains the following critical pedagogy-informed outcome: Students should be able to "[u]nderstand the relationships among language, knowledge, and power," which has no counterpart in the CCSS. In keeping with the emphasis on rhetoric, context, and genre, most of the theory and research in writing pedagogy would have us as teachers and students attend to social, political, and economic power dynamics in the uses of language. Critical pedagogy would have us ask: Whose interests are being served in the writing of a document? Whose interests are being dismissed? The language in the outcome from the WPA OS suggests that students should be asked to reflect on the concept of power within and around writing: the micropolitics of the classroom as well as the ideologies embedded in knowledge claims and claims about knowledge (Berlin 1988). Often the most productive and illuminating ways to think about power and discourse are to engage cultural difference: race, sexuality, gender, class, ability/disability, nationality, and religion.

The CCSS do not address the idea of power directly. The closest the CCSS come to a statement about difference is in the introduction to the ELA standards, in a description of "Students Who Are College and Career Ready in Reading, Writing, Speaking, Listening, & Language." The heading reads, "They come to understand other perspectives and cultures":

> Students appreciate that the twenty-first-century classroom and workplace are settings in which people from often widely divergent cultures and who represent diverse experiences and perspectives must learn and work together. Students actively seek to understand other perspectives and cultures through reading and listening, and they are able to communicate effectively with people of varied backgrounds. They evaluate other points of view critically and constructively. Through reading great classic and contemporary works of literature representative of a variety of periods, cultures, and worldviews, students can vicariously inhabit worlds and have experiences much different than their own. (CCSSO and NGA 2010)

Difference is treated here as an unavoidable fact of life. Perspectives and cultures are simply different, equal in power, unlike the critical approach of the WPA OS that recognizes writing as a technology of power. By eliding the issue of power, the CCSS suggest that everyone has equal status and is in an equally strong position from which to evaluate and critique. Thus, the CCSS fail to recognize writing as a technology of power. The political and economic tightrope the authors of the CCSS walk forces a deferential and passive gesture to cultural diversity, whereas the WPA OS authors are more candid about awareness of power, treating it as a key part of any rhetorical context, and as a high-priority outcome for college-level writing.

Conclusion: The WPA OS and College-Level Writing

As one whose job involves close contact with local high schools and professors in our College of Education, and as a parent of preschool-aged children, I have a lot at stake in the CCSS initiative, and I have serious reservations about the implementation of the CCSS, most having to do with funding to support instruction for students who do not seem to be on track for a "college- and career-ready determination." In comparing the WPA OS and the CCSS, I don't mean to suggest that all first-year writing courses are designed according to these outcomes. Certainly some college-level writing courses are still designed according to a current-traditional philosophy, with very little attention to rhetorical matters of audience, purpose, and genre, choosing instead to focus on sentence-level correctness, MLA documentation style, the MEAL plan, and the 5PE. Schools that align ELA instruction to the CCSS in creative, engaging, locally rich ways like those suggested later in this volume will surely be providing students with a better learning experience than some college-level writing programs.

Therefore, I'd like to end with a challenge to both high schools and colleges for how we might do a better job teaching rhetoric and argument in our writing courses. I see two main problems at work in how we currently approach argument in first-year writing. The first is a conflation between civic and academic argument, as I illustrate in Figure 6.1.

Civic argument is associated with several areas of research in writing studies: contact zones (Pratt 1991), civic literacy (Lazere 2005), critical pedagogy (Giroux 2011), cultural studies (George and Trimbur 2000), feminist pedagogy (Jarratt 1991), and more. *Academic argument* is associated with academic discourse (Bartholomae 1985), collaborative pedagogy (Bruffee 1984), genre studies (Berkenkotter and Huckin 1994), and discourse communities (Bizzell 1992), among others. There are areas of overlap, of course: Both spheres of rhetoric involve critical thinking and the knowledge of rhetorical techniques. Many teachers want to do both civic and academic argument at once, resulting in a conflation. This conflation has consequences; in the attempt to teach both academic and civic discourse, students get mixed messages, which inhibits knowledge transfer. I suspect that what students hear from us is something to the effect of, "OK, you've taken first-year writing. You have learned MLA format, and you know what ethos, pathos, and logos are. Now go forth and write in your chosen major, and be an agent of change in the world!"

Second, I see a disconnect between the genres students are asked to read and the genres, or non-genres, or "mutt genres" as Elizabeth

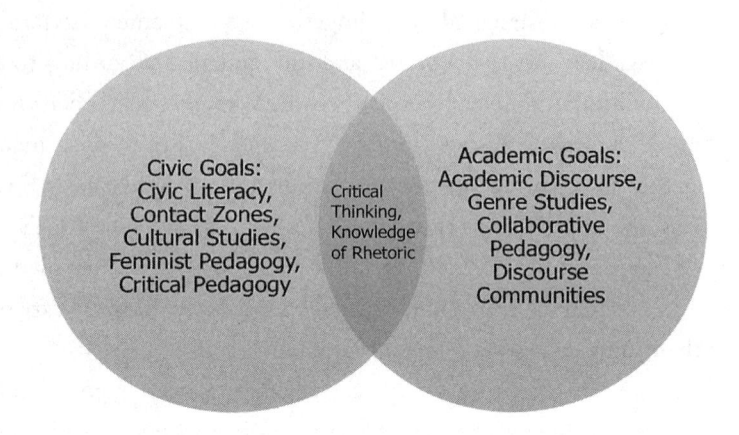

Figure 6.1 Conflation between civic and academic argument

Civic Goals: Civic Literacy, Contact Zones, Cultural Studies, Feminist Pedagogy, Critical Pedagogy

Critical Thinking, Knowledge of Rhetoric

Academic Goals: Academic Discourse, Genre Studies, Collaborative Pedagogy, Discourse Communities

Wardle (2009) calls them, that they're asked to write. The genre we're often really asking them to write is a short scholarly journal article (the genre with which we are most familiar), but we don't usually ask students to read such texts. As we know, op-ed pieces from newspapers handle sources very differently from scholarly journal articles, but we don't always make those differences explicit for students. Textbooks usually contain far fewer "sample student essays" than newspaper and magazine readings, but even those are not the actual genres we're invoking. We're not advancing past that inchoate "critical thinking and analysis" stage. We're saying to students, "You need to make an argument," but students aren't realizing, "I need to make an argument." This isn't a criticism of students, only a statement that they don't often have the real-life motivating occasion in many first-year writing classrooms. Here we can see the way the CCSS handle argument:

- Write arguments to support claims in an analysis of substantive topics or texts, using valid reasoning and relevant and sufficient evidence (W.11–12.1).

- Introduce precise, knowledgeable claim(s), establish the significance of the claim(s), distinguish the claim(s) from alternate or opposing claims, and create an organization that logically sequences claim(s), counterclaims, reasons, and evidence (W.11–12.1a).

- Develop claim(s) and counterclaims fairly and thoroughly, supplying the most relevant evidence for each while pointing out the strengths and limitations of both in a manner that anticipates the audience's knowledge level, concerns, values, and possible biases (W.11–12.1b).

Again, here we're just seeing those techniques for undifferentiated "argument"; while there's a gesture to audience, the arguments aren't situated in civic contexts or academic contexts.

We need to bring genre to the CCSS: While genres do overlap, a goal of teaching civic, public argument should require public genres such as a blog post (for a particular blog, like The Moderate Voice, The Huffington Post, or Hit and Run), an infographic, an action letter to representatives of Congress, or a preface to a petition.[3] A goal of teaching academic argument should require academic genres such as the annotated bibliography, literature review, review essay, book review, and scholarly journal article. Assignment handouts can be presented as calls for papers, just like the ones we write, read, and respond to on our professional listservs. If this is our goal, then we need to give appropriate caveats about what we can reasonably promise to do. "Academic writing" here really means "academic writing in English studies." As Wardle's research shows, scholars in English studies cannot really know the genres that academics in other disciplines write (2009). But even "public, civic argument" and "academic writing in English studies" is a step toward getting rid of the conflation.

What can we do, then, as teachers of high school ELA, teachers of college writing, and as librarians at the high school and college level? High school and college teachers alike should help students distinguish civic and academic arenas of rhetoric by emphasizing genre more, especially in assignment design. Librarians can help students see this distinction by helping students find information sources and clarifying who the intended audience is for each source, effectively helping the students understand the rhetorical context of each source. Perhaps the

CCSS, including the problems we recognize in them, offer a challenge to us all to improve our teaching.

Endnotes

1. According to PARCC, governing states "will administer the assessment system statewide during the 2014–15 school year" as well as "pilot and field test components of the assessment system during the development period." Louisiana, as a governing state, has agreed to "use the results from the proposed assessment system in their state accountability systems" (PARCC 2014).
2. See the excellent collection *What Is "College-Level" Writing?* edited by Patrick Sullivan and Howard Tinberg (2006), which contains chapters written by high school teachers and college teachers, for thoughtful analyses of these issues.
3. Change.org has a remarkable tutorial for users who want to create a petition.

References

Ballenger, Bruce. 2011a. *The Curious Writer*. 3rd edition. New York: Pearson.

———. 2011b. *The Curious Researcher*. 7th edition. New York: Pearson.

Bartholomae, David. 1985. "Inventing the University." In *When a Writer Can't Write: Studies in Writer's Block and Other Composing-Process Problems*, edited by Mike Rose, 273–285. New York: Guilford.

Behm, Nicholas, Gregory R. Glau, Deborah H. Holdstein, Duane Roen, and Edward M. White. 2012. *The WPA Outcomes Statement: A Decade Later*. Anderson, SC: Parlor Press.

Berkenkotter, Carol, and Thomas N. Huckin. 1994. *Genre Knowledge in Disciplinary Communication: Cognition/Culture/Power*. New York: Routledge.

Berlin, James. 1988. "Rhetoric and Ideology in the Writing Class." *College English* 50 (5): 477–494.

Bizzell, Patricia. 1992. *Academic Discourse and Critical Consciousness*. Pittsburgh: University of Pittsburgh Press.

Bruffee, Kenneth. 1984. "Collaborative Learning and the 'Conversation of Mankind'." *College Composition and Communication* 46 (7): 635–652.

Connors, Robert. 1981. "The Rise and Fall of the Modes of Discourse." *College Composition and Communication*. 32 (4): 444–455.

Council of Chief State School Officers and National Governors Association. 2010. *Common Core State Standards for English Language Arts and Literacy in History/Social Studies, Science, and Technical Subjects*. Washington, DC: National Governors Association Center for Best Practices, Council of Chief State School Officers. Accessed February 10, 2014. www.corestandards.org/assets/CCSSI_ELA%20Standards.pdf.

Council of Writing Program Administrators. 2008. *WPA Outcomes Statement for First-Year Composition*. Accessed February 10, 2014. wpacouncil.org/positions/outcomes.html.

George, Diana, and John Trimbur. 2000. "Cultural Studies and Composition." In *A Guide to Composition Pedagogies*, edited by Gary Tate, Amy Rupiper, and Kurt Schick, 71–91. New York: Oxford.

Giroux, Henry A. 2011. *On Critical Pedagogy*. London: Continuum Press.

Jarratt, Susan. 1991. "Feminism and Composition: The Case for Conflict." In *Contending With Words: Composition and Rhetoric in a Postmodern Age*, edited by Patricia Harkin and John Schilb, 105–123. New York: MLA.

Johnson, Kristine. 2013. "Beyond Standards: Disciplinary and National Perspectives on Habits of Mind." *College Composition and Communication* 64 (3): 517–541.

Lazere, Donald. 2005. *Reading and Writing for Civic Literacy: The Critical Citizen's Guide to Argumentative Rhetoric*. Boulder, CO: Paradigm Publishers.

Partnership for Assessment of Readiness for College and Careers. 2014 "Governing Board." Accessed February 10, 2014. parcconline.org/governing-board.

Pratt, Mary Louise. 1991. "Arts of the Contact Zone." *Profession* 91: 33–40.

Ramage, John, John Bean, and June Johnson. 2012. *Writing Arguments: A Rhetoric With Readings*. 9th edition. New York: Pearson.

Sullivan, Patrick, and Howard Tinberg, eds. 2006. *What Is "College-Level" Writing?* Urbana, IL: National Council of Teachers of English.

Wardle, Elizabeth. 2009. "'Mutt Genres' and the Goal of FYC: Can We Help Students Write the Genres of the University?" *College Composition and Communication* 60 (4): 765–789.

Yancey, Kathleen Blake. 2002. "A Comment on the 'WPA Outcomes Statement for First-Year Composition': Responds." *College English* 64 (3): 378–380.

CHAPTER 7

Media Literacy Principles and the Common Core State Standards in English Language Arts Teacher Education

James Cercone and David L. Bruce

In 2011, the National Council of Teachers of English (NCTE) celebrated its 100th year anniversary. Throughout that century, the teaching profession has been pulled by various tensions. Historically, these tensions have centered around what types of texts are worthy of attention in English Language Arts (ELA) classrooms and what students should be asked to do with them (Applebee 1974; Bates 1912; Barnes 1932; O'Sullivan 1962; Rosenblatt 1994; Scholes 1998; Squire 2003). Most recently, these same tensions have become embodied in the Common Core State Standards (CCSS), a national educational policy effort that has reignited debates on what counts as literacy learning in ELA classrooms.

As two former high school ELA teachers, we were often faced with the pressures of meeting various "standards"—board, state, national—

while also engaging our students in literacy work that was meaningful to them. Like most ELA teachers, we were required to teach literature that our students often found difficult and unrelatable. At the same time, we took note of the wide range of texts they engaged with outside of school. One way that we were able to deal with the dichotomies between classroom texts and adolescents' cultural capital (Bourdieu 1986) outside of school was to use *media literacy* (ML) principles as an interpretive framework to address the various gaps we encountered between our students' lived experiences and the texts we were asked to teach in our classrooms. Now as teacher educators, we find ourselves and our pre-service teachers still grappling with these same tensions.

Media Literacy: A Way Forward

In our experience, ML has offered a lens from which to see and attempt to mitigate these tensions, at both the secondary and college level. Though we taught in different states and did not interact prior to our collaboration in higher education, we each came from backgrounds teaching high school ELA, Media Studies, and Video Production. In those stand-alone media courses, we organized our content around the ML core principles. As we pursued our separate paths into teacher education, we integrated those ML principles into our teacher preparation courses.

Over the past 3 years, we have co-taught a 6-hour graduate ELA methods block (Cercone the first half, Bruce the second) based around a common set of readings that include pedagogical texts and selections in young adult (YA) and canonical literature. In designing and teaching these courses, we have encountered many of the same tensions about texts and activities within teacher education as we did in our own high school courses.

In what follows, we first provide an overview of the CCSS movement as the most recent incarnation of historical tensions within ELA education. We then examine the lengthy relationship ELA has shared with ML. We argue that ML principles provide ELA teachers a theoretical base from which to address the demands of the CCSS while at the same time engaging students in meaningful literacy practices. We then provide examples from our own teaching that illustrate how adopting a ML stance on ELA teacher education can help alleviate the tensions within our profession and address the concerns raised by the essentially nationwide adoption of the CCSS.

CCSS: Media Literacy and Historical Tensions Within ELA

The field of ELA has been a nexus of converging tensions from its inception. ELA coalesced into a recognized field in the late 19th century through the work of the National Education Association's Committee of Ten, in combination with the National Conference on Uniform Entrance Requirements in English (Applebee 1974; Squire 2003). Both groups focused on creating uniformity of high school ELA, particularly for the purpose of college entry requirements (Kliebard 2004). A focus on classical literature in the high school ELA curriculum took root during this time. Though a single list of required reading was never achieved, Arthur N. Applebee (1974) found that titles referred to as "'classics'… came to be used to describe the body of English standard authors" (35) and have carried this status ever since.

This dual focus of the Committee of Ten, on college readiness and classical literature, is threaded throughout the CCSS. The authors of the CCSS suggest in their opening remarks that the purpose of the CCSS is to "lay out a vision of what it means to be a literate person in the twenty-first century" (Council of Chief State School Officers [CCSSO] and National Governors Association [NGA] 2010, 3), and that one purpose of secondary ELA is to focus on college and career preparation. In fact, the phrase *college and career readiness* (3) is used throughout the document as the intended result of secondary education. The CCSS also offer a focus on canonical works of literature and "informational texts." Though the term *classics* is not used, an overwhelming majority of fiction authors listed in the CCSS are associated with canonical literature including Shakespeare, Brontë, Twain, Hemingway, Steinbeck, and Fitzgerald, with only one listed title published after the year 2000 (58).

Furthermore, the CCSS include limited references to popular cultural texts, such as film, with no mention of television programs, music, video games, and advertisements; in other words, the CCSS appear to ignore the kinds of texts that young people engage with daily (Alvermann 2005; Hull and Schultz 2002). This omission is curious, given the large body of research that positions adolescents' out-of-school literacy practices as complex, socially situated forms of learning (Beach and O'Brien 2008; Christenbury, Bomer, and Smagorinsky 2009; Moje et al. 2000; Snyder and Bulfin 2008). Such oversights tend to reinforce the erroneous concept that print is a superior form of meaning making over other forms of media (Alvermann 2005; Alvermann, Moon, and Hagood 1999; Brauer and Clark 2008; Scholes 1998).

These omissions are not accidental. Historically, print and nonprint texts have shared an uneasy co-existence within ELA, particularly on the issue of what constitutes a "text." As we have noted, there has been considerable focus on print-based definitions of texts in ELA. In addition to the traditional modes of reading and writing with print, many have argued throughout the history of ELA instruction that other media are valid texts for study and use in the classroom. In fact, as early as 1915, teachers called for the inclusion of film as appropriate content in the ELA classroom, stating, "moving pictures everywhere will become a valuable adjunct in the mastery of skill in English composition" (Gerrish 1915, 230).

It is interesting to note, however, that the word *adjunct* continues to describe the prevalent perception of media texts in the ELA classroom. Though various forms of media have been included in the curriculum—such as TV (Foster 1979), movies (Costanzo 1992; Monaco 1981), radio (Cushman 1973), and videogames (Gee 2007)—the profession tends to view them as add-ons to a predominantly print-based curriculum. Deborah Dashow Ruth (1977) makes this relationship clear when she writes:

> The primary function of nonprint media in English classrooms has traditionally been as an aid to the teaching of

the real, more important subject, rather than as valuable means of learning in and of themselves. And the "real, more important" subject being served always required that the nonprint media be "curriculum-related" to the printed word. (105–106)

Rather than taking a hierarchical view of print over nonprint texts, we argue for a more inclusive framework that perceives these as complementary and not competing modes of text. With this in mind, we briefly turn to the six core concepts of ML detailed by the National Association for Media Literacy (NAML 2007):

1. All media messages are "constructed."
2. Each medium has different characteristics, strengths, and a unique "language" of construction.
3. Media messages are produced for particular purposes.
4. All media messages contain embedded values and points of view.
5. People use their individual skills, beliefs, and experiences to construct their own meanings from media messages.
6. Media and media messages can influence beliefs, attitudes, values, behaviors, and the democratic process. (3)

These principles may appear incongruous within the canonical-based framework established by the CCSS, with the "back to print" focus and use of examples from canonical literature. However, stated within the CCSS introduction is a recognition that ELA teachers should provide students with the chance to "analyze and create a high volume and extensive range of print and nonprint texts in media forms old and new" (CCSSO and NGA 2010, 4). The ML principles then, it would seem, provide a conceptual framework for incorporating that range of print and nonprint texts within ELA classrooms.

A Next Digital Scholar Approach to Media Literacy and the CCSS

In this section, we propose a framework demonstrating how ML principles and the CCSS connect (Table 7.1). Rather than attempting to identify exact matches of the language between the documents, we recommend aligning ML principles with their reading and writing counterparts in the College and Career Readiness Anchor Standards within a Venn overlap. In presenting them in this form, it is evident that these standards have more in common with each other than not. Considering the CCSS' focus on canonical literature, we intentionally use examples of literature traditionally taught in secondary ELA classrooms throughout the chapter. We do this to address the curricular reality of many ELA teachers: Canonical literature still dominates required reading lists. By using these canonical works, we want to demonstrate how it is possible to adopt a next digital scholar (NDS) approach, even when using traditional readings. We do want to acknowledge, however, that we see many titles of YA literature, contemporary fiction, and other literary works meeting the demands of the CCSS and recognize a need for teacher educators to address this gap in further scholarship. The examples we provide could be adapted using a number of noncanonical texts.

As there are only six ML principles, we use those as the framework for the discussion. For each ML principle, we include a corresponding example of a traditional and NDS activity and discuss how the examples align with the Anchor Standards for Reading and Writing. We conclude the discussion of each of the six ML principles with a section on classroom extensions suggesting variations of our examples for teachers' and librarians' use.

Please note that for ease of language, the pronoun "we" includes projects we have done in both our classes as well as those done individually. Also, all of the examples we provide were from either our high school or college classrooms. As these were students in our classroom, we use "students" to denote both adolescent and adult learners.

Table 7.1 Media Literacy and CCSS Connections

ML (NAML 2007)	CCSS Reading and Writing Anchor Standards (CCSSO and NGA 2010)	Traditional ELA Assignment	NDS Activities
1. All media messages are constructed.	*Reading:* Read closely to determine what the text says explicitly (6). *Writing:* Produce clear and coherent writing in which the development, organization, and style are appropriate to task, purpose, and audience (4)	*Reading:* Close reading of poem *Writing:* Analysis of poem essay	*Reading:* Deconstruction of film text *Writing:* Constructing a blog
2. Each medium has different characteristics, strengths, and a unique "language" of construction.	*Reading:* Interpret words and phrases as they are used in a text, including determining technical, connotative, and figurative meanings, and analyze how specific word choices shape meaning or tone (4) *Writing:* Produce clear and coherent writing in which the development, organization, and style are appropriate to task, purpose, and audience (4)	*Reading:* Literary analysis *Writing:* Five paragraph essay; critical analysis and summarization of lines from *Rome ad Juliet*	*Reading:* Film scene comparisons *Writing:* Twitter scene and character summations
3. Media messages are produced for particular purposes.	*Reading:* Analyze how and why individuals, events, and ideas develop and interact over the course of the text (3) *Writing;* Write informative/ explanatory texts to examine and convey complex ideas and information clearly and accurately through the effective selection, organization, and analysis of content (2)	*Reading:* Historical speeches *Writing:* Persuasive essay	*Reading:* Political advertisements *Writing:* Bullying PSA
4. All media messages contain embedded values and points of view.	*Reading:* Assess how point of view or purpose shapes the content and style of a text (6) *Writing:* Write arguments to support claims in an analysis of substantive topics or texts, using valid reasoning and relevant and sufficient evidence (1)	*Reading:* Character analysis *Writing:* Persuasive essay	*Reading:* Music video *Writing:* This I Believe podcast
5. People use their individual skills, beliefs, and experiences to construct their own meanings from media messages.	*Reading:* Read and comprehend complex literary and informational texts independently and proficiently (10) *Writing:* Write narratives to develop real or imagined experiences or events using effective technique, well-chosen details, and well-structured event sequences (3)	*Reading:* Historical speeches *Writing:* Literacy Narrative	*Reading:* Wiki page about a novel that they read *Writing:* Literacy Narrative using Comic Life
6. Media and media messages can influence beliefs, attitudes, values, behaviors, and the democratic process.	*Reading:* Integrate and evaluate content presented in diverse media and formats, including visually and quantitatively, as well as in words (7) *Writing:* Gather relevant information from multiple print and digital sources, assess the credibility and accuracy of each source, and integrate the information while avoiding plagiarism (8)	*Reading:* Newspaper editorials *Writing:* Research papers	*Reading:* Website URL sources *Writing:* Multigenre, Multimodal Narratives

Also note that some of the examples we present or suggest include the use of copyrighted materials. These are appropriate for school and classroom usage under "fair use."[1]

All Media Messages Are "Constructed"

Reading

One canonical poem we have used in our classrooms is "To an Athlete Dying Young" by A. E. Housman ([1896] 1985). Our discussions have included drawing attention to the carrying of an athlete in victory as well as carrying the body of the athlete in a coffin. Aspects of rhyme and meter were also discussed. In particular, the poem's iambic pentameter mimics the rhythmic footsteps of both the runner as well as the funeral procession. In analyzing these language devices, the students read the highly constructed nature of the language and language conventions of the poem. This is an example of a traditional ELA approach to what is referred to in the CCSS as "read[ing] closely to determine what the text says explicitly" (Anchor Standard for Reading 1; CCSSO and NGA 2010, 10).

Applying an NDS framework to this Anchor Standard for Reading would have the students closely reading a media text. For example, one activity that we have used in high school and college classrooms is the close reading of a movie scene. Students pay attention to the construction of the scene, including such things as examining the number of edits, the camera angles, the sounds (including voice, music, and ambient), graphics, and special effects.

We have often used the opening scene from the film *Raising Arizona* (1987) as it employs rich visual and auditory textual features. Typically, we viewed the scene twice. The first was to orient the class about the context of the scene within the film. During the second viewing, we divided students into groups looking for specific details in the "constructedness" of the film segment. One group counted the number of edits, another looked for camera techniques, and another listened for the different audio layers being used. Afterward, the small groups were asked to share their findings on an online discussion board on our class webpage. Students were able to review the small group findings prior to our next class meeting. The conversation that took place both online and in our next class meeting demonstrated a productive, close reading of the text. As this activity demonstrates, students can post their work on class blogs, wikis, websites, and so on, and their classmates can then comment on their findings. In this way, the NDS approach provides an excellent opportunity to continue discussions around close readings of texts in synchronous and nonsynchronous spaces.

Reading media texts closely for constructedness involves looking at the component aspects of the media text. For example, in reading visuals (including artwork, photography, and magazine advertisements) attention must be given to the conventions that comprise visuals: framing, color, texture, contrast, use of light and darkness, etc. The same can be done for other forms of media as well. Music, for example, can be closely read for such things as rhythm, beat, lyrics, instrumentation, and arrangement. Whatever form of media text is used, one huge benefit of closely reading a media text is that it reinforces the concept of multiple reads.

Writing

Along with the close reading of a poem example previously mentioned, a corresponding writing activity we have used asks students to compose an analytic essay detailing Housman's use of language, rhyme, meter, and scheme in the text. In this activity, we encouraged students to attend to the constructed elements of an essay, including thesis statements, previews and transitions, paragraph structure, and supporting details. In our experience with this form of writing, the teacher is the primary audience. While common, this model does not build on years of research on the writing process and the important role writing for real audiences plays in student writing development (Ede and Lunsford 1984). Moreover, the CCSS are explicit in their call for students to "produce clear and coherent writing in which the development, organization, and style are appropriate to task, purpose, and audience" (Anchor Standard for Writing 4; CCSSO and NGA 2010, 18), and this audience can and should be, on most occasions, one beyond solely the classroom teacher.

An NDS approach to writing using multimodal composing in online spaces addresses this gap. As students write their responses in a multimodal format, they are attending to the constructedness of the modes in which they are working. Moreover, such an assignment extends the audience beyond the teacher, often beyond the classroom walls. In our classrooms, students construct blogs that communicate their responses to literary texts, serve as publishing venues for their own creative work, and provide a medium in which to broadcast their own research and inquiry into teaching and learning in the 21st century. For example, in one of our teacher education classes, students were asked to create a glog (graphical blog) detailing their thoughts on a literary work and how they might approach teaching it in their own classrooms. In creating their glogs, students analyzed and selected a variety of texts including images, hyperlinks, music, videos, and words for inclusion in their projects. In making their own glogs, they attend to the constructedness of the component modes with which they are working. In this way we are asking students to "produce clear and coherent writing in which the development, organization, and style are appropriate to task, purpose, and audience" (Anchor Standard for Writing 4) while at the same time asking them to "use technology, including the internet, to produce and publish writing and to interact and collaborate with others" (Anchor Standard for Writing 6; CCSSO and NGA 2010, 18). Here, linking the CCSS with the literacy practices of digital scholars provides our students with meaningful opportunities to think through how teachers might best address the demands of the CCSS while attending to the literacy skills students will need to be "college and career ready" in the 21st century.

Classroom Extensions

Classroom teachers and media specialists can also ask students to share their analysis of a poem on a class blog by constructing a multimodal response and posting it online. Media specialists and classroom teachers could co-teach a lesson on the various blogging platforms available for student use and help students set up and navigate through their blogs, teaching them how to design their blogs as well as post and edit content on their blogs and other aspects of composing in online spaces. This multimodal assignment would involve any combination of media, including words, images, music, hyperlinks, and video clips, that reflect the students' analysis. For example, a student's multimodal analysis of William Carlos Williams's poem "The Red Wheelbarrow" ([1923] 1985) might focus on how the poem represents values of the imagist movement in poetry, the utilitarian nature of the wheelbarrow as well as the setting of the poem itself. Teachers and media specialists might ask students to embed a contemporary photograph or video clip that they think relates to their interpretation of the poem. In these instances librarians can teach a mini-lesson on copyright, evaluation of online resources, and other relevant aspects of information literacy. Students would then be asked to comment on at least two of their classmates' posts and discuss the connections they see between the photograph and/or video clip their peers included in their interpretations.

Finally, students could then explain the connections they made between the poem and images they included as a follow-up activity and compare their reasoning to their classmates' comments. Again, these 21st-century literacy activities are especially important, as students will be required to do more work with digital technologies in college and throughout their careers. It is important for teachers and media specialists to note that these activities still do meet the demands of the CCSS. Here, for instance, students meet the requirements outlined in Anchor Standard for Writing 8, for they are asked to "gather relevant information from multiple print and digital sources … and integrate the information" (CCSSO and NGA 2010, 18).

Each Medium Has Different Characteristics, Strengths, and a Unique "Language" of Construction
Reading

In teaching Shakespeare in our ELA classes, one way we examined the text was to look at the constructedness of language. Most of our students were not familiar with conventions of either Elizabethan English or theatre. Thus, we spent time examining different ways Shakespeare used language along with various theatrical customs, including script conventions, soliloquies, and stage directions. In teaching *Julius Caesar* ([ca. 1599] 1969b), for example, we engaged students in staging the assassination scene (3.1), so that they could envision how the text's stage directions and language helped convey the scene. Thus, examining *how* something was said (i.e., the language and theatre conventions), helped students figure out *what* was said.

Using an NDS variation of this concept involves having students analyze the constructedness of film texts. In this activity, multiple versions of the same film scene were posted to our class iTunes U site where the students could compare ways in which the directors used the language of film as a means to interpret the passage. For example, in teaching *Hamlet* ([ca. 1602] 1969a) we highlighted the scene (3.3) in which Claudius confesses to the murder of his brother. Hamlet observes Claudius praying but does not hear the content. We provided three different versions of the same scene in order to compare interpretations. We posted a graphic organizer on a Google Doc that had three columns, one for each film. While each version shared the same content, each director made choices regarding their representation of that passage. For example, the Michael Almereyda version (2000) put the emphasis on Claudius, cutting Hamlet's dialogue completely. The Franco Zeffirelli version (1990) emphasized Hamlet, with Claudius on the periphery. Kenneth Branagh (1996) included the entire text of the scene, emphasizing both characters. Through looking at all three, students examined what text the directors included/omitted, camera angles, audio conventions, costuming, lighting, etc. In analyzing the constructedness of film, students were able to see how altering the language of film affected how the scene could be interpreted. Moreover, students saw that there were a number of valid interpretations of the same scene. The NDS twist on traditional ML film activity had the students conducting this class conversation in a nonsynchronous environment by individually accessing the film clips through iTunes U and posting their collective responses and observations on a class Google Doc. Doing a similar activity with the clips on YouTube, as we suggest with the following example, would also take students' work further out into the digital landscape.

Classroom Extensions

Given the number of different film adaptions of canonical texts, teachers have a tremendous selection from which to choose. Teachers often feel obligated to show the entire film, yet selectively viewing key scenes is a powerful use of movies in the classroom. The film scene can be read along with the text or, as with the earlier example, multiple versions of the same scene can be compared. Finding these clips is relatively easy through sites such as YouTube. Though some versions are not posted due to studio copyright issues, there is a tremendous repertoire of scenes from movies adapted from books available online.

Librarians can be an important resource in this regard, particularly in identifying film clips and advocating the appropriate use of media texts to the district. As schools often limit and/or block sites such as YouTube, librarians and media specialists could offer a workshop for students and teachers to help them navigate the school's internet policy and locate the appropriate film clips for the lesson. In addition, there are programs that allow downloading online clips. These could then be saved to a portable drive or embedded in a PowerPoint presentation to be viewed in those classrooms that do not have internet access.

Writing

Reading comprehension can be a problem for students when studying Shakespeare's plays. Students often lament that Shakespeare's use of language is difficult to understand and prevents them from enjoying the play and fully understanding the plot and themes the play addresses. One traditional example of attempting to support our students' understanding of a Shakespearean play like *Romeo and Juliet* (ca. 1597/1969c) was to offer them opportunities to summarize passages in their own words or engage them in writing activities that ask them to rewrite scenes using "modern" English. In this case, students read passages from the original text and rewrote those passages in the common everyday language of today.

Using Twitter is an NDS approach attending to the constructedness of writing as the form deals with communicating with 140 characters or less. These tweets can be tagged and shared with a global audience. Tagging allows Twitter users the opportunity to search for posts related to their interests. This process is referred to as *hashtagging*, a term related to the practice of placing a hash mark (#) before the words used to tag the post. For example, an ELA teacher might search for Twitter users' posts related to *Romeo and Juliet* by searching for the term *#romeoandjuliet* on the Twitter website or mobile app. All public tweets tagged *#romeoandjuliet* will then appear (see Chapter 10 by R. Spencer

Atkinson in this volume for other NDS approaches to teaching *Romeo and Juliet*).

In order to help the pre-service teachers in our ELA Education Methods courses develop instructional practices that use Twitter as a teaching tool, we asked them to tweet scenes from *Romeo and Juliet*. Students were placed in groups and assigned a scene and character from one specific act of the play. Students were then asked to assume the role of that character and tweet versions of their lines from the play. In this way, each group "acted" out their scene on Twitter through a series of tweets that sought to convey the meaning of the language as well as the plot of the scene. Students were asked to provide hashtags that captured the mood of the character or identified the larger ideas, themes, and issues at work during the scene. For example, after having previously declared his love for the unseen character Rosaline, Romeo falls in love with Juliet at first sight, announcing, "Oh she doth teach the torches to burn bright" (1.4.44). To engage our students in deeper thinking, we asked them to tweet this scene in their own words. We modeled the activity using Romeo's quote, asking students to rephrase his declaration in their own words and adding hashtags that either captured the subtext of the scene (*#loveatfirstsight*) or illustrated their understanding of Romeo's character (*#fickleteen*). The conventions of 140 characters in Twitter required that they use language in a parsimonious manner. As such, they had to pay close attention to how they constructed their tweets.

Classroom Extensions

Before beginning the project, librarians and teachers should co-teach a lesson on how to set up and use Twitter. During the lesson students should be made aware of their "digital footprint," and other aspects of posting and sharing personal information and other content online. As such, media specialists and ELA teachers can help students further develop information literacy while supporting their learning of classroom content.

Using tweets as a writing activity can be used with any work of fiction (or any text for that matter, including student texts). Students can, for example, tweet scenes from John Steinbeck's *Of Mice and Men*

([1937] 1993) to demonstrate their understanding of the plot. Close readings, however, call for careful attention to the words as well as the subtext of a literary work. In this case, hashtags are particularly useful in determining students' reading comprehension. Not only are they asked to read and understand the printed word in their tweets, they are asked to read the subtext of the scene or passage and demonstrate their close reading through the use of appropriate hashtags. More so, the CCSS stipulates in Anchor Standard for Writing 4 that students should "[p]roduce clear and coherent writing in which the development, organization, and style are appropriate to task, purpose, and audience" (CCSSO and NGA 2010, 18). Twitter's limit of 140 characters per post will help students develop as writers by compelling them to choose their words carefully in order to communicate their ideas. ELA teachers are often asking students to be attentive to the words they choose when they write, and Twitter provides a useful platform to explore that practice.

Media Messages Are Produced for Particular Purposes
Reading

With this principle, one traditional approach we have taken is reading historical speeches. For example, in our classes, we have had students read Martin Luther King Jr.'s *I Have a Dream* speech (1963). In addition to reading the text, we studied the historical, geographical, and social context in which it was delivered. In examining the situated nature of the text, students examined the various purposes of King's speech and the impact it made on society. In doing so, students "analyze how and why individuals, events, and ideas develop and interact over the course of a text" (Anchor Standard for Reading 3; CCSSO and NGA 2010, 10).

An NDS variation of reading historical speeches is similar to the media reading exercises mentioned previously. However, we suggest using other texts, such as political advertisements, as well. The activity could examine the production features of a political ad and seek to determine how well they convey the ad's purpose. One example we have used is George H. Bush's presidential ad, "Family/Children"

(1988). The spot features sparse political footage and instead focuses on numerous images of Bush surrounded by extended family and friends at social gatherings, juxtaposed with the reoccurring slow-motion image of him holding up his baby granddaughter. The voiceover by his wife tells the audience what a good man he is, how he is respected by a wide range of people, and how important family is to him. Our classes discussed how the intent of this ad focused on the character and personality (ethos) of the candidate rather than political issues (logos). During discussions, students indicated that this ad appeared to be an attempt to humanize a man who was having difficulty connecting to a portion of the voting public.

Advertisements can be rich texts for teaching audience and intent. Teachers can select from print ads in magazines or ads from commercial TV. Many current and classic commercials as well as images of print campaigns are available online. Teachers may have students read these through the perspectives of potential audiences. They also may want to have students pay close attention to audio in commercial texts, as the music and sounds selected are often subtle but powerful audience cues. Librarians can be helpful in compiling websites and archives that contain a variety of advertising examples. These can range from content and subject matter to stylistic examples. In addition, older magazines are great repositories for examples of print advertising that teachers and students can use to cut out and analyze.

Writing

A writing activity we used had students identifying a social issue (school, community, state, nation, and/or international) they felt needed to be changed. With this activity, students wrote a variation of a persuasive paper in which they selected an issue of concern, found appropriate support, and then wrote it up. We had students peer-edit each others' drafts and turn the final version in to us.

An NDS variation of this type of writing we used was to have students produce a public service announcement (PSA) video. Traditionally, PSAs have been 30-second TV spots providing identification and commentary of a social problem, such as littering, smoking, and drinking and driving. Using the TV format of PSAs as a guide, we had students identify a social issue and create a video. One example of this is when our students created responses to bullying. Working in small groups, the students identified a specific aspect of bullying, such as physical, verbal, or cyber. They found information, researched pertinent statistics, wrote their script, and shot and edited their videos. The audience for the PSAs went beyond the teacher as the viewership included the class, the school, and the community through the local public access TV channel.

Classroom Extensions

Librarians can help provide a range of samples of topical PSAs. Finding good models, guidelines, and rubrics for PSAs can provide teachers with a variety of examples from which to begin such a project. Teachers and media specialists may also reach a potential global audience by publishing student work on YouTube, a class website, blog, or wiki. In this aspect, as teachers and librarians collaborate in having their classes create PSAs, librarians can help create an online database that shares and features PSAs. As noted earlier, we use iTunes U as a way to host and share class work. Posting student work in an online space allows for the storage, organization, and control of student-created content.

Teachers can also use PSAs in tandem with the literature being read in their classroom. Creating PSAs is an excellent way for ELA teachers and media specialists to address the CCSS by ensuring that students "write informative/explanatory texts to examine and convey complex ideas and information clearly and accurately through the effective selection, organization, and analysis of content" (Anchor Standard for Writing 2; CCSSO and NGA 2010, 18). As readings tend to bring up social issues, the PSA assignment can be tailored to those present in the literature. For example, one teacher in a local school district was studying the industrial revolution. Her students created PSAs dealing with the social conditions, such as child labor, housing, and working environments. Another local teacher had students create PSA posters on date rape after their class read the YA novel *Speak* (Anderson 1999). Both classes had their work displayed throughout the school or shared online. Through using the formats of PSAs, both teachers were able to have their students craft a persuasive argument as well as provide a broader audience for their work.

All Media Messages Contain Embedded Values and Points of View
Reading

Analyzing characters in literary works is a staple of the ELA curriculum. For example, one traditional approach to examining a canonical text we have used is a close reading of Steinbeck's *Of Mice and Men* ([1937] 1993). We asked students to examine how Steinbeck portrayed the only female character, Curly's wife, in his novella through his use of imagery, dialogue, setting, and other literary devices. Students completed a worksheet identifying those literary devices in the text and explained their answers. In doing so, students were introduced to feminist criticism and asked to use this lens to examine Steinbeck's story in a formal essay at the end of the unit.

Analyzing a music video is an NDS approach to examining embedded values and points of view. In our courses, we often pair the critical analysis of a popular music video with the study of canonical literature. We use these pairings to model how different modalities of texts can be used to support critical examinations of literature. One example we used was comparing Katy Perry's "California Gurls" (2010) with Steinbeck's *Of Mice and Men*. We watched the video and discussed the images of women it portrays through its constructedness (camera angles, set designs, costumes, lighting, etc.). In the ensuing conversations, students identified instances of objectification and sexual imagery they saw at work in the video. Students then used the basis of those discussions as a framework to examine *Of Mice and Men* in a similar way. Our class examined the language Steinbeck used to describe Curly's wife, noting the specific language about her (including the descriptive adverbs Steinbeck used to describe her gestures and her lack of a proper name) that demonstrated a point of view about this female character. Students explored the principle of embedded values in texts, and in doing so, "[a]ssess[ed] how point of view or purpose shapes the content and style of a text" (Anchor Standard for Reading 6; CCSSO and NGA 2010, 10).

Classroom Extensions

Common digital technologies readily available in networked classrooms and libraries make a wide range of popular culture texts accessible for instructional purposes. Students can analyze popular music videos and then compare and contrast those texts with other canonical works of literature. Teachers can look for intersections of popular culture and the literature they are teaching. While music videos remain an important tool to support and encourage students, close readings of other popular culture texts are also useful, including film, television, and commercials. Given the amount of information available through the internet, librarians are an important collaborator on such projects. Media specialists and classroom teachers can develop curricular materials together. When working within an NDS framework, familiarity with texts (both canonical and popular), online resources, and other media are quite valuable. Helping teachers choose texts that compliment and complicate inquiry in their classrooms is an important component in creating a rich classroom environment of close reading. Teachers and media specialists can work together to co-teach lessons on conducting online research and accessing content through various websites.

Writing

Like literary analysis, persuasive writing is common to ELA and college writing classrooms. Students are required to take a position on a topic, gather supporting evidence, organize the material in a sensible way, and write a paper that seeks to persuade an audience. Students are asked to select a position on a controversial topic and write their opinion on it as supported and illustrated by their research. To encourage critical thinking in this process, we require students to investigate other viewpoints and to include those in their paper.

Like most other traditional writing assignments, teachers tend to be the primary audience for these persuasive papers. An NDS approach to this genre of writing is to have students create podcasts based on their persuasive writing. For example, we have used a variation of *This I Believe* with our teacher educators. Edward R. Murrow started *This I Believe* in 1951 in order to create public statements on what various Americans, both famous and ordinary citizens, believe. National Public Radio revived the radio format, and a number of the earlier statements were published online (Allison and Gediman 2006).

The format of the *This I Believe* essay is similar to a persuasive paper: Students are asked to make a statement and provide necessary support. In doing so, students "[w]rite arguments ... using valid reasoning and relevant and sufficient evidence" (Anchor Standard for Writing 1; CCSSO and NGA 2010, 18). Students began the assignment by reading a number of *This I Believe* essays from the website, before writing one that stated a deeply held value about education. They then used audio programs such as the free program Audacity or Apple's Garage Band to create podcasts of their essays. In doing so, they focused not only on the writing, but also on the spoken word performance of their work. We found that as students heard their writing in spoken form, they often edited their texts to improve the overall delivery. We then created an archive of these podcasts to make available for our entire class. In addition, we created a forum on a discussion board where students responded to the content of other classmates' podcasts.

Classroom Extensions

Media specialists and classroom teachers can work together to help students conduct research on their topic, investigating differing positions and collecting and evaluating supporting evidence on all sides of the issue. Students can create podcasts on any number of topics or issues, making it a good companion to persuasive writing. One approach ELA teachers can capitalize on through the use of podcasts is the teaching of *voice*. Students often have a difficult time understanding this concept through print. However, in connecting their spoken word to their written work, teachers can use the audio conventions as a means to help students understand how voice works with the printed word. In fact, it is not unusual for students to revise their essays as they perform their podcasts because they hear awkward phrasings and other difficult passages in their writing.

People Use Their Individual Skills, Beliefs, and Experiences to Construct Their Own Meanings From Media Messages
Reading

For this principle, where people construct meaning from media messages based on their own backgrounds and beliefs, a traditional approach we have used is to ask students to read an historical speech such as the Gettysburg Address. Specifically, we have had them examine Lincoln's use of parsimony in the speech and then asked them to cite relevant evidence from the text to support their argument about the speech.

An NDS approach might ask students to create a wiki page about the speech. While many wikis are text based, they also use multimedia, including video, photography, and hyperlinks to communicate meaning. We used a wiki project on Lincoln's famous speech to have students investigate the president's use of parsimony and cite relevant evidence from the speech to support their argument. We next attempted to deepen students' engagement with this activity by asking them to include examples of uses of parsimony in popular media. In this case, students included a section on the use of concise language in modern advertising. Here, they were able to use television commercials, magazine advertisements, and various types of web content to develop and support their argument. In doing so, they demonstrated the ability to "read and comprehend complex literary and informational texts independently and proficiently" (Anchor Standard for Reading 10; CCSSO and NGA 2010, 10).

Classroom Extensions

Teachers and librarians can collaborate to help students research other historical and contemporary speeches for comparison. For example, when studying Lincoln's speech, it can be compared to Aristotle's appeals of argument (ethos, logos, and pathos) and then framed for classroom inquiry as a series of questions posed to students: How does

Lincoln use ethos, logos and pathos in his address? What was Lincoln's purpose for delivering the speech? Was Lincoln aware of his audience? How do we know? Students can be asked to cite relevant information from the text to back up their arguments. Teachers and librarians could then turn to contemporary political speeches, commercials, and online argumentative and persuasive texts asking students to engage in similar analysis.

Students could then create wikis that detail their analysis of how Aristotle's framework has been used across a wide variety of historical and contemporary texts. As creating and maintaining online content such as wikis can be overwhelming, librarians can assist students and teachers in developing their wikis. Students can also include hyperlinks and/or embed video files and other media to illustrate their ideas. In addition, students can research other historical and contemporary speeches for similar features and post their findings to their wikis.

Writing

Students also construct meaning through personal experience, and this meaning-making can be brought out through a literacy narrative assignment in the ELA classroom. Karen Gallas (2003) defines the latter as "unique, usually unarticulated and unexamined stories that represent cultural perspectives on learning, culled from home, the public world, and past experiences on classrooms" (140). Our use of literacy narratives have asked our students to consider who they are as readers and writers, and to explain the role that language and story have played in their lives. We ask them to consider memorable moments, favorite texts (books, movies, magazines, etc.), and other defining points in their literacy journey.

An NDS variation of the written literacy narrative we have used is to have teachers create their narratives using the program Comic Life, a comic book-like word processor, in which student writers have a number of visual conventions in addition to traditional narrative at their disposal. Users shape the frames on the page, access their digital photo library, manipulate the photos with special effects, select speech/thought bubbles, and add various text boxes. We have found that in focusing on these different compositional choices, students attend to their stories in different ways, considering what aspects can be told visually and what aspects need written clarification. Some of our students scanned actual photos for their narratives. However, other students who did not have access to photos from events in their lives often reconstructed the events by recreating scenes and recording them using a digital video camera. Students also used images from online sources. Even though students did not take these photos or create the images, they still made complex compositional decisions with their selection and integration of existing images. Regardless of the technique for content creation, students used multiple modes in order to narrate an aspect of their lives. In doing so, they addressed the CCSS directive to "[w]rite narratives to develop real or imagined experiences or events using effective technique, well-chosen details, and well-structured event sequences" (Anchor Standard for Writing 3; CCSSO and NGA 2010, 18).

As with our video files, we have used the Dropbox feature in iTunes U to create a repository of Comic Life literacy narratives so that we can compile a number of stylistic and content variations as examples. In addition, this feature allows us to extend the audience beyond our classroom walls.

Classroom Extensions

Again, these classroom activities provide librarians and classroom teachers meaningful opportunities to help students develop information literacy. Media specialists and ELA teachers can co-teach lessons focused on the ethical use of online content, examining fair-use policies and copyright laws, and investigating online resources that offer copyright free materials for students to use when working on their multimodal compositions. Media specialists will also be of tremendous help in providing support in two ways. The first is to check for purchasing and licensing of programs such as Comic Life. However, there are also online programs (some free) that have similar features as the paid programs. The second way is to consider photo options for classroom use. These include access to DV still cameras, internet access to online photo archives that offer non-copyrighted photos for student use, as well as scanners to convert print photos to digital copies.

Media and Media Messages Can Influence Beliefs, Attitudes, Values, Behaviors, and the Democratic Process
Reading

A traditional manner in which we have approached this sixth ML principle, which reinforces that media messages influence democratic processes, is to use editorials from newspapers and magazines as means of examining issues of fact and opinion. Editorials are current and offer a variety of topical interests that can be chosen from community, regional, and national publications. We have had students read these relatively short pieces and prompted them to consider how the editorial uses a mix of fact and opinion for the purpose of swaying attitudes in the format of a published column.

One way we have varied the editorial assignment in an NDS approach is to examine website sources as a means to critique credibility. A specific activity we have used is to look at an issue through the different URL sources such as .com, .org, .gov, and .edu. In doing so, students "[i]ntegrate and evaluate content presented in diverse media and formats, including visually and quantitatively, as well as in words" (Anchor Standard for Reading 7; CCSSO and NGA 2010, 10). For example, one Google search we did with a class on this topic of environmental issues yielded the following results:

- The Department of Environmental Services (.gov) website offering state-generated information and resources
- A university's agricultural program website (.edu) that offered research and training programs
- An organization (.org) dedicated to environmental conservation awareness and advocacy
- A news site (.com) that focused its content on environmental issues

The sheer volume of information available online is often overwhelming for students. For example, when our class entered the search term *environment* in Google, it registered 380,000,000 hits. Therefore, reading the URL and recognizing the differences between governmental, educational, organizational, and commercial websites is an important skill.

Classroom Extensions

Librarians have traditionally played a vital role in helping students learn how to conduct print-based research. Using an NDS approach, librarians and ELA teachers can work together to help students become critical consumers as they evaluate online information and websites. Librarians can introduce students to various databases they can use during their research. In addition, they can teach students how to conduct online searches using keywords, quotation marks, and Boolean search terms. Classes can examine and evaluate information from online sources together and learn to ask meaningful, critical questions about the information they find online.

Reading URL sources can be easily adapted to a variety of lessons. ELA teachers can take an issue that has multiple perspectives and examine how the different URL sites approach the topic. Reading the material, layout, graphics, text-flow, and commercial content all provide students with critical tools to navigate the internet, arguably their number one source of information.

Writing

We have used variations of the traditional research paper in numerous ways over the years. No matter what the topic of the day was, the process usually followed this procedure: Students select a topic, conduct research (which can include print or internet sources as well as interviews with experts), and compile the research into an organized written product. Students, of course, may not find this to be the most interesting or engaging process.

An NDS composition entails our students composing in a multigenre format. Tom Romano (2000) defines multigenre writing as a text "composed of many genres and subgenres, each piece self-contained, making a point of its own, yet connected by theme or topic and sometimes by language, images and content" (x–xi). For example, in a writing methods course, our pre-service teachers were assigned this prompt: "Who are you as a teacher of writing?" In answering that question, students were required to use at least five genres. Using iBook Author (a free app on the Mac platform), our class created an anthology of their responses in the form of an EPUB. One course assignment was to videotape themselves teaching a writing lesson and edit the video into a 2-minute synopsis. Most teachers embedded that video in their responses, a feature not possible with traditional research papers. Thus, the affordances of the EPUB format allowed for the integration of print, visuals, and videos. What resulted was a multimodal, multigenre response that explored the notion of their identity as a writing teacher. Once again, as with other NDS writing assignments, the audience for the research papers went beyond us as teachers. Since these were compiled into an electronic version of a class anthology, the entire classroom viewed the final versions. Moreover, since we published the anthology in the iBooks store, the potential audience was well beyond our classroom walls.

Classroom Extensions

ELA teachers can vary this assignment quite a bit. The multigenre essay can be composed entirely with print sources, just varying the genre of responses.[2] Depending on the research requirements, teachers may want to consider the different compositional, viewing, and sharing affordances that EPUB formats (like iBook) offer. Students can take videos of their interviews or topics and embed them within their document. The multigenre format still affords the same components as a research paper, but incorporates multiple modes and sources to do so. In doing so, students address the CCSS' directive to "gather relevant information from multiple print and digital sources, assess the credibility and accuracy of each source, and integrate the information while avoiding plagiarism" (Anchor Standard for Writing 8; CCSSO and NGA 2010, 18). The latter issue is particularly advantageous with multigenre research. Using this approach to the research paper makes plagiarism a relatively minor issue as each piece has to be tailored specifically for the topic. While the content of the paper stays much the same, the format is customized according to genre conventions (i.e., recipe, advertisement, want ad, etc.). Because of this, it makes traditional "cut and paste" plagiarism nearly impossible.

Conclusion

Throughout our careers as teachers, we have used with our students each of the traditional and NDS reading and writing activities we have described in this chapter. In doing so, we have found worth in applying the intellectual and scholarly activities valued by the traditional approach to ELA instruction. Drawing from an already long history of collaboration, ELA and ML educators can inform each other's work in developing instructional frameworks that encourage and support close readings and compositions of texts of all kinds while at the same time meeting the requirements of the CCSS. Our work using core ML principles within the ELA education classroom helps underscore how teachers might approach implementing the CCSS while remaining true to research-based, pedagogically sound practices. In fact, the ML approach is a necessary balance to the print-centric tone of the CCSS. Given the wording of a passage from the introduction, the CCSS seem to condone this sort of approach: "Teachers are thus free to provide students with whatever tools and knowledge their professional judgment and experience identify as most helpful for meeting the goals set out in the Standards" (CCSSO and NGA 2010, 4). This passage, which explicitly acknowledges that teachers can use "whatever tools and knowledge their professional judgment and experience identify as most helpful," gives us hope that under the CCSS teachers will continue to have the professional license to choose which activities and texts will most meaningfully engage students.

Endnotes

1. "Fair use" is defined by the Center for Social Media (2009) as "the right to use copyrighted material without permission or payment under some circumstances—especially when the cultural or social benefits of the use are predominant" (1).

2. See users.muohio.edu/romanots for examples of assignments, papers, and rubrics.

References

Allison, Jay, and Dan Gediman. 2006. *This I Believe: The Personal Philosophies of Remarkable Men and Women*. New York: Henry Holt.

Alvermann, Donna E., ed. 2005. *Adolescents and Literacies in a Digital World*. New York: Peter Lang.

Alvermann, Donna E., Jennifer S. Moon, and Margaret C. Hagood. 1999. *Popular Culture in the Classroom: Teaching and Researching Critical Media Literacy*. Newark, DE; Chicago, IL: International Reading Association.

Anderson, Laurie Halse. 1999. *Speak*. New York: Farrar Straus Giroux.

Applebee, Arthur N. 1974. *Tradition and Reform in the Teaching of English: A History*. Urbana, IL: National Council of Teachers of English.

Barnes, Walter. 1932. "A Curriculum of Literature Experiences." *English Journal* 21 (3): 191–199.

Bates, Herbert. 1912. "The School and Current Fiction." *English Journal* 1 (1): 15–23.

Beach, Richard, and David G. O'Brien. 2008. "Teaching Popular-Culture Texts in the Classroom." In *Handbook of Research on New Literacies*, edited by Julie Coiro, Michele Knobel, Colin Lankshear, and Donald J. Leu, 775–804. New York: Routledge.

Bourdieu, Pierre. 1986. "The Forms of Capital." In *Handbook of Theory and Research for the Sociology of Education*, edited by John Richardson, 241–258. Westport, CT: Greenwood.

Brauer, Lydia, and Caroline T. Clark. 2008. "The Trouble Is English: Reframing English Studies in Secondary Schools." *English Education* 40 (4): 292–313.

Bush, George H. 1988. *Children/Family*. George Bush Presidential Library. 4PresidentTV. Accessed February 10, 2014. tv.4president.us/tv1988.htm.

Center for Social Media. 2009. *The Code of Best Practices in Fair Use for Media Literacy Education*. Accessed February 10, 2014. www.centerforsocialmedia.org/fair-use/related-materials/codes/code-best-practices-fair-use-media-literacy-education.

Christenbury, Leila, Randy Bomer, and Peter Smagorinsky. 2009. *Handbook of Adolescent Literacy Research*. New York: The Guilford Press.

Costanzo, William. 1992. *Reading the Movies: Twelve Great Films on Video and How to Teach Them*. Urbana, IL: National Council of Teachers of English.

Council of Chief State School Officers and National Governors Association. 2010. *Common Core State Standards for English Language Arts and Literacy in History/Social Studies, Science, and Technical Subjects*. Washington, DC: National Governors Association Center for Best Practices, Council of Chief State School Officers. Accessed February 10, 2014. www.corestandards.org/assets/CCSSI_ELA%20Standards.pdf.

Cushman, Janet. 1973. "'Old Radio' in the English Class: It Can't Miss!" *English Journal* 62 (2): 244–249.

Ede, Lisa, and Andrea Lunsford. 1984. "Audience Addressed/Audience Invoked: The Role of Audience in Composition Theory and Pedagogy." *College Composition and Communication* 35 (2): 155–171.

Foster, Harold. 1979. *The New Literacy: The Language of Film and Television*. Urbana, IL: National Council of Teachers of English.

Gallas, Karen. 2003. *Imagination and Literacy: A Teacher's Search for the Heart of Learning*. New York: Teachers College Press.

Gee, James. 2007. *What Video Games Have to Teach Us About Learning and Literacy*. Rev. ed. New York: Palgrave Macmillan.

Gerrish, Carolyn. 1915. "The Relation of Moving Pictures to English Composition." *English Journal* 4 (4): 226–230.

Hamlet. 1990. Directed by Franco Zeffirelli. Burbank, CA: Warner Home Video, 2004. DVD.

———. 1996. Directed by Kenneth Branagh. Burbank, CA: Warner Home Video, 2007. DVD.

———. 2000. Directed by Michael Almereyda. Burbank, CA: Buena Vista Home Entertainment, 2001. DVD.

Housman, A. E. (1896) 1985. "To an Athlete Dying Young." Reprint, *English Journal* 74 (2): 75.

Hull, Glenda, and Katherine Schultz. 2002. *School's Out! Bridging Out-of-School Literacies With Classroom Practice*. New York: Teachers College Press.

King, Jr., Martin Luther. 1963. "I Have a Dream." Speech, Lincoln Memorial, Washington, DC, August 28. American Rhetoric. Accessed February 10, 2014. www.americanrhetoric.com/speeches/mlkihaveadream.htm.

Kliebard, Herbert. 2004. *The Struggle for the American Curriculum: 1893–1958*. 3rd ed. New York: Routledge.

Moje, Elizabeth Birr, Josephine Peyton Young, John E. Readence, and David W. Moore. 2000. "Reinventing Adolescent Literacy for New Times: Perennial and Millennial Issues." *Journal of Adolescent and Adult Literacy* 43 (5): 400–410.

Monaco, James. 1981. *How to Read a Film: The Art, Technology, Language, History and Theory of Film and Media*. New York: Oxford University Press.

National Association for Media Literacy Education. 2007. *Core Principles of Media Literacy Education in the United States*. Accessed February 10, 2014. namle.net/wp-content/uploads/2013/01/CorePrinciples.pdf.

O'Sullivan, Jr., Eugene J. 1962. "What the English Teacher Should Know about Film and Television Drama." In *An English Teacher Reader: Grades 7 Through 12*, edited by M. Jerry Weiss, 73–84. New York: The Odyssey Press.

Perry, Katy. 2010. "California Gurls." Directed by Matthew Cullen. YouTube. Accessed February 10, 2014. bit.ly/swwwDw.

Raising Arizona. 1987. Directed by Joel Coen and Ethan Coen. Los Angeles: 20th Century Fox, 2002. DVD.

Romano, Tom. 2000. *Blending Genre, Altering Style: Writing Multigenre Papers*. Portsmouth, NH: Heinemann.

Rosenblatt, Louise M. 1994. *The Reader, the Text, the Poem: The Transactional Theory of the Literary Work*. Carbondale, IL: Southern Illinois University Press.

Ruth, Deborah Dashow. 1977. "The Next Language Arts: Views of Nonprint Media." In *The Teaching of English*, edited by James R. Squire, 96–125. Chicago: University of Chicago Press.

Scholes, Robert. 1998. *The Rise and Fall of English: Reconstructing English as a Discipline*. New Haven, CT: Yale University Press.

Shakespeare, William. (ca. 1602) 1969a. *Hamlet, Prince of Denmark*. In *William Shakespeare: The Complete Works*, edited by Alfred Harbage. New York: Viking Press.

———. (ca. 1599) 1969b. *The Tragedy of Julius Caesar*. In *William Shakespeare: The Complete Works*, edited by Alfred Harbage. New York: Viking Press.

———. (ca. 1597) 1969c. *The Tragedy of Romeo and Juliet*. In *William Shakespeare: The Complete Works*, edited by Alfred Harbage. New York: Viking Press.

Snyder, Ilana, and Scott Bulfin. 2008. "Using New Media in the Secondary English Classroom." In *Handbook of Research on New Literacies*, edited by Julie Coiro, Michele Knobel, Colin Lankshear, and Donald J. Leu, 805–837. New York: Routledge.

Squire, James R. 2003. "The History of the Profession." In *Handbook of Research on Teaching the English Language Arts*, 2nd ed., edited by James Flood, Diane Lapp, James R. Squire, and Julie M. Jensen, 3–17. Mahwah, NJ: Lawrence Erlbaum Associates.

Steinbeck, John. (1937) 1993. *Of Mice and Men*. Reprint, New York: Viking Penguin.

Williams, William Carlos. (1923) 1985. "The Red Wheelbarrow." In *William Carlos Williams: Selected Poems*, edited by Charles Tomlinson. New York: New Directions.

PART THREE

Classroom Assignments to Meet the Common Core State Standards

CHAPTER **8**

Browsing With Intent
Digital Information Literacy and Distant Reading Practices

Laura J. Davies

The internet hasn't merely affected how students conduct research—it has upended how our students think about research. It's easy, as teachers and librarians who remember relying on printed books, bound journals, and library shelves and archives for our own research projects, to dismiss our students' digitally mediated research processes as lacking in rigor and deficient in depth. I have my own qualms about their seemingly exclusive reliance on pixels: I fear it leads our students to believe that the only information that's worthy of their attention is found on a computer (or a cell phone) screen. The anecdotes we've heard in hallways about students' digital research habits could be pieced together to form a compelling case against some of the research habits of this digital generation.

Until recently, anecdotes were all we really had to form opinions and develop strategies to target the information literacy needs of our students. However, in June 2012, the British Library and the Joint Information Systems Committee (Jisc), an organization in the U.K. that investigates the adoption and use of digital technologies, published a report on their longitudinal joint study that examined doctoral students' attitudes and habits of research. Their research, which was based on three annual surveys of more than 17,000 doctoral students at 72 higher education institutions, sheds considerable light on how Generation Y, or NextGen, graduate students (those born between 1982 and 1994) find information and conduct research. One of their most significant findings is that the most valuable information source for these students is the ejournal, or digitally available journal articles (Jisc and British Library 2012, 6). Related to that finding are two others: One, other than ejournals, Google was the most often used information source across all disciplines, and, two, if students were unable to access the full-text of a journal article through an online database, more than half the students stated that they would make do with the abstract instead of searching for alternative means to access the full-text (6, 23).

Though the study focuses on doctoral students, I believe its conclusions are valuable to secondary school teachers and librarians. If doctoral students turn regularly to Google and rely on digitally mediated resources and secondary sources over printed texts, archival documents, and other primary sources, as the Jisc and the British Library research concludes, then I think it's likely that our middle school and high school students, our next digital scholars, depend just as much (maybe more?) on both Google and other online resources for their research. Additionally, I think it's disturbing that doctoral students choose not to follow up on their digital research, to locate the full text of the articles that aren't available in the database they are using. Or, perhaps it's not a matter of choice. It might be that they lack the skills and strategies of an inquiry research process. If graduate students reach an impasse in their research when scholarship is unavailable online, then it seems likely that secondary students have difficulty knowing how to track down sources that are not immediately accessible digitally.

I believe, however, that it would be preemptive to see our students' digital research habits negatively only because they don't match the methods we were taught and believe credible. To this end, this chapter explores the digital research habits our secondary school students bring to the classroom in order to determine how their intuitive online behaviors might be harnessed and extended to deepen their digital information literacy. Specifically, this chapter investigates the digital behavior of browsing, an online habit regularly practiced among the current generation of secondary school students. In this chapter, I analyze how our students browse through search engines and databases and, with screenshots, show what kinds of information are uncovered in the process of browsing. I then offer ways teachers and librarians can help students in their classrooms browse more purposefully and productively. I argue in this essay that we, as educators, can use our students' browsing skills to introduce them to practices of distant reading that can help them become more critically aware of the information they find online.

Distant Reading, Close Reading, and the Common Core State Standards

The Common Core State Standards (CCSS) for English Language Arts (ELA) emphasize the importance of building students' information literacy skills, especially in grades 7–12. Specifically, in the standards for writing, educators need to ensure students demonstrate competence in several related kinds of research and evaluative skills (Council of Chief State School Officers [CCSSO] and National Governors Association [NGA] 2010):

- Conduct short as well as more sustained research projects to answer a question (including a self-generated question) or solve a problem; narrow or broaden the inquiry when appropriate; synthesize multiple sources on the subject, demonstrating understanding of the subject under investigation. (W.9–10.7)

- Gather relevant information from multiple authoritative print and digital sources, using advanced searches effectively; assess the usefulness of each source in answering the research question; integrate information into the text selectively to

> maintain the flow of ideas, avoiding plagiarism and following a standard format for citation. (W.9–10.8)

The cultivation of *online distant reading skills*, a term I define as learning how to systematically investigate and analyze the large amount of information gathered through digital browsing and search results, explicitly addresses portions of these two standards. Distant reading skills help students narrow and broaden their research inquiries, gather relevant information from digital sources, use advanced search techniques effectively, and assess the usefulness of sources.

Distant reading is opposite in scope to close reading. The practice of close reading is familiar to ELA teachers: Close reading asks students to focus on a particular text, using techniques of literary analysis, not outside interpretation, to discover how the author constructed the text and the text's larger meaning. The practice helps cultivate both attention to detail and deep analytical skills. Close reading, as N. Katherine Hayles (2010) explains, is a common tool and inquiry method used in the discipline across literary genres and time periods (63). Hayles describes close reading as "detailed and precise attention to rhetoric, style, language choice, and so forth through a word-by-word examination of a text's linguistic techniques" (64). It's no wonder that close reading functions as a cornerstone of ELA curricula, especially in middle school and high school, because the practice helps improve reading comprehension since it requires reading and re-reading a text. Furthermore, close reading grounds the work of critical thinking in a concrete text: Critical thinking processes—those elusive and abstract habits of mind which are so central to making good, thoughtful decisions—remain difficult to define and describe.

My argument for the integration of distant reading practices in the secondary ELA curriculum does not negate the importance of teaching this kind of close reading. Sandra Jamieson and Rebecca Moore Howard's Citation Project (2013), a data-driven study of how college students use sources in their research writing, demonstrates the necessity of focusing on close reading skills. Their study shows that college writing students struggle with paraphrasing and summarizing, two techniques that depend on close reading skills, and that when students cite sources in their paper, almost 75 percent of the citations come from the first three pages of the source. Clearly, our students are not reading as closely and as deeply as we expect them to when writing research essays (Jamieson and Howard 2013, 122–23).

I think of the two kinds of reading that I describe here in this essay, close reading and distant reading, as two useful, necessary, but distinctly different camera lenses. Professional photographers have a variety of lenses in their camera bags, ready to use depending on the subject or circumstance of the shot. Close reading is like a macro lens: designed to focus on minute details, able to magnify small objects, and calibrated to adjust to subtle changes in the depth of field. Distant reading is more like a wide-angle lens, which produces panoramic photographs that display a wider angle of view than the human eye. Wide-angle photography requires just as much skill as macro photography: The photographer has to overcome distortion, maintain steady exposure, and stitch together individual shots to create a coherent whole. Close reading zooms in; distant reading zooms out.

My concept of distant reading blends together the ideas of several literary and writing studies scholars who are interested in investigating how the strategies we use while reading affect what we see in and learn from texts. Hayles, who I cited previously in my description of close reading, also defines two other kinds of reading: hyperreading and machine reading, which she argues are important reading practices to teach alongside close reading. Hyperreading, according to Hayles, is "a strategic response to an information-intensive environment" and emphasizes scanning and skimming documents quickly (2010, 66). As opposed to the slow, linear practices of close reading, hyperreading is by nature purposefully disruptive: flipping through a book to read the conclusion first or constructing new narratives by following a trail of hyperlinks. The goal of hyperreading is to quickly acquire information and to engage a state of "hyperattention," which allows the reader to quickly shift between different ideas and move rapidly among texts (68, 72). Machine reading, as Hayles describes, is "computer-assisted human reading," whereby readers use a computer's ability to run mathematical algorithms and word-count frequencies to understand the patterns internal to the text (72–73). Hayles argues that all three kinds of reading—close, hyper, and machine—have their own set of advantages for readers of literary texts, and the primary differences among the three kinds of reading is scale and context (74).

My conception of distant reading contains attributes from both Hayles's definitions of hyperreading and machine reading, as both the practices of hyperreading and machine reading focus on finding patterns across multiple texts. Although I'm not arguing that high school students need to compose and use sophisticated computer algorithms to research and read texts, there are ways in which students can rely on computer-mediated technologies to trace words across texts and use numerical and contextual information usually provided in search engine keyword searches that will allow them to participate in a kind of machine reading which Hayles describes.

The term *distant reading* was first defined in literary studies by Franco Moretti, a Stanford professor of literature. Distant reading borrows on quantitative research methods and visual displays of information to allow students to see a text (and a collection of related texts) in a larger context. Moretti's 2005 monograph, *Graphs, Maps, Trees*, demonstrates how distant reading can help scholars understand large yet subtle movements in literary history. His book is divided into three chapters that illustrate three separate methods of distant reading: graphs, maps, and trees. He develops these methods of distant reading from the quantitative and visual modeling methodologies commonly practiced in geography, evolutionary biology, quantitative history, and the social sciences (2). For example, in his first chapter, he uses a series of graphs, developed from 300 years' worth of publication records, to trace the rise and the fall of the novel as a genre in five countries: Britain, Japan, Italy, Spain, and Nigeria. The graphs allow him to notice patterns that would have been impossible to see through a focus on close reading.

Moretti's distant reading methodologies are currently being employed in the Stanford Literary Lab, a research group working with digital library collections and Google Books to trace words and phrases across thousands of texts (Parry 2010). Furthermore, his methods have been adopted by other writing studies scholars, such as Derek Mueller (2012), who used graphs, lists, and tables to aggregate data about the most cited-authors in the journal *College Composition and Communication*. The patterns he discovers shed light on writing studies' growth and specialization as a field of study (210). These distant reading methodologies, which Mueller defines as "a deliberate adjustment in the level of detail at which we ordinarily experience texts," are also related to the practices of data mining and economic macroanalysis (197; see also Lang and Baehr 2012, 178). The point of distant reading is to deliberately bring into focus associations and patterns that are not noticed through close reading methods. These patterns and associations do not necessarily make arguments, but they do spur new questions and observations. And it is that practice—formulating new questions—which is, on the one hand, essential for good research and also, on the other, very difficult for secondary students to learn how to do. In fact, the CCSS name this skill of creating new "self-generated" questions as a central, recurrent part of the research process (CCSSO and NGA 2010, W.9–10.7).

Cultivating Digital Information Literacy

How can distance reading, a technique, as Moretti argues, "where distance is however not an obstacle, but *a specific form of knowledge*," be brought into the middle school and high school ELA classroom? (2005, 1, emphasis in original). How can we adapt this quantitative method of reading so that it is valuable to secondary students? How can we teach them to recognize and use this form of knowledge? How does distant reading reflect the reading, writing, and researching skills outlined in the CCSS?

As stated previously, I believe we can reframe our students' digital habit of browsing (which Hayles would describe as a method of hyperreading) as a form of distant reading if we teach students both how the information they see on their screens is constructed and also how to look for and describe patterns that emerge during internet searching.

We all know the typical picture of a high school student researching online: scanning through Wikipedia, checking out the first few links that pop up on Google, hopping from site to site and link to link. This skimming—zipping "along the surface like a guy on a Jet Ski," as Nicholas Carr so aptly put it in his 2008 essay from *The Atlantic*, "Is Google Making Us Stupid?"—seems at first something we, as librarians and ELA teachers used to close critical reading, should discourage. Just the thought of internet-based research makes our internal research alarms go off. We imagine our students seduced by fancy HTML coding and streaming videos, rejecting the vetted electronic databases our libraries subscribe to in favor of the familiarity and ease of commercial search engines.

Part of the problem our students face is one of excess. Data surrounds them as a cloud; information is cheap. Johndan Johnson-Eilola (2005) defines this new 21st-century reality as the *datacloud*, and he calls attention to the fact that our digital surface interfaces hide and belie the complexity and vastness of information available to us (4, 12). Richard Lanham points out this phenomenon in his 2007 book *The Economics of Attention*: "Information is not in short supply in the new information economy. We're drowning in it. What we lack is the human attention to make sense of it all" (ix). Brian Ballentine (2013) echoes Lanham's argument that in the 21st century we are faced with seemingly boundless amounts of information and limited human attention. Ballentine contends that the abundance of information available online has changed how we read and think about that information, and he argues that to counteract this shallowness, as Carr describes it, teachers need to design new research assignments that will help students deeply engage with information. The arguments of Ballentine, Lanham, Carr, and Johnson-Eilola illuminate the particular challenges secondary ELA teachers and librarians face as they develop ways to teach their students online research strategies and digital information literacy skills articulated in the CCSS.

Another challenge our students face is that the search engines they typically turn to during their research processes are constructed differently than the research tools available in libraries, yet that difference is not always obvious to our students. Search engines and all digital media are acts of rhetoric: They are socially constructed for a specific purpose, audience, and context. The algorithms that search engines like Google and Yahoo! use to retrieve and display information are grounded in specific values, and these values are not those associated with academic research. Rather, search engines, like much of the internet, were built by largely commercial interests and demonstrate that subjectivity (Fabos 2008, 844). Even Google Books, one of the primary search tools used at the Stanford Literary Lab, was not built for scholarly research. The books catalogued in Google Books are riddled with incorrect tags and inaccurate metadata, because the search engine "was built to create more content to sell ads against" (Parry 2010). These errors frustrate the work of Moretti and his fellow researchers at Stanford and also unknowingly trip up student researchers, who might trust at face value the information that pops up on the screen.

The amount of faith students put in familiar search engines like Google is shown through Eszter Hargittai and colleagues' 2010 study of the online research habits of first-year college writing students. Hargittai and his colleagues found through surveys and observations of students conducting online research that students judge the credibility of a web source based on the assumed credibility of a favorite search engine (470). For example, students will defend their use of the first hit on a Google search because it is the first hit on their Google search (481). Students' routine familiarity with certain search engines, or "brand-name perception" as Hargittai and colleagues define it, has the potential of misleading students into assuming a credible academic ethos for search engines (482).

David Buckingham, a British scholar of education, explains that true information literacy "means asking questions about the sources of that information, the interests of its producers, and the ways in which it represents the world" (2007, 46). Buckingham's definition here connects with Sidney Dobrin's argument that pedagogical discussions about digital technologies need to move past the idea of "writing technology as tool or apparatus" that can either improve or inhibit instruction (2011, 175). Instead, Dobrin claims that technology is more of a concept, a way to do and think about writing that is inseparable from our larger local and global contexts. In Buckingham's argument, he describes the evaluation checklists that are so often introduced to students as ways to assess the credibility of certain websites as narrowly conceived, focused on safety precautions, and unable to help students understand the rhetorical nature of the internet, that larger global and local context Dobrin explains (Buckingham 2007, 45–46). The literacy skills we need to teach our students so that they can successfully and purposefully mediate digital information must instead take the form of a *metalanguage*, Buckingham contends, which is an understanding of the rhetorical and systematic nature of the internet, a habit of mind to rely on during the research process (45, 48).

ELA teachers and their librarian colleagues can begin to develop this metalanguage by showing students how browsing can illuminate the ways in which the internet is constructed and, through this understanding, the ways in which this construction creates systems of information. Browsing is a form of distant reading, which I define by borrowing Hayles's concepts of hyperreading and machine reading and Moretti's and Mueller's definition of distant reading. Moretti's and Mueller's illustrations of distant reading techniques focus on how scholars can use distance and scope to find new associations and patterns, and my adaptation of distant reading applies these concepts to the work of student researchers.

Not all browsing can be portrayed as distant reading. Often, students mindlessly jump from link to link, using browsing as a way to pass the time instead of paying attention to how they are moved through data online and questioning why the information they see is structured in the way that it is. However, by teaching students online browsing practices that draw on the principles of distant reading—skimming websites, quickly skipping through links and search results pages, manipulating search terms, and paying attention to how search results pages are constructed—teachers and librarians can help meet the specific information literacy objectives in the CCSS' Anchor Standards for Writing: thoughtful, systematic browsing can help students narrow and broaden their research inquiries (CCSSO and NGA 2010, W.9–10.7), and gather relevant information from digital sources; use advanced search techniques effectively; and assess the usefulness of sources (W.9–10.8).

Browsing as Distant Reading

The English word *browse* itself derives from the French word *broust* (buds or young shoots), and so takes its meaning from the idea of animals cropping or feeding off the most peripheral parts of plants, the edible, accessible buds and young shoots ("Browse" 2014). Online browsing is very similar, at least conceptually. When people browse online, they move quickly from site to site, following their interests and appetites, biting off bits of information here and there. The most accessible information is quickly retrieved; rarely do people scroll down or click over to another page unless compelled by driving curiosity or hyperlinks.

In order to see how browsing can function as a form of distant reading—a method that uses distance as a way to see new patterns and acquire information—this section will investigate what happens when a student browses online to find research for a school project. For this example, we'll imagine that the student is in 10th grade and writing a research paper about Wangari Maathai, the recipient of the 2004 Nobel Peace Prize. I will trace how that student might browse for information about Maathai on Google and Opposing Viewpoints in Context, a popular high school and college library database hosted by Gale/Cengage Learning. This exercise will help illuminate the ways browsing functions as a method of distant reading, a way of noticing associations and how search engines work at a macro-level.

First, I search *Wangari Maathai* on Google. Figure 8.1 shows some key features of the Google search. The first result is for the Wikipedia entry for Maathai. Wikipedia is a conundrum for librarians and teachers. On the one hand, its open-editing policy makes us understandably nervous about our students using it and citing it as a source. On the other hand, research has shown that Wikipedia entries are as reliable as vetted, peer-reviewed encyclopedias like *Britannica* (Giles 2005, 900). Although Wikipedia is not an ideal authoritative source for students to cite in an academic essay, Wikipedia entries are valuable starting places for researchers to go to because they provide ideas about an issue or topic, links to other sources about that topic, and search terms researchers can use to expand their search (Purdy 2010, 209), one of the proficiencies addressed in the CCSS (CCSSO and NGA 2010, W.9–10.7). My point here is not to argue whether or not our students should use Wikipedia in their research process.[1] What I think is important here, in discussing browsing as a form of distant reading (and therefore as a way to notice patterns and associations across texts and links), is that Wikipedia is the first result for not just this Google search but for more than 80 percent of all one- or two-word informational Google searches (Miller 2012).

Google ranks its results on its search engine results page based on its complicated algorithms, which take into account, among many things, the number of links to a page from other websites and how well the user's search terms match the key terms of the site. Google maintains a master index of words, compiled through Google's Googlebot, which is Google's web crawling bot that searches the web for updated or new webpages that need to be added to the master index ("Google Basics" 2014; "Googlebot" 2014). Important for teachers and librarians, who are helping their students learn how to navigate information online, is that Google's algorithms aren't searching for peer-reviewed or vetted webpages: The search engine results page is a popularity (and accuracy) contest, and Wikipedia wins that competition most of the time (Segal 2011).

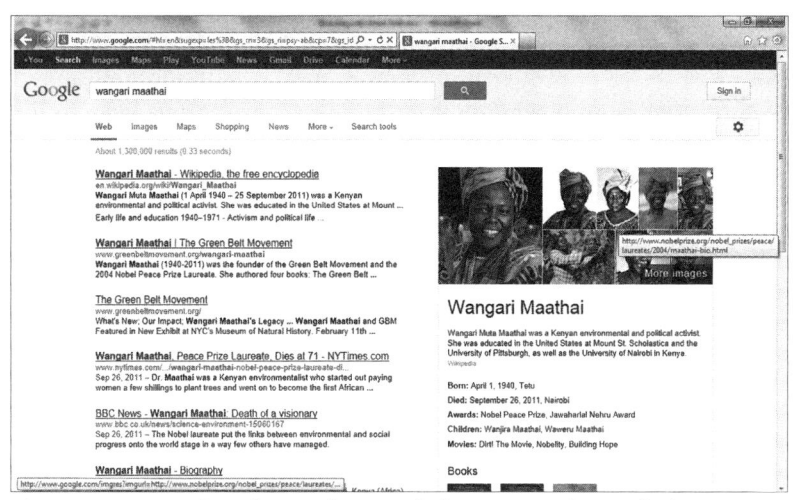

Figure 8.1   Results of Google search for *Wangari Maathai*

Google's methods for organizing and combining search terms are different than electronic databases like Opposing Viewpoints in Context. Google returns results from any and all information available to index online. In contrast, academic databases limit the sources from which they draw results. Also important is that databases do not rely on commercial profits because libraries pay to subscribe to databases. Commercial interests underline the structure and purpose of the internet and internet search engines like Google, and these interests, sometimes made manifest in business deals to cram sites with internal links to raise a particular site's visibility on the search results page, impact what information is privileged and what information is buried (Segal 2011).

The next two links on the Google search results page shown in Figure 8.1 direct the user to the About page and the homepage of the Green Belt Movement, the organization that Maathai founded and that many believe led to her Nobel Peace Prize. The next two results are her obituary, published on NYTimes.com and BBC.com respectively, and the sixth result is her biography on the Nobel Prize website. The biographies and obituaries don't apply a critical lens to her work; they, like the Wikipedia entry, are a collection of facts about Maathai.

What is also notable about the Google search is the sidebar on the right side of the results page, which, in this case, displays images of Maathai, her basic biographical information, images and links to her books, and images and links to other people associated with Maathai, such as Daniel arap Moi and Shirin Ebadi (the latter is cut off and not seen in the screenshot, but was on the results page). This sidebar, a relatively new feature for Google, is the representation of a larger Google project, the Knowledge Graph. With the Knowledge Graph, which Google dubs part of the "future of search," Google has created a database of the most searched-for people, events, places, and things, with the understanding that users are searching for answers, not just facts ("The Knowledge Graph" 2014). Instead of searches based on key terms and internal links—data out of context—the Knowledge Graph traces the relationships between search words, aggregating the associations among search terms by following user searches.

It is helpful to think of the Knowledge Graph as a "bottom up" search, one based on how people jump from site to site during the research process. In this way, the Knowledge Graph is a visual representation of collective distant reading, as it displays the associations a multitude of researchers make as they browse through search results pages. Teachers and librarians can introduce students to the Knowledge Graph as another search engine embedded within Google. What's especially helpful about the Knowledge Graph is that the way it succinctly summarizes key information and offers direct links to relevant information can help students meet two of the proficiencies listed in the CCSS (CCSSO and NGA 2010, W.9–10.8). The Knowledge Graph facilitates the process of gathering relevant information from multiple authoritative digital sources, and, because it relies on user data instead of out-of-context algorithms and internal link formulas, it is a kind of advanced search technique readily available to students on the Google platform.

Now, going back to Figure 8.1, we know that most students would dive into one of the first six links listed on the search results page (and likely choose Wikipedia first, since they are familiar with Wikipedia as

Browsing With Intent 243

a genre) and not scroll down to see the other four links on the page or click over to the second or third results page. However, if they did, Figure 8.2 shows what they would find.

Here's what the second half of the first page of results contains: Maathai's page on BrainyQuote, a link to *Taking Root*, the film based on her Green Belt Movement in Kenya, another obituary, and another biography. Even more important, Google offers alternative searches on the bottom of the first page of search results, based on what search terms other people used in conjunction with *Wangari Maathai*.

Patterns, Anomalies, and Surprises on the Search Results Page

Let's look at the first page of search results on Google shown in Figure 8.1 through a distant reading lens to notice patterns and associations that emerge when we cluster these ten links together. We know just from looking at this results page, which contains both titles of websites

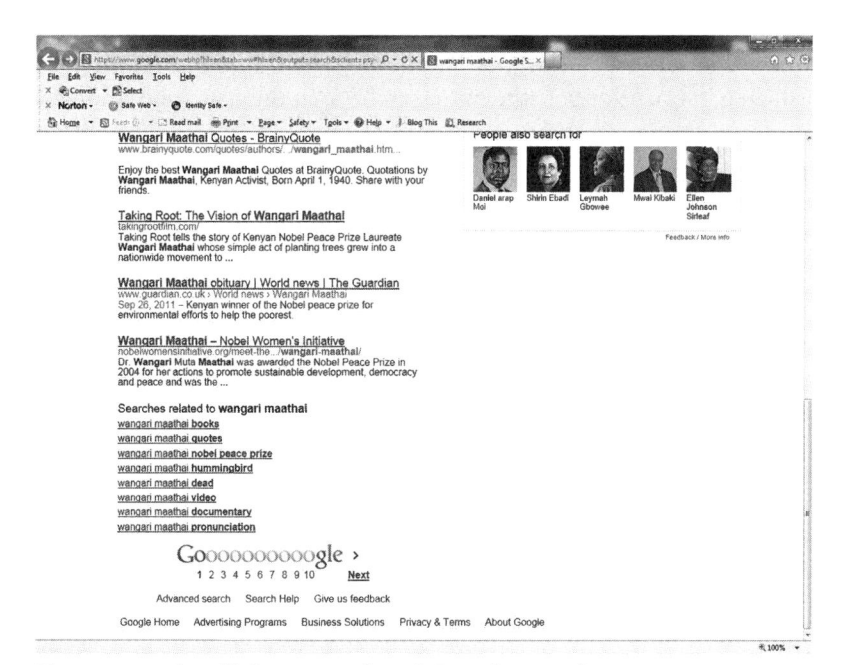

Figure 8.2 Scroll down results of Google search on *Wangari Maathai*

and short, truncated excerpts from them, that Maathai is a Kenyan woman who received the Nobel Peace Prize. Maathai founded the Green Belt Movement, died at age 71, and was considered a "visionary" in sustainability and environmental movements, and her work of planting trees was featured in a film. Before even reading any of the webpages themselves, the Google's search results page gives the student researcher valuable information about Maathai and directs the student to other promising searches related to Maathai. The search results page has unexpected information, too—anomalies in the general pattern gleaned from these 10 links. The suggested search *Wangari Maathai hummingbird is* one of these surprises. If the student clicks on that link, the new results page lists links to YouTube videos, blog posts, and explanations of Maathai's allegory of the hummingbird, which she shared in her speeches in order to encourage people to have hope and do what they could in order to enact change, no matter how small their effort might be.

What I am pointing out here is that the search results page itself, as a kind of digital table of contents or card catalogue drawer, contains valuable information for student researchers. In the space of 5 minutes, by clicking through the suggested searches and over a few pages here and there, I learned (beyond what I discovered in the first search result page) the titles of Maathai's books; that she was jailed and then became a member of the Kenyan Parliament; that she was educated in the United States; that she died of ovarian cancer; and that she served as an activist for women, education, social justice, and the environment. By using distant reading techniques (scanning, skimming, following links, and consciously noticing associations and patterns), students can find valuable background information and search terms even before they read a specific webpage. Research happens among the search results. I am not suggesting that we encourage our students to stay distant and only skim the search results page for their research projects. Rather, I am suggesting that if we can teach our students to be cognizant of the information that appears on a Google search results page, and explain to them the reasons why some links appear above others, then we are one step closer to helping them better negotiate their online research process.

Being mindful of how information is displayed and organized on a Google search results page helps students meet the CCSS in writing. First, by relying on Google's Knowledge Graph to generate search terms and new questions, students can practice narrowing or broadening a search inquiry when appropriate (CCSSO and NGA 2010, W.9–10.7). Second, by understanding how search engines like Google rank their search results, students are better able to assess the usefulness of certain websites in answering their research question (W.9–10.8). Third, encouraging students to browse through the search results page facilitates their ability to gather information from multiple sources instead of solely focusing on the first site listed on the search results page (W.9–10.8).

Now, let's turn to a library database, Opposing Viewpoints in Context, and see how the search for *Wangari Maathai* takes a different path than the Google search. This database brings together content across various media, including audio podcasts, video streams, images, maps, full-text academic journal articles, and newspaper and magazine reports. The database also has tools directed to student researchers, including interactive Web 2.0 platforms, and was designed to imitate the layout of a webpage, since that interface is familiar to students. The purpose of the database, as its title suggests, is to provide users with sources that speak to many of the most hotly debated issues in society today ("Opposing Viewpoints in Context" 2013).

Figure 8.3 shows a screenshot of my basic search for *Wangari Maathai* in Opposing Viewpoints in Context. The Opposing Viewpoints in Context search results page divides the results into types of sources, which is a valuable categorization for a researcher. For this search, there are seven results from academic journals, one image, six videos, 17 audio clips, 805 news articles or editorials, 17 magazine articles, and four reference links (links to primary source indices or encyclopedias). It's obvious from scanning this search result page, a distant reading technique, that Wangari Maathai has had more coverage in popular

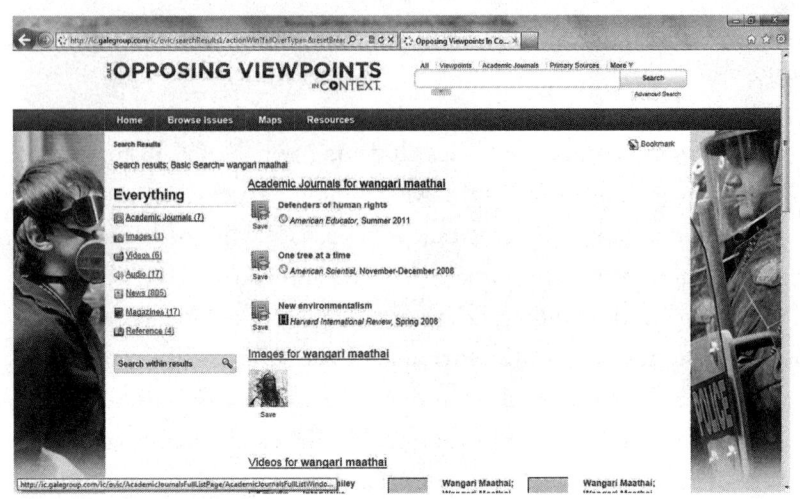

Figure 8.3   Basic search for *Wangari Maathai* in Opposing Viewpoints in Context

news outlets than in academic journals or texts. That may be because she is a recent figure of study, having won the Nobel Peace Prize less than 10 years ago. The Opposing Viewpoints in Context database also allows students to limit their search results from the get-go; in the search bar at the top of the page, students can decide to only search academic journal articles, primary materials, or other specific kinds of sources. Google allows this limitation to a degree through its Google Images and Google Scholar searches (though Google Scholar results have large gaps in content and coverage), yet the Opposing Viewpoints in Context database instantly classifies sources for students in recognizable ways that are useful for the research process.

When students click on the tab Academic Journals on the sidebar, they see what is shown in Figure 8.4. Opposing Viewpoints in Context gives the student researcher abundant information just on the search results page. Not only do all seven entries list the title, publication, and publication date, but the database also categorizes how difficult the reading level of each article is (indicated by the shape at the right-hand side of each entry) and the specific type of article: a brief article, book review, article, or children's review. This explicit contextual information is absent in Google. In a Google search, the researcher must intuit the

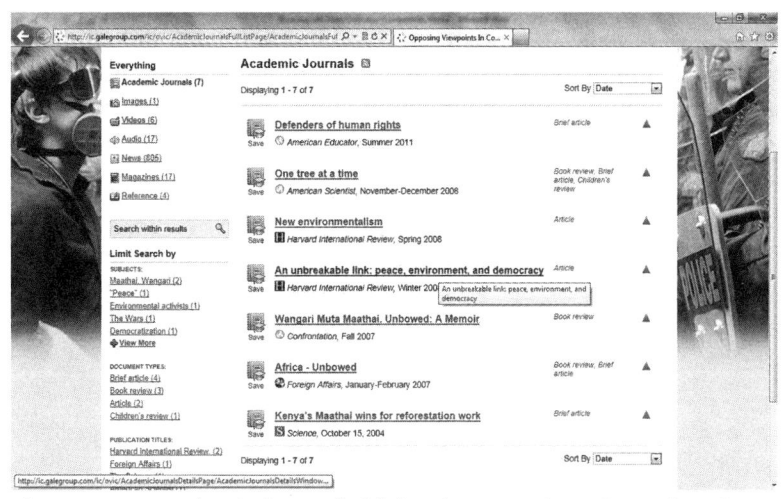

Figure 8.4 Academic journal sidebar in Opposing Viewpoints in Context

kind of source, its audience, and its purpose (a review or an argument, for example) based on the title of the webpage and its short description. Databases fill in some of the blanks.

Also, just glancing at the journal titles or article titles listed in this search results page gives the student researcher valuable information: The journal titles suggest that Maathai's academic influence extends across disciplinary boundaries—education, science, and foreign affairs—and the article titles imply that her work makes connections among issues of peace, violence, gender, and the environment. Researchers who use distant reading techniques, like skimming and noticing patterns in journal subject areas, can learn valuable information about Maathai relatively quickly.

The type of source that has the most results for a *Wangari Maathai* search is news articles. When students click on that category on the left sidebar, they see what is shown in Figure 8.5. Further down on the left sidebar, the database offers student researchers possible limitations for their search, restricting results by subject, document type, or publication title. These suggested limitations are also useful for seeing patterns among the 805 news article results. Opposing Viewpoints in Context draws from 279 periodicals, yet 738 results, or 91.7 percent of the news

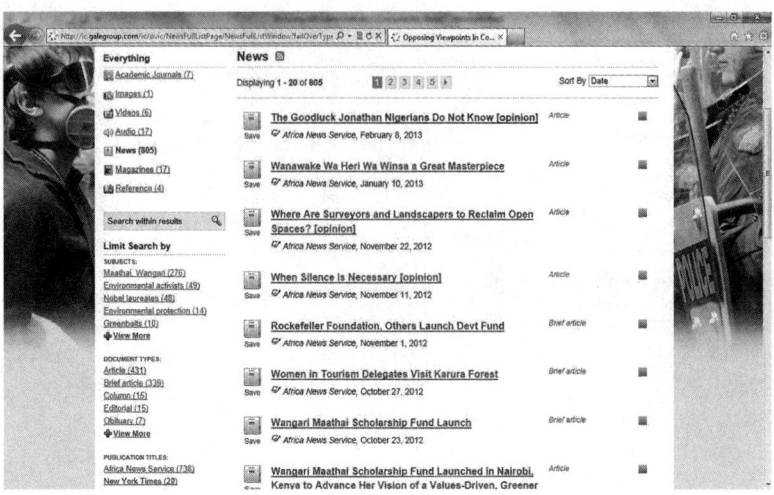

Figure 8.5 News article sidebar in Opposing Viewpoints in Context

articles gathered in this search for *Wangari Maathai*, are drawn from *Africa News Service*. The other publication titles for this search include the *New York Times*, *Christian Science Monitor*, and *Toronto Sun*. The fact that the vast majority of articles about Maathai are from *Africa News Service*, an organization that collects news and information from over 130 African news organizations, is interesting ("Publishers" 2014). It's difficult to make an argument about this pattern, but it does raise a new question: Does this pattern suggest that international or Western news outlets have ignored Maathai's work, or does it suggest that Maathai's work is primarily suited to the African context?

As I did with the Google search on Maathai, I spent 5 minutes doing a "free search." Instead of reading individual sites or articles closely, I purposefully spent time staying on the surface, clicking the different sidebars and through the search results pages to see what other information about Maathai I could glean just from the results pages themselves. On just the page of podcasts, I discovered that Maathai spoke out in favor of Barack Obama's election in November 2008 and that she refused to carry the Olympic torch out of protest. Again, these facts aren't conclusions. Instead, they are anomalies in the larger pattern of coverage about environmental and justice issues, so these variances are valuable because they help lead to new research questions. These anomalies are critical parts of the research process, because new inquires often emerge from discovering ideas or data that do not fit the hypothesized pattern.

Though the database search has far fewer results than the Google search (857 total results in Opposing Viewpoints in Context versus 1.3 million hits on Google), that's not a bad thing. More is not necessarily merrier or better. The Boolean searches that drive database and library searches help researchers calibrate, control, and limit their search results. Limiting search results assists in defining and narrowing a researcher's search inquiry, one of the proficiencies listed in the CCSS (W.9–10.7). The goal of research is not to gather information for the sake of padding a works cited page, though students often get that message when we require a specific number of sources for an essay assignment. Teachers and librarians must work to help students understand the value of relevancy over quantity, helping them choose useful sources for their search inquiry (W.9–10.8). Students value research resources that return scholarly results, not necessarily those that return *relevant* scholarly results, as demonstrated through James P. Purdy's 2012 survey of the reasons why first-year university writing students turn to certain online research resources. The real challenge of research is to choose the right sources, and the limited results in a database help students begin that selection process.

This section, which explored the information students could collect during the process of browsing both Google and an electronic library database, demonstrates that the search results page itself—its hierarchal listings, its suggested alternative searches, its sidebars that include categories, images, and contextual data—is a valuable but often overlooked source of information. Instead of seeing the search results page as a link to other objects of analysis, the search results page can be an object of analysis in and of itself. Looking for patterns and anomalies in the search results page is a kind of distant reading: The researcher purposefully moves away from individual links to look at the panoramic picture as a whole.

Moreover, when the student-researcher combines this kind of distant reading with an understanding of how commercial and academic search engines are constructed, students are able to be more critical of the influences and assumptions that lead to the content and organization of their search results page. This is exactly the kind of critical information literacy that both Buckingham (2007) and Fabos (2008) argue that teachers and librarians need to help cultivate among today's students, and it fits with the goals listed in the CCSS for writing. Students who know how search engines select and categorize data can more efficiently gather *relevant* information on their research topic (W.9-10.8). As Purdy illustrates through his 2012 survey, students are primarily concerned with finding sources that are considered "scholarly," whether or not that source is relevant to the research inquiry. Coupling discussion of how search engines work—developing critical information literacy—with instruction on how to navigate search engine results pages can help students meet the CCSS standards for conducting research for writing.

Clouds, Links, and Tags: Other Information-Rich Avenues for Distant Reading

Thoughtful browsing as a form of distant reading can also take other forms. For instance, by entering a site like The Green Belt Movement and clicking from hyperlink to hyperlink, the student researcher can begin to notice, with instruction from teachers and librarians, what kinds of alternative narratives are constructed and what analytical connections are forged through those links. Hyperlinks are rhetorical devices unique to the digital environment and deliberately tracing where they lead helps researchers develop scope, context, and further inquiry questions for their research. Tags and tag clouds on blogs can also be followed in a similar way, allowing a researcher to see how others categorize information and make larger associations about issues. Search results pages, as digital media interfaces that combine words and images, are a visual display of hierarchal information and function much like the systematic visualizations used by scholars such as Moretti and Edward Tufte (2001). Student researchers can use browsing as a distant reading practice when they are cognizant of the larger context the results emerge from and move systematically and analytically through the copious amounts of data that surface during the browsing process.

Suggestions for the Classroom

In the beginning of this chapter, I argued that online distant reading skills can help students meet some of the CCSS for writing. Specifically, I believe that browsing can help students narrow and broaden their research inquiries, gather relevant information from digital sources, use advanced search techniques effectively, and assess the usefulness of sources, competencies taken directly from the CCSS' Anchor Standards for Writing 7 and 8, which are grouped under the subheading "Research to Build and Present Knowledge" (CCSSO and NGA 2010, 18).

Using Patterns and Anomalies to Narrow and Broaden Searches

Students can learn how to narrow and widen their research inquiries by paying attention to the anomalies that emerge across the pattern of search results on either an online search engine like Google or an electronic database like Opposing Viewpoints in Context. For instance, the suggested search *Wangari Maathai hummingbird* on Google helped me discover one of Maathai's most influential speeches. If I were a 10th-grade student writing a research paper on Maathai, this discovery could help expand my inquiry to include research on the underlying philosophies informing Maathai's activist work. Teachers and librarians can help students widen or focus their research inquires by teaching students to pay attention to similar kinds of information available on almost every search results page, thus becoming an heuristic invention and leading students to new research-writing questions.

Relying on the Search Results Page to Discover a Range of Relevant Sources

Browsing, practiced as a form of distant reading, can also help students gather relevant information from digital sources. In my search in Opposing Viewpoint in Context, for example, I learned about the range of sources available to me—both traditional print-based articles and news reports and multimedia sources, like audio podcasts, images, and video clips—by just paying attention to the sidebars of the search results page, which categorized sources by genre, and clicking through those tabs. By exploring the right sidebar of my Google Search, which contained the connections with Maathai drawn together from Google's Knowledge Graph, I found links to other relevant sources, such as the people associated with Maathai's work and the titles to her publications. It's obvious that electronic library databases like Opposing Viewpoints in Context contain sources that are immediately relevant to academic research, but that's not to say that Google's search results were not also valuable, though the onus to sort out what links are useful and appropriate for research lies more on the student when they use a commercial search engine.

Taking Time to Explore With a "Free Browse"

Valuing browsing by giving students dedicated time for it is important for teaching students how to find information online. Archival historians spend considerable amounts of time browsing through boxes and papers; students need to be shown the usefulness of this first step of research. Good research requires thorough surveying. Teaching students specific "navigational" strategies for following links and evaluating sources and search engines prepares them for thorough surveying, as Mary Lourdes Silva's (2013) study of the research habits of college students shows (180). It's important to not only teach students these surveying skills, but also to allow them repeated time in class to practice these skills, which might be different from the kinds of strategies they use to surf the web for personal purposes.

In order to help students gather relevant information from digital sources, teachers and librarians can ask students to perform "free browses," which can be compared to freewrites. In a freewrite, students are asked to write for a set length of time without stopping. Sometimes, the teacher assigns a prompt for the free write. During a free browse, the student browses online for a set amount of time, either using an online search engine or an academic database or both. In this scenario, the teacher or librarian could give students a research prompt, such as "See what you can find about *X*." The point of the free browse is for the student to click from link to link, page to page, not stopping to read a particular result. Students are asked to pay attention to what they discover during the free browse, and after the time limit has passed, they can either write down what they found through the search process or discuss what they uncovered with their teacher or classmates.

Learning How Search Engines Work

Teaching students how search engines are constructed also helps them learn how to use advanced search techniques effectively. Although both of my searches for Maathai in this chapter only utilized the basic search functions in both Google and Opposing Viewpoints in Context, teachers and librarians can show students how to calibrate their searches using advanced search techniques—such as excluding words in a Boolean search or limiting results to include only certain kinds of documents, like PDFs, on an online search engine. In order to be effective researchers, students need to be aware of what drives the research tools they use: They need to know how Google sorts and stacks results, how advertising plays a role in creating internal links, and how a search engine built for and regulated by commercial and governmental interest and an academic database built for scholarly research are different. We need to demonstrate to our students the larger economic, social, and political contexts in which their research happens. One way to do this is to introduce students to the conversations about search engine optimization and discuss how corporations—like J.C. Penney in 2010 and 2011—have manipulated search engines to maximize their online exposure and commercial profits (Segal 2011).[2]

Discussing What "Usefulness" in Research Means

Teaching students how to use browsing as a distant reading practice can help them develop skills to evaluate the usefulness of sources, links, and websites they find during their research process. Usefulness in academic research means that the source presents information and an argument that is not found elsewhere, and/or the source achieves a level of general relevance because it is frequently cited or linked. It's difficult to discern the first kind of usefulness on the search results page of either Google or an academic database, though with the restricted number of hits on a database like Opposing Viewpoints in Context, it is possible to sort through titles and short descriptions to find sources that could possibly give an alternative perspective on a person or an issue, like the NPR clip in which Maathai speaks out in support of Obama's election. The other kind of usefulness is a bit easier to determine through search results pages: Though the websites themselves must be researched and vetted for reliability and accuracy, the hierarchical listing of sites on commercial search engines like Google do show what links other researchers have visited while searching for similar sources.

Asking students to browse intentionally, and giving time in class or assigning browsing exercises to students as a way to introduce them to online research, opens up the opportunity to talk about degrees of usefulness. For instance, the high-profile placement of Wikipedia on Google's search results page for most one- and two-word searches can lead to frank discussions about the usefulness and relevancy of Google and Wikipedia, two resources students commonly turn to in the beginning of the research process. As Randall McClure (2011) argues, "Wikipedia and Google are so much a part of the research process for writers today that to ignore their role and refuse to work with these tools seems ludicrous" (223). During or after a free browse, teachers and librarians can ask students questions about the nature of online research:

- Why are free services like Google sometimes more useful than library subscriptions?
- What are the benefits of relying on a tertiary source like Wikipedia to start the research process?
- What are the drawbacks of only depending on the top five links for research?
- How can less frequently visited sites and lesser known academic sources enhance research?

Discussing all these questions help students think more critically about what happens when they browse for sources, either online or through an academic database. The goal is to help them reject the knee-jerk acceptance so many students have of the first few results that arise in their searches for sources.

Conclusion

Teaching students to browse as a form of distant reading can help them become savvier, more thoughtful, and more effective researchers. What we do as teachers and librarians when we encourage our students to browse with intent is showing them how an online habit that they regularly practice can be transformed from a passive activity to a new habit of mind that enhances their research.

Distant reading techniques show students how to systematically sort, categorize, and evaluate the large amounts of information generated during online searching. Distant reading asks students to pay attention to how information is presented and structured. Often, students zoom in on specific sources early in the research process, truncating their searches prematurely. When students are able to resist this early focus on a handful of sources, they can instead zoom out and put meaningful distance between themselves and the array of information available to them either online or in electronic databases. Distance allows students to gather new and valuable information about the larger context within which sources operate. The practice of distant reading helps emphasize analytical skills because it teaches students to pay attention to both patterns and anomalies within patterns, critical observation work that leads to new inquiry questions and better research.

It's no surprise that the CCSS emphasize critical information literacy in their writing standards: Good argumentative writing depends on good research. Teachers and librarians ought to harness browsing and other instinctive practices the next digital scholar brings to the classroom in order to help students hone and strengthen their digital literacy, critical research, and college- and career-ready writing skills. By browsing, students may just be sampling the surface, but this surface knowledge can help guide and define their research and their writing.

Endnotes

1. Teachers and librarians who are dealing with that question in their classrooms would be benefited by reading James P. Purdy's scholarship on ways students and teachers can use Wikipedia productively in the classroom (2009; 2010).

2. In late 2010 and early 2011, during the months surrounding and encompassing the high-profit online holiday shopping season, J.C. Penney engaged in a large-scale search engine optimization strategy, which resulted in the J.C. Penney website becoming the first or second website on Google's search result page for a wide variety of search terms, including *Samsonite carry-on luggage*, *home décor*, and *skinny jeans*. Google determined that those in charge of the J.C. Penney website and its search engine consulting firm were paying to have links to the J.C. Penney company website placed on thousands of websites. Furthermore, many of these websites were placed on sites not related to the search terms, sites or "link hovels" that exist merely to advertise. Since the Google search engine takes into account the number of internal links in determining the hierarchy on the search results page, this optimization strategy led to J.C. Penney skyrocketing up the search results page. Google does not condone this kind of "black hat" optimization. When Google finds organizations disrupting the integrity of their search algorithm by selling links and setting up link hovels, Google manually demotes (and in some cases, outright removes) a company or organization from its search results page (Segal 2011).

References

Ballentine, Brian. 2013. "Fighting for Attention: Making Space for Deep Learning." In *The New Digital Scholar: Exploring and Enriching the Research and Writing Behaviors of NextGen Students*, edited by Randall McClure and James P. Purdy, 83–104. Medford, NJ: Information Today, Inc.

"Browse." 2014. *Oxford English Dictionary*. Accessed February 10, 2014. www.oxforddictionaries.com/us/definition/english/browse?q=browse

Buckingham, David. 2007. "Digital Media Literacies: Rethinking Media Education in the Age of the Internet." *Research in Comparative and International Education* 2 (1): 43–55.

Carr, Nicholas. 2008. "Is Google Making Us Stupid?" *The Atlantic*. July 1. Accessed February 10, 2014. www.theatlantic.com/magazine/archive/2008/07/is-google-making-us-stupid/306868.

Council of Chief State School Officers and National Governors Association. 2010. *Common Core State Standards for English Language Arts and Literacy in History/*

Social Studies, Science, and Technical Subjects. Washington, DC: National Governors Association Center for Best Practices, Council of Chief State School Officers. Accessed February 10, 2014. www.corestandards.org/assets/CCSSI_ELA%20 Standards.pdf.

Dobrin, Sidney I. 2011. "Ecology and Concepts of Technology." *Writing Program Administration* 35 (1): 175–198.

Fabos, Bettina. 2008. "The Price of Information: Critical Literacy, Education, and Today's Internet." In *Handbook of Research on New Literacies*, edited by Julie Corio, Michele Knobel, Colin Lankshear, and Donald J. Leu, 843–874. New York: Lawrence Erlbaum Group.

Giles, Jim. 2005. "Special Report: Internet Encyclopaedias Go Head to Head." *Nature* 438: 900–901.

"Google Basics." 2014. *Google: Webmaster Tools.* Accessed February 10, 2014. support.google.com/webmasters/bin/answer.py?hl=en&answer=70897.

"Googlebot." 2014. *Google: Webmaster Tools.* Accessed February 10, 2014. support.google.com/webmasters/bin/answer.py?hl=en&answer=182072.

Hargittai, Eszter, Lindsay Fullerton, Ericka Menchen-Trevino, and Kristin Yates Thomas. 2010. "Trust Online: Young Adults' Evaluation of Web Content." *International Journal of Communication* 4: 468–494.

Hayles, N. Katherine. 2010. "How We Read: Close, Hyper, Machine." *ADE Bulletin* 150: 62–79.

Jamieson, Sandra, and Rebecca Moore Howard. 2013. "Sentence-Mining: Uncovering the Amount of Reading and Reading Comprehension in College Writers' Researched Writing." In *The New Digital Scholar: Exploring and Enriching the Research and Writing Behaviors of NextGen Students*, edited by Randall McClure and James P. Purdy, 109–132. Medford, NJ: Information Today, Inc.

Joint Information Systems Committee and British Library. 2012. *Researchers of Tomorrow: The Research Behaviour of Generation Y Doctoral Students.* Accessed February 10, 2014. www.jisc.ac.uk/publications/reports/2012/researchers-of-tomorrow.aspx.

Johnson-Eilola, Johndan. 2005. *Datacloud: Toward a New Theory of Online Work.* Cresskill, NJ: Hampton Press.

"The Knowledge Graph." 2014. *Google: Inside Search.* Accessed February 10, 2014. www.google.com/insidesearch/features/search/knowledge.html.

Lang, Susan, and Craig Baehr. 2012. "Data Mining: A Hybrid Methodology for Complex and Dynamic Research." *College Composition and Communication* 64 (1): 172–194.

Lanham, Richard A. 2007. *The Economics of Attention: Style and Substance in the Age of Information.* Chicago: University of Chicago Press.

McClure, Randall. 2011. "Googlepedia: Turning Information Behaviors into Research Skills." In *Writing Spaces: Readings on Writing.* Volume 2, edited by Charles Lowe and Pavel Zemliansky, 221–241. Fort Collins, CO and West Lafayette, IN: WAC

Clearinghouse and Parlor Press. Accessed February 10, 2014. wac.colostate.edu/books/writingspaces2/mcclure--googlepedia.pdf.

Miller, Miranda. 2012. "3 More Studies Examine Wikipedia's Page 1 Google Rankings." *Search Engine Watch*. March 26. Accessed February 10, 2014. searchenginewatch.com/article/2163432/3-More-Studies-Examine-Wikipedias-Page-1-Google-Rankings.

Moretti, Franco. 2005. *Graphs, Maps, Trees: Abstract Models for a Literary History*. London: Verso.

Mueller, Derek. 2012. "Grasping Rhetoric and Composition by Its Long Tail: What Graphs Can Tell Us About the Field's Changing Shape." *College Composition and Communication* 64 (1): 195–223.

"Opposing Viewpoints in Context." 2013. Gale Cengage Learning. Accessed February 10, 2014. www.gale.cengage.com/InContext/viewpoints.htm.

Parry, Marc. 2010. "The Humanities Go Google." *Chronicle of Higher Education*. May 28. Accessed February 10, 2014. chronicle.com/article/The-Humanities-Go-Google/65713.

"Publishers." 2014. *AllAfrica*. Accessed February 10, 2014. allafrica.com/list/publisher/editorial/editorial/type/pub.html.

Purdy, James P. 2009. "When the Tenets of Composition Go Public: A Study of Writing in Wikipedia." *College Composition and Communication* 61 (2): 351–373.

———. 2010. "Wikipedia Is Good for You!?" In *Writing Spaces: Readings on Writing*, Volume 1, edited by Charles Lowe and Pavel Zemliansky, 205–224. Fort Collins, CO and West Lafayette, IN: WAC Clearinghouse and Parlor Press. Accessed February 10, 2014. writingspaces.org/essays/wikipedia-is-good-for-you.

———. 2012 "Why First-Year College Students Select Online Research Resources as Their Favorite." *First Monday* 7 (3). Accessed February 10, 2014. www.uic.edu/htbin/cgiwrap/bin/ojs/index.php/fm/article/view/4088/3289.

Scholes, Robert J. 2002. "The Transition to College Reading." *Pedagogy* 2 (2): 165–172.

Segal, David. 2011. "The Dirty Little Secrets of Search." *New York Times*. February 12. Accessed February 10, 2014. www.nytimes.com/2011/02/13/business/13search.html?pagewanted=all&_r=0.

Silva, Mary Lourdes. 2013. "Can I Google That? Research Strategies of Undergraduate Students." In *The New Digital Scholar: Exploring and Enriching the Research and Writing Behaviors of NextGen Students*, edited by Randall McClure and James P. Purdy, 161–188. Medford, NJ: Information Today, Inc.

Tufte, Edward R. 2001. *The Visual Display of Quantitative Information*. 2nd ed. Cheshire, CT: Graphics Press.

CHAPTER 9

Blogging as Public Writing
Meeting the Common Core State Standards Through Community-Centered Writing

Christina Saidy and Mark A. Hannah

> So I kinda saw why blogs help. For once I felt proud of what I do. I was happy to put effort in my work. — Claudia, Age 15

In this quote, Claudia, a participant in the research we describe in this chapter, reflects on her experiences with a blogging curriculum in her high school class. Although Claudia's experience with blogging is recent, teachers have been creating their own blogs for a number of years. Some teachers have made the move toward integrating blogging into the writing curriculum via student blog projects. Although blogging itself has become fairly mainstream, there is still often an underlying assumption in schools that blogs, and other Web 2.0 technologies, are for "techie" teachers, those with specialized technological skills. However, with the introduction of the Common Core State Standards (CCSS) specifically focused on using technology to produce and publish student writing, even less "techie" teachers have opportunities to integrate Web 2.0 technologies into their teaching in meaningful ways. For teachers, Web 2.0 technologies, specifically blogging, create opportunities for innovative teaching. For students like Claudia, the integration of blogs provide the potential both to meet the CCSS and find pride and value in their work.

In this chapter, we specifically focus on the ways that blogging can be used to help meet the following standard in the CCSS that calls for students to:

> Use technology, including the internet, to produce, publish, and update individual or shared writing products, taking advantage of technology's capacity to link to other information and to display information flexibly and dynamically. (Council of Chief State School Officers [CCSSO] and National Governors Association [NGA] 2010, W.9–10.6)

We acknowledge that in order for students to meet this particular standard they must also meet other writing standards. However, we believe this particular standard, because of its focus on the use of technology for producing, publishing, and updating writing, provides a new and unique challenge for classroom teachers as they adopt the CCSS. Not only are teachers tasked with covering the writing standards, but they also must meet these standards using technology that invites students to make their writing digital and take it beyond the classroom.

Specifically in this chapter, we provide findings from a study of a ninth-grade blogging unit developed in an established university–secondary school partnership, wherein students blogged about public and community issues of importance to them. We frame our discussion of this blogging unit within what is often referred to as a "public writing" pedagogy, or community-focused writing that moves it beyond the teacher and the classroom into communities both local and global. We argue that the standard focusing on producing, publishing, and updating writing provides a unique opportunity for teachers and students to incorporate technology, in our case blogging, in meaningful ways to meet the CCSS, while at the same time offering opportunities for students to develop writing that engages other students and their communities. In this chapter we will review literature regarding blogging in the classroom to illustrate the need for a public writing curriculum that employs blogging. We will then discuss our specific work and research in a secondary–university partnership in which a blogging curriculum was used in a ninth-grade class and make specific connections between this blogging curriculum and the CCSS. Finally, we will offer tips and strategies for teachers and librarians interested in integrating blogging into the English Language Arts (ELA) curriculum to meet and exceed the CCSS.

Blogging in the Classroom

In one regard, the early appeal of blogs in the classroom was simply tied to the emergence of the technology. As Greg Weiler (2003) notes, blogs provide fairly simple platforms for instant web publishing. In essence, blogs respond to the call from earlier writing scholars and teachers (Elbow 1968; Murray 1972) who assert that students write more intentionally and value their writing more when it is published, in some form, and read by real audiences. Blogs, as Weiler notes, provide the "ability to publish instantly to a wide audience" (2003, 74). The ability to publish instantaneously and for a *real* audience is what commonly attracts teachers to blogging for classroom purposes and what keeps students interested in blogging, even despite its fairly simplistic architecture in the increasingly complex digital landscape that is home to the next digital scholar.

One particular way that blogs both extend classroom learning and help make classrooms more student-centered is by inviting a multiliteracies approach. The multiliteracies approach is not new; the New London Group coined the term about 20 years prior to publication of this volume (New London Group 1996). However, this approach provides a pedagogical lens that many teachers and scholars continue to find useful in discussing the role of blogging in the classroom because of its student-centered nature. Though not specifically discussing blogging, Carlin Borsheim, Kelly Merritt, and Dawn Reed (2008) argue that "teachers who use a variety of media and technologies in their teaching do more than familiarize students with specific technologies or motivate them with the latest cool tool: They prepare students with multiliteracies for the twenty-first century." The authors argue that "sophisticated engagement" with technology equips students with the full range of literacies they need in their lives (88).

Beyond simply considering skills or literacies students need for engagement in school and their communities, Kathleen C. West (2008) in her discussion of blogs in her classroom describes how students enjoyed learning through their blogging unit. West reports "[e]njoyment was paramount in these class periods" (588). West argues that blogs provided her students with freedom and novelty. She reports that her students felt freer in expressing their beliefs and in engaging with texts on the class blog than in other learning forums and venues. Will Richardson (2003) reports on the use of blogs in his teaching of *Secret Life of Bees* in which the novel's author, Sue Monk Kidd, read the student blogs from Richardson's class. He argues that blogs are interesting to students because they provide opportunities for connections between readers and writers and because blogs provide a potential forum for building community. Finally, Richardson notes that all of his students, even his typically reticent students, engage each other via blogs.

Students often are willing to engage in blogs since this genre builds on student expertise and offers students choices in their writing. Richard Beach and David O'Brien (2005) argue that forms of multimedia, including blogging, are successful because they acknowledge "the importance of literacy practices the kids are already good at in the mediasphere, the multimediating world they live in, and most of these practices are more complex than 'print-centric' practices" (48). Similarly, Alex Reid (2011) claims that blogs are "an excellent opportunity for exploring and developing intrinsic motivations for writing" because in blogging, students "control the subject matter, the length, the format, the timing of [their] posts, and all the other characteristics of [their] writing" (303). Reid as well as Beach and O'Brien illustrate the ways that multimedia composing shifts the focus of the classroom to a more student-centered approach to composing because of the focus on student expertise and choice. This expertise may be technological, as students may have more experience with blogging and other multimodal technologies than their teachers, or it may simply be that multimodal assignments motivate students since students have more control over their writing. Ultimately, since blogs build on student expertise and choice, even students unfamiliar with blogging can participate meaningfully in a blogging curriculum.

Seeing students as technology experts in the classroom exposes one particular challenge of classroom blogging—teacher preparation. Aaron Doering, Beach, and O'Brien (2007) call for in-service and pre-service teachers to expand their repertoire of technological skills to accommodate the technological skills of their students. The authors specifically call for exposing teachers to Web 2.0 tools in their teacher preparation programs. While teacher expertise may be a challenge (see Chapters 15, 16, and 17 in this volume), we argue that the benefits of blogging, especially in regard to meeting the demands of the CCSS, outweigh the discomfort of teachers learning alongside their students. Furthermore, teachers who invite themselves to be learners in front of their students may actually provide effective models of learning for their students. This is especially true for public writing where students and teachers must be attuned to the needs of the community in order for meaningful writing to occur.

Public Writing, Blogging, and the CCSS

Working off the premise that student writers are at their best when they are genuinely interested in the types of writing they do, we argue that a blogging curriculum should provide opportunities for students to identify and work on topics of public concern relevant to their daily lives. This move to public writing was influenced by the "public turn" in writing studies (Flower 2008; Weisser 2002; Wells 1996) that emphasized students working with real audiences to effect change in local communities. The challenge for adapting the public turn to secondary writing contexts centers on rearticulating the theoretical and pedagogical aims of public writing to meet the CCSS. In particular, we need to be attentive to how a blogging curriculum creates opportunities for students not only to produce texts, but also to publish and update their writing in response to the rhetorical demands placed on their writing by public audience(s).

Generally, public writing positions students as advocates in a variety of public spaces, including schools, communities, and workplaces. The primary difference between public writing and traditional academic writing is the former's insistence on students producing writing that has the potential to be actionable and move beyond the classroom space. The emphasis on positioning their writing to move beyond the classroom invests students differently in their work in that it encourages them to be active writers who bring about change with their writing through the production, publication, and updating of their texts. More specifically, it prompts students to see the writing process as dynamic and recursive, as requiring attention to how their writing both potentially links with other information and spurs the circulation of ideas to address issues with which they are concerned. Ultimately, in positioning student writing in this manner, public writing demands that students be attentive to practices of *publishing* and *updating* that extend the initial *production* of their writing, three essential practices outlined in the CCSS for the "Production and Distribution of Writing" (CCSSO and NGA 2010, W9–10.6).

Learning as Partners

To investigate meaningful public writing in secondary schools, we established a secondary–university partnership. The study and the connected partnership occurred in a large metropolitan city in the Southwest at an urban high school we refer to as Center City High School. The name of the school, teachers, and students are all pseudonyms. The ethnic composition of the school population for the 2013–2014 school year was 94.8 percent Latino, 1.9 percent White, and 1.6 percent Black; the remaining 1.7 percent identify as multiracial or Native American. The state does not report specific numbers/percentages for racial groups with less than 10 students reporting (Arizona Department of Education 2014). The school's "Facts and Figures" sheet reports that 86.1 percent of students receive free and reduced lunch and that the school's 4-year graduation rate is 88.2 percent, which is measurably higher than the state average (Center City High School 2012).

The partnership with Center City High School was formed out of the authors' interest in the ways in which the curriculum may change in response to the CCSS. Specifically, the authors were interested in working with a teacher or small group of teachers and exploring new pedagogical approaches in response to the career and college ready writing emphasis in the CCSS. Karen, a veteran teacher with 16 years of teaching experience, expressed an interest in working with us. To forge the work of the research study and of the partnership, we began by observing Karen's classes, surveying her students, and interviewing Karen and her co-teacher, Laura, a teacher double certified in ELA and Special Education. In the observation year, Karen and Laura taught inclusion classes with students ranging from special education to honors. In the study year, Karen and Laura's inclusion classes included only special education and general education students. Karen and Laura did much of their classroom planning together. However, Karen was the lead teacher in the classroom. Throughout the study year, we collected data in the form of field notes, pre and post surveys, student interviews, teacher interviews, sample student work, and videotaped lessons.

Along with Karen and Laura, we articulated a partnership in which we collaboratively designed and implemented curriculum, and the authors studied the effects of this implementation. While the authors entered Karen and Laura's classroom with specific interests, we followed Karen's lead in the direction of the curriculum. To this end, Karen expressed interest in establishing class blogs that would be used throughout the year, but she felt that she lacked the technological knowledge to infuse blogging into the curriculum. The authors, interested in career- and college-ready writing, as well as public writing, worked with Karen to develop a blogging curriculum. The next section details some of the highlights of this blogging curriculum, particularly focusing on ways that students met the requirements of the CCSS: producing, publishing, and updating their blogs.

The Blogging Curriculum

The blogging curriculum in Karen's class was intended both to introduce the students to blogging as a writing genre and to transition them into a larger community-focused research writing unit. Therefore, the blogs in Karen's class were an integrated and integral part of learning for students. The blog was neither an afterthought, nor was it just for fun. The blog was an embodiment of all the learning the students were doing. For the blogs to function in this way, Karen and her students had to rethink some of their conceptions about learning to research and learning to write. This was primarily the case because a blogging curriculum is often nonlinear, while the teaching of writing and researching is typically presented in a linear fashion. That is, production, publishing, and updating were processes in which the students engaged repeatedly, and not in order, as we moved through the blogging unit. Interestingly, the students never questioned this nonlinear writing process. It was more challenging from an instructional planning standpoint than it seemed to be for the students. This appears to confirm Beach and O'Brien's (2005) claim that multimedia learning builds on existing student practices and experiences. Students seemed unfazed by a nonlinear curriculum because we were asking them to think and work in ways that they often worked.

In the sections that follow, we describe how producing, publishing, and updating—the specific elements of the CCSS (CCSSO and NGA 2010, W.9–10.6)—are part of this blogging for public writing curriculum. However, since producing, publishing, and updating are nonlinear processes, the discussion about these elements overlaps in ways that are productive for students in their learning. Finally, we offer the students' own words as illustrations of how the work of producing, publishing, and updating functions in the ELA classroom.

Producing

Due to its mere web presence, a blog has the inherent ability to reach broad and diverse audiences. This fact alone is what draws many writing teachers to use blogs in their curricula, as blogging offers students the opportunity to produce writing for an audience other than their teachers. Admittedly, our blogging curriculum was motivated by this same impulse, but we wanted to be intentional with the students about specifically understanding and articulating who made up the broad and diverse audiences of their blogs. That is, we worked with students to target the production of their texts to named, identified audiences. How we accomplished the goal of targeted writing was by focusing on the principle tenet of public writing—that it be actionable. We asked students to produce meaningful writing for audiences who had the capacity to act in response to the issues they were examining, and by capacity we mean not simply a base understanding of public issues, but an ability to intervene in the local community and affect change regarding such issues. To help students determine audiences' capacity to intervene, we drew from the CCCS for argumentative writing that calls for students to: "Develop claims and counter claims fairly, supplying evidence for each while pointing out the strengths and limitations of both in a manner that anticipates the audience's knowledge level and concerns" (CCSSO and NGA 2010, W9–10.1b). In particular, we focused on the students' attention to the knowledge level of the audience.

An early challenge we faced in reorienting the students' view of producing texts away from a teacher-centric view to a community- or audience-centric view was in helping students understand what it means for a text to be "actionable." Early student responses to questions about what it meant to be actionable revealed their general belief that an audience must care about or be emotionally connected to the issue under discussion, and that the issue mattered to the audience in some way. We acknowledged this initial recognition of caring and emotion as essential to effective community-based writing, as caring is what motivates citizens to act, but we pushed the students to think about "actionable" beyond emotion, to identify new pathways of understanding the act of producing writing that compels action in a local community. To motivate the students to extend their thinking, we devised, with Karen, a classroom activity based on illegal immigration enforcement, a hotly contested issue in the students' community, which prompted the students to think about the different ways that issue impacted lives in their community.

Using the local and controversial county sheriff, whose anti-immigration views and policies had been widely publicized, as the focus of the activity, we asked students to compose a written response to the statement: "The sheriff is an excellent sheriff who has served our county well, and he deserves to be re-elected in November." Admittedly, we knew this was a loaded question. In conversations with Karen, we discovered that the students held a general animosity toward the sheriff (a sentiment that is shared widely in the county, we might add) due to the threat his enforcement policies posed to their friends and families. Yet, despite the loaded nature of the question, we saw value in using it for its ability to make clear the difference between producing texts for individual expression and producing texts to prompt action. We recognize that these two types of production are not mutually exclusive, but we wanted to emphasize that despite their overall validity, the students' personal feelings about the sheriff were not enough to affect community change; the students needed to link their concerns and arguments with other voices in the community to affect such change.

When asked to share their written responses with the class, the students unsurprisingly responded very strongly to our prompt and across the board emphatically denied that the sheriff had served his constituents well; he had failed them and needed to be removed from office. Examples of their writing include statements such as "he is racist," "he hates Mexicans," "his morals are wrong," and "he has destroyed families!" A number of the students even took to the visual to express their disagreement through drawing devil horns and a forked tongue on the picture of the sheriff that we affixed on the writing prompt. Overall, the texts these students produced merely affirmed their prior distaste for the sheriff and did not position them to alter their viewpoint in any way or motivate them to design a plan for achieving what they wanted: a county police force free of the sheriff's influence.

The sheriff activity became interesting when we asked students how their response to the prompt would change if they wrote it on a blog. The previous week, we had introduced students to the "anatomy of blog writing," so they were familiar with the general design and style of blogs. As part of the anatomy lesson, we paid special attention to the linking mechanics of a blog, or how a blog connected to other texts on the web. Examples of these mechanics included the blog roll, use of hypertext links, use of social media profiles, blog archives, and the blog comment box. For the most part, feelings of general dislike for the sheriff persisted in the hypothetical blog response we asked them to think about; however, there were a number of instances where we saw students emphasize how they would use the blog to get the "facts out there about the sheriff."

While most of these examples ended with a simple, general assertion of the desire to get the truth out, a small number of students in each class referenced specific facts about the sheriff. For example, some students noted the millions of dollars the county has wasted defending the sheriff in lawsuits. Other students commented on the sheriff's makeshift open-air jail in the desert known for its excessively high temperatures in the summer, and yet another group discussed how they would link to articles, videos, and other information that demonstrate what the sheriff has done. What we saw in these latter examples was recognition by the students of the need to make adjustments to the "opinion" statements they initially wrote in the activity. They needed something specific to support their claims, and the resources for such support came from linking to other texts. Granted, the need to establish claims and present claims and counterarguments fairly is part of most ELA curricula and part of the CCSS (CCSSO and NGA 2010, W.9–10.1, W.9–10.1a, W.9–10.1b). However, what is unique about blogs is the ease of linking and the ability to link to a variety of sources. Described another way and using the language from the CCSS section we cited at the opening of this chapter, these students understood they needed to leverage "technology's capacity to link to other information" when producing text (W.9–10.6). Their text alone was not enough.

What was noteworthy with the sheriff exercise was how it revealed to students the differences between producing text via traditional writing and producing texts via blogs. More specifically, they came to see the writing they would do on a blog as provisional and tentative; it would require external support via links. It would be research.

This is the case in the blog post shown in Figure 9.1. In this blog post on child abuse, which was completed after the sheriff activity,

Design to Engineer
Started with ideas and became a Engineer

Home   The Engineer

Solution

January 26, 2013

My group and I are doing a research about Child Abuse and this is an enormous problem. We came up with a solution to help and put a stop to child abuse by informing those who have little knowledge about this significant topic through a power point during advisory on Fridays. We will give statistics, numbers of reports, resources, and ECT.

We want to help prevent child neglect, sexual abuse, physical abuse, ECT. We want to inform teenagers about this topic of how important it is and how it affects our community and social life. Did you guys know that every ten seconds theirs a report of child abuse? Did you know that every day 3 children/teen die of abuse? This topic might not be IMPORTANT for you because you assume you'll never be abused, but think again anything can happen. We want to aware children's/teens about this terrifying topic and how to reach for help. 1 out of 3 children are abuse can that be you and do you know how to stop it?

Posted by
Filed In Uncategorized | Edit
No Comments »

Figure 9.1   Example of a sheriff activity blog

the student illustrated an understanding of the lessons of the activity. Specifically, the student anticipated the type of information his audience would be looking for in order to be persuaded, so he integrated questions to spur a particular type of response from his readers. Ultimately, what we came to understand through the blogging unit, and the prepatory sheriff activity more specifically, was the importance of helping students transition between traditional forms of production for school writing to forms of production for writing for the blogs.

Publishing

The act of publishing a text is what prompts the circulation of ideas, which is a necessary component for bringing about change locally. More specifically, publishing creates the nexus point for interaction, where students join public conversations. More importantly, publishing generates opportunities for linking to other information and inviting others to link with their texts, which is a key tenet of the CCSS. While students often have experience sharing writing with their peers via peer response, writing for and responding to blogs requires a different set of skills and perceptions. Students must learn to think of their audiences as dynamic and expansive, rather than the fairly limited audience (teacher and peers) in traditional classroom writing. The publishing step takes this dynamic nature of audience into account.

To transition students into thinking about audience broadly, the students began by posting responses to a teacher blog post. Students were given the following mnemonic for thinking about qualities of effective responses:

> **T**rue
> **H**opeful
> **I**nspiring
> **N**ecessary
> **K**ind

They then responded to the teacher post while the responses were projected on the screen in the classroom. This yielded two important results. First, students were able to see others' responses, which helped students who were less certain about quality responses formulate more thoughtful responses of their own. Second, students came to see the dynamic nature of the blog. While all students responded to the initial post by the teacher, some students also responded to the comments of other students. Many of the students typed with an eye on the screen, watching their—and others'—responses pop up.

In this activity, students experienced the nonlinear nature of research and writing, a stark contrast to how they had been taught to do other academic forms of writing. For example, in this school, all of the students are required to learn how to write a Summary Analysis Paragraph, a fairly formulaic approach to writing in which students move through the paragraph step-by-step. In the blog response activity, by contrast, students produced meaningful written comments for their teachers and peers before ever writing an "official" blog post. That is, they did not have to master a step-by-step process before they could participate and write on a blog.

Furthermore, through this commenting activity, students came to see writing as dynamic and not limited to formal isolated settings. For example, the content of comments changed as additional comments were added, and students learned to appreciate the full range of responses that were possible in blogging. Finally, this particular activity expanded the students' notion of audience tremendously. That is, since all of the students responded to the teacher's post, the audience was quite large. The students were able to see what happens when the audience expands beyond one or two people (the teacher and peer reviewers) to well over 100 readers. Ultimately, writing that is nonlinear and dynamic has the potential to help students meet the "Range of Writing" standards in the CCSS: to "[w]rite routinely over extended time frames (time for research, reflection, and revision) and shorter time frames (a single setting or a day or two) for a range of tasks, purposes, and audiences" (CCSSO and NGA 2010, W.9–10.10).

Early activities, such as the one described here, prepared students to think about the utility of blogs as sites for public writing. As students became more comfortable blogging, they clearly came to see their blogs as resources for their classmates conducting similar community-based inquiry, and they were eager to link to one another's blogs. For example, a small group of girls in one class asked us how to create a blogroll. A blogroll is a list of links, typically in a sidebar, to blogs that the blog owner either reads or identifies with in some way. A blogroll is an endorsement, of sorts, of the linked blogs. We showed this small group of girls the fairly simple process for creating the blogroll, and by the end of the class period the word had spread. Within a few days, the majority of students in all sections had a blogroll in which they linked to the blogs of friends, group members, and people in other classes. Some students even chose to link to blogs that were not school related. This behavior showed us that students had an interest in making their work public. They saw the blogs as mechanisms for sharing and creating networks of information. Furthermore, this illustrated the students' interest in and ability to meet the audience requirements that are part of the CCSS for argumentative writing. The overwhelming interest in the blogrolls suggests that students had a broader interest in "anticipat[ing] the audience's knowledge level and concerns" (W.9–10.1b).

The sharing of texts among students is an important element of the blogging curriculum. More important, however, is the potential for blogs to move beyond the classroom. It is an understanding of this potential that is at the heart of the public writing blogging curriculum. Blanca, a student blogger, reports, "When I would write [the blog entries] I would feel like I was talking to the world." Blanca's comment illustrates her understanding of the potential for blogs. It was not simply that she imagined the reach of her words, but that her words did hold the potential for reaching broad audiences. When asked what she was proud of, Blanca commented that she was proud of writing about child abuse in her community and how she "let the world know about it." Blanca understands her role in circulating information on a much larger scale than her own class, school, or even immediate community.

As part of the larger research-based writing unit, students were required to reach out to experts in the community for interviews. It was during this interview that Claudia, another student in the class, came to see the value of the blogs. Claudia comments:

> At the beginning with the blogs I wondered what was this for. But now she [the interviewee, a social worker] asked me about our blogs and about the situation. And she told us that she wanted to see our blogs. So I thought somehow this is working you know? Other people can see it. And we might be bad at English or whatever you want but the information is out there. You know?

Claudia's comments show an awareness of what happens when blogs are "out there" and ideas are in circulation. Furthermore, her comments show a progressive process of coming to understand the potential in publishing. At first, Claudia assumed the blogs were, like many of her other school assignments, restricted to the classroom. However, in reaching out to her community, Claudia saw the potential in blogs to move beyond the classroom into the community, and potentially beyond. While Claudia recognizes the limitations of her prose ("We might be bad at English"), she understands that the reach of her blog has the potential to overcome her limitations.

In this particular blogging unit, it seems that students began by thinking of blogs as any other form of schoolwork. They assumed the audience for their writing would be closed and small. However, through a series of mini-lessons and activities tied to the curriculum, many students came to see the value of blog publishing and its potential to circulate information and ideas beyond the classroom.

Updating

As described in the preceding sections, blog writing positioned the students to see their writing as dynamic, as shifting in its emphasis and direction based on how the students connected their writing to other texts. Students became aware that the initial display of their ideas was not static and required adaptations that were responsive to the ways in which other texts affected the meaning or intent of what they wrote.

In our observations, we noted examples of student blogs changing over time. The majority of student blogs changed in appearance. When the blogging unit initially began, students relied heavily on the standard themes and options provided by the blogging platform. They demonstrated little initiative in, or knowledge of the skills for, developing their blog's appearance beyond these default choices. However, as the students grew in their blog identity, they adapted their blogs' appearance to reflect that identity. For example, students customized their blogs via color and font choices they deemed appropriate and relevant to the public issue they were addressing. They also learned to integrate relevant images as backgrounds for their blogs.

For example, in Figure 9.2, the author, whose nickname was Kay, originally named her blog *Designing Kay* because of her interest in design and fashion. Initially, she used one of the simple and standard backgrounds for her blog. As the project moved along and Kay's blog focused more on her topic of drug abuse, she continued to alter the appearance of her blog to maintain her design sensibilities. This showed a meshing of her original intent and her passion for her topic. The "Never let go of your DREAMS" graphic represents Kay's personality, complements her blog's appearance, and communicates her passion for ending drug abuse in her local community and family (Kay shared in her interview that her brother had problems with drugs). In addition to customizing the appearance of blogs, we observed students customizing their blog titles to cultivate interest in their blogs and provide more details about the nature and content of their blogs.

The author of the blog *Justice Will Be Served* originally started with a completely different blog title. As he worked in the group focusing on The Dream Act and alternative paths to citizenship, he changed the title of his blog. Concurrently, he chose a chalkboard background to emphasize the education focus of this community issue (Figure 9.3). The students continuously worked to revise the appearance and titles of their blogs to more effectively communicate with each other and their audience while cultivating their own online identities.

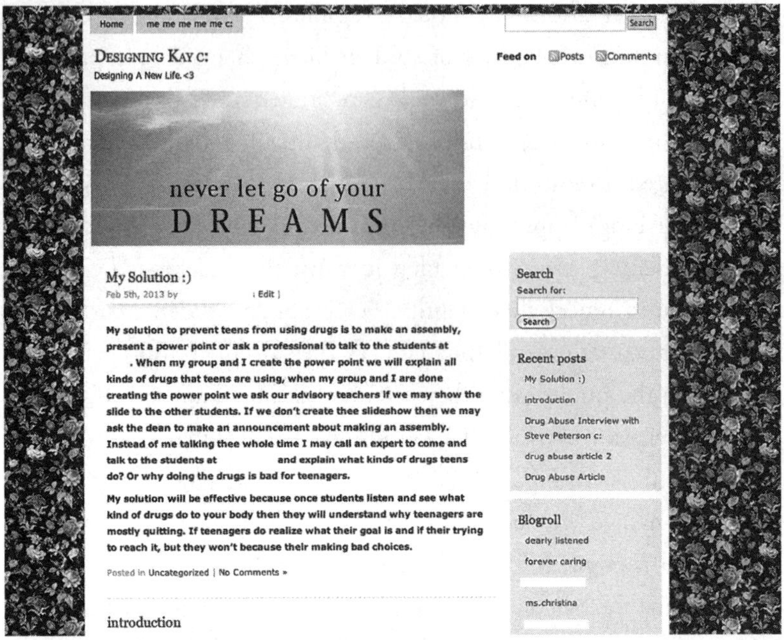

276 The Next Digital Scholar

Figure 9.2 *Designing Kay* blog

Figure 9.3 *Justice Will Be Served* blog

While revisions to the appearance of the blogs were common, students did not necessarily make substantive revisions to posts during the blogging unit. In part, this was due to the fact that the particular blogging platform we used did not have tools to aid in revision, such as a spelling or grammar checks. Accordingly, the lead teacher encouraged her classes to compose, revise, and edit their blog posts in a word processing file and then copy and paste it to their blogs. Likely because of this, we did not observe substantive revision to the blog posts, although it may have occurred. Secondly, since the blogging unit was new, there was a learning curve for all involved. Because of this learning curve, we did not spend as much time on some parts of the writing process, namely formal revision. Despite the lack of observable, formal revision in the posts, the revisions to the blog appearance showed us that students generally understood and cared about the value of revision in creating a public blogging identity, which is tied to the CCSS' call for students to "Produce clear and coherent writing in which the development, organization, and style are appropriate to task, purpose, and audience" (CCSSO and NGA 2010, W.9–10.4).

Ultimately, students came to see their blog identity as being just as important as the words they wrote in their postings, and that identity was the primary source of the students' credibility. It was the mechanism that invited engagement from other writers. When asked in an interview what she was most proud of in her blog, Blanca responded, "That it was free. You can write anything you like about your topic and what it's about." Blanca's response showed she understood the blog was topically focused, but she saw the potential in updating and making changes. To her, the blog was a free space that reflected her identity while meeting the assignment. Like the other students, Blanca saw the updating of the blog's appearance, and the freedom that came with that, as powerfully linked to the content and topic. Her updating reflected an understanding of this connection.

In addition to appearance, we observed students engage in a recursive process with their blogs; their blogs served as a springboard for writing in other contexts. For example, we observed students pull text from their blogs and use it in other class projects. What is noteworthy about this process is that students did not rely on simple copy-and-paste moves. Instead, we observed students sitting in groups, looking at blogs, and negotiating what information was relevant to other course work. The students came to see the blogs as part of a larger community-based writing unit, much in the way we hoped they would. As they pulled from their blogs and consulted other blogs for information, we saw the potential in updating. While blogs are, of course, updated by new blog posts or additions to other posts, they are also updated with use. The blogs themselves became resources for knowledge and information students needed; thus, students created their own research repositories and networks through this blogging unit.

Ultimately, the blogging unit required responses from the students that were not in the vacuum of the classroom environment. More specifically, the unit compelled students to reconsider how they viewed the act of revising texts. Rather than seeing their texts as something to be corrected for grammar and usage, the students saw their texts as constantly in flux. Texts were used to generate ideas and other texts. Additionally, texts were used to construct classroom and community identity, which changed throughout the unit. Ultimately, the act of updating is a continual process of pushing the envelope of change.

Where to Begin

In our informal weekly meetings, Karen often reported being pleased with the quantity and quality of student work on the blogs. In one particular meeting, she shared that the school principal was so pleased with the students' work on the blogs that the principal was considering requiring blogs in all ninth-grade English classes the following year. As we illustrated in the previous "Updating" section, students generally reported being proud of the work they did on the blogs, especially since they saw the work as an extension or reflection of themselves and their commitments to issues in their local communities. However, as with all uses of technology in the classroom, the blogging unit was messy at times while we all navigated the technology learning curve. Throughout the project, we discussed changes to the blogging unit that the teachers would implement the next year. For example, Karen said that she hoped to introduce the blogs at the very beginning of the school year so that students would have more time to develop their personal blogs prior to moving on to school-specific work. As we mentioned, the researchers also hoped to see more substantive revision to blog posts during the unit. To lessen the learning curve for other teachers, we have provided some information to help teachers interested in classroom blogging implement these technologies in their own classrooms.

Decisions About Use

In this particular blogging unit, we worked with ninth-grade teachers and their students, so we referenced the ninth- and 10th-grade CCSS. However, a blogging unit such as the one we describe is appropriate for all secondary grade levels. Of course, teachers at other grade levels would need to adjust content and expectations to meet the needs and abilities of their students, and school librarians and media specialists may be able to assist teachers in adjusting the curriculum in this way. Furthermore, since the CCSS scaffold instruction from grade-to-grade, many of the standards we reference in this chapter are also covered, to some extent, at other grade levels.

Teachers desiring to implement a blogging curriculum should begin by deciding how blogs will be used in the current curriculum. Karen originally planned to simply use a teacher blog on which students posted comments. However, when she considered the connection between the blogging project and the larger community-based public writing research project, she decided that individual student blogs would be better in facilitating and tracking student learning. Teachers who use blogs in their classrooms will need to make similar decisions as did Karen.

Teacher blogs or class blogs in which the entire class participates on one blog give students experience with blogging technology. On a teacher blog, students typically participate by commenting on posts written by the teacher. These posts may include links to other information on the web or responses to other student comments. Class blogs afford students the opportunity to compose full blog posts. However, this occurs infrequently since the whole class, or multiple classes, participates on one blog. Although extended posts are few and far between, class blogs extend the potential for participation beyond that on a teacher blog.

Individual student blogs, like the ones employed in this curriculum, offer students a greater degree of flexibility and potential for completing more in-depth writing. They also offer an opportunity for personalization, which typically appeals to students. If teachers hope to integrate blogs into the curriculum over a long period of time, individual student blogs are likely the best option. However, individual blogs require more attention on the part of the teacher. If a teacher plans to use individual student blogs, then we suggest the blog work replace other graded writing rather than be added onto existing writing assignments.

Teachers who like the idea of individual blogs but are leery of the time commitment for grading or have other concerns may choose to have students establish group blogs. In these scenarios, groups of four or five students compose blogs on similar topics with students rotating the responsibility for posting. This may be a good option for teachers trying blogs for the first time.

Beyond decisions about the types of blogs (teacher, individual student, student group), teachers will also need to make decisions about blog content. In the ELA classroom, blogs can be used for a variety of purposes, including personal writing, literary response, technological instruction, and research-based writing. In this way, blog-writing is uniquely situated to meet a rather large number of the CCSS for the ELA. Moreover, blogging for research positions teachers to work jointly with librarians and media specialists to create innovative learning experiences in which research is an integrated practice, rather than a series of discrete skills.

Choosing a Blogging Platform

Once teachers have decided which types of blogs and purposes best meet their needs, it is time to decide on a blog platform. There are a number of free blog platforms available to the general public. Examples of these include Blogger (blogger.com) and WordPress (wordpress.com). These particular platforms also have educational functions that teachers may use, such as an ability to view all student blogs or to create class blogrolls. Additionally, there are blog sites specifically intended for education. Education-focused blog sites include Edublogs (edublogs.org), SchoolRack (schoolrack.com), and 21st Century School Teacher (21stcenturyschoolteacher.com). Some of these sites allow for individual student blogs while others focus primarily on teacher blogs. Additionally, depending on the types of services, some of the education-focused blog sites require a fee—another consideration for teachers. While many of the blog platforms provide similar services, teachers should consider items such as the platform's ability to meet school and district security requirements and the teacher's ability to access and assess student blogs. Finally, using the blog platform's user manuals and tutorials, teachers will want to explore the technical and creative elements of the blog, including possible backgrounds, layouts, and the amount of storage space that users receive.

In the case of Karen's class, we decided on an education-focused blog platform. Because of her lack of blogging knowledge, Karen wanted to use a platform specifically intended for teachers and students that provided quality support, along with a fairly simple way to view and collect student work. Finally, Karen was interested in the range of security capabilities that the education-focused site provided should the district require tighter security.

Seeing the Students as Experts

Perhaps one of the most challenging aspects of incorporating blogging into the classroom is knowing that students may have more expertise than the teacher. In the case of Karen and Laura's class, few, if any, of the students had blogged previously. However, because of the multimodal and technological nature of students' daily lives, the learning curve for students was shallow while the learning curve for the teachers was noticeably steeper. Karen and Laura chose to embrace the students' expertise. In addition, they found that students completed required blog posts thoroughly and on time with greater frequency than regular assignments. More importantly, students enjoyed the blog assignment.

Conclusion

Toward the end of the first semester, Karen described a discussion she had with her students in which she asked them what they would like to do differently next semester. Some students indicated they wanted to stop doing the blogs. "So you want to go back to the way we did things before?" Karen asked. She said a student loudly responded, "And have nobody read our work? Forget it." Karen reported that the students then all agreed that they wanted to continue doing the blogs. This example illustrates that many of Karen's students came to value the public audiences for their work. With public audiences, their writing became actionable.

As the CCSS begin to ask teachers to consider integrating technologies into their writing curriculum in innovative ways, new opportunities emerge for introducing students to complex writing tasks that require advanced critical thinking skills. Rather than limiting students' scope of inquiry to standard classroom writing genres and limiting audience to their teachers, public writing pedagogies promote a vision of writing that situates it not simply as a mode of personal expression, but instead as a vehicle for preparing citizens for action in the public sphere. Viewing writing in this way increases student access to and involvement in the communities in which they engage.

References

Arizona Department of Education. 2014. "2013–2014 October 1 Enrollment." Accessed March 27, 2014. www.azed.gov/research-evaluation/arizona-enrollment-figures.

Beach, Richard, and David O'Brien. 2005. "Playing Texts Against Each Other in the Multimodal English Classroom." *English in Education* 39 (2): 44–59.

Borsheim, Carlin, Kelly Merritt, and Dawn Reed. 2008. "Beyond Technology for Technology's Sake: Advancing Multiliteracies in the Twenty-First Century." *Clearing House* 82 (2): 87–90.

Center City High School. 2012. "Facts and Figures." Accessed January 31, 2013.

Council of Chief State School Officers and National Governors Association. 2010. *Common Core State Standards for English Language Arts and Literacy in History/Social Studies, Science, and Technical Subjects*. Washington, DC: National Governors Association Center for Best Practices, Council of Chief State School Officers.

Accessed February 10, 2014. www.corestandards.org/assets/CCSSI_ELA%20 Standards.pdf.

Doering, Aaron, Richard Beach, and David O'Brien. 2007. "Infusing Multimodal Tools and Digital Literacies into an English Education Program." *English Education* 40 (1): 41–60.

Elbow, Peter. 1968. "A Method for Teaching Writing." *College English* 30 (2): 115–125.

Flower, Linda. 2008. *Community Literacy and the Rhetoric of Public Engagement.* Carbondale, IL: Southern Illinois University Press.

Murray, Donald. 1972. "Teaching Writing as a Process, Not Product." *The Leaflet*: 11–14.

New London Group. 1996. "A Pedagogy of Multiliteracies: Designing Social Futures." *Harvard Educational Review* 66 (1): 60–92.

Reid, Alex. 2011. "Why Blog? Searching for Writing on the Web." In *Writing Spaces: Readings on Writing,* Volume 2, edited by Charles Lowe and Pavel Zemliansky, 302–319. Anderson, SC: Parlor Press.

Richardson, Will. 2003. "Weblogs in the English Classroom: More than Just Chat." *English Journal* 93 (1): 39–43.

Weiler, Greg. 2003. "Using Weblogs in the Classroom." *English Journal* 92 (5): 73–75.

Weisser, Christian. 2002. *Moving Beyond Academic Discourse: Composition Studies and the Public Sphere.* Carbondale, IL: Southern Illinois University Press.

Wells, Susan. 1996. "Rogue Cops and Healthcare: What Do We Want From Public Writing?" *College Composition and Communication* 47 (3): 325–341.

West, Kathleen C. 2008. "Weblogs and Literary Response: Socially Situated Identities and Hybrid Social Languages in English Class Blogs." *Journal of Adult and Adolescent Literacy* 51 (7): 588–598.

CHAPTER **10**

Wherefore Art Thou Not Updating Thy Status?
Facebook, the Common Core State Standards, and the Power of Meaningful Work

R. Spencer Atkinson

Practical and Theoretical Context

The first time I tried incorporating Facebook into my ninth-grade English class, it was a total failure. It was the fall of 2011 in the small Midwestern town of Lakeside (a pseudonym), where I taught English Language Arts at Lakeside High School—a school of about 650 students in an upper-middle-class bedroom community. The school had a block schedule of four 90-minute periods per day, and the main focus of my course load was English 9, the required English course for all freshmen. That fall, my English 9 class consisted of 18 students: a little more than half female, predominantly white, and intentionally untracked by ability group.

It was my sixth year teaching, and the course curriculum was handed down to me by the retiring teacher I had replaced the previous year, with a traditional reading list that included *To Kill a Mockingbird* and *Romeo and Juliet*. Because all teachers of English 9 in the department were expected to teach the same lessons on the same schedule, it was a course that changed very little from year to year. As a result, the course still included a few handouts that were created on a dot matrix printer and photocopied ad infinitum year after year. However, the state's recent adoption of the Common Core State Standards (CCSS) had triggered an examination of the content and methods in our coursework school-wide. We as a department agreed that some change was in order in English 9, and I took this as an opportunity to try some new ideas. In this chapter I explain one of those new ideas: creating an assignment that draws on students' predilection for and use of social networking sites, particularly Facebook. After discussing this assignment and presenting two student examples, I explore the implications of taking such an approach to meet the CCSS.

In the fall of 2011, my students were reading *To Kill a Mockingbird*, and I wanted them to conduct character analyses in accordance with CCSS RL.9–10.1 ("Cite strong and thorough textual evidence to support analysis") and RL.9–10.3 ("Analyze how complex characters [...] develop over the course of a text") (Council of Chief State School Officers [CCSSO] and National Governors Association [NGA] 2010). I started to look online for a creative way to achieve this, and I came across a PowerPoint template designed to look like a Facebook profile (Figure 10.1). David Ashby (2010), the template's creator, suggested it could be used for historical figures or literary characters. Considering how much time my students spent on Facebook, I figured this would be a fun way to get them engaged while requiring them to use details from the text to complete the characters' profiles.

As I was putting some finishing touches on the activity one day after school, a few students came into my room to ask about an assignment. One student glanced at the "profile" on my computer screen,

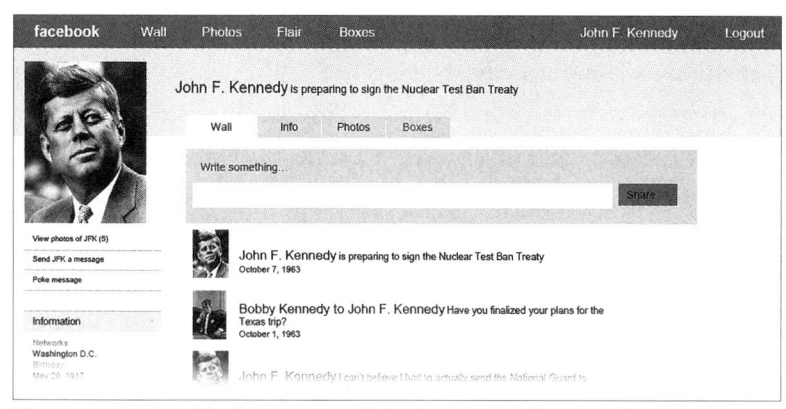

Figure 10.1 Ashby's (2010) original PowerPoint template

unimpressed, and said, "Facebook doesn't look like that now. That's the old version."

"Oh, okay," I replied. "But it's still pretty cool, right?"

"Um, I guess. We're not going to do that in class, though, are we?" Others nodded.

I was struck by their dismissiveness. Rather than be excited about this activity, as I had expected, it was clear they were put off by its inauthenticity.

If I had charged ahead with the idea for a "Facebook" PowerPoint template, in spite of my students' candid disapproval, I may have been able to say I "covered" CCSS standards RL.9–10.1 and RL.9–10.3 (CCSSO and NGA 2010), but I certainly would have done so at the expense of some meaningful learning and in a way that put the CCSS above student practices rather than using student practices to drive my response to the CCSS. This was not the curricular change I hoped the CCSS would inspire, so I scrapped the idea and went back to the drawing board. I realized that I had been misguided in my approach to social media, that I wasn't quite getting what this technology meant for my students. Yet I still believed in the potential power of Facebook as a learning tool, particularly given the growing body of scholarship that reveals the promise and challenges of using Web 2.0 and social media in the classroom. Gina Maranto and Matt Barton (2010), for instance, describe online social networks' possibilities for youth participation in civic engagement, ranging from silly community building opportunities to confronting serious political and social issues. They find that Facebook and other social networks are a medium of engagement in which otherwise disaffected youth have willingly participated, creating a powerful learning space that is different from conventional media. Randall McClure (2011) finds that Web 2.0 technologies create opportunities for research and writing tasks to become more personal, collaborative, and social than in the more static first generation of the internet. His work locates digital spaces within an iterative process of "writingresearchwriting," asking students to draw connections between their sources of information and their chosen methods of accessing that information. He suggests having students "explain and justify their selections of information sources [...] in ways that articulate how the sources are related to one another" (324). Such work made me excited to persist in my desire to use social networking sites in productive and creative ways to meet the CCSS. Thus, as my students and I moved to the next unit in the course, which was centered around *Romeo and Juliet*, I was determined to discover how social media could achieve meaningful, authentic learning *within* the new framework of the CCSS.

In the pre-CCSS plan for *Romeo and Juliet*, the unit had always included a project, but its purpose was never entirely clear. Out of all the major components of the unit, students got most excited about the project and often put the most work into it, but the products rarely demonstrated meaningful learning. Nor were they actually expected to: The *real* assessment took the form of a multiple choice final unit exam, which far outweighed the project in the gradebook. This felt backward to me. If a major component of the unit was to be a project, then it seemed like folly to squander the students' enthusiasm and effort on silly, insignificant work. It occurred to me that using Facebook in ways more reflective of student practice might allow me to revamp the project and use it as an opportunity for students to demonstrate deeper thinking about Shakespeare and his play.[1]

In their book *Understanding by Design* (2005), Grant Wiggins and Jay McTighe provided a framework for approaching the new CCSS-inspired unit. At the core of Wiggins and McTighe's work is the idea of backward design—starting with the end in mind, so as to reverse engineer what content, skills, and activities will help students to arrive at that end. In order to achieve this, they recommend articulating "big ideas," which they define as "a concept, theme, or issue that gives meaning and connection to discrete facts and skills" (5) and "enduring understandings," which are "the specific inferences, based on big ideas, that have lasting value beyond the classroom" (342). For the new project, an essential question (EQ) helped define the big idea: What role does social and family pressure play in the choices we make? Not only would this "big idea" question address CCSS W.9–10.7 ("Conduct short as well as more sustained research projects to answer a question") (CCSSO and NGA 2010), it would provide a much-needed focus to the project students so relished. The EQ gave students a lens to discuss the text (e.g., why is Tybalt so offended when Romeo intrudes on his family's party?), understand Shakespeare's choices as a writer (e.g., why are there so many references to Greek mythology?), and connect the text to students' lives (e.g., how would teenagers and their parents today react differently/the same in this situation?).

With the EQ as a compass, I presented the new project as the students' opportunity to demonstrate how *Romeo and Juliet* provides a possible answer to the EQ. Because the question is intentionally open-ended, I encouraged students to consider multiple angles and develop multiple possible answers before beginning their work. I also gave them a wide range of ways to respond, leaving the choice of medium open-ended and allowing for the EQ to be implicit or explicit in the final product. In the end, students presented their projects to the class, at which time they more fully explained their answers to their EQ, if necessary.

Overall, the new, EQ-driven project was more successful than in previous years, and I was proud to see the kind of creativity and critical thinking that emerged. The proportion of thoughtful and effective projects was significantly higher, which I believe was the product of building on students' existing social networking practices and utilizing students' existing enthusiasm about choice and creativity in the project and then providing a clarity of purpose that had been missing before. To illustrate students' productive responses for readers of this chapter, I highlight in the next section a project by two students, Amanda and Edaline (pseudonyms), which they gave me permission to share because of the range of learning outcomes that it demonstrates.

Results of the Project

Amanda and Edaline began by creating Facebook accounts for all the main characters in *Romeo and Juliet*, with the premise that they would retell the story as it might occur in today's digital world. They populated the characters' profiles with biographical information, familial connections, personality traits, and more. This was exactly the kind of character analysis I had envisioned for *To Kill a Mockingbird*, requiring close reading of the text for accurate profiles and careful inferences to fill in any gaps in their personal information. Amanda and Edaline then invented status updates that provided succinct plot summaries from each character's first person viewpoint.

This project addressed three major CCSS in depth: RL.9–10.1 ("Cite strong and thorough textual evidence to support analysis of what the text says explicitly as well as inferences drawn from the text"), RL.9–10.2 ("Determine a theme or central idea of a text and analyze in detail its development over the course of the text, including how it emerges and is shaped and refined by specific details; provide an objective summary of the text"), and RL.9–10.3 ("Analyze how complex characters develop over the course of a text, interact with other characters, and advance the plot or develop the theme") (CCSSO and NGA 2010). The characters' Facebook profiles used *textual evidence* to support character *analysis* of both explicit and inferred details. The characters' *motivations* and interactions were explored through their connections to one another online. The EQ required students to track a *central theme* throughout the text, and their status updates provided a concise *summary* of the plot. There were some fun elements, too, like posting Juliet's relationship status as "it's complicated" and using a shirtless Zac Efron as Romeo's profile picture (he looks a lot like Leonard Whiting, the actor in the 1968 film).

The Facebook medium allowed Amanda and Edaline to embed a response to the EQ, which they elaborated when they presented their project to the class. What they wanted to show, they explained, was the ways that the characters attempted to influence one another's actions throughout the play. Sometimes they were subtle, such as when they would like each other's statuses; other times they were more direct, such as when Mercutio minimized Romeo's swooning by saying, "You met her Sunday ... it's barely Monday morning" (see the bottom right of Figure 10.2). These patterns of interaction reinforce research findings on the ways that the effects of peers' behavior on one another play out in both on- and off-line social networks (e.g., Lomi et al. 2011; Wang, Yu, and Wei 2012).

Amanda and Edaline's efforts to fit the story to the medium resulted in some impressive evidence of metacognition and critical thinking, which are two crucial intellectual skills for any college-ready student, according to the Framework for Success in Postsecondary Writing

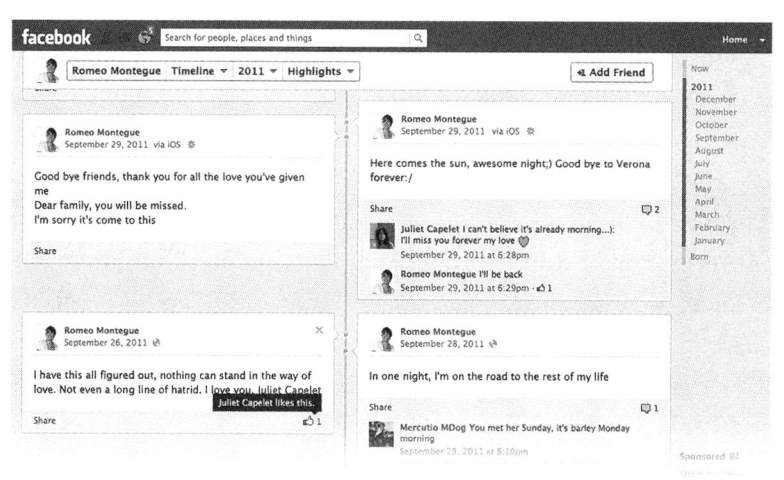

Figure 10.2 Screenshot of Romeo's profile[2]

(Framework) (Council of Writing Program Administrators [CWPA], National Council of Teachers of English [NCTE], and National Writing Project [NWP] 2011), and are implicit in the CCSS.[3] They knew that a post from a cell phone displays differently on Facebook than a post from a PC, and they used that information to create a post for Romeo, who, while in exile in Mantua, updated his status with, "Goodbye friends. I'm sorry it's come to this" (see the top left of Figure 10.2). In another example, they adjusted Romeo and Juliet's privacy settings so that their parents would be blocked from seeing them post about their secret rendezvous—a stealth tactic that is a common practice for adolescents. In perhaps the most intriguing example from the project, Tybalt's hatred of Romeo was demonstrated through cyberbullying—that is, sending him threatening messages and passive-aggressively commenting about him to his friends. This is a concept with which many students are unfortunately familiar. According to the results of the Youth Internet Safety Survey (Ybarra et al. 2006), about one in 10 adolescents has been the target of internet harassment. They also found that almost half (45 percent) of targets knew the harasser in person before the incident (1169). By bringing this contemporary social issue into their project, Amanda and Edaline opened the door for their classmates to critically examine their engagement with social media in their own lives.

What made this project an even further success was its demonstration of what Deborah Meier calls "habits of mind." While this term has been applied to a variety of intellectual skills, here I use Meier's list: *evidence, viewpoint, connections, supposition,* and *relevance* (1995, 49–50). These terms also appear in the standards already cited in this chapter. In Amanda and Edaline's project and presentation, all of these habits of mind were manifest. They selected textual *evidence* to create the characters' profiles, such as the familial relationship (cousins) between Tybalt and Juliet, and Romeo's description "I always follow my heart, and I act on a whim." They employed the various *viewpoints* of each of the characters through their first person postings on each other's walls (Figure 10.3), such as when Benvolio attempts to mediate an ongoing

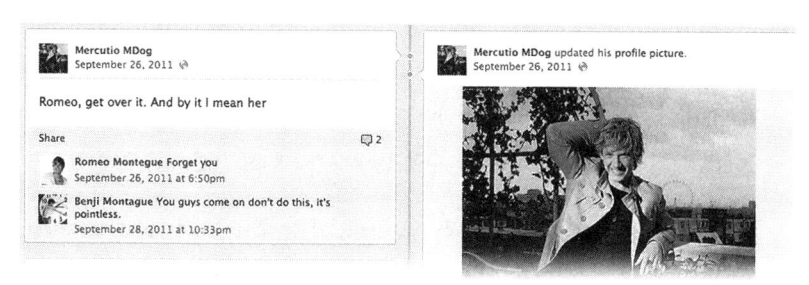

Figure 10.3 Benvolio "Benji" Montague, ever the mediator, comments on Mercutio's post to Romeo

argument between Romeo and Mercutio by posting, "You guys, come on [...] it's pointless." They drew *connections* between the characters' actions and their own lived experiences, such as the previously mentioned example regarding privacy settings and parental supervision. They made *suppositions* about how the story would change in a digital world, and they made the story *relevant* to their peers through a contemporary social issue (cyberbullying).

Meeting the CCSS

While the CCSS were *implicit* in this project in the ways I have described, they did not *drive* the project. Instead, the project was built on authentic inquiry, on remaining open to what unanticipated learning occurred. Such an approach helps students and teachers to achieve the ideals of the CCSS through skill application, not just demonstration.

In fact, my reading of the CCSS is that they already suggest a need for this kind of work. The introduction to the CCSS makes this clear, although it is the part of the document most likely skipped over by an audience of teachers and administrators feeling overwhelmed about (and hurried into) implementation. First, it makes explicit the limitations of the document—paramount among them being that it doesn't specify *how* to teach:

> For instance, the use of play with young children is not specified by the Standards, but it is welcome as a valuable

> activity in its own right. [...] Students require a wide-ranging, rigorous academic preparation and [...] attention to such matters as social, emotional, and physical development and approaches to learning. (CCSSO and NGA 2010, 6)

These declarations strike me as essential to the spirit of the document, and they should be heeded in tandem with the CCSS themselves. Furthermore, the document paints a portrait of the ideal "college and career ready" student: "They comprehend as well as critique. They respond to the varying demands of audience, task, purpose, and discipline. They use technology and digital media strategically and capably" (7). Yet this brief enumeration of what college and career ready students should know and be able to do only minimally addresses the intellectual qualities that such students need for future success—leaving "room for teachers, curriculum developers, and states to determine how those goals should be reached" (4). As such, the CCSS have given educators and administrators a lens through which to see our practice anew, just as their adoption in our state led those at my school to reexamine their curricula and inspired me to explore fresh ideas.

The Framework attempts to define the qualities of thought that educators should cultivate in their students. This document, like Meier's work, employs the term "habits of mind" (CWPA, NCTE, and NWP 2011, 4). When John Dewey (1916) first coined that term, he was intentional about his choice of the word *habit*: "The habits of mind involved in habits of the eye and hand supply the latter with their significance. Above all, the intellectual element in a habit fixes the relation of the habit to varied and elastic use, and hence to continued growth" (57). These intellectual behaviors require frequent practice to become habitual, automatic responses in the way a person approaches his or her world. Once ingrained, these habits of mind endure beyond the specific task, assignment or technology, ensuring their application throughout an individual's "continued growth."

I point out these features of the CCSS in order to make the case that myopic attention to *covering* the CCSS—without due deference to the bigger picture of which they are a part—can stifle the very skills that the CCSS declare are important to college and career readiness. Instead, the approach I tried to take with the project described in this chapter was meant both to address the CCSS and stay true to the spirit of meaningful work that I believe is implied by them. For instance, the project description I gave to students emphasized the importance of creative and critical thought in their work. This is underscored by the EQ (What role does social and family pressure play in the choices we make?), which is intentionally open-ended and value-neutral: What kind of role? What choices? For better or for worse? Students' interpretations of the characters' actions helped define their answers to the question. Then the choice of medium for the project was left up to the students. They were asked to consider what medium would best demonstrate their learning and their answer to the question, and they submitted proposals to me to ensure they were setting themselves up for success. Finally, as mentioned, the project ended with presentations to the class where they explicated their responses to the EQ. This requirement served as a means to address CCSS SL.9–10.4 ("Present information, findings, and supporting evidence clearly, concisely, and logically such that listeners can follow the line of reasoning") and SL.9–10.5 ("Make strategic use of digital media […] in presentations to enhance understanding") (CCSSO and NGA 2010). These presentations produced a "positive peer effect": As students saw each other's differing interpretations and approaches, they also saw their own work in context. Research studies on peer effects show a significant benefit to students' academic performance when the work of their high-achieving peers is made available for analysis (Sacerdote 2011). For example, a student in my class named Landon (a pseudonym) had done a similar Facebook-based project, but he immediately recognized and commented on the lack of depth in his own work as compared to the work of Amanda and Edaline. As he presented his work to the class, Landon acknowledged what the rest of us quickly saw: He focused mostly on basic plot summary, so his project was missing the interactivity of viewpoints and metacognition that made Amanda and Edaline's project so dynamic. Of course, Landon didn't say it that way; he expressed that theirs "just had more to it" than his did. In a conversation with him later, though, he and I discussed what he thought that meant, and we explored what lessons he might take away from the experience. In the next project, I saw drastic improvement in the quality of Landon's work.

As I reflect on my students' learning outcomes from this project, I am also aware of the learning that their work inspired in me. Reflecting on my initial failure with *To Kill a Mockingbird* led me to revise my thinking about Facebook as a learning tool. Born in 1982, I was raised in a Web 1.0 world, when the internet was a source of information to be looked at and read, not to be interacted with. Meanwhile, my students are what have been called "digital natives" (NWP with DeVoss, Eidman-Aadahl, and Hicks 2010; Prensky 2001a): Having grown up immersed in the world of Web 2.0 and social media, they are native speakers of the language of today's internet. Our students use Web 2.0 tools like wikis and social networks to access and interpret knowledge the way their parents' generation used yearly encyclopedia sets and the nightly news. Those of us in Gen-X fall somewhere between, with a foot in both generations.

The way our students process and interact with their world is fundamentally different from that of most of the people teaching them. For example, digital learning specialist Marc Prensky draws an analogy to social psychology: "People who have grown up in different cultures do not just think about different things, they actually think differently. The environment and culture in which people are raised affects and even determines many of their thought processes" (2001b, 4). Prensky's description of digital media as a totally new "environment and culture" (2001b, 4) from that of previous generations conveys just how distinct this worldview is. Something I had misunderstood in my earlier attempt with Facebook—and something that my students understood implicitly—was that the medium is useful for what one can *do* with it, not for what it looks like. By simply replicating the appearance (and badly, at that), a PowerPoint template could not achieve the layers of interconnectivity that made social networking technology so powerful in the first place. What's more, the way it was used in the real world informed how it was used in the project, ultimately giving the students' work its depth and creativity. As I learned from this project, the "read-write Web" (McClure 2011) represented by social media opens possibilities for teachers to continually re-teach and re-learn digital literacy alongside their students, keeping in mind that further technological evolution is already occurring.[4]

Implications for Future Practice

This project showed me that, while I was teaching my students about important mental habits like creativity, critical thinking, and metacognition, they were teaching me about how those habits can be applied to their digital world. However, being digital natives doesn't mean that our students know how best to navigate their information-rich world. In his groundbreaking book *Amusing Ourselves to Death* (1985), Neil Postman cautioned that the world had become more Huxleyan than Orwellian: It was not the strict control of information, but the sheer glut of it that was a danger to society. Yet Postman was writing at a time when the internet felt more like sci-fi than reality. Statistician Nate Silver, in an interview the day after he successfully predicted the vast majority of November 2012 election results, provided an updated variation on that sentiment: "According to IBM, 90 percent of the data in the world was created within the last 2 years. So one problem is what we call the signal-to-noise ratio. The amount of meaningful information relative to the overall amount of information is declining […] and that means the real skill now is learning how to pick out the useful information from all this noise" (National Public Radio 2012).

This is what the American Library Association (ALA) calls "information literacy"—those skills and competencies needed to navigate the sea of data and chart a meaningful course of thought or action. The ALA cautions, "increasingly, information comes to individuals in unfiltered formats, raising questions about its authenticity, validity, and reliability. […] The sheer abundance of information will not in itself create a more informed citizenry without a complementary cluster of abilities necessary to use information effectively" (2000,

2).[5] The CCSS document frames the issue this way: "Students need the ability to gather, comprehend, evaluate, synthesize, and report on information and ideas [...] and to analyze and create a high volume and extensive range of print and nonprint texts in media forms old and new" (CCSSO and NGA 2010, 4). The educational implication here is that we can't have content retention as a goal without teaching students how to evaluate that content. When we do the work of selecting all the "important" information for our students, then provide it for them pre-sorted and pre-packaged, we do them a disservice. This is what James P. Purdy (2010) means when he affirms, "Many students have been trained to limit the resources they consult to those already vetted by academic professionals (i.e., those in libraries); therefore, they lack the strong analytical skills to make judgments for themselves. [...] Teachers need to help students develop the perceptual lenses with which to use these [Web 2.0 tools] productively" (56). In today's world, students need to be able to do their own sorting of information and make their own decisions about which information and tools are important to their purpose—and their classroom experiences can help them learn to do so more thoughtfully.

Educators who allow their students to utilize social media and explore their appropriate academic uses, while being supported by thoughtful curriculum and practice, can equip students with crucial critical thinking skills. The creativity evident in the work of Amanda, Edaline, and their peers can be a response to cynics who question, as Stanford professor Andrea Lunsford quips, "whether Google is making us stupid and whether Facebook is frying our brains" (Haven 2009). Lunsford's own work demonstrates quite the opposite: This generation, she finds, does more writing than any previous in history—it just isn't the kind of writing their parents or their teachers understand. According to our students, Lunsford says, "Good writing [...] doesn't just sit on the page. It gets up, walks off the page and changes something" (Haven 2009). Educators can validate these forms of writing and engagement through thoughtful opportunities to incorporate them into students' classroom experiences.

This is what projects like the *Romeo and Juliet* Facebook assignment can do for our students: They can provide the kind of intellectually rigorous work required to make coverage of the CCSS transcend the school walls. My *Romeo and Juliet* project aimed to make explicit through public presentation the thinking skills utilized by the most successful examples. If content retention is a goal, then, yes, a multiple-choice test can demonstrate content retention. But this project demonstrated more—including creativity, metacognition, critical thinking, and other important intellectual skills promoted by the CCSS. After high school, knowledge of the specific content of *Romeo and Juliet* will, at best, be anecdotally useful to my students (unless they become English teachers). Instead, it is the habits of mind—a term coined by John Dewey almost 100 years ago and reframed in the CCSS' recommendations for cultivating college and career ready students—that will persist and transform into lifelong learning.

Endnotes

1. In thinking about the redesign of this project, I was already cognizant of the role the CCSS played in other parts of the unit. For instance, a lesson on allusions to Greek mythology in the play addressed RL.9–10.9 ("Analyze how an author draws on and transforms source material in a specific work") and analysis of the various figures of speech in Shakespeare's writing addressed L.9–10.5a ("Demonstrate understanding of figurative language, word relationships, and nuances in word meanings: Interpret figures of speech in context and analyze their role in the text") (CCSSO and NGA 2010).

2. At the time of this project, students were forced to misspell characters' names in order to accommodate Facebook's user agreement against creating fake accounts. It is worth noting that major publishing companies have created accounts for fictional entities, including Richard Castle and Lemony Snicket, as a way to publicize books. Facebook has since realized the demand for this use of their product, and they have added a "fictional character" category to their profile offerings.

3. For a more extensive discussion of the Framework's habits and their connection to CCSS, see Angela Clark-Oates, Allyson Boggess, and Duane Roen (Chapter 4) and Rachel Bear, Heidi Estrem, James E. Fredricksen, and Dawn Shepherd (Chapter 5) in this volume.

4. For more discussion on trends in digital literacy instruction, see Elizabeth Homan and Dawn Reed (Chapter 2) and Tawnya Lubbes and Heidi Skurat Harris (Chapter 16) in this volume.

5. In Chapter 3, Amanda Nichols Hess and Katie Greer further explore how library standards documents intersect with the CCSS.

References

American Library Association. 2000. *Information Literacy Competency Standards for Higher Education*. Chicago: ALA. Accessed February 10, 2014. www.ala.org/acrl/sites/ala.org.acrl/files/content/standards/standards.pdf.

Ashby, David. 2010. "Facebook Project and Template." Accessed February 10, 2014. techtoolsforschools.blogspot.com/p/facebook-project.html.

Council of Chief State School Officers and National Governors Association. 2010. *Common Core State Standards for English Language Arts and Literacy in History/Social Studies, Science, and Technical Subjects*. Washington, DC: National Governors Association Center for Best Practices, Council of Chief State School Officers. Accessed February 10, 2014. www.corestandards.org/assets/CCSSI_ELA%20Standards.pdf.

Council of Writing Program Administrators, National Council of Teachers of English, and National Writing Project. 2011. *Framework for Success in Postsecondary Writing*. Accessed February 10, 2014. wpacouncil.org/files/framework-for-success-postsecondary-writing.pdf.

Dewey, John. 1916. *Democracy and Education: An Introduction to the Philosophy of Education*. New York: The MacMillan Company.

Haven, Cynthia. 2009. "The New Literacy: Stanford Study Finds Richness and Complexity in Students' Writing." *Stanford News*. October 12. Accessed February 10, 2014. news.stanford.edu/news/2009/october12/lunsford-writing-research-101209.html.

Lomi, Alessandro, Tom A. B. Snijders, Christian E. G. Steglich, and Vanina Jasmine Torló. 2011. "Why Are Some More Peer Than Others?: Evidence from a Longitudinal Study of Social Networks and Individual Academic Performance." *Social Science Research* 40 (6): 1506–1520.

Maranto, Gina, and Matt Barton. 2010. "Paradox and Promise: MySpace, Facebook, and the Sociopolitics of Social Networking in the Writing Classroom." *Computers and Composition* 27 (1): 36–47.

McClure, Randall. 2011. "WritingResearchWriting: The Semantic Web and the Future of the Research Project." *Computers and Composition* 28 (4): 315–326.

Meier, Deborah. 1995. *The Power of Their Ideas: Lessons for America from a Small School in Harlem*. Boston: Beacon Press.

National Public Radio. 2012. "'Signal' and 'Noise': Prediction as Art and Science." October 10. Accessed February 10, 2014. www.npr.org/2012/10/10/ 162594751/signal-and-noise-prediction-as-art-and-science.

National Writing Project with DeVoss, Danielle N., Elyse Eidman-Aadahl, and Troy Hicks. 2010. *Because Digital Writing Matters: Improving Student Writing in Online and Multimedia Environments.* San Francisco: Jossey-Bass.

Postman, Neil. 1985. *Amusing Ourselves to Death: Public Discourse in the Age of Show Business.* New York: The Penguin Group.

Prensky, Marc. 2001a. "Digital Natives, Digital Immigrants Part 1." *On the Horizon* 9 (5): 1–6.

———. 2001b. "Digital Natives, Digital Immigrants Part 2: Do They Really Think Differently?" *On the Horizon* 9 (6): 1–6.

Purdy, James P. 2010. "The Changing Space of Research: Web 2.0 and the Integration of Research and Writing Environments." *Computers and Composition* 27 (1): 48–58.

Sacerdote, Bruce. 2011. "Peer Effects in Education: How Might They Work, How Big Are They and How Much Do We Know Thus Far?" In *Handbook of the Economics of Education,* Volume 3, edited by Eric A. Hanushek, Stephen Machin, and Ludger Woessmann, 249–227. San Diego, CA: Elsevier B.V.

Wang, Xia, Chungling Yu, and Yujie Wei. 2012. "Social Media Peer Communication and Impacts on Purchase Intentions: A Consumer Socialization Framework." *Journal of Interactive Marketing* 26 (4): 198–208.

Wiggins, Grant P., and Jay McTighe. 2005. *Understanding By Design.* 2nd ed. Alexandria, VA: Association for Supervision and Curriculum Development.

Ybarra, Michelle. L., Kimberly J. Mitchell, Janis Wolak, and David Finkelhor. 2006. "Examining Characteristics and Associated Distress Related to Internet Harassment: Findings from the Second Youth Internet Safety Survey." *Pediatrics* 118 (4): 1169–1177.

CHAPTER **11**

Technology, the Common Core State Standards, and School Budgets
A Recipe for Necessary Innovation

Amanda Stearns-Pfeiffer

Curricular Shifts and Technology Demands

Teachers are working hard to figure out what the Common Core State Standards (CCSS) require of them and identify the curricular shifts they may need to make to demonstrate the standards. I use the phrase *curricular shifts* in order to acknowledge that much of what teachers are already doing in the classroom is effective and engaging for their students and already meets much of the CCSS. Our schools' curricula need not be completely overhauled; however, there is a newfound focus on the inclusion of technology in the English Language Arts (ELA) classroom.

My recommendation in this chapter is that free websites such as Weebly and Storify[1] can help bridge the gap between what is expected at many universities in terms of digital literacy (what the CCSS call "college readiness") and the (sometimes) lacking resources available to secondary students in some school districts. In this chapter, I first outline the ongoing economic issues associated with technology use in the secondary classroom, especially as highlighted in the CCSS. I then propose the use of Weebly and Storify to help teachers and librarians engage students in digital literacy. I argue that with no major financial commitment required to use them, sites like Weebly and Storify can easily be experimented with in the classroom, and, more importantly, become valuable tools for teachers as they shift the curriculum to address the CCSS in ways that acknowledge the next digital scholar.

More Technology + Career and College Readiness = One Curricular Shift

One potential curricular shift is an increased focus on digital literacy in the classroom. Of the 32 Anchor Standards in Reading, Writing, Speaking and Listening, and Language for grades 6–12, six make direct mention of technology, digital sources, or media (Wood 2011). One could argue whether this is an increased focus on the use of technology in the classroom (perhaps depending on how your state's previous set of standards addressed technology), but one thing is clear: The types of jobs our students are going to compete for will more than likely involve some aspect of digital literacy, either in production (creating websites, composing on blogs, communicating digitally) or consumption (gathering data online, reading digital sources) or both. Few can argue with the CCSS' intimation, through its use of the phrase "college and career ready," that keeping up with 21st-century literacy needs requires becoming literate within digital spaces. What, then, can this look like in the ELA classroom?

This increased focus on digital literacies is not only a shift away from traditional notions of print-based "school writing," but also a shift that requires school districts to have a reasonable amount of technology resources available for student use. Inequality in these resources will inevitably create disparities between school districts and their ability to demonstrate and fulfill the goals of the CCSS. In "Common Core Technology Demands Raise Budget Worries," Leslie Harris O'Hanlon

(2012) discusses the issue of increased need for technology in order to achieve the online testing goals set forth by the CCSS. But the conversation does not end with how to accommodate online assessments. O'Hanlon summarizes the bigger picture regarding technology and the CCSS:

> Some education experts say that common-core online testing is bigger than just taking a test at a specific moment in time. Rather, it's part of a larger movement to infuse more technology into schools, changing how teachers teach and how students learn. So, the same technology used to test students should also be used to teach students. Therefore, the question isn't just where the money will come from to do online assessments, […] but where it will come from to increase technology resources and usage in schools.

Our goals in the classroom should reflect the financial hardships many school districts face. One way to do so is to make use of the many free applications on the web, utilizing the very tools that consume our students' digital lives.

Technology Accessibility: Still a Concern

The most recent data set for technology accessibility in schools was collected by the National Center for Education Statistics (NCES) in 2009, with just over 2,000 schools participating in the survey (Gray, Thomas, and Lewis 2010). The NCES routinely conducts national surveys for the U.S. Department of Education; the use and accessibility of technology in schools is just one segment of the study. Of the myriad pieces of data collected, two points are especially pertinent in a discussion about technology accessibility and increased demands for digital literacy as established by the CCSS and the 21st-century workplace. The following two key findings of the study situate the argument put forth in this chapter and reinforce the reservations many of us have about assuming schools have adequate resources to keep up with these changing demands:

1. Ninety-seven percent of teachers had one or more computers located in the classroom every day, while 54 percent could bring computers into the classroom. Internet access was available for 93 percent of the computers located in the classroom every day and for 96 percent of the computers that could be brought into the classroom. The ratio of students to computers in the classroom every day was 5.3 to 1.

2. Results differed by low and high poverty concentration of the school for the percentage of teachers that reported their students used educational technology sometimes or often during classes to prepare written text (66 and 56 percent, respectively), learn or practice basic skills (61 and 83 percent, respectively), and develop and present multimedia presentations (47 and 36 percent, respectively). Percentages are based on the teachers reporting that the activity applied to their students (Gray, Thomas, and Lewis 2010, 3).

While the first finding appears overwhelmingly positive, it should be underscored that the 97 percent of teachers who responded positively had a minimum of one computer in their classroom, which means there are still some classrooms without a single computer. Only slightly more than half (54 percent) of the classrooms had some form of mobile cart teachers could use to bring computers into the classroom. Internet access was high (93 to 96 percent) for all computers (but this means 4 to 7 percent of computers do not have internet access), suggesting that the real need is with actual computer access (assuming internet access is mostly available once computers are present).

However, a student to computer ratio of 5:1 puts that initial percentage (97 percent) into perspective and suggests that, while there may be some classrooms with enough computers for each student, the overwhelming majority of classrooms do not and likely bring the overall ratio down. The ratio of five students to one computer hardly creates a suitable environment for students to engage fully in a digital learning experience. The second finding suggests that in high poverty school districts students engage in these skills less often (except, it seems, when learning or practicing "basic skills").

This data is now a few years old, and as we await the next study's results, we can hope for better news. In the meantime, the focus should be on providing viable ways for educators and librarians to make the best use of available technological resources, especially as districts move forward with the implementation of the CCSS.

School districts approach these economic problems in a variety of ways. Some district leaders believe the best way to counteract a lack of resources is to find third party funding—mainly technology grants. Grant writing, though, takes time, another precious resource. Other schools have turned to BYOD ("Bring Your Own Device") strategies; however, as Audrey Watters (2012) points out, "Of course, BYOD also means that parents—instead of schools—may end up footing the bill for computing devices in the classroom. That's a concern to people like educator and author Gary Stager, who thinks that BYOD may be the 'worst idea of the 21st century,' because it 'enshrines inequality.'" BYOD policies may work for some students, but not for the students who are already disenfranchised by poverty. Instead, this approach widens the gap between those who have access to technology and those who do not.

I offer a different solution. With the financial limitations of many school districts and other economic barriers in mind, I propose that teachers and librarians instead adopt two free web-based tools that offer digital spaces for composition and many possibilities in the classroom: Storify and Weebly.

Websites and Weebly in the Classroom

Digital literacy is a phrase that may have become a cliché in its overuse, but this does not diminish the importance of preparing our students for the unique demands of communicating digitally in the 21st century. We must make sure students have avenues in which their voices can be heard, as this opportunity is at the heart of the democratic education we aim to provide for all students. Web design projects also have the potential to provide real audiences for student writing, which is something ELA teachers have been struggling to do for students for decades (Tchudi and Tchudi 1999; Zemelman, Daniels, and Hyde 2005) and is an outcome recognized as important by the authors of the CCSS. When students are faced with the task of writing for a public audience, their concerns over their writing inevitably change. Their concerns deepen, as they are faced with a situation that is more complex than simply answering the question, what does my teacher want? For what may be the first time in many of their lives, they may wonder how to best entertain, inform, or persuade an audience *outside* of the classroom.

Incorporating a user-friendly web-building site such as Weebly into the classroom can be helpful in teaching students website design and construction. Weebly introduces students to the architecture behind web design without teachers having to spend large amounts of class time on the mechanics. Weebly works mainly through a drag-and-drop interface. By using Weebly, students are able to get a genuine sense of web design strategies. They can reap the educational benefits of engaging in digital literacy by writing within the architecture of the web and writing for authentic audiences on it, even as teachers need not commit much curricular time to learning and teaching the functions behind building a website. With sites like Weebly, more attention is spent on composition and design, and less attention is paid to the functions and mechanics of website building.

I do not mean to suggest that Weebly, or any website building interface, is a perfect tool for the ELA classroom teacher interested in working with digital writing. There are definite limitations with using Weebly, especially in terms of design options. Because Weebly forces the use of provided templates, there is a compromise with user choice (mainly in terms of how information can be displayed). These limitations have been elaborated upon by composition scholars such as Anne Frances Wysocki, Kristin L. Arola, and Kathleen Blake Yancey. They argue that the split between content and design is not something that should be overlooked, as both provide students with important rhetorical choices. Empowering students with an online voice is not complete unless they are empowered with the literacy of design. Arola (2010) writes, "The belief that design is simply a 'vessel' or a 'container,' and that content is the *real* meat of the Web, threatens to make the effects of design invisible" (13). While I appreciate the concerns raised by Arola and others, I believe as an introduction into web composing, sites like Weebly are an important bridge for students to compose for larger audiences (aside from composing on social media sites, which most of them already do). The benefits of relinquishing some creative prowess for the ease of use will probably outweigh the shortcomings, especially for secondary students who might not otherwise have access to composing online. And as a resource for students learning how to navigate composing on a website within the confines of limited classroom time, the ease of use with Weebly is vital.

Many of our students already know about certain online avenues of expression, especially forms of social media (Twitter, Facebook, etc.). A few may even have ventured into the blogosphere, although probably not as many as we might imagine. This seems to be true for both our college bound, more "privileged" students, as well as for our less economically privileged (and therefore often less technologically privileged) students. Regardless, few students appear to embark on web design; the process just seems far too daunting. The process was, no doubt, daunting in the earlier 2000s when "speaking" HTML was necessary for website production. Today, however, there are a number of design sites on the web that simplify the process of website creation. Drag-and-drop technology has made website building more accessible. It is still, however, a learned literacy. A website is a medium with its own set of rules and constraints that students must learn in order to master the mode of communication. The CCSS reinforces this notion in Anchor Standard for Writing 6:

> Use technology, including the internet, to produce, publish, and update individual or shared writing products, taking advantage of technology's capacity to link to other information and to display information flexibly and dynamically. (Council of Chief State School Officers [CCSSO] and National Governors Association [NGA] 2010, 18)

Although technology is not specifically mentioned in Anchor Standard for Writing 4, the skills needed to identify the modes of a genre are explicated: "Produce clear and coherent writing in which the development, organization, and style are appropriate to task, purpose, and audience" (CCSSO and NGA 2010, 18). These two Anchor Standards can be met by allowing students the opportunity to create websites in the ELA classroom.

Creating a Literature Class Website

The first time a teacher embarks on web design in his or her classroom, creating a group webpage might be a good place to begin. This assignment can be used in any teaching unit centered around an overarching theme (e.g., "What It Means to Be a Hero") or around a single common text (e.g., *To Kill a Mockingbird*, *Catcher in the Rye*, etc.). The idea behind the group-created webpage is that it scaffolds the traditional kinds of writing about literature common to the ELA classroom with the audience demands of 21st-century writing and publishing. Some of the items students could address include the following (which are further articulated in Figure 11.1):

- Character analysis
- Theme exposition
- Close readings of important events/sections/texts
- Comparisons of texts read in the class (including poetry, nonfiction, etc.)
- Current events that speak to the timeless theme(s) present in the text(s)

As the parameters of the project are further identified, more Anchor Standards for Writing can be met. Based on the project guidelines previously outlined, in addition to Standards 4 and 6, this project now has the potential to meet four more Anchor Standards for Writing (CCSSO and NGA 2010, 18):

- Standard 1: Write arguments to support claims in an analysis of substantive topics or texts, using valid reasoning and relevant and sufficient evidence.

- Standard 5: Develop and strengthen writing as needed by planning, revising, editing, rewriting, or trying a new approach.

- Standard 9: Draw evidence from literary or informational texts to support analysis, reflection, and research.

- Standard 10: Write routinely over extended time frames (time for research, reflection, and revision) and shorter time frames (a single sitting or a day or two) for a range of tasks, purposes, and audiences.

Building a website as a class project is one way to scaffold into independent website creation. It might also be the most feasible way to introduce students to website production if a school district lacks

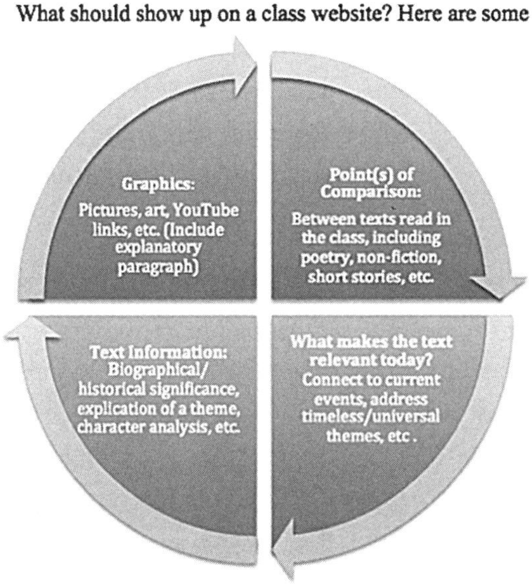

What should show up on a class website? Here are some ideas:

- Graphics: Pictures, art, YouTube links, etc. (Include explanatory paragraph)
- Point(s) of Comparison: Between texts read in the class, including poetry, non-fiction, short stories, etc.
- Text Information: Biographical/historical significance, explication of a theme, character analysis, etc.
- What makes the text relevant today? Connect to current events, address timeless/universal themes, etc.

Figure 11.1 Potential material teachers and librarians can ask students to include on their Weebly sites

the necessary resources to provide each student with his or her own computer to use during class time. In these circumstances, teachers still have some options. While students may compose their individual components of the website in a traditional mode (i.e., on paper), it will be important for them to see their final product published on the website. Equally valuable for students is to see their teacher work through the various issues that arise while creating a website and to see what troubleshooting entails. Observing and taking part in the uploading of information to the website, weighing in on design choices, and dealing with unforeseen challenges all make for a more authentic experience for students. If teachers allow the actual production of the site to be collaborative and transparent, then students have a more accurate understanding of what goes into building a website. Students should be better prepared to build their own websites when the time comes. Admittedly, allowing students to engage in the creation of the website will take more class time as opposed to an independently teacher-created site; however, including students in the uploading and design choices of web production is what really establishes this class project as digital literacy instruction. Without student collaboration, the digital aspect of the project becomes an abstraction. As with any learned skill, it is a more effective practice to have students *engage* in the activity rather than to *tell* them about the activity.

Moving From Class Project to Independent Website

It is important to keep in mind that building a website as a class project (with the teacher at the helm) requires that the classroom be equipped with some sort of projection technology (either mobile or permanent) with which the teacher can display what is on his or her computer screen. Only one classroom computer is necessary, though, which makes this project accessible for teachers and students in financially challenged districts.

Moreover, when students are given complete control over the composition and construction of their webpages, additional CCSS are met as well. Three Anchor Standards for Language, in addition to the previously mentioned writing standards, can be met, including (CCSSO and NGA 2010, 18):

- Standard 1: Demonstrate command of the conventions of standard English grammar and usage when writing or speaking.

- Standard 2: Demonstrate command of the conventions of standard English capitalization, punctuation, and spelling when writing.

- Standard 3: Apply knowledge of language to understand how language functions in different contexts, to make effective choices for meaning or style, and to comprehend more fully when reading or listening.

These standards point to the important rhetorical decisions that students must make when they become the sole contributor to their websites: Language choices must reflect both the professional, standardized format that an educational website assumes and also the nuances of website writing as opposed to traditional academic writing (including attention to differences in tone, voice, word choice, organization, and visual layout).

So, How Do We Get Started With Weebly?

Both the education and classic version of Weebly will work for the purposes outlined in this chapter, and both versions are free. Weebly users are given the opportunity to buy a web domain address, whereby they will be free of the weebly.com designator in their web address. However, if users do not object to weebly.com in the address, this is a completely free tool. Figure 11.2 shows what the Weebly for Education homepage looks like. It takes moments to sign up for a free account (an email address is all that is needed). Once users have created an account, they are immediately able to experiment with building a page. Exploring the various theme options is a great place to start. There is a theme option available for most any desired impression that users want to establish.

Figure 11.2 The Weebly for Education homepage

Rather than provide a step-by-step tutorial in this chapter, however, I will instead suggest that readers spend some time on the actual site. Because of the site's straightforward user-friendly interface, its inner workings are more easily learned through experimentation with the templates than by reading a set of directions.

Bye, Bye Index Cards. Hello, Storify!

Storify is a second free web-based technology that can assist teachers and librarians in meeting the CCSS. As a high school teacher for 7 years, I admit that I assigned more than one research paper in which I required students to track their sources on index cards. I'm not sure what it is about an index card that begs for them to be used as a resource-tracking device, but I suspect many readers have also assigned similar research projects. Perhaps it is because this is a tried and true method; we like the idea of organizing our own research this way and therefore want to instill these same habits in our students.

But if we think about the way researching has evolved over the last decade, it seems our mode of tracking that research should likewise change. Many of us no longer scribble notes in a notebook as we read through an online source; instead we might have multiple windows open on our computer screen. We download PDFs to read later, we follow hyperlinks from one source to another, and we do not necessarily read a source in its entirety. This is often what an organic (and digital) research path looks like, yet what we ask students to produce for us often reflects only the final product of that path (i.e., an annotated bibliography, or an index card with the quick and dirty information on a source).

This is where Storify can be helpful. Websites like Storify have the potential to redefine the way we ask students to conduct research in the classroom. Say goodbye to those index cards, as these sites allow us to focus on the narrative nature of a more authentic research process.

Storify is an online tool where users compose "stories." These stories can include anything: YouTube videos, websites, links to academic articles, Facebook posts, Twitter feeds, and any other web-based information source of which a reader can envision. The original purpose of Storify was to provide a space for users to write their own narratives through a mash-up of interspersed internet links and commentary, as Wikipedia explains in its definition of "Storify" (2013): "Storify is a social network service that lets the user create stories or timelines using social media such as Twitter, Facebook, and Instagram." I was first introduced to Storify by my writing studies colleagues at the University of Wisconsin-Eau Claire. Searching for ways to help our writing students creatively tell digital stories about current events, we found Storify to be the perfect option. Some of my colleagues also believed Storify could aid students in the organization of their research, which inspired this section of the chapter. While online sites like Storify are perhaps easier to implement in a classroom of college students (where computer and online access are less pressing issues thanks to the existence of on-campus computer labs), I see benefits of introducing secondary students to sites like this as well.

The Research Process as a Narrative

There are some captivating examples of narrative writing on Storify—narratives that are personal, educational, social, and simply aesthetically pleasing. This site could potentially be used for all types of digital storytelling. However, I also see Storify serving a very practical role in the storing of research data. Research paths tell a story, too, though perhaps not in the traditional definition of the word "story." My interest here is to explore how Storify could be used as a meaningful part of the research process, to explain how writers can utilize this resource as a means of storing, organizing, and narrating their research paths.

Take, for example, my own research in writing this chapter. In my daily life, I come across myriad articles, website postings, and op-ed pieces that interest me. These sources may relate directly or indirectly to my ongoing research interests regarding standards, technology, and school budgetary concerns. When I come across one of these sources, I link it to my Storify account for later perusal. I always try to write a few sentences explaining why I linked to the source or how it might connect to my research. Later, when I go back into my Storify account to thoroughly read the source, I replace those sentences (or add to them) with a brief summary of the source, add an important quote or two, and include a discussion of how the source might contribute to my research.

Figure 11.3 shows two sources I read in preparation for writing this chapter. Although I didn't use either source directly in this chapter, both served to shape my understanding about standards in some way. The first source, "Schools Must Help Educators Transform 'PD' into Personal Discovery" (2012) by Rob Mancabelli, helped me understand how school districts are implementing standards via personal development experiences. I wrote a one-sentence summary before the source link: "This article looks into the ways that PD experiences can become personalized and meaningful for teachers, rather than just limited to one-day workshops that often don't translate into helpful change in the classroom." This quick summary is enough to remind me of how the source pertains to my writing and research. At some point, I may want to revisit this piece, in which case it will be easily accessible for me.

The same is true for the second source, "Adaptive Testing Evolves to Assess Common-Core Skills" (2012) by Michelle Davis, which is also

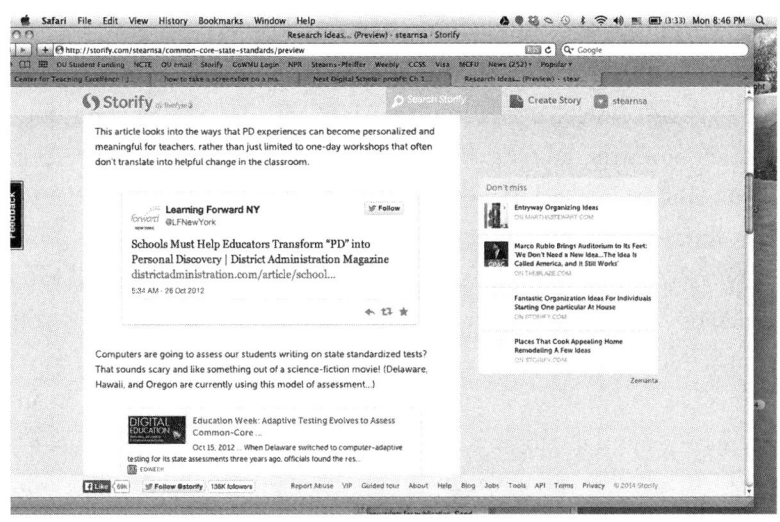

Figure 11.3 The research organization methods offered by Storify

captured in Figure 11.3. While this source addresses a general concern of mine (how computers are being used to assess student writing on standardized tests), this information was also not *directly* used in this chapter. Note the personal system of organization I have established here: a brief summary, followed by the link, followed by significant quotes. In the next section, I offer an example for the secondary ELA classroom of how students can adopt these organizational strategies for their own research paths. My goal here is to show how making research strategies more transparent for students can help them establish habits of mind and of practice that are more reflective of current research methods. Teaching students simple research strategies such as these, and making the research process more transparent, can help students engage in more authentic ways of conducting and tracking research; they can create systems of organization that perhaps match their actual research paths more closely. Copying and pasting a link is an action many students have grown up performing. It is second nature for them, and it reflects the faster paced condition of research that is mostly conducted online.

The Updated Annotated Bibliography Project

Few of us have probably made it through high school or college without having completed an annotated bibliography. We have dutifully written down the source's citation and summarized what the source is about. But as our techniques of researching evolve, the ways we track that research should also change.

Websites like Storify give students a forum where they can still write a description of the source, but also include a narration of how the source informed their research/knowledge about the topic. This feature allows them to more easily show connections between sources. Perhaps the most important characteristic that Storify offers students is that it is easily accessible and updatable; the website provides a more fluid way of tracking research progress and changing needs/interests, rather than the static method of an annotated bibliography. While annotated bibliographies generally have shown the post-product (i.e., where students end up after their long, often tangential research paths), Storify can be more involved in the research *process* by helping students organize and visualize their research as it is being conducted. In other words, Storify can offer students a place where their research is ongoing and more personalized than what an annotated bibliography can offer. In response, students recognize that their "school" research methods reflect their personal research methods more than they perhaps previously acknowledged. Students may then become more engaged with the research they do for school projects in the same ways they "research" their personal interests (such as investigating their favorite actors or musicians, learning how to play a song via a YouTube video, or figuring out which car or shoes they want to purchase) and in the same ways they conduct what scholars Alison Head and Michael Eisenberg (2009) have termed *everyday life research* (such as investigating a health concern, learning about career opportunities, or catching up with the local news or the latest in national politics) (3). For example, Storify may help students establish the "big picture" and identify "the common knowledge about a topic area," both characteristics of *everyday life research* (6), by tracking websites visited, recurring information, and changing perspectives on the topic. In this way, students can sift through, organize, and more easily synthesize what many report to be overwhelming amounts of information, especially in the beginning stages of research, and especially in "course-related research" with its strict deadlines and time-sensitive demands (4).

When students track their research in fluid, adaptive ways, such as on Storify, they meet several Anchor Standards. The 18 Anchor Standards listed in Table 11.1 provide an idea of the extensive curricular goals that can be covered with Storify-based assignments.

Many students already engage in research strategies that would help them succeed with school research projects (or "course-related research"). Often, though, they have not been encouraged to think about the research they do *in* class as connected to their "everyday life research" strategies; a constructive place to begin is with identifying the "big picture" of their research (Head and Eisenberg 2009, 6). This specifically reflects the goals outlined in Reading Standards 2 and 7. Storify can provide a bridge between school and personal research methods by organizing the many different avenues of information in one place. Moreover, when students organize their sources in an interactive interface such as Storify, teachers and librarians are better able to help students analyze the different types of information resources they are likely to encounter online (which meets Writing Standard 8 and Speaking and Listening Standard 2). Because using Storify to track one's research invites students to investigate a wider array of texts (e.g., students are not limited to only academic journals or books), evaluating the validity of sources is even more important (outlined in Reading Standard 8 and Writing Standard 8). Multiple points of view on one topic can be addressed, and this requires a more critical approach to reading and understanding the texts chosen. Asking students to use Storify to document their research process can help them see how researching is a complex and multi-faceted activity (Reading Standards 7 and 10). Researching a topic by reading multiple sources from varying types of media, and illustrating how those sources relate to one another and inform the whole picture, provides a more holistic

Table 11.1 Anchor Standards (CCSSO and NGA 2010, 10, 18, 22, 25)

	Anchor Standards for Reading
2	Determine central ideas or themes of a text and analyze their development; summarize the key supporting details and ideas.
7	Integrate and evaluate content presented in diverse media and formats, including visually and quantitatively, as well as in words.
8	Delineate and evaluate the argument and specific claims in a text, including the validity of the reasoning as well as the relevance and sufficiency of the evidence.
9	Analyze how two or more texts address similar themes or topics in order to build knowledge or to compare the approaches the authors take.
10	Read and comprehend complex literary and informational texts independently and proficiently.
	Anchor Standards for Writing
2	Write informative/explanatory texts to examine and convey complex ideas and information clearly and accurately through the effective selection, organization, and analysis of content.
4	Produce clear and coherent writing in which the development, organization, and style are appropriate to task, purpose, and audience.
5	Develop and strengthen writing as needed by planning, revising, editing, rewriting, or trying a new approach.
6	Use technology, including the internet, to produce and publish writing and to interact and collaborate with others.
7	Conduct short as well as more sustained research projects based on focused questions, demonstrating understanding of the subject under investigation.
8	Gather relevant information from multiple print and digital sources, assess the credibility and accuracy of each source, and integrate the information while avoiding plagiarism.
9	Draw evidence from literary or informational texts to support analysis, reflection, and research.
10	Write routinely over extended time frames (time for research, reflection, and revision) and shorter time frames (a single sitting or a day or two) for a range of tasks, purposes, and audiences.
	Anchor Standards for Speaking and Listening
2	Integrate and evaluate information presented in diverse media and formats, including visually, quantitatively, and orally.
3	Evaluate a speaker's point of view, reasoning, and use of evidence and rhetoric.
4	Present information, findings, and supporting evidence such that listeners can follow the line of reasoning and the organization, development, and style are appropriate to task, purpose, and audience.
5	Make strategic use of digital media and visual displays of data to express information and enhance understanding of presentations.
	Anchor Standard for Language
6	Acquire and use accurately a range of general academic and domain-specific words and phrases sufficient for reading, writing, speaking, and listening at the college and career readiness level; demonstrate independence in gathering vocabulary knowledge when encountering an unknown term important to comprehension or expression.

representation of any given subject (highlighted in Reading Standard 9, Writing Standard 2, and Speaking and Listening Standard 3). Furthermore, reading the world through critical eyes is perhaps the ultimate goal of public education, and creating a research narrative via Storify inspires a critical awareness that perhaps does not exist with more traditional modes of research organization (articulated in Writing Standards 7 and 10).

Conclusion

There is no quick solution to the ongoing problem of limited school resources, especially in terms of technology. However, if ELA teachers, librarians, and information science professionals—as well as ELA teacher educators, administrators, and other stakeholders—think in terms of curricular *shifts* while implementing and meeting the CCSS, then ways to incorporate digital learning in the classroom that do not require significant economic investment can more easily be explored. As I have suggested here, one way to help the implementation of digital learning work in every classroom is to investigate the use of free web resources.

In closing, the projects outlined here meet all six Anchor Standards that mention incorporating technology in the ELA classroom along with several other CCSS. However, aside from meeting a quota of state standards, these projects reflect several best practice strategies that would likely engage students in new and exciting ways. Effective teaching and student engagement should be at the heart of every pedagogical decision we make; Weebly and Storify provide two economical ways to offer students digital spaces in which thoughtful composition may take place.

Endnote

1. As of September 2013, Storify changed its name to Livefyre. The website continues to function in the same way described in this chapter, and remains a free resource for users.

References

Arola, Kristin L. 2010. "The Design of Web 2.0: The Rise of the Template, the Fall of Design." *Computers and Composition* 27 (1): 4–14.

Council of Chief State School Officers and National Governors Association. 2010. *Common Core State Standards for English Language Arts and Literacy in History/Social Studies, Science, and Technical Subjects*. Washington, DC: National Governors Association Center for Best Practices, Council of Chief State School Officers.

Accessed February 10, 2014. www.corestandards.org/assets/CCSSI_ELA%20Standards.pdf.

Davis, Michelle R. 2012. "Adaptive Testing Evolves to Assess Common-Core Skills." *Education Week*. October 15. Accessed February 10, 2014. www.edweek.org/dd/articles/2012/10/17/01adaptive.h06.html.

Gray, Lucinda, Nina Thomas, and Laurie Lewis. 2010. *Teachers' Use of Educational Technology in U.S. Public Schools: 2009* (NCES 2010-040). Washington, DC: National Center for Education Statistics, Institute of Education Sciences, U.S. Department of Education. Accessed February 10, 2014. nces.ed.gov/pubs2010/2010040.pdf.

Head, Alison, and Michael Eisenberg. 2009. "What Today's College Students Say About Conducting Research in the Digital Age." *Project Information Literacy*. February 4. Accessed February 10, 2014. projectinfolit.org/pdfs/PIL_ProgressReport_2_2009.pdf.

Mancabelli, Rob. 2012. "Schools Must Help Educators Transform 'PD' into Personal Discovery." *District Administration*, November 10. Accessed February 10, 2014. www.districtadministration.com/article/schools-must-help-educators-transform-"pd"-personal-discovery.

O'Hanlon, Leslie Harris. 2012. "Common Core Technology Demands Raise Budget Worries." *Education Week*. October 15. Accessed February 10, 2014. www.edweek.org/dd/articles/2012/10/17/01budget.h06.html.

"Storify." *Wikipedia*. 2013. Wikipedia.org. Accessed February 10, 2014. en.wikipedia.org/wiki/Storify.

Tchudi, Susan J., and Stephen N. Tchudi. 1999. *The English Language Arts Handbook*. 2nd edition. Portsmouth, NH: Boynton/Cook Publishers, Inc.

Watters, Audrey. 2012. "What Tech in Schools Really Looks Like." *The Digital Shift*. April 30. Accessed February 10, 2014. www.thedigitalshift.com/2012/04/digital-divide/what-tech-in-schools-really-looks-like.

Wood, Joe. 2011. "Digital Writing and Common Core." *Joe Wood Online*. Accessed April 10, 2014. www.joewoodonline.com/digital-writing-common-core.

Wysocki, Anne Frances. 2004. "The Sticky Embrace of Beauty: On Some Formal Problems in Teaching about the Visual Aspects of Texts." In *Writing New Media: Theory and Applications for Expanding the Teaching of Composition*, 147–198. Logan, UT: Utah State University Press.

Yancey, Kathleen Blake. 2004. "Made Not Only in Words: Composition in a New Key." *College Composition and Communication* 56 (2): 297–328.

Zemelman, Steven, Harvey Daniels, and Arthur Hyde. 2005. *Best Practice, Today's Standards for Teaching and Learning in Schools*. 3rd edition. Portsmouth, NH: Heinemann.

PART **FOUR**

Curricular Initiatives to Meet the Common Core State Standards

CHAPTER **12**

The Saving Our Stories Project
Pushing Beyond the Culturally Neutral Digital Literacies of the Common Core State Standards

Antero Garcia and Cindy O'Donnell-Allen

As English educators and former high school English teachers, when we first heard about the widespread adoption of the Common Core State Standards (CCSS), we were resistant to the idea that teachers nationwide would be asked to implement yet one more mandate. When we read the standards more closely and asked ourselves whether we would be satisfied if a student finishing high school had met the standards, we had to admit that we would not only be satisfied, but also confident that the student was ready to meet the demands of college-level work. As self-proclaimed technophiles, we were also initially pleased to see that many of the standards alluded to students reading, writing, and producing text fluidly in digital environments.

A conversation in a Las Vegas taxi at the 2012 National Council of Teachers of English (NCTE) Conference, however, prompted us to revisit the standards with a more critical eye. On our way back from dinner with our colleague Louann Reid, we learned that a resolution opposing the CCSS had been presented by teachers at the NCTE business meeting. Reid explained that a friend who had attended the meeting had spoken out against the resolution, even though she understood the spirit of it. During her turn at the microphone, Reid's friend shared her perspective as a high school English teacher from a small Midwestern town: "If this resolution passes, it will be very, very bad for me. It will not send the message that we intend." She went on to explain that members from her community would misinterpret the good intentions of those proposing the resolution. She worried that community members would read the measure as an attempt to thwart educational reform rather than seeing it as teachers' opposition to a mandate they feared would compromise their work with students. Our taxi ride ended before Reid had a chance to explain other objections that were raised at the meeting, but we left the conference determined to think more deliberately about responding to objections to the CCSS as well as to the content, limitations, and language of the CCSS themselves.

Ever since, we have looked for opportunities to critically examine the CCSS in our work with pre-service teachers, our National Writing Project (NWP) colleagues, and teachers in local schools with whom we partner for professional development. In particular, we have been interested in exploring how we might develop socially relevant and civically proactive education for marginalized students in our community that still meet the expectations of the CCSS. Toward these ends, we focus this chapter on the Saving Our Stories (SOS) Project, a summer digital-storytelling program aimed at elementary-aged English Language Learners (ELLs), with the following questions in mind:

- What is missing from the CCSS in terms of digital literacy, cultural relevancy, and language diversity?
- How might the SOS Project provide a useful framework for thinking about how teachers can address these important considerations while meeting the CCSS at the same time? What are the key elements of that framework?

- What important questions and implications must teachers address in order to move beyond the CCSS and help students employ "second mindset" literacies and acquire the equivalent of what we term "21st-century standard English"?

We begin this chapter by reviewing what we see as the limitations of the CCSS regarding digital literacies as well as cultural and linguistic diversity. Next, we describe how we purposefully addressed these areas in the SOS Project while helping students meet the CCSS at the same time. Using SOS as a case in point, we then offer a framework to help readers think about ways to design similar standards-based programs and instruction appropriate for professional development contexts aimed at helping students produce culturally relevant print and digital texts.

What's Missing in the CCSS?

As we have revisited the CCSS with our students and colleagues, we have identified three significant areas that we believe are either under-conceptualized, given short shrift, or are missing altogether in the actual standards. The first of these areas concerns digital literacy. We contend that the CCSS problematically privilege what Colin Lankshear and Michele Knobel (2007) refer to as "first mindset" literacies; that is, the CCSS refer primarily to the typographic use of digital tools like word processors and web-searching applications. "Second mindset" literacies, on the other hand, acknowledge that

> [t]he world is being changed in some quite fundamental ways as a result of people imagining and exploring new ways of doing things and new ways of being that are made possible by new tools and techniques, rather than using new technologies to do familiar things in more "technologized" ways (first mindset). (10)

The perpetuation of a first-mindset orientation is evidenced by the fact that of the 32 CCSS at the fourth-grade level, digital tools are referenced just six times—twice in Reading, twice in Writing, and twice in Speaking and Listening. Furthermore, only Standard 6 in the "Production and Distribution" section of the Writing standards explicitly acknowledges students' agency in composing digital texts and using digital tools to connect with others:

> With some guidance and support from adults, [students will] use technology, including the internet, to produce and publish writing as well as to interact and collaborate with others; demonstrate sufficient command of keyboarding skills to type a minimum of one page in a single sitting. (Council of Chief State School Officers [CCSSO] and National Governors Association [NGA] 2010a, W.4.6)

The presence of student agency also might be extrapolated from Standard 5 in the section of the Speaking and Listening standards called "Presentation of Knowledge and Ideas": "[Students will] add audio recordings and visual displays to presentations when appropriate to enhance the development of main ideas or themes" (CCSSO and NGA 2010a, SL.4.5). It is unclear, however, if students are creating their own "audio recordings and visual displays" or simply culling these texts from pre-recorded sources.

The other four references to digital tools indeed focus on "using new technologies to do familiar things in more 'technologized' ways" (Lankshear and Knobel 2007, 10), describing such skills as keyboarding, taking notes, and recalling, gathering, and integrating information from visual texts, digital sources, and diverse media. Based on our own teaching (and learning) experiences as well as our work in the SOS Project, we believe the CCSS could have pushed beyond a primary emphasis on reception and consumption to more fully honor students' potential for production and agency as writers in a digital age.

Another sticking point for us in the CCSS is the apparent positioning of digital tools and the reading and writing practices that go along with them as "culturally neutral." In her landmark book on culturally responsive teaching, Geneva Gay (2010) points out that teaching is a "contextual, situational, and personal process ... [that is] most effective when ecological factors, such as prior experiences, community settings, cultural backgrounds, and ethnic identities of teachers and students, are included in its implementation" (4). She dispels the "fallacy of cultural neutrality and the homogeneity syndrome in teaching and learning" for students of color by arguing in favor of "instructional reforms ... that are grounded in positive beliefs about the cultural heritages and academic potentialities of these students" (23). While we applaud the intent inherent in the CCSS that *all* students be held to high expectations in order to increase their chances for post-secondary success, we are bothered that the authors appear to minimize, obscure, or omit the ecological factors Gay mentions. This discomfort is again rooted in our teaching experiences.

While teaching high school in South Central Los Angeles, Antero Garcia (co-author of this chapter) found it important to avoid approaching culturally responsive lessons and academically supported content as an "either/or" decision. Instead, he integrated lessons around youth culture and local histories with canonical literature and writing performances so that his students could better grasp "the language of power" (Delpit 2006). For example, in one lesson, Garcia's students read Mary Shelley's *Frankenstein* while collaborating with the Los Angeles Department of Cultural Affairs to investigate the roots of graffiti within South Central. Creating a custom map on Google Maps, Garcia's students traced their routes to school and "pinned" each instance of graffiti they encountered (some students even uploaded photos using their phones). Exploring the social construction of "monsters" in the graffiti of the present and the creature in *Frankenstein* not only increased student knowledge of a classic literary text, but also affirmed and built upon their existing knowledge about the innate, human understandings present in their everyday world. What's more, students were so invested in their work that they went out and bought their own copies of *Frankenstein* (the very inexpensive Dover Thrift Editions) in order to annotate the text on their own (our academic form of "graffiti" you might say), furthering a classroom culture rooted in reading that at the same time helped them develop important college-readiness skills.

We acknowledge that the CCSS would not preclude either of us from teaching in a similar fashion today, yet since we taught high school English in a pre-CCSS era, our practice was instead shaped by the International Reading Association (IRA)/NCTE standards (IRA and NCTE 1996). Garcia's instruction described here, for instance, clearly addresses the IRA/NCTE standard requiring students to "read a wide range of literature from many periods in many genres to build an understanding of the many dimensions [e.g., philosophical, ethical, aesthetic] of human experience" (3). Our familiarity with these standards makes us hyper-aware of what is missing from the CCSS regarding cultural and linguistic diversity.

The IRA/NCTE standards explicitly direct students to read texts from varied cultures and draw on their prior (presumably varied) experiences "to build an understanding of texts, of themselves, and of the cultures of the United States and the world" (3). In regard to language, the IRA/NCTE standards suggest all students "develop an understanding of and respect for diversity in language use, patterns, and dialects across cultures, ethnic groups, geographic regions, and social roles" (3). A separate IRA/NCTE standard refers specifically to ELLs, guiding them to use their first language to develop competency in English and understand curricular content. Taken together, the IRA/NCTE standards make it explicit that students benefit when their lived experiences and home language come to bear on their classroom literacy practices. And in fact, these intersections are not just useful and encouraged, but actually required if teachers are to help students meet the standards.

Contrast this with the Anchor Standards of the CCSS, where the word *diverse* appears only three times, referring to "conversations and collaborations with diverse partners" (Anchor Standard for Speaking and Listening 1; CCSSO and NGA 2010a, 22) and to the integration of "content presented in diverse formats and media" (Anchor Standard for Reading 7; CCSSO and NGA 2010a, 35). Granted, oblique references appear to cultural diversity in other references to the CCSS. We are concerned, however, that busy educators will focus solely on reading the CCSS themselves rather than on the introduction and other ancillary materials available on the CCSS website, especially in states like Colorado where the CCSS are embedded in a separate document that makes no mention of these materials. Notably, the Language Standards refer only to "standard English," though a separate statement on the "Application of Common Core State Standards for English Language Learners" is available on the CCSS website (CCSSO and NGA 2010b). Like the IRA/NCTE standards, this brief addendum notes that ELL students' first language can be used as a resource to help them acquire English. The statement offers additional advice about the instructional conditions that will help ELLs meet the high expectations outlined in the CCSS, such as extra time and support to complete their work. The only other explicit references to culture and diversity occur in the CCSS introduction: once in naming the importance of "understand[ing] other perspectives and cultures" as one of seven capacities demonstrated by students who are college and career ready (CCSSO and NGA 2010a, 7), and again in acknowledging that it is "beyond the scope of the Standards to define the full range of supports appropriate for English language learners" (CCSSO and NGA 2010a, 6).

We are further persuaded by our research (Garcia 2013; O'Donnell-Allen 2006, 2011) and teaching that students are likely to have more powerful literacy learning experiences when their cultural identities and linguistic diversity are viewed as valuable resources. We also know that we can teach in ways that will help students use their literacy practices to read, write, and re-write both the "word" and their surrounding "world" (Freire and Macedo 1987). Our firm conviction that teachers must move beyond the culturally neutral rendition of digital literacy and language practices apparent in the CCSS is reflected in the design of the Saving Our Stories Project.

The Saving Our Stories Project

The SOS Project is a summer enrichment program offered by the Colorado State University Writing Project (CSUWP) in partnership with local elementary schools that have high ELL populations. The fourth and fifth graders participating in the digital storytelling workshop engage in creative problem-solving and youth-driven research with innovation in cultural practices and community change in mind. The description that follows focuses on two summers when we held the program in a suburban elementary school with an English Language Acquisition designation for second language learners. With one exception, all of the ELLs participating in the SOS Project spoke Spanish as their first language.

During SOS, the students learned to record and edit videos, podcasts, and slideshows to document the history and everyday experiences of the Fort Collins Latino community. Students recorded their own stories as well as those of family members, first-generation CSU students and staff, and other members of the Latino community. During the workshop, students visited El Museo de Las Tres Colonias, a restored adobe home built in the 1920s when the Great Western Sugar Company established a colony for its Hispanic workers (Thomas and Smith 2004). Students wrote extensively in writer's notebooks, shared their work in writing groups, and worked with published writers. They also read and emulated creative writing by Latino authors, including Sandra Cisneros, Gary Soto, and Pablo Neruda. As well, they read excerpts from *The Dreamer* by Pam Munoz Ryan, a fictional biography of Neruda's childhood. As a result, they became enamored with the ode, a poetic form particularly suited to our emphasis on documenting the everyday. You can hear some students reading their work on the NWP website *Digital Is* (O'Donnell-Allen, 2012). Students published their digital stories online and selected their favorite pieces to share with family, friends, and community members at a celebratory reading at the conclusion of the workshop.

Students met multiple CCSS for reading and writing through their participation in the SOS Project and often achieved several standards in a single project activity, such as the five-frame story. As the name suggests, authors of a five-frame story construct a complete narrative in five images. To introduce students to the genre, Cindy O'Donnell-Allen (co-author of this chapter) distributed a simple one-page storyboard and challenged students to tell a story using just five pictures. Beside each of the five frames of the storyboard, students had space to respond to these prompts:

1. Who is in the story? Where does it take place?
2. What *might* happen in your story?
3. What happens first?
4. What happens next?
5. How does your story end?

At the bottom of the storyboard, they responded to one final question: *What's a good title for your story that will give your audience a clue without giving the story away?*

In serving as lead teacher, O'Donnell-Allen modeled planning a story by displaying her own storyboard on a document camera. She asked students to help her decide what pictures she might include as well as a title. Next, she introduced basic film vocabulary and shooting techniques, asking students to create a paper "camera" by rolling their storyboard into a tube. By doing so, students learned what a *frame* was by looking through their cameras to focus on an object across the room. Next, they practiced "zooming in" by tightening the roll of the paper camera to achieve a "close-up shot," then "panning out" to capture a "landscape" by loosening the roll of their cameras. Students discussed the effects of various shots and considered which ones might be most appropriate for each phase of their story (e.g., using a "capturing shot" for the first frame to establish setting).

Next, students formed groups of three in order to plan a five-frame story using their storyboards. O'Donnell-Allen provided each group with a digital still camera and demonstrated how to zoom, pan, delete photos, and so on. After students were familiar with the equipment and their storyboards were complete, they visited the playground to shoot their stories. O'Donnell-Allen encouraged them to take more shots than they thought they needed so they would be able to select from their best images. When students returned to the classroom,

O'Donnell-Allen and the other workshop teachers helped students transfer their photos to a computer and demonstrated how to create a slideshow in iPhoto. Students quickly caught on to how to order photos and engaged in tough negotiations with one another over which five photos to use. Students then assembled their images, added a title slide, and then selected music from iPhoto that complemented their stories. Finally, students eagerly shared their work with the entire class. As a testament to the success of the activity, several groups created additional five-frame stories during the week (voluntarily using extra storyboards we had copied) and shared their five-frame stories with friends and family at the celebration to end the SOS workshop.

In the course of this activity, students meet multiple CCSS for reading and writing including (CCSSO and NGA 2010a): analyzing narrative structure (RL.4.5, RL.5.5); considering how visual elements contribute to meaning (RL.5.7); using effective techniques and event sequences to craft narratives (W.4.3, W.5.3); enthusiastically engaging in all phases of the writing process (W.4.5., W.5.5); and using technology in meaningful ways to produce and share their work (W.4.6., W.5.6).

Table 12.1 illustrates other examples of how SOS students combine print-based, digital, and spoken texts to address many of the grade-level expectations in all four areas of the CCSS: reading, writing, speaking and listening, and language. For ease of reference, we have used the same coding system employed in the CCSS document to identify grade-specific standards in a particular strand (i.e., RL 4.2 refers to Reading Literature, fourth grade, standard 2; W.4.3 refers to Writing, fourth grade, standard 3).

As Table 12.1 illustrates, the SOS Project allowed us to align the CCSS with innovative practice that took full advantage of students' enthusiasm for digital literacies along with their cultural and linguistic resources. Although SOS was a summer enrichment program, we believe that many of its elements would translate well into a standalone unit during the regular school year. Offering the project during the summertime, however, afforded us the opportunity to be

Table 12.1 How Students Met CCSS in the SOS Project

Skills Addressed in Reading Standards	SOS Project Activities
• Determining themes of literary texts, including how characters in a story or drama respond to challenges or how the speaker in a poem reflects upon a topic; summarizing the text (RL.4.2, RL.4.9, RL.5.2) • Determining literary and figurative meaning of words and phrases (RL.4.4, RL.5.4) • Writing and speaking about structural elements of narratives and poems (RL.4.5, RL.5.5) • Understanding how a narrator's point of view influences content (RL.4.6, RL.5.6) • Analyzing how visual elements contribute to meaning, tone, or beauty of a text (RL.5.7) • Reading and comprehending literary and informational texts appropriate for grade level from diverse cultures (RL.4.10, RI4.10, RL.5.10, RI.5.10) • Explaining events in historical texts (print and digital sources), including what happened and why, in order to answer questions and read or speak about the subject knowledgeably (RI.4.3, RI.4.9, RI.5.7, RI.5.9) • Purposefully reading and comprehending on-level texts (Foundational Skills 4.4, 5.4)	• Reading and discussing the content and stylistic techniques present in vignettes by Sandra Cisneros and odes by Gary Soto and Pablo Neruda • Reading and discussing excerpts from *The Dreamer*, a fictional biography of Pablo Neruda's childhood • Studying the chronological structure of five-frame stories to determine opening incidents, rising action, climax, and resolution • Analyzing the visual effectiveness of five-frame stories created in IPhoto • Reading informational texts, including digital archives, on the history of Latino workers in the sugar beet industry in the 1930s
Skills Addressed in Writing Standards	**SOS Project Activities**
• Writing narratives to develop real experience or events using effective technique, descriptive details, and clear event sequences (W.4.3, W.5.3) • Producing clear and coherent writing in which the development and organization are appropriate for task, purpose, and audience (W.4.4, W.5.4) • With guidance and support from peers and adults, developing and strengthening writing as needed by planning, revising, editing, rewriting, or trying a new approach. (W.4.5., W.5.5) • With some guidance and support from adults, using technology […] to produce and publish writing (W.4.6., W.5.6) • Conducting short research projects that use several sources to build knowledge through investigation of different aspects of a topic (W.4.7, W.5.7) • Recalling relevant information from experiences and gathering relevant information from print and digital sources; summarizing or paraphrasing information in notes from print and digital sources (W.4.8, W.5.8) • Writing routinely over extended (time for research, reflection, and revision) and shorter time frames (a single sitting or a day or two) for a range of discipline-specific tasks, purposes, and audiences (W.4.10, W.5.10)	• Emulating stylistic techniques in vignettes by Sandra Cisneros and writing personal narratives capturing their own experiences as well as those of family and friends (e.g., using "Hair" from *The House on Mango Street* as a mentor text, students wrote about the hair of family members) • Emulating odes by Gary Soto and Pablo Neruda capturing their own imaginative perspectives on ordinary objects • Observing chronological structure and integrating dialogue, description, and figurative language in narratives and poetry • Posting print and digital writing to a private Ning that could be accessed by friends and family members and presenting writing at celebratory reading • Using storyboards that combined print and sketches to plan five-frame stories and videos • Creating and editing five-frame stories in IPhoto • Recording and editing podcasts in GarageBand • Revising and editing their print and digital texts based on feedback from members of their writing groups and teachers • Writing to daily prompts in an exercise called "Morning Pages" in order to develop fluency • Recording research notes in their writer's notebooks regarding the history of Fort Collins • Writing interview questions for community members and first-generation university students and staff • Using Flip cameras, still cameras, and podcasting equipment to document field trip to El Museo

Table 12.1 (*cont.*)

Skills Addressed in Speaking and Listening Standards	SOS Project Activities
• Engaging effectively in a range of collaborative discussions with diverse partners, building on others' ideas and expressing their own clearly (SL.4.1, SL.5.1) • Summarizing the points a speaker makes (SL.4.3, SL.5.3) • Adding audio recordings and visual displays to presentations when appropriate to enhance the development of main ideas or themes (SL.4.5, SL.5.5) • Speaking clearly at an appropriate pace and adapting speech to a variety of contexts (SL.4.4, SL.5.4, SL.4.6, SL.5.6)	• Discussing literature, participating in writing groups, interacting with teachers from the Teaching with Technology workshop • Discussing guest speakers' presentations • Recording podcasts and underlaying music in five-frame stories and podcasts • Interviewing community members and CSU students and staff • Presenting work in final reading
Skills Addressed in Language Standards	**SOS Project Activities**
• Demonstrating command of the conventions of standard English grammar and usage when writing (L.4.1, L.5.1) • Demonstrating command of the conventions of standard English capitalization, punctuation, and spelling when writing (L.4.2, L.5.2)	• Editing final drafts of work to be published to a social network at the final reading

ambitious in our span and reach by involving multiple stakeholders in the community. In order to build capacity within and beyond the SOS students, we deliberately designed the program to include pre-service and practicing teachers and take advantage of CSUWP's alliances with the host school and the NWP. We describe these efforts in the following section.

Building Capacity Through Partnerships

In the semesters prior to the SOS Project, pre-service teachers who enrolled in O'Donnell-Allen's course on teaching writing participated in a service-learning project to create standards-based curricula and resources for teachers that were later adapted for use in the SOS Project. The university students worked in groups to complete the Coherent Assignment Sequence, a collection of instructional materials that would support students, especially ELLs, in completing a major assignment associated with a particular focus in SOS. O'Donnell-Allen's intent for the project was to provide students with authentic opportunities to develop digital pedagogies, to integrate reading and writing instruction, and to shape curricula with the notion of culturally responsive teaching in mind.

Each group had a particular instructional focus aligned with the SOS Project. For instance, the All Things Digital group developed materials for teaching students how to use digital storytelling tools, such as video and still cameras, podcasting equipment, and social networks. Other groups focused on historical research, documentary production, and writing print-based poetry and prose based on mentor texts written by Latino authors. Students also participated in some activities parallel to those of the SOS students, such as a field trip to El Museo, workshops with published authors, creating digital stories, daily writing activities, and creating social networks to feature project work. Additionally, each group piloted its curriculum with students in a nearby alternative high school with the understanding that adaptations would be necessary for use in the SOS Project. The CSU students were then eligible to apply for scholarships to fund their participation in a week-long CSUWP summer workshop on teaching with technology that coincided with the launch of the SOS Project.

Held concurrently in the SOS students' elementary school, the workshop allowed the pre-service teachers to work alongside practicing elementary and secondary teachers from various content areas to examine issues and methods related to integrating technology in their respective classrooms. Like the SOS elementary students, teachers wrote online and learned to record and edit digital stories in iPhoto and GarageBand. They then applied these skills immediately by working with the SOS students in the afternoons. They also accompanied students to El Museo and attended the reading at week's end.

The site where we held the SOS Project and the workshop was also crucial to the project's success. In prior years, CSUWP had developed a positive ongoing relationship with the elementary school by offering professional development related to writing and recruiting several teachers from the school for participation in the annual summer institute. Along with support from the principal of the school, O'Donnell-Allen received a small grant from a local foundation and gained the cooperation of other community partners, including a local restaurant, to help supply books, food, and supplies for SOS. Because the school was also working toward a goal of integrating digital tools in literacy instruction, the principal also paid for a team of teachers from the school to attend the weeklong workshop. In return, CSUWP was able to leverage this partnership with NWP to secure a small grant to help pay for some of the workshop expenses associated with teachers' professional development.

The reciprocal nature of all of these partnerships ensured that participants personally reaped professional benefits for the common goal of enriching ELLs in developing valuable 21st-century literacy skills. We even extended the reach of the project by contacting the school district office (which created a mini-documentary on the project), the local newspaper (which published a feature article), and the NWP (which featured the project on both the NWP website and *Digital Is*). For this reason, we encourage individual classroom teachers and librarians to cultivate similar relationships locally with parent–teacher organizations, community partners, professional organizations, and colleagues at different grade levels whose students might be interested in mentoring or serving as mentors.

Key Elements of the Framework

We believe that the SOS Project offers a promising framework for addressing the needs of ELLs in ways that meet, and move beyond, the culturally neutral practices and limited conception of digital literacies required by the CCSS. This framework includes four interrelated elements that encourage teachers to intersect students' lived experiences, cultural resources, and social contexts with their production of culturally relevant print and digital texts. As described in the following section, these elements include design-based teaching, civically proactive curricula, effectual partnerships, and transformative definitions of Standard English.

Design-Based Teaching

Grant Wiggins and Jay McTighe's book *Understanding by Design* (2005) holds a hallowed place on the bookshelves of many teachers, and for good reason. The book takes on traditional but well-meaning approaches to instructional design that emphasize engaging activities or content coverage at the expense of student understanding. Instead, the authors encourage teachers to frame units around essential questions, create assessments that will allow students to explore and demonstrate their understanding about those questions, and then to "plan backward" to create learning experiences that will build toward those assessments. In short, a backward-design curriculum enables teachers to "meet standards without sacrificing goals related to student understanding" (5).

We see parallels between Wiggins and McTighe's approach to instructional planning and the broader movement called *design thinking*, a generative process to create innovative solutions to problems or challenges arising in a particular context. Like innovators in architecture, business, engineering, technological industries, and other fields, we draw on design thinking to describe our methods for creating learning experiences in the SOS Project.

The five-step method we used in the SOS Project is well-documented in the work of the Stanford University Institute of Design, where students and faculty from various disciplines in the Institute apply design thinking to real-world problems. The Institute of Design's approach is unabashedly oriented toward learning by doing. As explained on the Institute's website, "Our bias is toward action, followed by reflection on personal discoveries about process" (2014). The Institute's method involves five stages:

1. Empathize: In this stage, innovators immerse themselves in the context to develop a deep understanding of participants' needs related to a problem that needs solving.

2. Define: In this stage, innovators drill down into the abstract problem in order to determine a concrete "actionable need."

3. Ideate: This stage involves brainstorming a range of possible solutions to the problem and selecting those that seem most promising.

4. Prototype: In this stage, designers field-test solutions alongside users on a small scale to determine their effectiveness in meeting the actionable need.

5. Test: The final stage incorporates the feedback generated by designers and participants during prototyping to carry the solution out in full.

This cycle is repeated as many times as necessary, with a constant eye toward refinement. Throughout the process, reflection is key to tweaking the design and maintaining an empathic perspective.

We contend that design thinking holds great potential for teaching. While complementing Wiggins and McTighe's approach to unit planning, it offers a deliberate method to address more broad-based problems in education. In relation to the SOS Project, design-based teaching allowed us to *empathize* with ELLs' capacity for accessing their cultural identity to support their literacy development. The actionable need we *defined* was the necessity of addressing the deficiencies in the CCSS regarding digital literacies and cultural and linguistic diversity. Along with our CSUWP colleagues, we *ideated* possible solutions that moved beyond CSUWP's tradition of helping teachers develop theoretically sound pedagogy that supported students' acquisition of culturally neutral literacy practices like those required in the CCSS. Out of the array of possible solutions we generated (e.g., developing instructional materials, convening study groups, offering more professional development workshops), we ultimately decided to confront the problem head-on by creating a program that would reach students directly while simultaneously helping teachers address the "actionable need" in their own contexts.

We *prototyped* SOS and the concurrent Teaching with Technology workshop on a small scale the first summer, offering the programs in a limited fashion to a small number of fourth-graders, pre-service teachers, and members of CSUWP. Throughout the process, we combined student and teacher feedback with reflections on our own practices to make necessary refinements. The subsequent summer, we *tested* an expanded program to include fifth-graders and opened the workshop up to teachers outside of CSUWP. We more closely aligned students' reading of culturally relevant literature to their production of more complex digital texts and expanded their contact with community members to include interviews with first-generation students and staff from CSU.

Based on the lessons learned during these iterations, we are now extending the program to three weeks, embedding it fully in a summer school program, and including an additional community partner, the city's new science and history museum. We have expanded the service-learning project for pre-service teachers to incorporate an additional course on teaching reading, and we also have plans to replicate SOS and the Teaching with Technology workshop within a rural context in another school district. Additionally, O'Donnell-Allen has presented the work at professional conferences and, along with a pre-service and practicing teacher who participated in the programs, has created online resources for the NWP. This far-reaching impact—from local students to national audiences—has convinced us of the power of design-based teaching. As one of the four main components of this framework, we see design-based teaching as a necessary component of one's pedagogy in an era of CCSS.

Effectual Partnerships

Drawing on civic literacies, teaching in culturally proactive ways, and helping students meet and exceed the expectations of the CCSS are daunting tasks for any teacher to tackle alone. The success of the SOS Project has been dependent on partnerships that are not just *effective*, but *effectual*. That is, they involve more than cordial relationships and incidental cooperation between participants. Rather, these partnerships are deliberately entered into in order to bring about change.

Consider the different results that might have occurred if the partnerships formed during SOS were merely effective: The principal might have agreed to let CSUWP use the facility because students would attend; the pre-service teachers might have simply completed the course project as an exercise in curriculum development; teachers in the workshop could have enrolled in the workshop to learn more about technology and earn some graduate credit.

Instead, SOS partnerships were based on *actionable needs* and a *shared purpose* with *transformative ends* in mind for all participants. The ELL students needed to develop digital composing skills that would allow them to strengthen their academic knowledge and leverage their cultural identities at the same time. Pre-service and practicing teachers needed to acquire and learn how to implement culturally responsive digital pedagogies. The principal wanted to actualize the school's mission statement regarding education of the whole child. In CSUWP, we needed to enact our commitment to increasing equity and access to high-quality literacy experiences for all learners. First-generation university students and staff needed meaningful opportunities to reinforce CSU's position as the state's only land-grant institution. Members of the Latino community in Fort Collins needed to share their stories in order to preserve an often marginalized history.

Working in symbiotic relationships, SOS partners reciprocally and simultaneously met these overlapping needs by using digital media to achieve meaningful impact in both the immediate context of the SOS Project and the public sphere.

Civically Proactive Education

Civics is traditionally seen as a single course taken near the end of high school. Much as research and discourse about public education point to an achievement gap, civic education researchers Joseph Kahne and Ellen Middaugh (2008) have described a "civic opportunity gap" that exists between marginalized youth and their more privileged peers. Our experiences with SOS suggest that opportunities exist for English Language Arts (ELA) teachers to consider more deliberately the potential civic lessons lying latent within our curricula.

In a 2004 study of how students learn civic lessons in various U.S. schools, Joel Westheimer and Kahne noted various forms of citizenship promoted through education programs. Our SOS framework delineates an approach to a "justice-oriented" model of civic education in ELA classrooms, building student civic activity on exploring root, systemic causes to the challenges and inequities students see in the world around them. In conceptualizing civic literacies, we want to underscore that we do not see them as yet another responsibility heaped on top of what teachers already do. Instead, we want to suggest that the concept of civic literacies can inform the underlying questions, ideas, and lines of inquiry that students pursue in classrooms.

Our previous reference to Gay's (2010) notion of culturally responsive teaching is also relevant here. Instead of envisioning standards and classroom practices only as ways to prepare students for traditional academic assessments, Gay writes that "[m]oral, social, cultural, personal, and political developments are also important" (16). However, instead of simply *responding* to the cultural needs of students and the literacies they bring into our classrooms, we see civic literacies reframing this approach more proactively. Culturally proactive teaching requires identifying salient social issues, underrepresented histories, and opportunities for digital and physical exploration within a school's community. A justice-oriented approach to this work would not simply look at surface-level solutions (e.g., holding a canned food drive for those in need) but would instead focus on challenging the systemic roots of inequality and injustice (e.g., utilizing youth literacies to articulate and amplify knowledge about the reasons some people in a city are hungry and others are not).

Teaching beyond the culturally neutral assumptions of the CCSS must rely upon a deliberate civic engagement with students and their surrounding communities. The civic literacies students enacted in the SOS Project were determined by our local context. The social and cultural factors salient to our community will differ from those explored by students in other schools. Still, we want to underscore that the civic literacies we are emphasizing as key tenets of our framework are proactive in nature; students must be able to do more than read about or reflect upon injustices and historically exceptional factors in books. Instead, civic engagement is a process learned through action. Drawing on civic literacies in ELA classrooms to teach in culturally proactive ways, teachers can provide opportunities for youth to be generative in their learning by creating socially substantive outcomes. In so doing, students develop valuable practices that will enable them to fluidly engage as civically active members of society.

Within the SOS Project, civic literacies are an integrated and crucial component designed to increase student engagement. The SOS Project afforded the opportunity for students to learn first-hand about the migrant working community and the role of Latinos in the sugar beet industry through their interactions with Chuck Solano, a guide at El Museo de las Tres Colonias. Solano shared stories from his childhood about growing up in a family of migrant laborers, describing the long days of back-breaking work he endured in the sugar beet fields north of Fort Collins when he was only 10 years old, the same age as most SOS students. He also described instances of persecution within the city, including signs that were posted in local stores that read "Whites Only" and "No Mexicans, No Dogs." Audible gasps by students are not uncommon when they hear these stories because they are so shocked to learn of the troubling history of our often idealized community. Students inevitably leave the museum committed to documenting and sharing a fuller picture of Fort Collins' past that exposes the roots of racism and white privilege that are typically downplayed in sunnier views of Colorado's past. This experience stands in stark contrast to the one offered by another museum in the city that mentions aspects of the farming history as part of the city's past only through a single wall of difficult-to-hear video segments.

Projects like SOS provide students with the civic literacies necessary to explore and expose a history of marginalization. Providing a powerful outlet for youth to foment "political anger" (Ruitenberg 2009), such projects can productively channel the "indignation one feels when decisions are made and actions are taken that violate the interpretation and implementation of the ethico-political values of equality and liberty that, one believes, would support a just society" (277). A framework that includes civic literacies can help students counteract prevailing narratives and replace them with more critical histories. Saving stories like these acknowledges the collective power of younger citizens to help a community confront its difficult past and move forward to a more inclusive future.

Transformative Definitions of Standard English

As noted in the CCSS, guiding the development of Standard English within our classrooms is a clear and necessary charge for teachers. However, we want to challenge what 21st-century Standard English looks like, arguing instead for a more inclusive instantiation that reflects the shifting and more diverse population of America and broadens the notions of language practices in light of the constant flux of digital technologies. The rich and robust forms of spoken and written language we encounter in our classrooms, online, and in society strain the restrictive seams of traditional Standard English. New definitions must be multivocal and must more fluidly integrate print, imagaic, and digital literacies that each have grammars and conventions of their own.

As described earlier in this chapter, cultural diversity is merely glossed over in the CCSS and is completely absent from the Language standards. We surmise this omission is due to the authors of the CCSS aiming at producing students who are college and career ready in ways that they can successfully negotiate and use what Gee (2012) calls discourses of power in these contexts. While we agree that students need to be facile with power codes, we intentionally propose a more transformative definition of Standard English that promotes language diversity. As Paulo Freire and Donaldo Macedo (1987) describe, powerful literacy begins with "reading the world," learning the codes appropriate for diverse contexts, and using these codes intentionally to rewrite it. These intentional practices are necessary components in authentic 21st-century Standard English. The role we see educators playing in broadening definitions is one of leveraging existing cultural knowledge within the classroom (Fecho 2003). In SOS, for example, we encouraged students to code-switch for rhetorical and stylistic effect in their writing, just as Cisneros (1991), Junot Diaz (1997), and Soto (1992) frequently do.

Another problem with the CCSS is that it frames digital technology as a layer of information for students to be able to parse and sift through. The authors of the CCSS miss the malleability of today's digital tools and resources—many of which our SOS students are familiar with in creating multimodal texts. Building upon the CCSS, our framework integrates digital technology not simply as a source of information, but as a context within which new forms of learning and writing occur. Digital tools like YouTube and Flickr and social networks like Facebook and Twitter contribute to what Henry Jenkins and colleagues call a "participatory culture" (2009): "Participatory culture is emerging as the culture absorbs and responds to the explosion of new media technologies that make it possible for average consumers to archive, annotate, appropriate, and recirculate media content in powerful new ways" (8; see also Chapter 5 in this volume for more discussion of Jenkins). As he notes, communicating, accessing, and producing within these digital spaces is increasingly a part of how youth are working, learning, and engaging civically. These activities and spaces, then, should be part of what "counts" as Standard English in the 21st century. To be clear, while we recognize that it is important for students to "habitually perform the critical reading necessary to pick carefully through the staggering amount of information available today in print and digitally" (CCSSO and NGA 2010a, 3), this alone is not enough. A fuller definition of Standard English represented in such a standards document must also consider the *relational* nature of communicating and shifting contexts and discourses in digital environments.

The CCSS authors' understanding of technology is stalled in earlier forms of digital literacies. Standard English today must embed technology as a contextual tool for communication (including speaking differently in text and Facebook messages), as production tools (for generating and sharing personally meaningful information), and as opportunities for remix (adapting existing texts as resources to write upon). Within the SOS Project, existing Fort Collins narratives provided opportunities to expand and interrogate through digital technology. Instead of merely looking at and reading about the history of our community, the students clicked, recorded, and edited their way to disseminating multimodal texts in online and offline environments. These are not simply digital gimmicks; the access to digital tools and online contexts of learning are increasingly necessary for academic and career success. In our various classes for pre-service teachers, we often require our students to communicate via Twitter, share their writing publicly, and engage in larger online networks of current teachers. As these are standard practices for a large part of the U.S. population, these are the kinds of writing and communication skills that are transforming how we define Standard English. Twenty-first century Standard English includes fluent communication online and the ability to produce multimodal texts with digital tools.

A Heuristic for Addressing Diverse Student Needs in the Age of the CCSS

The teachers with whom we work often express frustration with the restrictive interpretations of the CCSS and their effects on the classroom. Though popular rhetoric often demonizes the CCSS as a step backward with regard to meeting diverse student needs, we are optimistic that we as educators can help students meet CCSS expectations without abandoning our commitment to progressive and powerful teaching. Drawing from the four components of the framework upon which the SOS Project is based, we have developed central questions teachers and librarians can apply directly to the actionable needs present in their professional contexts. It is our hope that working through the questions that follow will help teachers and librarians push against culturally neutral assumptions of technology integration and linguistic diversity within the CCSS.

Design-based teaching:
- What professional contexts do you inhabit that are constrained by the CCSS (your classroom, library, school, district, professional organizations, and/or community)? How might you apply the methods of design-based thinking in one of those contexts to a problem related to digital literacies and cultural and linguistic diversity?

- As you empathize with the participants in that context, what is a concrete actionable need you can define?
- What broad array of solutions might be taken to solve the problem?
- How could you move forward in a small way to prototype the most promising solution and determine whether it will meet the actionable need?
- Reflecting with participants on the implementation of the prototype, what refinements do you need to make before you test out the solution in full?

Civic literacy:

- What are local social, cultural, or political issues for student inquiry?
- From a justice-oriented approach to civic education, how can students explore the systemic roots of the issues being taught?
- How do writing and text play into the civic purpose of your lessons? How might student texts effect change?
- Are the kinds of products students perform reflective of their cultural practices and responsive to the socially relevant topics salient within the local community?

Effectual partnerships:

- Who else shares your interest in helping ELL youth use their digital literacies to achieve impact in meaningful ways in their lives, local community, and the broader public sphere?
- How does this shared purpose intersect with these potential partners' needs?
- How might partners leverage their resources, energies, and time with reciprocal benefits and transformative intent in mind?

Transformative Standard English:

- How are students' diverse linguistic practices supported within the classroom and library?
- How are the needs of ELL students authentically incorporated into the literacies of the curriculum?
- Are technologies integrated in ways that reflect the practices and realities of participatory culture?

Conclusion

We offer the framework described in this chapter as an alternative way to nurture the human needs of diversity and social engagement within our classrooms and libraries. Informed by this framework, the SOS Project demonstrates one model for not only meeting, but exceeding the CCSS related to digital technologies and cultural diversity. As such, it pushes ELA teachers and librarians alike to problematize potentially limiting interpretations of digital literacies in CCSS while at the same time addressing the standards' omission of important considerations like cultural relevancy and language diversity.

By employing methods of design-based teaching similar to those we used in the SOS Project, we propose that other teachers enlist allies interested in effectual partnerships that bolster students' development of civic literacies. Students can meet the CCSS as they construct and share personally meaningful texts and manipulate and remix culturally relevant academic content in ways that demonstrate their prowess with 21st-century Standard English. They can increase their potential for success in and beyond school and develop as community advocates at the same time.

Thinking back to the objections to the CCSS we discussed with our colleague in that fateful taxi ride and other problems we have considered since, we view the CCSS as merely a starting block for students. For if the CCSS are conceived of as a finish line, students will cross it with a stunted view of literacy that prohibits them from seeing how to use their language practices as tools to effect change in their lives and the world.

References

Cisneros, Sandra. 1991. *The House on Mango Street*. New York: Vintage.

Council of Chief State School Officers and National Governors Association. 2010a. *Common Core State Standards for English Language Arts and Literacy in History/Social Studies, Science, and Technical Subjects*. Washington, DC: National Governors Association Center for Best Practices, Council of Chief State School Officers. Accessed February 10, 2014. www.corestandards.org/assets/CCSSI_ELA%20Standards.pdf.

———. 2010b. *Application of Common Core State Standards for English Language Learners*. Accessed February 10, 2014. www.corestandards.org/assets/application-for-english-learners.pdf.

Delpit, Lisa. 2006. *Other People's Children: Cultural Conflict in the Classroom*. 2nd ed. New York: New Press.

Diaz, Junot. 1997. *Drown*. New York: Riverhead Press.

Fecho, Bob. 2003. *Is This English?: Race, Language, and Culture in the Classroom*. New York: Teachers College Press.

Freire, Paulo, and Donaldo Macedo. 1987. *Literacy: Reading the Word and the World*. New York: Routledge.

Garcia, Antero. 2013. "Utilizing Mobile Media and Games to Develop Critical Inner-City Agents of Social Change." In *Critical Digital Literacies as Social Praxis: Intersections and Challenges*, edited by JuliAnna Ávila and Jessica Zacher Pandya, 107–125. New York: Peter Lang.

Gay, Geneva. 2010. *Culturally Responsive Teaching: Theory, Research, and Practice*. 2nd ed. New York: Teachers College Press.

Gee, James Paul. 2012. *Social Linguistics and Literacies: Ideologies in Discourses*. 4th ed. New York: Routledge.

International Reading Association and National Council of Teachers of English. 1996. *Standards for the English Language Arts*. Accessed February 10, 2014. www.ncte.org/library/NCTEFiles/Resources/Books/Sample/StandardsDoc.pdf.

Jenkins, Henry, Ravi Purushotma, Margaret Weigel, Katie Clinton, and Alice J. Robison. 2009. *Confronting the Challenges of Participatory Culture: Media Education for the 21st Century*. MacArthur Foundation. Cambridge, MA: MIT Press.

Kahne, Joseph, and Ellen Middaugh. 2008. *Democracy for Some: The Civic Opportunity Gap in High School*. CIRCLE Working Paper 59. Washington, DC: The Center for Information and Research on Civic Learning. Accessed February 10, 2014. www.civicyouth.org/PopUps/WorkingPapers/WP59Kahne.pdf.

Lankshear, Colin, and Michele Knobel. 2007. "Sampling the 'New' in New Literacies". In *A New Literacies Sampler*, edited by and Michele Knobel and Colin Lankshear, 1–24. New York: Peter Lang.

O'Donnell-Allen, Cindy. 2006. *The Book Club Companion: Fostering Strategic Readers in the Secondary Classroom*. Portsmouth, NH: Heinemann.

———. 2011. *Tough Talk, Tough Texts: Teaching English to Change the World*. Portsmouth, NH: Heinemann.

———. 2012. "Saving Our Stories: Digital Storytelling With ELLs." *Digital Is*. National Writing Project. Accessed February 10, 2014. digitalis.nwp.org/resource/4419.

Ruitenberg, Claudia W. 2009. "Educating Political Adversaries: Chantal Mouffe and Radical Democratic Citizenship Education." *Studies in Philosophy and Education* 28 (3): 269–281.

Soto, Gary. 1992. *Neighborhood Odes*. Harcourt: Orlando.

Stanford University Institute of Design. 2014. "Innovators Not Innovations." Stanford University. Accessed February 10, 2014. dschool.stanford.edu/our-point-of-view/#design-thinking.

Thomas, Adam, and Thomas Smith. 2004. *The Sugar Factory Neighborhoods: Buckingham, Andersonville, Alta Vista*. Durango, CO: SWCA Environmental Consultants. Accessed February 10, 2014. www.fcgov.com/historicpreservation/pdf/sugar-factory-doc.pdf.

Westheimer, Joel, and Joseph Kahne. 2004. "What Kind of Citizen? The Politics of Educating for Democracy." *American Educational Research Journal* 41 (2): 237–269.

Wiggins, Grant, and Jay McTighe. 2005. *Understanding by Design*. 2nd ed. Alexandria, VA: ASCD.

CHAPTER **13**

UnCommon Connections
How Building a Grass-Roots Curriculum Helped Reframe Common Core State Standards for Teachers and Students in a High-Needs Public High School

Stephanie West-Puckett and William P. Banks

A one-medium user is the new illiterate. (Zingrone 2001, 237)

Equipping students to write in only one mode—traditionally, black ink on white paper in scripted genres—will not serve students in their higher education experiences or in the workplaces of the future. (National Writing Project [NWP] with DeVoss, Eidman-Aadahl, and Hicks 2010, 5)

Use technology, including the internet, to produce, publish, and update individual or shared writing products in response to ongoing feedback, including new arguments or information. (Council of Chief State School Officers [CCSSO] and National Governors Association [NGA] 2010, W.11–12.6)

Without a doubt, the teacher who carefully reads the Common Core State Standards (CCSS) will discover that something feels different from previous outcome articulation documents. While the CCSS themselves are not necessarily more complex or sophisticated than previous local or state standards, they articulate those standards in ways that can seem alien or off-putting, both because there are so many standards and because the discourse around them has involved more talking *around* or *at* teachers than *with* them. Further complicating the issue, some standards focus on actual outcomes, while others focus more on micromanaging classroom activities and teacher practices than on measurable outcomes (or standards) of student learning. As teacher-educators, we have worried significantly about how we should begin approaching the CCSS with both pre- and in-service teachers, as well as how we might help experienced teachers to understand and, if possible, engage these new standards critically and professionally.

One element of the CCSS that we have been excited to see is a concern for 21st-century digital literacies. Having worked for years on local, state, and national professional development projects centered on digital literacies, we see the CCSS as a space where English Language Arts (ELA) teachers should be encouraged to integrate new literacy practices throughout the curriculum in order to engage learners in more meaningful ways than previous standards and educational policies have allowed. Standards like Anchor Standard for Writing 6, which focuses on using "technology" for writing, gesture toward a more collaborative, digitally aware curriculum (CCSSO and NGA 2010, 18).

In part, our thinking on new literacies has been influenced by researchers like Henry Jenkins and colleagues who argue in *Confronting the Challenges of Participatory Culture* (2006) that "Participatory culture shifts the focus of literacy from one of individual expression to community involvement. The new literacies almost all involve social skills developed through collaboration and networking" (4). While these networks in previous generations were interpersonal and hyperlocal, the networks that Jenkins and colleagues' work has explored are built on the awareness that tomorrow's (and even today's) networks are global and intercultural. As such, it is not enough simply to have two students from the same class swap papers for peer review; young composers need spaces to think about their work in terms of how various networks—from the hyperlocal to the global—might impact writing, from invention and exploration to production, from research and discovery to design and delivery (see Chapter 5 in this volume for an extended look at connections between Jenkins and the CCSS).

In order to explore more fully the intersections of the CCSS, "best practices" in the teaching of writing, and student experiences with digital media, the Tar River Writing Project partnered with a local high school on a grant-funded initiative to help rebuild the school's "Graduation Project" from the ground up as a "born-digital" project aimed at addressing the writing standards of the CCSS and serving, for the most part, as the primary writing curriculum for senior English (English IV). This chapter explores how we developed this project, in conjunction with teachers, media specialists, and students at the high school, as a grass-roots response to the new standards. We argue that teachers, like any group of professionals, both want and need to have some degree of agency in the construction of the curriculum that they teach, an agency that is far too often denied them in the current educational climate. Likewise, we demonstrate that students benefit from being involved in the creation of a new curriculum. Ultimately, we provide a rationale for why teachers and students should be allowed space and time for engaging the CCSS, a rationale that brings these standards into conversation with other equally important standards for literacy and learning.

Historicizing Old Connections

The Tar River Writing Project (TRWP) and J. H. Rose High School (JHR), both located in eastern North Carolina, have forged a connection by working on several projects over the years. Through TRWP summer institutes, we've come to know, value, and support the 21st-century literacy work that strong teacher-leaders at JHR have been doing in their classrooms long before the CCSS were even a blip on the North Carolina education radar. As a high-needs high school in eastern North Carolina, with a racially and economically diverse population of students, JHR teachers and students have their fair share of successes and challenges. Despite JHR's colloquial reputation as the region's flagship public school because of its geographical positioning inside the region's only micropolitan area, as well as its community reputation, diverse curricular offerings, and award-winning band and athletic programs, JHR has struggled with racial parity and a higher than average dropout rate. In addition, JHR has struggled to graduate its lower-achieving students, and increasing its graduation rate is a top priority for the school over the next few years.

To address the high drop-out rate that plagued each of its six high schools including JHR, the Pitt County School District voted in 2012 to abolish the mandate that all seniors must complete and score satisfactorily on a tightly conscripted research project, one managed and taught as a major element of the state's pre-CCSS English IV curriculum. The former Graduation Project required students to find a project mentor in the school or community, work with him or her to complete 20 hours of carefully documented work on a physical project that would teach the student something new, write a five- to eight-page researched academic essay on a topic loosely connected to that physical project, and prepare and deliver a 10-minute oral report with a visual accompaniment that demonstrated the physical project to a group of judges from the school and the community. Citing the difficulty many students, especially those who are already underresourced and under-achieving, had in finding mentors, arranging transportation to complete the work, producing an error-free five- to eight-page academic argument during the course of one semester, and learning effective oral and visual communication skills, the school board dropped the system-wide requirement, effective for the 2012–2013 academic year.

This action sent a conflicting message to many secondary ELA teachers in the district as some felt they were being asked to lower their expectations while at the same time prepare to meet the new CCSS with rigor and relevance. One of our JHR colleagues has called this conundrum the "fancy dance" of public education, a representation of the complex work that professional educators have to do when faced with conflicting imperatives to provide access to education to all students while simultaneously being the "standard bearers" of education.

While many of the former Graduation Project demands did seem like undue burdens, the principal at JHR and a few of the school's teacher-leaders, some already connected with TRWP, recognized the value of a capstone project that could provide authentic writing and research experiences for both college- and career-track students. Thus, they called on TRWP to help enact a space in which English IV teachers could conceptualize a curriculum that promotes (1) authentic inquiry, (2) experiential learning, and (3) making and doing—in short, a curriculum that provides rich literacy instruction with embedded opportunities to read, write, speak, and listen in both virtual and face-to-face environments. While the former Graduation Project had been designed with college-bound honors students in mind, JHR school leadership wanted to invest in a project that could meet the needs of multiple student groups, conceptualizing literacy as a tool for success and empowerment as opposed to a sorting device for social stratification around which we must, as John Trimbur (1991) argues, periodically create a crisis.

Imagining New Connections

David Barton and Mary Hamilton (1998), in articulating the new literacies that will play a key role in students' lives in the 21st century, argue that:

> Literacy is primarily something people do; it is an activity, located in the space between thought and text. Literacy does not just reside in people's heads as a set of skills to be learned, and it does not just reside on paper, captured as texts to be analyzed. Like all human activity, literacy is essentially social, and it is located in the interaction between people. (3)

Likewise, as Kathleen Blake Yancey reminded the audience during her Chair's Address to the 2004 Conference on College Composition and Communication, to teach new literacies requires new strategies, to move away from old models and old logics of teaching writing. To collaboratively develop a new logic that would operate in the English IV classroom, teacher-leaders at TRWP and JHR convened for one week during the summer of 2012 to explore collaboratively the CCSS for writing as well as the MacArthur Foundation's Connected Learning Principles (2011) and the Framework for Success in Postsecondary Writing (Framework), jointly authored by the Council of Writing Program Administrators (CWPA), the National Council of Teachers of English (NCTE), and the NWP (2011).

While JHR teachers had some familiarity with the CCSS for writing, none had had an opportunity to explore the textures of writing and teaching in a networked world, an inquiry that is taken up in the Principles. Built on Jenkins's (2006) concept of participatory cultures, the Principles (MacArthur Foundation 2011) work to articulate and showcase how teachers and schools can design student-centered learning experiences that harness the power of networked digital technologies to support learning for academic, economic, and social achievement. While the Principles position students as makers and collaborators, focusing on the act of doing with others in community, the Framework focuses on individual habits of mind that can be cultivated through a rich writing education (see also Chapters 4, 5, and 6 in this volume). Authored by educators representing our most reputable professional organizations, these habits of mind include curiosity, openness, engagement, creativity, persistence, responsibility, flexibility, and metacognition. These are habits that research into writing studies has identified as crucial to the practice of writing (and thinking) well in higher education. Taken separately, these materials provide a limited understanding of "doing digital" in writing classrooms, but taken together, these three approaches provide a theory of action and a practical vision for how student-centered writing pedagogy might operate in an ELA classroom.

We developed our initial leadership team out of existing professional partnerships that had developed among the following people:

- JHR's Digital and Print Media teacher from the Career and Technical Education Department
- JHR's Instructional Coach with ELA teaching experience and a writing studies background
- A college-level writing instructor and doctoral student in Rhetoric, Writing, and Professional Communication

All three teacher-leaders had completed the TRWP Summer Institute and were active teacher consultants with the NWP. But we knew we had to build new connections to prevent this initiative from being seen as the pet project of a few insiders. To build those connections, we invited two of JHR's English IV teachers: one, the former Graduation Project coordinator, and the other, an ELA teacher and an academic counselor working to increase the success rates of low-performing students. Together, we used the Principles as well as our own local knowledge of student digital literacies to envision a capstone student experience and develop what came to be known as Project Connect (learn more at sites.google.com/a/pitt.k12.nc.us/project-connect/home).

Collaborative Critique: Professionalizing Teachers Around the Standards

Since North Carolina had planned to implement the CCSS in the coming fall, the school district and JHR administrators were intent on being "CCSS-ready" and were eager to support Project Connect, seeing it as a possible model for how teachers could enact these standards, thus bringing some recognition to the school, its teachers, and its students. As we started our leadership institute, however, it became clear that only the instructional coach—who, by virtue of his position, had attended several state and district-level CCSS training events—enjoyed a thorough understanding of these standards; thus, our early discussions about standards centered on reading and collaboratively interpreting the 12th-grade writing standards. Through this experience, and conversations with teachers across our state and at national meetings of NCTE and NWP, we know that most teachers have had little direct experience working with the CCSS. Information about the standards has trickled down to teachers in hallway conversations and informal (often uninformed) spaces. We have come to believe that more teachers need both direct access to the CCSS and what their implementation might look like, and critical spaces to engage and question the CCSS with their colleagues. By providing teachers at JHR such a space, we were able to collaborate on Project Connect in more meaningful ways.

As a group, we agreed with the notion that students should have experience writing academic arguments, explanatory texts, and narratives—positions that are articulated by the first three writing standards for grades 11–12 (CCSSO and NGA 2010, 45–46). When we further explored those text types and purposes, however, we started to wonder about the lingering allegiance to the 19th-century modes of writing over more socially shaped, emerging genres; we also questioned the overly prescriptive and narrow ways that these text types were being constructed by the standards. We began to wonder, for example, why the Toulmin model of argumentation was scripted into the description of W.11–12.1a, in which students are asked to introduce claims, establish their significance, and create an organization that logically sequences claims, counterclaims, reasons, and evidence.

Furthermore, we worried that this standard might restrict options for authentic argumentation, redeploying the trope of the five-paragraph essay as students (1) introduce and tell the significance of a claim; (2) provide reason 1 with three types of evidence; (3) provide reason 2 with three types of evidence; (4) provide reason 3 with three types of evidence; and (5) refute counterclaims and summarize the claim. With the extreme focus on organization instead of negotiation, a singular model of argumentation as opposed to the rich and multiple genres of persuasion at work in the world, and the lack of more complex models of student writing, we worried that fidelity to such a structure might circumscribe the habits of openness, flexibility, and metacognition that are outlined in the Framework. Similarly, the description in W.11–12.1d struck us as problematic: While W.11–12.1b asks students to consider the audience's "knowledge level, concerns, values, and possible biases," W.11–12.1d asks students to adopt a "formal style," "objective tone," and write in the norms and conventions of a particular "discipline," again showing a lack of awareness of the diversity in academic audiences, purposes, contexts, and forum conventions (CCSSO and NGA 2010, 45).

If the CCSS are intended to foster a rhetorical approach to composition, which is suggested in the CCSS introduction with the phrase, "they [students] respond to the varying demands of audience, task, purpose, and discipline" (7), then why are the standards circumscribing students' construction of rhetorical situations, preventing student choice regarding audience and appropriate tones and styles for those audiences? Why, we wondered, are students, particularly those who are preparing for civic- and career-readiness, being asked to write discipline-specific arguments more appropriate for college students and/or professional academics? We don't expect first-year writers at the university to write like field botanists or John Donne scholars as they could not yet be appropriately "disciplined" to do so in first-year writing courses. Why, then, would we value this outcome for the diverse range of high school students being measured by the CCSS?

Similarly, we wondered why students writing informative/explanatory texts should, as W.11–12.2 suggests, employ the literary techniques of metaphor, simile, and analogy listed in W.11–12.2d. While we appreciated the attention to "precise language" spelled out there, we also imagined how a young entrepreneur preparing a business plan—one example of an informative and explanatory text type regularly practiced in Career and Technical Education—might use the stylistic devices of simile and metaphor inappropriately in context. We imagined the potential failures of constructing a sentence like the following, which uses vocabulary appropriate to the discipline, as well as various metaphors (e.g., simile, personification): "I quite expect my profits, Mr. Capital, to grow like the morning sun out of a dark horizon." Again, this focus in W.11–12.2e on "formal style," "objective tone," and disciplinarity causes us to question what kinds of rhetorical contexts these documents imagine for high school students—visions that seem quite disconnected from the ways that we and our students use language in social practice. The conversations that we engaged in as professionals allowed us to ask these user-centered questions before entering the classroom with the CCSS. Thus, we've learned that work with teachers around the CCSS should move beyond comprehension of complex (and contradictory) texts and into collaborative critique, which creates opportunities for teachers to build capacity and exercise agency in conversations about curriculum reform.

Reframing the Standards

These discussions helped set the tone for our group's work as we began to think about the CCSS for writing as the lowest common denominator for the kinds of writing students might do in English IV. And while we could critique the constraints of this document, we also seized on one particular affordance: a clear justification for constructing a digital writing curriculum articulated in Anchor Standard for Writing 6. As the NWP with DeVoss, Eidman-Aadahl, and Hicks (2010) assert in *Because Digital Writing Matters*, "[D]igital writing matters because we live in a networked world and there's no going back. Because, quite simply, *digital is*" (ix). In the former senior project at JHR, however, *digital wasn't*. Students did use technology in the form of word processing programs to produce informative and explanatory texts that would be printed and collected in shiny plastic sleeves, yet the former project largely ignored the participatory, collaborative, networked nature of students' digital writing practices. Working from characteristics that are outlined by Project New Media Literacies (2014) as play, performance, simulation, appropriation, multitasking, distributed cognition, collective intelligence, judgment, transmedia navigation, networking, negotiation, and visualization, the Project Connect leadership team needed to challenge the notion that a digital writing curriculum is about students interacting with machines. Digital writers do, of course, *seem* to interact with machines, but we wanted to recognize in our curriculum revisions that this human–computer interaction is really about using a set of tools to interact with other people by actualizing a digital communication framework, one that is about making, doing, creating, collaborating, connecting, and ultimately being *present* in the world with others.

To achieve this vision, we had to look beyond the CCSS, working to synthesize what we were learning from our other professional conversations. Thus, we collaboratively read and discussed the Framework as well as the Principles. In contrast to standards that, as Tom Fox (2009) argues, are more about excluding students than granting them access to literacy tools and experiences, the Framework and the Principles seemed to us more inclusive and student-centered. At the very least, the authors begin with the assumption that students have agency in digital composing environments, agency which is often denied them in the documents that teachers and EduCorps write about students. While the Framework and the Principles are explicit about developing college-ready writers, we think the habits of mind they address are actually well-suited for both college- and career-ready students as they embody the notion that learning is both intellectual and practical, an activity that happens both in and outside of school.

As we discussed the habits, we continually asked ourselves about the kinds of experiences with texts and technology that foster curiosity, openness, engagement, creativity, persistence, responsibility, flexibility, and metacognition. Were some of these experiences already seeded in our classrooms? How might we build on what was already there, working from the ground up to effect change as opposed to thinking about reform as a top-down mandate over which we had little or no control? This process of working from teacher expertise as a primary fund of knowledge separated our professional development program from others led by local or state education bureaus and created a comfort zone for educators who were working with the cognitive dissonance of being hit with yet another initiative to fix what others perceive as a broken system.

We found some intriguing answers to our questions about putting theory into practice in the wide variety of resources available through the Principles website, ConnectedLearning.tv. The Principles focus on two areas: learning and design. Based on research conducted by members of the Digital Media and Learning Research Hub at the University of California, Irvine, this framework asserts that learning happens when students and their peers are actively engaged in knowledge-sharing and ongoing feedback loops, when students are supported in pursuing their interests and passions, and when students are able to translate skills and experiences into academic success. When learning is intentionally designed to shape students as contributors, makers, and producers, to draw on the power of digital platforms and open networks that allow students to synchronize learning in home, community, and school settings, and to connect students with adults who share their interests and passions, students are well-positioned for transformative educational experiences. None of this language, however, is a central part of the CCSS.

As a framework, the Principles push us to consider when and where authentic learning occurs and promote the values of equity and networked learning through a lens that redefines "digital" as both a set of tools *and* a way of knowing and being in a networked world. The Principles, and the case studies that illustrate them, gave us a way to envision how we might design an ELA capstone experience that could engage all students at JHR in designing self-constructed writing experiences through the creation of socially meaningful genres, writing with digital tools for, with, and about communities (Deans 2003) who share their passions and interests. Through these experiences, students could develop the "habits of mind" that would serve them well for writing in communities, whether academic or not.

Out of these conversations and critical questions, the Project Connect team began the task of composing the texts that would articulate its shared curricular vision. These curricular documents were "born digital," collaboratively written and rewritten in Google Docs as we sat at the large conference table in the Writing Program office at East Carolina University with our letters and pictures joining in cyberspace and displaying on our screens. In stark contrast to the 150-page Graduation Project manual, with its formal tone and authoritative directives, we produced a web text that could lessen the rhetorical distance between readers and writers, playing with the fluid and dynamic boundaries of digital texts. As Colin Lankshear and Michele Knobel (2007) argue, shifts in literate identity require new literacy identities that are participatory, collaborative, and divergent from the ways we have historically understood authorial control. As the teachers in the room worked to embody these new identities, we worked to create a text that could provide space for writing new roles for teachers, media specialists, administrators, parents, and community members, reframing the work of curriculum development and school reform as hypersocial practice. Again, this professional development strategy of having teachers engaged as makers and contributors in digital spaces reinforced the kinds of learning experiences we envisioned for students: building shared purposes, literacies, and identities through connectivity and interactivity.

Building Project Connect

Out of the August professional development retreat, Project Connect team members built a framework for a project that would replace the long-running Graduation Project. While the leadership team wanted Project Connect to remain flexible, it recognized the need to sketch out the broad outlines of the project so that teachers and students knew where they were headed. The new central text of Project Connect would be the Contribution, which the leaders articulated to students as follows: "You will decide what you want to learn and how you want to contribute that learning back to the world around you. The Contribution may be something you share, something you do, something you produce. It may be a solo effort, or it may be a group project. The important thing is that you learn, and that you share that learning with the world." The past Graduation Project had been overly prescriptive and had been fairly teacher-directed, despite discourse that suggested the project focused on student choice. It was important for Project Connect to make sure students engaged their Contribution on their own terms and found a project into which they could invest time and resources. This Contribution involved the students' putting together, on their individual Google Sites website, a series of texts that made up this Contribution: shorter and longer pieces of writing, multimodal digital texts, videos, podcasts, and so on, as well as a researched paper that would be designed to share inquiry with a larger community than just the teacher or class. Ultimately, the students would then participate in a large public symposium in which they would share their research/inquiry with an audience of their peers, teachers, administrators, families, and community members who were invited to participate. Unlike the Graduation Project presentations, however, audience members were not there to judge or evaluate the quality of the project so much as to offer genuine feedback (e.g., critique, praise, suggestions).

Likewise, while the Graduation Project had, ostensibly, been an extracurricular activity, worked on outside of class yet evaluated by teachers to determine whether or not students graduated, Project Connect was built to be part of English IV; the work of connected learning meant that "school" was part of that connection. One of the goals of the team involved disrupting the traditional boundaries of the classroom and providing a space where teachers and students worked together, along with community mentors, to help focus and direct students' interests into positive and meaningful inquiry projects.

Projects presented at the first symposium ranged from the history and value of sewing/needle-craft in the military to the social-historical implications of super-hero comics to the scientific and business aspects of hair styles in African-American communities. Many of these projects stood rather outside traditional research papers but each demonstrated a connection both to traditional disciplinary inquiry practices and to projects and professions that contribute to the world in important ways. Students presented their Contributions by sharing video interviews they conducted with professionals in fields related to their projects, by sharing digital projects (e.g., Prezi presentations, Bitstrips comic strips) that explored key findings of their work and repurposed them for different audiences, and by showcasing websites and blogs they created to connect their research with real nonacademic audiences. While Project Connect is still a new and developing project, the success of the Contributions and the presentations at the Symposium has suggested that both teachers and students have expanded their perceptions of research and writing in ways that better prepare them to capitalize on digital resources for learning and distributing learning.

Taking It Back to the Building

Key to developing a sustainable project at JHR was using a professional development and engagement model that reflected the sort of networked subjectivities that we had explored in the summer visioning institute and built into the initial design of Project Connect. Therefore, after that institute, the Project Connect leadership team and the school principal identified seven additional teacher-leaders across the curriculum and grade level to bring into the program; these included the school's Media Coordinator, the English Department Chair, a second Career and Technical Education instructor teaching in the Business Department, and two additional English IV teachers and two English III teachers. To support the new Project Connect curriculum both vertically and horizontally, we began an intensive but flexible professional development program that would investigate digital writing and literacy, focusing on the concept and practice of digital writing and the act of teaching digital writers.

We based our programming on successful NWP models of teachers-teaching-teachers and the belief that effective teachers of (digital) writing are (digital) writers themselves. We also leaned heavily on the Critical Elements Framework, which Laura DeSimone (2009) has explored at length. While three members of the Project Connect leadership team had had significant experience in NWP summer institutes, they were far less experienced in developing ongoing, embedded professional development programs and found DeSimone's framework useful as she broadens the working definition of *professional development*, noting that it is both formal (workshops, conferences, meetings) and informal (conversations, co-teaching, mentoring, collaborative inquiry); as DeSimone argues, it is not the structure of the professional development but the "features" that make it effective. These features include a focus on participating teachers' content concerns; the use of active learning practices, a coherence that is consistent with teachers' beliefs and knowledge as well as local, state, and national initiatives; sufficient duration (some studies suggest semester-long or greater than 20 hours); and collective participation from a group in the same school, grade, or department. All participating teachers were interested in exploring writing in their classrooms, were engaged as thinkers and makers, and worked from a position of exemplary local practice to standards. And since we were a school cohort working together for the year, we felt fairly confident in our professional development design.

Our fall semester programming included a half-day workshop each month during which we discussed readings and ideas from *Because Digital Writing Matters* (NWP with DeVoss, Eidman-Aadahl, and Hicks 2010), slowly developing a shared vocabulary for talking about the digital. Through our reading and resource sharing, we were again introduced to policy statements on digital literacy by other groups (e.g., the International Technology Education Association), and we started to situate Project Connect at the intersections of conversations that were circulating in multiple educational circles including media literacy, high-needs urban schools, educational technology, service-learning and community engagement, ELA, and writing studies. In short, we were engaging in a rich and complex *network* of texts and ideas, all of which were exploring what it means to compose within digital environments; we were doing what the CCSS expect students to be doing as they explore "claims," outlined in W.11–12.1a and 1b (CCSSO and NGA 2010, 45), that are central to arguments that circulate among (networks of) readers and writers. Our logic here of practicing the language arts we are teaching is central to the NWP philosophy of "writers teaching writing"—to teach a practice well requires recent, relevant experience with that practice. This is where many professional development programs fall short: They operate from logics of indoctrination and enforcement rather than logics of participation and collaboration.

During these workshops, we also spent a good deal of time playing with open-source digital writing tools such as Google Docs, Google

Sites, WordPress, VoiceThread, Piktochart, YouTube Video Editor, and Tagxedo. The leadership team worked to model the functional, rhetorical, and critical support for digital writing that Stuart Selber (2004) articulates in *Multiliteracies for a Digital Age*. We reflected on our digital writing practices and worked to identify iterations of those practices in the CCSS. We found much of what we did as digital writers and digital writing teachers could be interpreted as CCSS practices, and we developed our collective capacity to argue for teacher- and student-centered interpretations of the writing standards. This method, however, was grass-roots: We looked at our own practices as writers and digital composers, and from those practices, we asked, "How do our practices connect to the CCSS?"

To answer that question, we started a collaborative Google Doc that contained the CCSS for writing and asked teachers to summarize a teaching strategy, activity, or unit that they currently used to build capacity for particular standards. What we found here was that teachers were already using digital technologies, mainly Google Docs, "to produce, publish, and update individual or shared writing products in response to ongoing feedback, including new arguments or information" (CCSSO and NGA 2010, W.11–12.6), and the media coordinator had developed a set of resources that could be used to scaffold academic research practices outlined in W.11–12.7 and W.11–12.8, particularly gathering and evaluating a variety of print and digital sources. Because subject-area Professional Learning Communities had cordoned off ELA teachers from media coordinators, there had been little room to share instructional strategies and bring relevant experience and expertise to bear on the interdisciplinary problems of producing source-based writing. Project Connect programming, then, provided a space for teachers and media coordinators to learn from each other and find ways to strengthen interdisciplinary partnerships inside the building.

This grass-roots, collaborative approach to uncovering what was already there allowed us to engage students, when they returned to school in August, in similar grass-roots inquiry: How do you use technologies? Which technologies? To what end? From that inquiry, we could begin to see the CCSS as standards that we already met and, at times, exceeded, when we tapped into our school networks of learners, rather than as some set of external impositions or abstract learning principles. This model is antithetical to most professional development in K–12 environments and is absolutely contradictory to the sort of top-down, outsider-as-expert models that EduCorps use in order to manufacture literacy crises for which they also seem to have "the cure." In those models, which range from tests, standards, and professional development materials developed by Pearson and Educational Testing Service/College Board to for-profit products like Study Island and Accelerated Reader, the teacher and student are both seen as ignorant; they do not know what they are supposed to know based on terms and formulas that have been created without engaging them. In our model, teachers and students both have agency and voice; both have knowledge of digital literacies (though sometimes in conflict) that can be tapped to develop processes and products that meet whatever mandated outcome might come along. NWP models start with the assumption that students and teachers are intelligent, purposeful agents who wish to learn and understand themselves and their world. Because we started with this assumption, we were better positioned to develop Project Connect based on a network model of knowledge and language that privileges digital literacies like play, performance, simulation, appropriation, distributed cognition, collective intelligence, judgment, and negotiation.

In addition to more structured events, the English IV teachers and the Project Connect Leadership team met weekly to share stories and brainstorm strategies to strengthen the Project Connect program. As one of our team members said, "I've been doing everything from fixing webcams on brand new laptops to using this portal or this site to post a video or host a video, [dealing with] issues with accessibility—on Google Sites you'll see something that is supposed to be viewable to the entire world, and still, for some reason, no one but that student logging in can access that document." Beyond an initial focus on the practical, this teacher went on to explain, "But far and away, the biggest impediment has just been getting these machines that we've all had for a decade now to actually do something substantive." We cannot understate the importance of that last statement, and how it gives voice to the research of scholars like Barbara Monroe, who noted many years ago in *Beyond the Digital Divide* (2004) that far too many schools have technologies but have no idea how to use them in "substantive" ways. She argues teachers are not given space or time to explore effective practices for integrating digital tools. By building a grass-roots, teacher- and student-led project, we have started collectively to unlock the potential of machines that have done little more than print and collect dust.

Between our face-to-face meetings, we also created and shared digital resources on the Project Connect collaborative blog site, and we planned and implemented several co-teaching and live demo lessons during which Project Connect team teachers could either observe digital writing workshops, participate as coaches leading small groups, or share full-group instruction around topics such as investigating genre conventions of YouTube videos, writing research proposals, or remixing text-based arguments with images and sound for popular audiences.

In this instance, the school media coordinator became a key part of our programming, prioritizing technology resources like laptop carts and computer labs for Project Connect teachers and students, privileging making and creating over content delivery modules and test administration, and working with us to plan and deliver workshops for multiple classes of English II, III, and IV students in the media center. After one of our workshops in the media center, in fact, she said that her work with Project Connect had helped her make sense out of what it meant to be a *media coordinator* as opposed to a librarian. She hadn't had the opportunity to explore digital writing and literacies alongside classroom teachers and reported that through our collaborative work she had come to understand how media coordinators were poised to help teachers and schools make the transition to digital literacies. In one reflection, she wrote:

> Students often don't understand that different groups of people put information on the internet and those groups

have different agendas. They are still in "textbook mode" assuming because it's there, it's credible. I can help with that. While teachers have particular visions about classroom assignments, I can handle basic information literacy—teaching students to use our media center resources ... to find information on a variety of topics and evaluate those sources for credibility, reliability, and usefulness to the classroom project.

These skills are central to literacies outlined in the CCSS as students are expected to "Research to Build and Present Knowledge" (CCSSO and NGA 2010, W.11–12.7 and W.11–12.8). When professional development programming is effective at surfacing the particular expertise of media coordinators and helping them make connections with subject area teachers, schools can learn to leverage existing knowledge as a catalyst for reform.

Project *Dis*Connect

For the Project Connect leadership team, this work has been intensive, exhausting, and invigorating as we've witnessed the immediate and tangible impacts of our work together on teacher practice and student production. Because we were able to connect at a kairotic moment when so many of these digital and education reform conversations were coalescing at the national, state, and local level, we have gained tremendous support from parents, students, teachers, and school administrators. That is not to say that this work has not had its challenges. While we have implemented a teacher-designed digital writing curriculum, the scaffold for that curriculum was constructed by a small cadre of teachers tasked with building a school-wide program, meaning teachers who were not in the Project Connect leadership institute were then asked to teach a curriculum that they hadn't helped to build. These teachers took longer to engage with Project Connect, which slowed down the project during the first semester.

And while we shared early drafts of our Project Connect website and asked for questions, critique, and feedback, working to incorporate what we received, the English IV teachers who were not part of the leadership institute have, at times, struggled to engage in the project. They have expressed frustration at what they saw as the sonic speed with which we've moved, wondering how to "fly a plane while we're building it." As we wanted all teachers to have a hand in developing the lessons and their own approach to integrating the project in their English IV classrooms, we didn't mandate due dates or produce pacing guides like those that had occupied a large space in the former Graduation Project manual. While the leadership team has referred to the week we spent together as the most enjoyable and transformative experience of the work we've done thus far, noting that the space for deep exploration and negotiated meaning-making was central in our conceptualizations of the project and our approaches to "doing digital" in our classrooms, we cannot stress enough how important it is for meaningful professional development around the CCSS to engage the broadest group of educators possible.

Too often, K–12 professional development, particularly in difficult economic times, has followed a "train the trainer" model: One person from a school or curriculum team receives "training" and then is expected to share materials and information with the rest of the school. While that model seems efficient—and may operate well in various corporate models of education—our experience demonstrates again and again that teachers (and students) want to be involved not merely at the end; they want to be part of building a curriculum that affects them, that reflects local needs and values, and that shapes their professional (or student) lives. Our experience reminds us that we can't underestimate the power of connection and conversation, for students or teachers. It matters who has access to those opportunities—and when. Our project has demonstrated the need for *connectivity*, for engaging curriculum as a networked project that follows the logics of digital literacies rather than those of a "master" project that can be "imported" to different locations.

Connectivity Not Portability

While much of the research that investigates the impact of professional development in schools has focused on how well teachers are able to operationalize an external model with strict fidelity (Biancarosa, Bryk, and Dexter 2010; National Institute for Excellence in Teaching 2012; Saunders, Goldenberg, and Gallimore 2009), the NWP has a strong history of working with teachers as co-researchers and co-makers. This stance positions teachers as knowledge-makers and recognizes teacher agency in the maelstrom of educational reform. Thus, our work in the Project Connect partnership was never about developing a packaged digital curriculum to be exported and implemented elsewhere; instead, it has been about developing a method for connecting teachers with common interests across contexts to "assess locally and validate globally" (Gallagher 2012).

Unlike other professional development organizations that build *for* instead of *with* teachers, our partnership method operates on contemporary notions of teacher-research as articulated by Lee Nickoson (2012) that challenge older notions of classroom-specific, individualistic, and positivistic constructions of teachers-as-researchers. Nickoson's definition of teacher-research acknowledges multiple sites of research and multiple ways of gathering and interpreting data. Most important, however, it is built on feminist research methodologies that foreground ethical stances involving collaboration and collective expertise in multiple research methods as well an understanding that teacher-research may happen in our own classrooms, in other's classrooms, or outside classrooms so long as that research provides "a deeper understanding of student writers" (111). This understanding of specific skill sets, particularly those skill sets built around writing with digital tools, is crucial for enacting the digital in ELA curricula. Thus, through systematic inquiry into the teaching and writing practices that were already positioning students for college and career readiness, our work with teachers at JHR has recognized the particular expertise of the classroom teacher and worked through teacher inquiry and reflection to identify and build on that expertise.

Reframing the CCSS: Making Networks Visible

Absent from previous conversations about the CCSS are discussions of how these new standards are operationalized in schools. The CCSS neither grew organically out of successful teacher practices or teacher inquiry, nor systematically from close observation of students' successes and struggles in the ELA classroom. So for us, Project Connect has been a slow, but meaningful, investigation into what the CCSS look like "on the ground." In the abstract, there is much to praise in the CCSS, including an obvious, if somewhat superficial, concern for genre, process-based writing, and meaningful inquiry/research. But we've also noticed what's *not* there, in large part because of how our project brought the CCSS into conversation with other equally important frameworks around 21st-century digital literacies. While we remain hopeful for what is expressed in the CCSS, we would be remiss if we did not mention the obvious gaps that Project Connect has made visible for us and our teacher colleagues at JHR.

Social Learning

Despite the fact that one of the key functions of a networked society as Manuel Castells (2010) elucidates is the connectedness of its nodes, there remains in the CCSS a lack of awareness of learning as a social activity, and certainly as a social activity that takes place across a network. While there is some superficial concern for writing practices that might involve peer response strategies or the notion that a teacher would comment on writing that would then be revised based on feedback, there remains an absence of any genuine sense that young writers might compose for audiences other than teachers. The hyper-reliance on three of the four modes of discourse (narration, exposition, and argument) as the only modes of communication, and the failure to recognize any audience beyond the classroom, further underscores how little the CCSS attend to issues of digital literacies.

With Project Connect, students recognized that there were audiences beyond the classroom that might be interested in their topics and ideas. While the Graduation Project that had been part of the curriculum before had always, in some way, assumed that students should be communicating with non-school audiences, those audiences, if they showed up at all, only showed up to judge how good the writing and presentations were at the end of the project; they were not really involved as collaborators or as peer reviewers. By bringing the Principles to the CCSS, and by using Google Sites and YouTube, the teachers helped students to imagine audiences beyond the hyperlocal. This shift is only just emerging, but it's one that we're excited about. Future analyses of student work may help us to better understand how they have made this shift as digital composers.

Public Rhetoric

Another major omission that we've observed in the CCSS involves the rhetorical practices that the standards value. While the phrase du jour is "college and career ready," it seems to us that the CCSS spend much more time working in pseudo-genres and formulaic writing activities that are mostly about outdated academic writing practices. From the mode-based articulation of writing pseudo-genres that are devoid of real (non–school-based) audiences or purposes for composing, to the preoccupation with writing practices that are about a very particular and limited concept of audience and purpose, the CCSS seems most interested in reproducing a very particular type of college student. This is a student who follows directions and acquiesces to the uncritical demands of disciplinary convention; this is a student who sees "school" and "life" as separate and distinct spaces, the latter for genuine engagement with real audiences/purposes and the former for superficial acceptance of authority figures; this is a student, in short, who *dis*connects from his/her meaning-making networks of invention, production, and consumption in order to offer lip service to the histories and modes of knowledge-making that do not challenge or disrupt the status quo.

Across the grade levels, the Anchor Standards for Writing 1d and 2e ask students to "establish and maintain a formal style and an objective tone while attending to the norms and conventions of the discipline in which they are writing" (CCSSO and NGA 2010, 45), but what does *discipline* mean to someone not going to college, or someone not planning to be part of a narrowly established academic community? What is the discipline of the auto mechanic? The offset printer? The bench chemist at a pharmaceutical plant? The cost accountant at a rural pulp mill? The professional hair stylist? While each of these individuals is part of a career, several of them well-paying, none of them represents a notion of discipline as defined in academic contexts. While we might generously read "discipline" in the CCSS as "discourse community," and therefore open to these different professional discourses, we think it's meaningful that the CCSS chose *discipline* over *discourse community*, primarily for the reasons we just articulated. The CCSS assumes an authority (and knowledge-making) structure that is hierarchical and imposed. *Disciplines* have histories and require that individuals modify their behaviors to become part of them on the terms of the discipline's boundary maintainers (e.g., teachers, researchers). While *discourse communities* assume that novice members have to learn conventions, they are typically more malleable and open for negotiation than academic disciplines. The CCSS' notion of *discipline* seems to us very much in keeping with Foucaultian notions (1995) of knowledge production and distribution. Central to both the *WPA Outcomes Statement for First-Year Composition* (CWPA 2008) and the Framework, however, is the concern for audience/purpose/exigency as they relate to public/civic rhetoric. Many of the writing standards in the CCSS, specifically those noted here, work against effective communication in civic spaces.

Synergy

As DeSimone (2009) notes, transformative learning can happen when, among other factors, professional development is able to realize a coherence that is consistent with teachers' beliefs and knowledge as well as local, state, and national initiatives. Part of Project Connect's momentum, we feel, comes from the synergy of converging interests. We know that top-down curricular mandates do not always impact actual classroom practice, and we also know that grass-roots approaches to teacher-centered classroom reform are not always recognized, supported, or encouraged in the tightly controlled hierarchies common in many of our school systems. Our Project Connect partnership, however, capitalizes on distributed expertise and networking at the intersection of multiple interests including:

- The administration's desire to be recognized as a clinical school whose teachers and student-teaching interns are involved in creating a culture of excellence through research and partnerships
- The teachers' desire to find higher ground in the flood of information rushing eastward from NC's Department of Public Instruction in Raleigh
- The TRWP's interest in digital writing and its potential for creating more participatory and equitable schools
- The local school district's push to become CCSS ready
- JHR students' desire to be recognized as knowledge makers and writers, and to be supported in developing the capacity to make connections with people, places, ideas, and texts through language

These convergences have enabled us to build a project that, while still in its infancy, has a presence that will endure after the buzz around the CCSS, the Principles, and the Framework has quieted and the professional development funding to support it has expired.

Future Directions: Forging Uncommon Connections

Despite the newness of Project Connect and of this particular partnership between TRWP and JHR, our work together has been both intensive and extended, meeting the timed standard set forth by DeSimone (2009) for effective professional development, and yet this duration seems far too short. The work of teacher-centered curriculum reform and professional development is not efficient. It takes time to read the multiplicity of frameworks that inform our work with digital literacies and investigate research-based teaching practices that can support those frameworks. It takes time to write and speak with students, families, community leaders, school administrators, and other teachers about the curriculum we've designed, and to make justifications and ask for commentary and critique. It takes time to listen actively to team members and those outside of our team, working to effect "forms of dialogue which facilitate open argumentation and forms of action in common which do not suppress difference" (Fairclough 1999, 153). And it takes time to develop a critical awareness about language in education and to apply that lens to understand how the language in standards and curriculum documents constructs both teacher and student identity.

As teachers, we both give and receive these educational discourses, and while this work is not efficient, it is central to helping us "examine the dialectical between the global and the local" (Fairclough 1999, 151). Ultimately, Project Connect has helped us and the teachers and students at JHR to explore the connections that are essential for 21st-century digital literacies. We believe that Project Connect has helped us to see the CCSS in more rigorous and relevant ways; certainly, it has helped us to discover where the CCSS misses the mark in the digital literacy needs of 21st-century students. This chapter highlights a model of professional development that's both grass-roots and network-based, a model that we think can help other teachers and schools to build curricular models by focusing on the networks of knowledge at their local sites. By connecting the CCSS with other frameworks, teachers, media specialists, and students can work together to build a model that meets both local exigencies and national norms, forging the (perhaps) uncommon connections that make networked literacies so valuable.

References

Barton, David, and Mary Hamilton. 1998. *Local Literacies: Reading and Writing in One Community*. London: Routledge.

Biancarosa, Gina, Anthony S. Bryk, and Emily R. Dexter. 2010. "Assessing the Value-Added Effects of Literacy Collaborative Professional Development on Student Learning." *Elementary School Journal* 111 (1): 7–34.

Castells, Manuel. 2010. *The Rise of the Network Society*. 2nd ed. Malden, MA: Wiley Blackwell.

Council of Chief State School Officers and National Governors Association. 2010. *Common Core State Standards for English Language Arts and Literacy in History/Social Studies, Science, and Technical Subjects*. Washington, DC: National Governors

Association Center for Best Practices, Council of Chief State School Officers. Accessed February 10, 2014. www.corestandards.org/assets/CCSSI_ELA%20Standards.pdf.

Council of Writing Program Administrators. 2008. *WPA Outcomes Statement for First-Year Composition.* Accessed February 10, 2014. wpacouncil.org/positions/outcomes.html.

Council of Writing Program Administrators, National Council of Teachers of English, and National Writing Project. 2011. *Framework for Success in Postsecondary Writing.* Accessed February 10, 2014. wpacouncil.org/files/framework-for-success-postsecondary-writing.pdf.

Deans, Thomas. 2003. *Writing and Community Action: A Service-Learning Rhetoric With Readings.* London: Longman.

DeSimone, Laura M. 2009. "Improving Impact Studies of Teachers' Professional Development: Toward Better Conceptualizations and Measures." *Educational Researcher* 38 (3): 181–199.

Fairclough, Norman. 1999. "Global Capitalism and Critical Awareness of Language." *Language Awareness* 8: 71–83. Reprinted in *The Discourse Reader*, edited by Adam Jaworski and Nikolas Coupland, 146–157. 2nd ed. New York: Routledge.

Foucault, Michel. 1995. *Discipline and Punish: The Birth of the Prison.* 2nd ed. New York: Vintage.

Fox, Tom. 2009. "Standards and Purity: Understanding Institutional Strategies to Insure Homogeneity." In *The Writing Program Interrupted: Making Space for Critical Discourse*, edited by Donna Strickland and Jeanne Gunner, 14–27. Portsmouth, NH: Boynton-Cook.

Gallagher, Chris W. 2012. "The Trouble With Outcomes: Pragmatic Inquiry and Educational Aims." *College English* 75 (1): 42–60.

Jenkins, Henry, Katie Clinton, Ravi Purushotma, Alice J. Robison, and Margaret Weigel. 2006. *Confronting the Challenges of Participatory Culture: Media Education for the 21st Century.* MacArthur Foundation. Cambridge, MA: MIT Press.

Lankshear, Colin, and Michele Knobel. 2007. "Sampling the 'New' in New Literacies". In *A New Literacies Sampler*, edited by Michele Knobel and Colin Lankshear, 1–24. New York: Peter Lang.

MacArthur Foundation. 2011. "Connected Learning Principles." Accessed on February 10, 2014. connectedlearning.tv/connected-learning-principles.

Monroe, Barbara. 2004. *Crossing the Digital Divide: Race, Writing, and Technology in the Classroom.* New York: Teachers College Press.

National Institute for Excellence in Teaching. 2012. "Beyond 'Job Embedded': Ensuring That Good Professional Development Gets Results." Accessed February 10, 2014. www.niet.org/assets/PDFs/beyond_job_embedded_professional_development.pdf.

National Writing Project with DeVoss, Danielle N., Elyse Eidman-Aadahl, and Troy Hicks. 2010. *Because Digital Writing Matters: Improving Student Writing in Online and Multimedia Environments.* San Francisco: Jossey-Bass.

Nickoson, Lee. 2012. "Revisiting Teacher Research." In *Writing Studies Research in Practice*, edited by Lee Nickoson and Mary P. Sheridan, 101–112. Carbondale, IL: Southern Illinois University Press.

"Project New Media Literacies." 2014. University of California, Irvine. Accessed on February 10, 2014. www.newmedialiteracies.org.

Saunders, William, Claude Goldenberg, and Ronald Gallimore. 2009. "Increasing Achievement by Focusing Grade-Level Teams on Improving Classroom Learning: A Prospective, Quasi-experimental Study of Title I Schools." *American Educational Research Journal* 50 (3): 1006–1033.

Selber, Stuart A. 2004. *Multiliteracies for a Digital Age*. Carbondale, IL: Southern Illinois University Press.

Trimbur, John. 1991. "Literacy and the Discourse of Crisis." In *The Politics of Writing Instruction: Postsecondary*, edited by Richard Bullock, John Trimbur, and Charles Schuster. Portsmouth, NH: Heinemann.

Yancey, Kathleen Blake. 2004. "Made Not Only in Words: Composition in a New Key." *College Composition and Communication* 56 (2): 297–328.

Zingrone, Frank. 2001. *The Media Symplex: At the Edge of Meaning in the Age of Chaos*. Toronto: Stoddart.

CHAPTER 14

Multimedia Composers, Digital Curators
Examining the Common Core State Standards for Nonprint Texts Through the Digital Expository Writing Program

Lisa Litterio

To be ready for college, workforce training, and life in a technological society, students need the ability to gather, comprehend, evaluate, synthesize, and report on information and ideas, to conduct original research in order to answer questions or solve problems, and to analyze and create a high volume and extensive range of print and nonprint texts in media forms old and new. (Council of Chief State School Officers [CCSSO] and National Governors Association [NGA] 2010, 4)

This quote from the "Key Design Considerations" of the Common Core State Standards (CCSS) for English Language Arts illustrates the need to prepare students for personal and professional success with a variety of media forms. Indeed, in today's technologically driven society, it is no longer sufficient for our students to be well versed in only one medium, such as a five-page written paper; they also must demonstrate the ability to conduct careful research, assess multiple systems of information, and analyze and create nonprint texts in familiar and unfamiliar media forms (i.e., written paper, video on the internet, speech with visuals).

However, the increased access to new forms of nonprint texts creates challenges for teachers and librarians as they consider developing relevant and meaningful assignments for their students. Some teachers have embraced the concept of implementing assignments within their classrooms that address new forms of visual and digital communication practices, specifically appealing to NextGen students, students who have been immersed in collaborative communication practices, informational technologies, and personal computers throughout their lives.

However, students often graduate high school unprepared for the research, creation, and analysis of digital, nonprint texts that are becoming more prolific in college classrooms. Researchers have already indicated the disconnect between college students' ability to *receive* information as readers and meaningfully *contribute* to these digital spaces as authors (Ball 2005; Selfe and Tayakoshi 2007; Wysocki et al. 2004), but they have not yet addressed ways that instructors can fulfill the CCSS' college readiness approach by preparing students for these digital writing environments.

In order to provide concrete suggestions for teachers and librarians on how to integrate nonprint assignments with diverse forms of media in the classroom, this chapter discusses assignments from the first-year Digital Expository Writing (DEW) Program at the College of Saint Rose. In Chapter 13 in this volume, Stephanie West-Puckett and William P. Banks have detailed practical advice for redesigning the high school curricula to support a teacher-generated digital writing curriculum. This chapter transitions from discussing high school programs to focusing on students in their first year of college, and, in doing so, it considers the ways in which teachers can prepare students to thrive in digital, first-year writing environments. First, this chapter explains the DEW Program and how the remix video assignment in particular challenges students to become critical composers by changing pre-existing materials into something new through iMovie, a movie editing software program. The second part of the chapter explores a multimedia project consistent with the CCSS, which invited students to conduct research about a particular subculture and represent their findings with writing and media elements. Ultimately, I argue that by introducing these kinds of assignments gradually, developing an awareness of the different research practices involved with them, and emphasizing collaboration and experimentation with the creation of nonprint texts, high school teachers can prepare students for the kinds of communication practices consistent with the CCSS, and valued in college and beyond.

The Digital Expository Writing Program at Saint Rose

The College of Saint Rose (located in Albany, New York) is a private, independent, co-educational school consisting of approximately 5,000 students, of which approximately 2,800 are undergraduates (U.S. News Education 2014). The DEW Program was developed as part of a pilot study within the First-Year Writing Program by three faculty members in the English Department: Megan Fulwiler, Jennifer Marlow, and Kim Middleton. As early as fall 2011, these teachers worked with one another to conceptualize a first-year composition course that would allow students to practice writing with various technological tools as well as consider how writing changes in digital environments. Each of these teachers experimented with integrating a digital media/video assignment in their previous classes, but the DEW program signified the first systemized effort at the college to create an alternative to first-year writing by offering a course that focused on digital writing, which is "compositions created with, and oftentimes for reading and/or viewing on, a computer or other device that is connected to the internet" (National Writing Project with DeVoss, Eidman-Aadahl, and Hicks 2010, 7). Through additional discussions in spring and summer 2012, the teachers developed and finalized the syllabus for DEW (English 105) to be implemented in fall 2012. They crafted the syllabus to focus on readings related to current technologies, multimedia assignments that incorporate website design, film production and visual arrangements, and the use of social media sites to discuss readings outside of class. Each instructor taught one section of DEW, for a total of three sections; the enrollment for these courses was 18 students each, for a total of 54 students. Data was collected through classroom observations, student interviews, and a compilation of drafts, peer reviews, and written reflections from students who opted to participate.

The course description for DEW reflects not only its focus on developing writing skills but also its consideration for how digital tools can be used in the classroom to facilitate the development of writing skills. The course description reads:

> DEW 105 will combine the best of traditional approaches to print-based writing (multiple draft assignments, rigorous textual and rhetorical analysis, peer workshops, one-on-one conferences) with guided, hands-on practice composing with text, image, hyperlinks and video across a range of platforms. The goal is to introduce you to the rhetorical and critical skills you will need in college, but also to the habits of mind and ways of composing that will prepare you to become creative, reflective, and critical digital citizens for the world beyond college. (Fulwiler, Marlow, and Middleton 2012, 1)

This course description depicts tenets woven throughout the CCSS, such as fostering media skills that involve critical analysis and production, employing technology thoughtfully, and evaluating viewpoints constructively (RI.11–12.5; RI.11–12.7; CSSO and NGA 2010, 7). It also reflects the CCSS' College and Career Readiness Anchor Standard for Reading 7, which emphasizes that students should be able to "integrate and evaluate content presented in diverse formats and media, including visually and quantitatively, as well as in words" (CSSO and

NGA 2010, 10). Although DEW is a first-year college writing course, findings from this pilot study can provide high school teachers and librarians with ideas to help their students achieve the CCSS and foster the technical and rhetorical skills necessary for them to thrive as 21st-century composers.

Remix Video Assignment: Rationale for Inclusion in a Writing Classroom

Gregg Gillis, an artist who works in the genre of mashup and remix videos, explains how our students are living in a remix culture. A *remix* refers to the concept of aggregating or collecting pre-existing information and then changing it in some way to craft a new idea, advance a critique of something, or call attention to common themes (Lessig 2008, 11). Similarly, Kirby Ferguson, a documentary filmmaker and creator of the web video series *Everything Is a Remix*, explained that the term *remix* was originally applied to hip-hop music to describe how musicians frequently sampled the bass line from one song to create the backbone for a new song. For example, the group Sugar Hill Gang used the bass line from Chic's "Good Times" in their 1979 song "Rapper's Delight." Although the foundation for the song was based on "Good Times," the Sugar Hill Gang used different song lyrics, instruments, and tempo to create a song that is unique enough to be considered an original rather than a copy.

Subsequently, with the introduction of the internet and the advent of the personal computer, remix as a genre of composing has extended more broadly to become a mainstream technique. The term now applies to the rearrangement of audio, video, images, and text to shape a message that often serves as a cultural/political critique, a fan-based video, a parody, or an illustration of themes common to the texts in the remix. Different from print-based texts, which consist of linear text arranged line-by-line, remixes overlap media forms, such as sounds over images, or video over text. The result of this manipulation of forms is a remix—a new, creative work. Although remixes can incorporate multiple elements, such as an image overlaid with text or with an audio track, the medium of this assignment at Saint Rose addressed remix videos, a type of project that called for the integration of film footage, audio clips, and textual elements layered over images, or used as transitions. The remix video, a type of writing assignment, required multiple drafts, conferences with the instructor, and peer review sessions. In this way, the remix video reflects three central tenets of the CCSS, which include the following goals for students: 1) "analyze and create a high volume and extensive range of print and nonprint texts in media forms old and new" (CCSSO and NGA 2010, 4); 2) use technology and the internet to publish and collaborate (Anchor Standard for Writing 6; 18); and 3) assess the credibility and accuracy of each source, being careful to consider issues with plagiarism and fair use practices (though the CCSS never use this exact term) (W.6–12.8).

The CCSS intend by design to extend and more deeply consider literacy practices in the 21st century; the remix video can serve as a gateway for teachers to explore these emerging literacy practices. For instance, Lawrence Lessig, Harvard Law Professor and founder of the Center for Internet and Society at Stanford Law School, explains how writing gathered from media forms such as television and video represent "the vernacular of today. They are the kind of writing that matter most to most" (2008, 68). This "most to most" refers to the idea that the majority of Americans, particularly young people between the ages of 15 and 19, spend more time watching television, playing video games, and surfing the internet than reading (Purcell et al. 2012). As a result of the amount of time younger people spend connected to the web and other social media forms, the concept of composing is changing in the 21st century. Lessig explains:

> These other forms of "creating" are becoming an increasingly dominant form of "writing." ... Using the tools of digital technology—even the simplest tools, bundled into the most innovative modern operating systems—anyone can begin to "write" using images, or music, or video. And using the facilities of a free digital network, anyone can share that writing with anyone else. (2008, 69)

Inherent in Lessig's claim, the remix video extends the notion of what is considered writing and allows for a more robust audience within a digital environment. The remix video, then, reflects one of the core tenets in the CCSS, "The Production and Distribution of Writing," which is to "use technology, including the internet, to produce, publish, and update individual or shared writing products in response to ongoing feedback, including new arguments or information" (CCSSO and NGA 2010, W.11–12.6). A remix video requires students to consider the creation of their video (i.e., constructing an argument with a different media form) and its reception (i.e., where and how it will be placed on the internet).

Teaching With Technology and Addressing Principles of Fair Use in the Age of Digital Freedom

One of the most significant contributions of integrating a remix video in a high school classroom is its ability to inform students about fair use practices in an age where the internet appears to be a repository of information available for the taking. Instead of viewing the internet as a global database where images or text can be downloaded instantly and without consequence, remix videos offer a viable opportunity for teachers to discuss the complexity of fair use practices and creative license in the digital age. These discussions surrounding fair use practices reflect Writing Standard 8 for Grades 6–12, which focuses on the ability to "gather relevant information from multiple print and digital sources, assess the credibility and accuracy of each source, and integrate the information while avoiding plagiarism" (CCSSO and NGA 2010).

At Saint Rose, the teachers envisioned the remix video assignment as a way to introduce students to the complex processes involved with video production, not only the technological skills necessary for completing these tasks, but also the rhetorical awareness of the choices that students make as they rearrange and recombine various media sources, such as text, images, video, and audio recordings. This assignment allowed students to engage with pre-existing information rather than having the daunting task of creating new multimedia elements for their videos. Teachers provided students with the following overview of the remix video assignment:

> A short video that will highlight your own knowledge of a specific subculture, by working with its associated artifacts (movies, books, games, TV, sports, celebrities, politicians, etc.) as you recombine and juxtapose video clips in order to create a "re-mixed" video. The aim of your remix is to fundamentally alter these materials to say something new and meaningful about the subculture. The focus will be on learning and adhering to the principles and practices of Fair Use, as well as learning how to rip clips, use iMovie, and reflect on the composing choices you make. (Fulwiler, Marlow, and Middleton 2012)

The goal of the assignment, and the processes involved, reflect the CCSS Anchor Standard for Reading 7, which emphasizes that at the end of each grade, students should be able to "[i]ntegrate and evaluate content presented in diverse formats and media, including visually and quantitatively, as well as in words" (CCSSO and NGA 2010, 10). The remix video encouraged students to consider the relationship among text, video, and audio elements in their work. Teaching the remix as a process rather than a one-time exercise reflects the CCSS' tenet that students must possess "the capacity to revisit and make improvements to a piece of writing over multiple drafts when circumstances encourage or require it" (41). The remix video can be viewed as a nonprint text that challenges students to analyze and reshape information with media forms beyond text. The students at Saint Rose had at least 2 weeks to work on the project after it was assigned, and a minimum of three class sessions devoted to working on their projects in a computer lab. Teachers required students to use the movie maker program iMovie, an Apple movie maker program compatible only with Macs, which were the only computers available in the lab. Other similar programs available as of this writing include Windows Movie Maker and a number of free and open source video editing software options, such as Avidemux, FileLab, StoryBoard Pro, VirtualDub, and VSDC.

Technical Proficiency

Technological programs used in the development of writing and multimedia assignments in the classroom are changing at a rapid pace. Within the past few years, teachers have integrated ePortfolios, blogs, Wikipedia, and microblogging sites such as Tumblr, Twitter, and Pinterest as part of digital writing assignment prompts and projects. Yet, due to the continual emergence of new programs, teachers sometimes feel as though they are expending more of their efforts toward mastering technology programs. There is also the issue of expectation; teachers often assume that students are proficient and able to use these programs because they are a part of the millennial generation (Selfe and Tayakoshi 2007; Winograd and Hais 2011). As a result, pedagogy sometimes becomes centered on the technological platform rather than on sound teaching practices.

From the data gathered at Saint Rose, it was clear that incoming first-year students were not prepared to use the technology involved in the creation of these works. The majority of students had never used a video editing software program before. In addition to observing classroom interactions, I interviewed four students to learn more about their experiences with the technology involved in making this remix video: Sam, Kate, Shannon, and Maeve (pseudonyms). Sam explained, "There were three people in the class who actually used [iMovie] before, while the rest of us were just playing with it and experimenting."[1] Many students were simply unfamiliar with the technical skills and even vocabulary (e.g., riffing, transitions) used in the process of downloading video files, converting them to mp3 files, then importing them into the program to manipulate them. A number of students had difficulty performing this initial task; as is the case with many nonprint projects, teachers were learning along with the students, and at times it was difficult to assist or be aware of each student's unique technological hurdle.

To learn the technical skills necessary for fluency and understanding of the software program, instructors provided students with a worksheet for their remix video editing in the early stages (see Appendix A at the end of this chapter), and classmates often began to share with one another interesting features of iMovie along with other programs that could help each other in the completion of the remix project. For example, Sam confided that she felt nervous at the beginning of the project, since she never used iMovie before. As a result, she turned to another classmate familiar with the program for assistance. Sam explained that her colleague "seemed to know a lot about the transitions and stuff and I wouldn't have discovered those if we didn't talk about it in class, and I know I would have been struggling with transition things and finding text and everything."[2]

Another student, Shannon, had a somewhat different approach. She was absent for the initial class session on downloading movie files and, even though she had a MacBook, was unable to download the program iMovie. As a result, she focused on using trial and error to discover how she could manipulate video files: "Basically what I did was I downloaded all the videos from YouTube that I needed and I just imported them and I played around with it and I was just like, oh what did this do?"[3] Similarly, another student, Kate, expressed that she visited Apple's website to watch tutorials on using iMovie.[4] These students accessed resources available to them, including soliciting advice from their peers, viewing tutorials, and spending time in class interacting with the system; their approach to acquiring the skill set needed to learn this technology program was multifaceted rather than limited to the ways the CCSS envision.

Since students will be at varying levels of technical proficiency, high school teachers and librarians should be aware that nonprint, digital texts require both teachers' and students' understanding and even mastery of the technology program specific to each assignment. As a result, they should encourage and foster opportunities for their students to experiment with video editing software, provide access to a computer lab outside of class time, and offer opportunities for students to interact and learn from one another in small group settings. Even more significant than what occurs peer-to-peer and instructor-to-student is the support of additional staff in the composing process. For example, we can apply Christina Murphy and Lory Hawkes's vision (2010) of writing center consultants as "digital content specialists who are adept at using technology and who understand the implications of technology for knowledge creation" (184) to the role of the librarians. Librarians at Saint Rose, as educational technologists, served as a valuable resource for students and provided additional assistance. Teachers in each class also collaborated together to provide students with technology support. By offering students the physical lab space to experiment with technology and responding to their questions and concerns, teachers, librarians, and information technologists can help students display and create information "flexibly and dynamically" and gather information from print and digital sources, as is stipulated by the CCSS (CCSSO and NGA 2010, W.9–10.6).

Fair Use Practices With Nonprint Texts

Another major component of this assignment was the attention given to the principles surrounding fair use practices, particularly how a video imparts a unique message—not just a rearrangement of preexisting materials on the internet. This type of nonprint assignment, then, offered a gateway for teachers and librarians to discuss fair use practices and illustrate ways to consider the complexity of citing digital sources. The student videos, averaging 3 minutes in duration, consisted of videos from reality television, the news, television, or films, recombining them in ways to create something new. Students could use footage, audio, and sound from other sources. The only items they were allowed to create themselves were slides of text to smoothly transition from one portion of the video to the next or to ask a question or show statistics; many of the students indeed chose to integrate these text/transition slides within their works and used them to transition between their ideas (Figures 14.1 and 14.2).

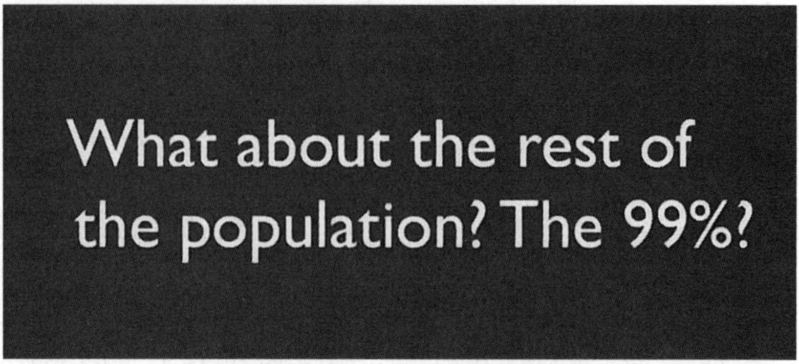

> What about the rest of the population? The 99%?

Figure 14.1 A transition slide introducing Sam's main argument

> Let's look at
> at how the 99% struggle today

Figure 14.2 A slide offering a transition to a discussion on statistical support

To introduce students to the complexity of using existing materials on the internet, teachers spent a full day discussing fair use practices, referencing the Center for Social Media's "Code of Best Practices in Fair Use for Online Video" (Jaszi et al. 2008, 1). This instructional document with an accompanying video, created by documentary filmmakers and a panel of experts in the fields of law, media studies, and creative writing, is not a reductive guidebook for citing video clips. Instead, it offers discussion items for students to consider and then interpret the copyright doctrine of fair use along with the rhetorical choices they must make as digital composers. As the authors explain, "Mashups, remixes, subs, and online parodies are new and refreshing online phenomena, but they partake of an ancient tradition: the recycling of old culture to make new" (2).

The creators offer a cautionary tale for students or those embattled in copyright issues: they must change pre-existing information to make it their own by providing readers with possible applications of fair use practices on the internet. These ways of making new meaning include the following:

1. Commenting or critiquing on copyrighted material
2. Using copyrighted material for an illustration or example
3. Capturing copyright information incidentally
4. Reproducing, reposting, or quoting in order to memorialize, preserve, or rescue an experience, an event, or cultural phenomenon
5. Recirculating a work or part of a work for purposes of launching a discussion
6. Quoting in order to recombine elements that make a new work (2–8)

Librarians and teachers can easily introduce these guidelines into their classrooms with examples of remix videos to inform students of the necessity for critically considering sources, integrating information into their work selectively, and following a standard format for citation (CCSSO and NGA 2010, W.9–12.8). Additionally, high school teachers can offer the option of crafting a student composer's statement or written reflection piece to accompany a nonprint text, which allows students to explain and defend their choices. As part of Saint Rose's remix video assignment, students were required to write a one-to-two page paper that explained the elements of their remix video and how they adhered to fair use practices. The writing that accompanied the nonprint text also afforded students the opportunity to reflect on the piece as a whole. This type of writing project, in conversation with the nonprint text, reflects the CCSS' Writing Standards of Production and Distribution, particularly Writing Standard 4 that students are able to "produce clear and coherent writing in which the development, organization, and style are appropriate to task, purpose, and audience" (CCSSO and NGA 2010, W.9–12.4).

In one of her written reflections, Sam discussed how she adhered to fair use practices in her remix video, which used clips from a reality television show highlighting the fashion mogul family, the Kardashians, and juxtaposed them with news clips about children starving in other countries to create a critique of reality television. She explained that her critique of the Kardashians' lifestyle reflected how "comment and critique are at the very core of the fair use doctrine as a safeguard for freedom of expression" (Fulwiler 2012b). Another student, Maeve, shared that she presented clips from *Dr. Who* out of context. In her reflection, she noted, "In the clip I showed where the Doctor is talking about one person you should never put in a trap, he is holding what looks like a gun. However, if the clip was to continue 2 seconds longer, the viewer would learn that it was only a flare gun, used to escape the trap."[5] The reflection aspect of this assignment offered students a thoughtful tool for thinking critically about the sources they used in order to avoid "plagiarism and overreliance on any one source" (CCSSO and NGA 2010, W.11–12.8), and at the same time integrated writing as an explanatory way to describe their rationale as creators. What is valuable about this assignment, and what high school teachers and librarians can use it to begin to accomplish, is that it approaches digital citation practices as complicated and nuanced, encouraging students to consider how their work challenges or reshapes pre-existing information on the internet into something new. Although this assignment explored video, specifically iMovie, as the technical platform, it could be easily adjusted to a collage of images and texts or another software program.

Integrating Multimedia Projects Into High School Classes: Research as Curation

Not only does the technology involved with nonprint texts call teachers to consider the integration of different technical platforms, but also composing texts in digital environments requires adjusting the focus of research practices. The CCSS acknowledge that research is an integral part of preparing high school students for academic and professional success, as evidenced by W.9–12.7–8, which appears under the heading "Research to Build and Present Knowledge." Some of the goals for students include:

> Gather relevant information from multiple authoritative print and digital sources, using advanced searches effectively; assess the strengths and limitations of each source in terms of the task, purpose, and audience; integrate information into the text selectively to maintain the flow of ideas, avoiding plagiarism and overreliance on any one source and following a standard format for citation. (CCSSO and NGA 2010, W.9–12.8)

Coupled with gathering sources and learning proper citations is the focus on developing strong research practices, which is outlined in W.9–12.7: "Conduct short as well as more sustained research projects to answer a question (including a self-generated question) or solve a problem; narrow or broaden the inquiry when appropriate; synthesize multiple sources on the subject, demonstrating understanding of the subject under investigation" (CCSSO and NGA 2010). These standards focus on gathering information from "print and digital sources" as well as carefully considering competing sources and types of research.

The final multimedia project at Saint Rose, which students spent almost 13 weeks researching, drafting, and discussing, can offer insights into digital research practices and generate successful components of multimedia projects by examining and defining these examples on the web.[6] This final research project asked students to combine print and media elements in order to understand a local problem or specific subculture. Students were encouraged to select any media platforms they wished to represent their project, but they were also invited to spend a considerable amount of time on the research process.

One of the ways in which teachers and librarians can began to assist students with the research practices involved with nonprint texts is to discuss students' roles as researchers. At Saint Rose, teachers began the discussion of the final project by inviting students to consider themselves curators of digital spaces. Research, students discovered, was the act of gathering information, but curation served a deeper, more critical function: Similar to an art curator, students were asked to shape and organize the information they found into organizing principles and patterns. One student explained that "being a good curator requires you to identify themes coming through social media streams and organize them for others" (Marlow 2012). As an example, the lens of research as curation allows for understanding Twitter use differently. Users on Twitter share articles or information about conferences, events, and current research relevant to their fields. They cull information deliberately and specifically. Curation, then, is an essential research skill that reflects W.11–12.3 as it calls upon students and teachers to filter, select, and arrange information effectively as well as discern accurate information (CCSSO and NGA 2010).

Activities for Researchers as Curators

Another aspect of the DEW Program was to focus on careful research practices in digital environments by focusing on triangulating different sources. Teachers integrated exercises in using digital, nonprint sources in class to teach their students the organizational skills involved in the research process and strategies to distinguish differences among sources based on their research topics, which included the use of iPads in a special needs classroom, the rising costs of private college institutions, and the effects of hydrofracking on the environment. Students were asked to bring a peer reviewed article from a database, an article from an online news source, and information from a website to class. Within small groups, they responded to questions relating to their sources (see Appendix B at the end of this chapter; Fulwiler 2012a). Students began to discuss and generate their own criteria for evaluating sources, observing that online sources seem to have a much more informal tone, while scholarly sources appeared more objective and data driven.

Another way in which instructors encouraged students to focus on their curatorial and research skills involved exercises on search engines.

When Marlow asked students to identify the search engine they most often use to locate information, the majority replied Google; only a few used Yahoo!, Dogpile, or Bing. This reliance on Google as the primary vehicle for research is consistent with the findings of Alison Head and Michael Eisenberg (2010) and James P. Purdy (2012), among others. According to the Pew Internet & American Life Project, the vast majority of Advanced Placement (AP) high school teachers (94 percent) surveyed explain their students are "very likely" to use Google or another online search engine in a typical research assignment, "placing it well ahead of all other sources" (Purcell et al. 2012, 4). Pew also reported that 57 percent of teachers "spend class time helping students improve search terms and queries, yet just [35 percent] devote class time to helping students understand how search engines work and how search results are actually generated and ranked" (4).

Creating an activity that harnessed dialogic collaboration and required students to think more critically about research practices, Marlow formed small groups and distributed a worksheet adapted from Johndan Johnson-Eilola's "The Database and the Essay: Understanding Composition as Articulation" (2004). Using this series of questions, students selected three different search engines and responded to questions that involved search results, hits and rankings, and the relationship among the search results (see Appendix C at the end of this chapter). Through the process of sifting through search engines, students at Saint Rose began to notice hits that were not relevant to their search process, sponsored pages, and several pages that ranked higher on one search engine results page but not another.

This type of exercise invites students to think more critically about their research practices in digital environments and connects to the research practices for digital spaces laid out in W.9–10.8, which includes gathering information from multiple print and digital sources, using advanced searches effectively, and assessing the usefulness of sources (CCSSO and NGA 2010). Rather than focusing on gathering information and analyzing its credibility, teachers can encourage students to consider how the frameworks of information, such as search engines, are also texts to be interpreted. For example, Johnson-Eilola (2004) recommends that instructors ask students questions about the order of search results and search engines themselves, including: "What does it mean, culturally, politically, economically, ideologically, for one type of result to come up higher in a search engine hit list than another site? Who made decisions that affected how the results looked—and why?" (228). By encouraging students to consider where research begins and ends, librarians and teachers invite students to conceive of research as embedded with difficulty and choices. In addition, librarians and teachers should caution students to consider Google as fast food—something quick and superficial, not comprehensive or, at times, beneficial. High school and college students may believe that search engines are the sites where their research occurs, but teachers and librarians must encourage them to consider multiple search engines, databases, and cross-referencing information as discerning curators.

As our students considered the scope of their research—on whatever subculture or community they selected—they were also encouraged to evaluate critically the kinds of nonprint projects they were seeing on the web. One of the methods by which teachers can begin to cultivate a deeper understanding of nonprint texts is by allowing students to generate and develop their own criteria for assessing and understanding these multimedia compositions (Adsanatham 2012). The Saint Rose teachers invited students to view a variety of multimedia research projects, including Faith in the Five Boroughs, a project that follows the immigrant city population of New York City and explores the connections between peoples' faith and their communities (Elliott and Elliott 2013). In one example, the filmmakers highlight Lady Rhea, a Bronx resident and a practicing Wiccan for 10 years. The video appears at the top of the website, followed by explanatory text and a map of the specific locations she visits (Figure 14.3).

Although produced by a professional filmmaker, the project served as a catalyst for discussing the integration of visuals, texts, and links as well as the reader's navigation among these elements.

Multimedia Composers, Digital Curators 401

Instead of a voice-over, the video begins with the soothing sound of wind chimes and then Lady Rhea's voice: "My name is Lady Rhea and I'm a Wiccan High Priestess, Witch Queen" (Elliott and Elliott 2013). The camera follows Lady Rhea as she commutes from her apartment in the Bronx to a shop that sells her oils, spell kits, and spiritual candles.

Figure 14.3   Faith in the Five Boroughs website featuring Lady Rhea

When instructors asked students about how they navigated through this multimedia project, a student explained that the title and the brief description initially sparked his interest, and then he clicked on the video for more information. Other students described how they clicked on the map of the Bronx, while some watched the video first. One student explained the function of the video was to "[give] a description of her everyday life and the text [gives] an in-depth analysis of her faith and who she is" (Fulwiler 2012b), distinguishing between the affordances of the video and text. The instructor then asked the students to describe how they moved through the work in search of more information; one student shared that she clicked the links pertaining to Lady Rhea's book publication on Amazon, another viewed her business page at Original Products, and another student clicked on the map to discover her location. These discussions of the navigation of this nonprint text reflect RL.11–12.7, which states that students should not only be adept at composing these texts, but also analyzing them.

Although it is advantageous to review professional examples of multimedia projects on the web, it is also beneficial to show successful student examples of nonprint projects, such as recent high school graduate Sam Bellavance's 2012 video, "The Root: Campaign Finance Reform and Citizens United v. FEC." As a high school senior, Bellavance developed his film with the goal of critiquing the Super PAC[7] process in American governmental campaigns. Throughout one class session, teachers at Saint Rose walked the students through each element of the composition: parsing the purpose of the audio, video, interviews, and images. Students observed that Bellavance seems to balance interviews from professors, authors, and politicians with visual elements of graphs, charts, and statistical images to support his research (Middleton 2012) (Figure 14.4).

They also discussed the role of narration in this video. The commentary provides context at critical moments, enhancing the relevance of the research. At one point in the video, Bellavance layers a chart that depicted the amount of money each corporation donated to political

Multimedia Composers, Digital Curators   403

Figure 14.4   An image Bellavance uses in his video to depict the corruption involved with the Super PAC process

campaigns with images of American currency. This resulted in a layered image of a chart and currency symbol (Figure 14.5).

As Figure 14.5 illustrates, these types of projects involve redirecting students' focus on nonprint texts to consider the creation process of the authors and decipher each element's (audio, visual, and textual elements) function within the piece. Generating discussions and

Figure 14.5   Chart of company donations overlaid with an image of U.S. currency

examining works that involve both writing and media elements reflect the CCSS' reading approaches, including RI.9–10.7, which invites students to "analyze various accounts of a subject told in different mediums (e.g., a person's life story in both print and multimedia), determining which details are emphasized in each account" (CCSSO and NGA 2010). The process of examining these particular nonprint texts encourages students to consider how digital composers like Bellevance use different media elements for a specific purpose and persuaded his audience of his argument relating to the PAC process.

Conclusion: The Future of Classroom Writing

The Saint Rose DEW Program offered a vibrant space for students who had graduated from high school and were entering writing classes at the college level to experiment and play with different forms of digital writing as well as consider how research practices are subject to significant changes within digital environments. Students in this particular program did not appear ready to assume some of the challenges involved with these types of alternative writing assignments, and their lack of familiarity with video editing programs could reflect the low-tech and print-based compositions still valued in high school classrooms. As colleges and universities increasingly transition toward digital writing, careful course preparation needs to be implemented at the high school level so that students will experience seamless transitions to collegiate writing environments with an understanding of the rationale and the technology necessary for creating nonprint assignments.

As this chapter concludes the section in this book on curricular initiatives to meet the CCSS, I end this chapter with the reminder that much of our future curricular discussions should center on teaching practices, support, and methods to assist students and institutions when integrating these nonprint forms of composing. We have moved past the initial introduction of these nonprint texts in our classroom into providing answers for the questions that remain, such as "What steps shall we take to prepare high school students to use the resources and tools available at their fingertips through the smartphones they hold, [those] devices that are rapidly expanding in their functionality in and out of the classroom?"

Since the CCSS stipulate that students must be "college and career ready in literacy no later than the end of high school" (CCSSO and NGA 2010, 3), educators must reach out to colleagues, librarians, and administrators to develop ways in which we can support our students, infuse experimentation and play in the classroom, and encourage learners to develop proficiencies with a variety of technology platforms—both those used now as well as those that will likely be commonplace for the next digital scholar.

Endnotes

1. Sam, interview with author, October 10, 2012, College of Saint Rose, Albany, NY.
2. Sam, reflection on program, October 15, 2012, College of Saint Rose, Albany, NY.
3. Shannon, email communication with author, October 17, 2012, College of Saint Rose, Albany, NY.
4. Kate, interview with author, October 10, 2012, College of Saint Rose, Albany, NY.
5. Maeve, reflection on program, November 17, 2012, College of Saint Rose, Albany, NY.
6. Because high school teachers are responsible for a significant amount of content, they will not have 13 weeks to devote to this assignment. I would recommend asking students to work collaboratively in groups and research a problem in their community using at least two media elements (e.g., visual and audio; text and visuals) in conjunction with a written reflection piece. Instructors can encourage their students to place their final reports on the web or an ePortfolio system. By limiting the elements involved with the project and coupling it with group task, students will still be able to experiment with creating a multimedia project.
7. PAC stands for a Political Action Committee, which refers to a private organization that provides financial support for or against "electing a political candidate or advancing a legislative agenda" ("Are Super PACs Harming U.S. Politics?" 2014). The title of Bellavance's video refers to the 2010 Supreme Court Case *Citizens United v. Federal Election Commission*. The court voted 5–4 to uphold the First Amendment, and ruled that "the government cannot prohibit spending by corporations and unions for political purposes." As a result, PACs were not closed, but there are regulations connected to them, such as disclosing the names of their donors ("Are Super PACs Harming U.S. Politics?" 2014).

References

Adsanatham, Chanon. 2012. "Integrating Assessment and Instruction: Using Student-Generated Grading Criteria to Evaluate Multimodal Digital Projects." *Computers and Composition* 29 (2): 152–174.

"Are Super PACs Harming U.S. Politics?" 2014. *U.S. News*. Accessed February 10, 2014. www.usnews.com/debate-club/are-super-pacs-harming-us-politics.

Ball, Cheryl. 2005. "Show, Not Tell: The Value of New Media Scholarship." *Computers and Composition* 21 (4): 403–425.

Bellavance, Sam. 2012. "The Root: Campaign Finance Reform and Citizens United v. FEC." May 31. Accessed February 10, 2014. www.youtube.com/watch?v=-D4q2lF_GDo.

Council of Chief State School Officers and National Governors Association. 2010. *Common Core State Standards for English Language Arts and Literacy in History/Social Studies, Science, and Technical Subjects*. Washington, DC: National Governors Association Center for Best Practices, Council of Chief State School Officers. Accessed February 10, 2014. www.corestandards.org/assets/CCSSI_ELA%20Standards.pdf.

Elliott, Scott, and Julia Elliott. 2013. "Faith in the Five Boroughs." Accessed February 10, 2014. faithinthefiveboroughs.org/video/a-city-witch.

Ferguson, Kirby. 2011. *Everything Is a Remix*. Accessed February 10, 2014. everythingisaremix.info/watch-the-series.

Fulwiler, Megan. 2012a. Digital Expository Writing. Lecture. November 5. St. Rose College, Albany, NY.

———. 2012b. Digital Expository Writing. Lecture. November 17. College of Saint Rose, Albany, NY.

Fulwiler, Megan, Jennifer Marlow, and Kim Middleton. 2012. Syllabus for English 105. College of Saint Rose.

Head, Alison J., and Michael B. Eisenberg. 2010. "Truth Be Told: How College Students Evaluate and Use Information in the Digital Age." Project Information Literacy Progress Report, University of Washington Information School. Accessed February 10, 2014. projectinfolit.org/pdfs/PIL_Fall2010_Survey_FullReport1.pdf.

Jaszi, Peter, Patricia Aufderheide, Michael C. Donaldson, Anthony Falzone, Lewis Hyde, Mizuko Ito, et al. 2008. *Code of Best Practices in Fair Use for Online Video*. Washington, DC: Center for Social Media. Accessed February 10, 2014. www.centerforsocialmedia.org/sites/default/files/online_best_practices_in_fair_use.pdf.

Johnson-Eilola, Johndan. 2004. "The Database and the Essay: Understanding Composition as Articulation." In *Writing New Media: Theory and Applications for Expanding the Teaching of Composition*, by Anne Frances Wysocki, Johndan

Johnson-Eilola, Cynthia L. Selfe, and Geoffrey Sirc, 199–236. Logan, UT: Utah State University Press.

Lessig, Lawrence. 2008. *Remix: Making Art and Commerce Thrive in the Hybrid Economy.* London: Penguin Press.

Marlow, Jennifer. 2012. Digital Expository Writing. Lecture. November 11. College of Saint Rose, Albany, NY.

Middleton, Kim. 2012. Digital Expository Writing. Lecture. November 5. College of Saint Rose, Albany, NY.

Murphy, Christina, and Lory Hawkes. 2010. "The Future of Multiliteracy Centers in the E-World: An Exploration of Cultural Narratives and Cultural Transformations." In *Multiliteracy Centers: Writing Center Work, New Media, and Multimodal Rhetoric*, edited by David M. Sheridan and James A. Inman, 179–190. New York: Hampton Press.

National Writing Project with Danielle N. DeVoss, Elyse Eidman-Aadahl, and Troy Hicks. 2010. *Because Digital Writing Matters: Improving Student Writing in Online and Multimedia Environments.* San Francisco: Jossey-Bass.

Purcell, Kristin, Lee Rainie, Alan Heaps, Judy Buchanan, Linda Friedrich, Amanda Jacklin, et al. 2012. *How Teens Do Research in the Digital World.* Washington, DC: Pew Internet & American Life Project. Accessed February 10, 2014. pewinternet.org/~/media/Files/Reports/2012/PIP_TeacherSurveyReportWithMethodology110112.pdf.

Purdy, James P. 2012. "Why First-Year College Students Select Online Research Resources as Their Favorite." *First Monday* 17 (9). Accessed February 10, 2014. journals.uic.edu/ojs/index.php/fm/article/view/4088/3289.

Selfe, Cynthia L., and Pamela Tayakoshi. 2007. "Thinking about Multimodality." In *Multimodal Composition: Resources for Teachers*, edited by Cynthia L. Selfe, 1–12. New York: Hampton Press.

U.S. News Education. 2014. "The College of St. Rose." Accessed February 10, 2014. colleges.usnews.rankingsandreviews.com/best-colleges/st.-rose-2705.

Winograd, Morley, and Michael D. Hais. 2011. *Millennium Momentum: How a New Generation Is Remaking America.* Piscataway, NJ: Rutgers University Press.

Wysocki, Anne Frances, Johndan Johnson-Eilola, Cynthia L. Selfe, and Geoffrey Sirc. 2004. *Writing New Media: Theory and Applications for Expanding the Teaching of Composition.* Logan, UT: Utah State University Press.

Appendix A: Remix Video Editing, Day 1

Work With Events Library

Import video into Events Library (make sure that you COPY the file, and NAME it).

Practice previewing your video in the Events Browser (click various events, use space bar to start and stop).

Practice splitting your events into clips (two options):

1. Follow directions in iMovie tutorial, using the "split event before selected clip" command in file menu.

2. If you have one long event that needs to be split into clips, you'll need to do the following:

   - You can split events by deleting (and discarding) a single frame at the point where you want to split the two clips.

   - In the Events Viewer, click to select where you want to split the event.

   - Drag the yellow handles to make the selection as small as possible (1 frame?). If you drag the thumbnail display slider to the left to show only ½ second intervals, it helps when selecting a single frame.

   - Right click and select Reject Selection. The clip is now split.

   - When you've completed all of your clip splitting, select Show: Rejected Only at the bottom of the Events Viewer to show all of the rejected frames.

   - Click on Move Rejected to Trash. This operation could take a while.

Work With Projects Library

Any of the clips in the Events Library can be dragged up to the Project Library (upper left corner) so that you can begin to put your remix together. Once you have a handful of clips assembled, hit the Swap button (see middle row) to place the projects into the editing pane (where the events were).

From here, you can practice splitting (cut into two pieces) and trimming (shaving off pieces from the ends) clips using the yellow "handles." Practice splitting two to three clips (see clip menu). Choose a place to divide the clip. Experiment: See how many fractions of a second *before* the place you want the split to occur you have to cut in order to have the scene split where you want it. Experiment with the "clip trimmer" function as well (highlight clip and click the blue gear menu that pops up).

Work With Texts and Transitions

In the middle row of the iMovie screen, on the right side, you'll see a row of buttons. One has a "T"—this will open the text menu and allow you to experiment with all of the options for including text in your video. Another has a rectangle with triangles inside it—this is the transitions menu, which allows you to make interesting relationships between your clips. Highlight a clip in your project, and experiment with elements from both menus to see the options that are available for your video.

Appendix B: Prompts for Group Work on the Research Process

Individual Work: Sources

Which of the author's sources is the most interesting and why? What made you want to learn more about the 5 sources?

Look carefully at the author's annotations for his/her sources together. What ideas or opinions or key terms begin to emerge as you look at all the sources at once? What other topics, key words, or ideas do you think the author should pursue in his/her research?

What is it you want to find out?

Group Questions for Sources

1. Compare your notes on each author's most interesting source. What makes for an interesting source? What differences do you see in the kinds of interesting sources in digital media versus scholarly sources?

2. Discuss the new suggestions that each of you had made for additional research for your group's authors. What are the reasons for locating new research? What specific instances in your existing research have motivated the search for new sources? What should people be on the lookout for in their research? When do they know to look into new areas of inquiry?

3. Discuss the ways that each author's inquiry question has shifted with reference to his/her curated sources. What kinds of patterns do you observe? What elements, considerations, themes, etc. help to change, narrow, or intensify an inquiry?

4. Phrase at least two questions that you now have about your own writing and research process as you go forward. What are you excited or concerned about? What tips and advice do you have for others?

Appendix C: Analyzing Search Engines and Search Results

Authors' Note: Assignment adapted from Johndan Johnson-Eilola (2004).

Search #1:_____
Search #2:_____
Search #3:_____

Search Engine Questions

Search Engine:			
How many hits did the search engine find?			
What were the top 10 hits?			
Did all the hits seem similar? How so? And/or how did they differ?			
Were there hits that seemed to make no sense? How/why not?			

Analysis

Summarize your findings. Provide concrete examples to illustrate your points. How did each search engine organize the information? Were there entries that were paid for (sponsored listings)?

Bonus

Did you find any poorly written headlines along the way? Write them down (and be prepared to explain why they are poorly written).

Compare (in Groups)

What are the major differences between search engines?

PART FIVE

Approaches to Teacher Training

CHAPTER 15

Preparing Pre-Service Writing Teachers to Enact the (Digital) Common Core State Standards in Secondary Writing Classrooms

Christine Tulley

As outcomes assessment movements gain traction, secondary English Language Arts (ELA) teachers are particularly vulnerable to the effects these initiatives have on the teaching of writing. Because such movements tend to focus on measurement and accountability, there is often a push to link student performance to teacher performance—a complex relationship at best. For one, writing is a nebulous enterprise that often resists measurement (Huot 2002). In addition, best practices in writing instruction such as prewriting, peer review, and revision typically take time and must be implemented across several years of writing instruction. These long-term, ongoing growth methods of teaching writing are increasingly at odds with a culture of immediate measurement and teacher accountability evidenced in previous state-based standards movements to the current Common Core State Standards (CCSS). Moreover, outcome movements to date typically ignore or downplay the largely digital contexts where today's students write, read, and research outside of school. Therefore, writing teachers are caught in a cycle of having less time to devote to writing instruction while being held more accountable for how students write in ways that often work against students' out-of-class literacies.

Clearly, writing teachers need strategies for navigating outcomes movements in a digital age. Chris Gallagher (2012) sums up the quandary for writing teachers in "The Trouble with Outcomes," which stresses that standards movements are requirements writing teachers must navigate. To do so, he suggests, "[W]e need methods for framing and using educational aims that allow us to avoid the problematic tendencies of outcomes while addressing institutional demands for assessment of student learning and achieving some measure of [writing] program coherence" (44). The recent widespread adoption of the CCSS by 46 states offers an opportunity for teacher education programs to rethink how they prepare novice writing teachers to approach outcomes movements. In a climate where new teachers must reconcile their teacher preparation with classroom realities such as outcomes assessment and with changing literacy practices of students, such instruction is vital.

Fortunately, the CCSS offer several benefits for writing teachers. According to Kristin Gehsmann and Shane Templeton (2012), the CCSS are praised for offering a coherent focus on "research, analysis, and presentation of knowledge" rather than a disconnected set of tasks (5). The CCSS also offer a more integrated model of literacy where all instructors in all subject areas have responsibility for teaching reading, writing, listening, and speaking within their disciplines, which, in theory, lessens the burden on writing teachers to be the sole instructors of literacy. Sally Valentino Drew (2012) argues that the most promising aspect of the CCSS for writing teachers is the tacit acknowledgement that "the changing nature of literacy [includes] nonprint text in new media forms" (323). In sum, the CCSS offer a more holistic approach to developing writing instruction that secondary teachers can work from in this digital age.

Still, the CCSS are criticized for a lack of deeper attention to explicitly digital concerns such as online reading, associated skills such as locating a source in an online search engine (Drew 2012, 326), and composing digital texts. While the CCSS recognize the growing importance of nonprint texts, digital literacies are treated as an ancillary concern rather than a focal point of instruction. Within the Anchor Standards for Reading, for example, only Standard 7 asks students to "integrate and evaluate content presented in diverse formats and media" (Council of Chief State School Officers [CCSSO] and National Governors Association [NGA] 2010, 35) and acknowledges explicitly that a "text" might be nonprint. The underlying assumption that writing is primarily print-centric puts writing teachers in a double bind: They must adapt the CCSS and make sure students are successful at meeting the reading and writing standards, but the CCSS handcuff teachers by not fully recognizing the online contexts where today's students read, research, and write outside of class. The CCSS also do not recognize the extent to which writing teachers already assign projects that rely on digital technologies such as podcasting, video production, or website development. As a result, the CCSS limit the range of literacy experiences students can have (Drew 2012, 327). Even if writing teachers faithfully address the CCSS, they are left unsure as to how to approach the apparent divide between print-focused, standards-based instruction and emerging digital composing tools and contexts.

Few training movements exist within teacher preparation programs to help pre-service writing teachers meet standards movements such as the CCSS. There is also little direction regarding how to address digital literacies standards such as those that the CCSS are beginning to recognize. Allison Jones and Jacqueline King (2012) point out that students are introduced to standards in education methods areas, yet as Dolores Brzycki and Kurt Dudt (2005) acknowledge, this instruction has not focused on adopting standards that relate to digital literacies.

The most logical place to prepare pre-service teachers to navigate the CCSS and the digital versus print concerns they will face when they start teaching is the undergraduate writing methods course (WMC) within teacher preparation programs. The WMC offers instruction in writing assessment, theoretical grounding, and a mix of tools to use with students. Despite these benefits, I have previously argued that preparation to meet standards using digital literacies within the WMC is addressed only marginally (Tulley 2013). Moreover, lack of attention to how writing instruction relates to standards in a digital age may be state dependent since, until now, states largely set their own standards. As a result of this fragmented training, writing teachers typically encounter standards in their first teaching jobs as something to be feared. Because novice teachers lack practice with working with standards in general, attempting to implement the standards in classrooms (where many students use varied technological devices to compose and publish writing) provides an additional challenge. In short, novice teachers must meet standards that often don't explicitly acknowledge technology use even though students often use technologies to complete many writing tasks.

The widespread adoption of the CCSS, however, allows for the possibility for writing teacher educators across the country to orient pre-service teachers to the complex nature of the CCSS in a thoughtful manner prior to entering the high stakes environment of a first teaching job. This chapter describes one assignment that can be used within the WMC that:

1. Invites pre-service teachers to critically adopt the CCSS that focus on digital literacy in the thoughtful manner Gallagher (2012) advocates for all outcomes assessment

2. Uses action research practice to test a writing strategy in consultation with specific CCSS that can easily be applied to a digital context (i.e., online searching, design of a video, etc.)

3. Asks pre-service teachers to publish such research using digital technologies and, in the process, practice meeting

four essential elements in the CCSS Anchor Standards for Writing that support digital literacy

Because they have to meet the CCSS themselves, pre-service teachers gain experience working with the standards. More importantly, pre-service teachers can see a clear link between the digital literacies their own students rely on to write and what the standards ask for them to teach.

Although practicing writing teachers also need help with standards adoption in a digital age, I purposefully focus on mentoring pre-service teachers in implementing the CCSS within the WMC for three reasons. One, the WMC is increasingly required within teacher preparation programs. Focused solely on the teaching of writing, this course is a logical place for an introduction to the CCSS. Two, a growing number of states require teacher preparation programs to align curricula to the CCSS (Sawchuk 2012). Three, it is more cost effective to train teachers before they begin teaching. As Sawchuk notes, "Why pay for [CCSS training] in professional development later, when it is much more costly?" (8).

If pre-service teachers have practice meeting the CCSS in a supported space prior to beginning their first teaching position, a better opportunity exists to align writing theory, practice, and standards. Tracy Hargrove and colleagues (2004) argue that standards adoption is typically a reactive measure for practicing teachers. Therefore, working with the CCSS in the undergraduate WMC offers new writing teachers some protection against that reactive response. In this chapter, I first describe an action research assignment that invites pre-service teachers to examine specific CCSS that can be applied to digital environments in detail and within the overall project design. Next, I break down the specific phases of the project and follow with project outcomes. Finally, I argue that new writing teachers need this type of project-based instruction to really understand the standards in order to implement them effectively in schools. Due to a selective project focus on the CCSS that can be applied to digital writing environments, pre-service teachers are better equipped to see how the CCSS can measure writing, reading, and researching in today's digital environments.

Using Action Research to Meet the CCSS Within the Writing Methods Course

Peter Smagorinsky, Leslie Cook, and Tara Johnson (2003) argue that effective teacher preparation occurs when theory is refined by practice and reflection. My previous research (Tulley 2013) has shown that the most effective WMC tends to bridge theory and practice using action research projects—projects that ask students to experiment with a writing strategy with actual students, report and reflect on the results, and then refine and theorize the writing strategy based on these findings within the context of the WMC to help pre-service teachers learn flexible problem-solving strategies.

I describe here an action research project focused on reading theory through the CCSS in order to demonstrate the specific goals covered in Anchor Standards for Writing 6 and 8, and the specific elements of online literacy instruction associated with these standards. Through the course of creating an action research project, pre-service teachers are required to do the following (I divide Anchor Standard for Writing 8 into three parts to highlight the multiple tasks it involves):

- W.6: Use technology, including the internet, to produce and publish writing and to interact and collaborate with others

- W.8: Gather relevant information from multiple print and digital sources; assess the credibility and accuracy of each source; integrate the information (CCSSO and NGA 2010, 18)

These standards were chosen as the project focus because they expand the concept of "writing" to recognize digital literacy. They explicitly acknowledge that writing is researched, composed, and published in digital contexts. Because the project asks pre-service teachers to work within a focused section of the CCSS (i.e., the few standards that directly deal with digital literacy), pre-service teachers understand where the CCSS and emerging digital literacies such as online searching can be reconciled. This project also teaches pre-service teachers how to implement the CCSS to construct learning experiences for all writing instruction using the flexible strategies of action research. At the same time, this project serves as a model pre-service teachers can modify for use with their students to meet the CCSS. (See the appendix at the end of this chapter for the full project assignment.)

Project Design

Prior to starting the action research project, I ask pre-service teachers to share particular problems with teaching writing that concern them as they think about moving into the ELA classroom. Common large scale challenges cited include:

- How do I teach creative writing when I am not a creative writer?
- How do I get students to revise papers?
- How do I teach grammar?

From broad initial queries, I ask novice teachers to focus on a more specific problem they have with teaching writing that they would like to study. Questions emerge such as "How can I get students to organize introductory paragraphs?" and "How do I evaluate blogs?"

After students have selected a "teaching writing" challenge to study, they proceed through five phases of an action research process in order to practice meeting some of the writing CCSS they will have to teach students to meet. Based on a chart modified from Drew (2012), Table 15.1 summarizes how the tasks within the action research project meet primary writing standards that relate to or assume digital literacy and the skills pre-service teachers must have their future writing students demonstrate. Each of these phases is described more fully in the following section.

Table 15.1 How Phases in Action Research Project Meet the CCSS

Phase in Action Research Project	(Digital) Skill Project Requires	CCSS Number	Specific Standard
I. Research a writing problem using search engines (e.g., stimulating reluctant writers, thesis development, a grammar element, etc.). Supplement with library instruction in effective searches. Find sources that offer multiple ways to "solve" this writing challenge in print, video, and audio contexts.	Locating	CCRA.W.8	Gather relevant information from multiple print and digital sources
II. Test two to three of the writing solutions on a first-year composition student to determine each source's usefulness.	Evaluating	CCRA.W.8	Assess the credibility and accuracy of each source
III. Develop a draft document of findings or "solutions" to the problem. Determine which solution(s) worked. Reflect on findings.	Synthesizing	CCRA.W.8	Integrate the Information
IV. Turn draft document into a video, podcast, or webpage about the writing challenge. Complete peer review activity where peers provide feedback based on a rubric. Publish the video in an online archive, at a conference, or within an online journal.	Communicating	CCRA.W.6	Use technology, including the internet, to produce and publish writing and to interact and collaborate with others

Phase I: Research a Teaching of Writing Problem

For this segment, I asked my librarian colleagues to lead a session on how to conduct online searches using library databases effectively, within the context of the action research project. The librarians received a list of topics pre-service teachers are researching ahead of this session and used several of these topics as models for online searches. This segment tends to take at least two class sessions: one for the librarian to offer instruction, and one for students to do some online searching and printing or saving articles on digital devices. I often build in a third session for exploring non-academic resources available with the help of librarians (e.g., homemade tutorial videos on YouTube, diagrams of study habits, or podcasts of ways to implement teaching strategies). This third session explicitly combats any assumption that online searching should be limited to print articles and recognizes that nonscholarly sources are essential for this project. The pre-service teachers were asked to collect 10 sources and select three that they would like to explore further. This process encourages novice writing teachers to locate and evaluate professional development resources—a skill they will need to rely on as practicing teachers when they do not have the support structure of a teacher preparation program and need to find their own answers.

In addition, locating sources for a "real" teaching problem encourages careful searching, as pre-service teachers are not pressed for time to find sources in a hurry to solve a problem. Because time is allotted for them to search closely and critically, I often encourage pre-service teachers during this stage to find three very different ideas for solving the problem in order for them to see the range of solutions available to them. To do this, I introduce the specific standard they must have students meet. For example, all students must meet Anchor Standard for Writing 8: "Gather relevant information from multiple print and digital sources" (CCSSO and NGA 2010, 18). Described more specifically within the Writing Standards for grades 9–12, this standard asks students to:

> Conduct short as well as more sustained research projects to answer a question (including a self-generated question) or solve a problem; narrow or broaden the inquiry when appropriate; synthesize multiple sources on the subject, demonstrating understanding of the subject under investigation. (W.9–12.7)

Translated into how pre-service teachers meet the standards within the action research project, here pre-service teachers attempt to "solve a problem" in the action research project. To find out how to solve it, they must enter search terms in the library databases and in search engines such as Google Scholar, and "narrow and broaden the inquiry" terms as needed. Once pre-service teachers have found sources, they must "synthesize [the] multiple sources" they have found to determine which strategies suggested in the sources that they would like to test. Pre-service teachers ultimately will be called to "demonstrate [an] understanding" of the writing challenge they are studying, therefore meeting each of the requirements embedded in the general standard that asks students to gather relevant information. As this example illustrates, pre-service teachers have practiced meeting every goal of the standard.

Furthermore, when pre-service teachers teach the research project to their own writing students, secondary school librarians can be brought in to show how to search for nonacademic resources such as videos and podcasts and evaluate the credibility of such sources. Phase I provides a useful tie-in with the library for the strengthening of digital literacy.

Phase II: Test Three Strategies

In this phase, which is the second step in Table 15.1, I asked pre-service teachers to test the credibility of the sources they identified in Phase I by trying out the strategies suggested by them. Prior to testing, pre-service teachers identify particular CCSS that the strategies they have found in their research might help to address. During the course of 2 weeks, the WMC student implements two or three different strategies with a first-year writing student to determine how well particular CCSS can be met using these strategies. For the testing phase, to provide practice, I matched pre-service teachers up with first-year writing (English 101) students because these students often make errors typical of secondary students. I matched students with pre-service teachers during the heaviest writing times in the first-year writing course to make sure students have texts with which the pre-service teachers can work. Pre-service teachers then figure out how to test the strategies suggested by their research within a student's writing.

As an example of how the process works, one WMC student tested a strategy that offered the student two choices for revising the end commentary on a paper. After reading his student's draft, he wrote an end comment with two choices for revision. Next the student returned the paper and the WMC student could see if the student chose A or B as a possible revision solution, did nothing, did something else, or did a combination of A and B. The pre-service teacher repeated the process with two other strategies suggested by sources he found.

In another example, one pre-service teacher tested out three different pieces of advice from sources for composing an effective blog entry. He asked a first-year composition student to integrate an anecdote, a quotation, and background on the subject of the blog in three different versions of the blog entry. The pre-service teacher then compared all three to determine which blog entry appeared to offer the most development and made a case for his choice based on the research he had found and synthesized from his sources.

To make sure that such research follows appropriate protocols, I have students complete the necessary human subjects research documents with the university's institutional review office before the project starts. Doing so also ensures that pre-service teachers can publish their research (Phase IV) and have the appropriate permissions to do so. This second evaluative phase could be modified for secondary students in English courses. Pre-service teachers can ask future students to test out any solution posited by research they have read or viewed on a video from ELA to math.

Phase III: Develop a Reflective Draft of Findings

Phase III took the loose shape of a research paper. For this part of the project, the pre-service teacher offered a short introduction to the particular writing challenge that was explored, provided a literature review of the five sources chosen for study, described the three sources that were chosen for further study and a rationale (including the CCSS met by the strategies), provided findings for each of the solutions tested, and reflected on what was learned about solving this writing challenge. Students synthesized their findings in an initial draft of five to 10 pages that is used to help develop the final publication phase described in the following section. Even in this print-focused phase, pre-service teachers always recognized that the project will be published digitally. For example, one pre-service teacher described three strategies to eliminate unclear pronoun references in a paper that she used to help her first-year composition student. As her rationale, she argued student papers often contain unclear reference words such as "this" and working to specify such words could strengthen a whole paper. To showcase her findings, she embedded actual before and after screen captures of the changes in her student's text within her print draft and analyzed these findings. These images were later used in the digital publication she devised.

The print draft is important in Phase III and meets many of the other CCSS such as the Anchor Standard for Writing 1: "Write arguments to support claims in an analysis of substantive topics or texts, using valid reasoning and relevant and sufficient evidence" (CCSSO and NGA 2010, 18). However, this project assumes that the final publication phase must happen on the internet as that is where information is most often accessed.

Phase IV: Publish the Findings

Many researchers including Carla Asher (1987), Richard Bullock (1998), Cathy Fleischer (1994), Eleanor Kutz (1992), and Ruth Ray (1993) have argued that future writing teachers need to be teacher-researchers and engage in the action research process, such as that described in the previous phases. They emphasize this work must involve publishing findings from classroom research. There is some agreement here with the CCSS. In Anchor Standard for Writing 6, the CCSS asks students to use technology "including the internet" to foster collaboration and to publish the findings (CCSSO and NGA 2010, 18). To make sure that pre-service teachers understand what publication of a research project means and how they actually practice meeting the CCSS themselves by pursuing publication, we spent two or three class sessions talking about an appropriate venue to distribute project findings. This discussion includes figuring out audience (typically in this case, other writing teachers) and reframing the idea of publication to include the internet. For this phase, students are specifically asked to publish their findings by composing/designing a digital text, a concern Drew (2013) argues is missing from the CCSS. The action research project is not considered complete until the work is not only developed in a digital venue such as a video production program, but also published in a digital forum such as YouTube, Podcast Alley, or an online journal specializing in undergraduate research. One pre-service teacher created a podcast tutorial that explained how to use transitions effectively so that a first-year writing student could listen to it while revising a paper. Another created a hypertext article that showcased snippets of student drafts in response to teaching strategies. While the print papers in Phase III certainly could have communicated this information through digital publication, the pre-service teachers recognized that the internet is emerging as the key medium for publishing work.

As part of the final publication phase, pre-service teachers read/viewed each other's final publications as a form of peer review and asked questions about implementation and findings to focus on the collaborative element of communication outlined in Anchor Standard for Writing 6: "Use technology, including the internet, to produce and publish writing and to interact and collaborate with others" (CCSSO and NGA 2010, 18). Though the research projects were not formal studies, the goal from the peer review was to make sure that each paper describes thoroughly what happened so another future teacher can replicate the study. Pre-service teachers often ended up revising the digital publications to portray results more clearly after collaborating with classmates in peer review. The end goal of this phase is to have pre-service teachers rethink the CCSS as more broad than past standards requirements that implicitly assumed all student-generated texts would be final print or "clean" copies.

Outcomes

The most effective writing teacher preparation programs 1) link theory and practice within the WMC, 2) prepare students to link theory and practice within the culture of accountability within the schools once they exit the WMC, and 3) link theory and practice while recognizing the digital contexts within which students compose. This action research project offers a first look at how new writing teachers might approach digital literacy while still meeting the CCSS. Because the action research project gives them experience meeting the CCSS that explicitly acknowledge digital contexts, there is an explicit connection for pre-service teachers between using digital tools to write, research, and publish. Most importantly, this work requires pre-service teachers to approach digital tools and design with more flexibility because they must consider an online audience for their work.

Several benefits emerge from developing an action research project that teaches pre-service teachers how to apply the CCSS and, better yet, expand them to recognize digital literacy practices common to the next digital scholar. Once pre-service teachers have completed the action research project, they will have accomplished following tasks:

1. Articulated a writing problem (e.g., one pre-service teacher might choose teaching figurative language, if he dislikes teaching creative writing, or teaching verb tense, if he is unsure about grammar rules).

2. Discovered what the CCSS are associated with regarding this particular topic (and as a result, learn to read the CCSS).

3. Researched how to solve a specific writing challenge by identifying workable solutions and finding multiple ways of solving it in academic articles, videos, and so on (because there is no single solution that will work with every student in every writing class).

4. Tested several of the most viable solutions and reflected on why one solution worked better than another or how one of the strategies might be fine-tuned to match the pre-service teacher's ability, personality, philosophy of teaching writing, and so on. According to Chris Anson (2002), "Such reflection often leads to changed (and improved) teaching practices and behaviors ... more importantly, the process of reflection can move [writing] teachers out of instructional complacency and can sometimes reenergize a teacher who has reached a point of career burnout" (39).

5. Drafted a document of findings (a reflection on which solutions worked and how other solutions might be refined).

6. Extrapolated the research from the document and designed a digital publication (e.g., webpage, video, podcast, glog, etc.).

7. Published the findings using digital media. Publication ensures that pre-service teachers think of themselves as

writing researchers, which Fleischer (1994), Doug Hesse and Kirsti Sandy (2002), and Miles Myers (1985) argue is the best way to keep new writing teachers from getting burned out, and provides an opportunity for them to reach other teachers like themselves who search online for answers on how to solve a specific challenge in the teaching of writing.

8. Developed a research model for meeting the CCSS with which students, depending on age and ability, can work. For example, eighth-grade students who struggle to compose a thesis or topic sentence could be taught to locate websites or sources and provided with tips summarize findings, test out several solutions, reflect on which worked best, and publish the findings in a digital medium. Projects can even be built as part of a student research database in order to help writing students learn to solve some of their own writing problems while at the same time becoming stronger online readers and researchers in the process.

Caveats

As with any research assignment, an action research project to teach writing teachers to implement the CCSS does have some drawbacks. For one, WMCs are notoriously overcrowded courses. As previous research I have conducted on WMCs found, many WMC instructors already feel the course is full of topics both within writing studies and externally related areas such as gender studies (Tulley 2013). Moreover, the action research cycle tends to take roughly 2 to 3 weeks for each phase, particularly because students need at least a full week to test three different strategies. The project is designed to be ongoing throughout the course of the semester in conjunction with other assignments and readings within the WMC, but it does add to the overall workload for the students. For the instructor, time is needed to set up IRB training for pre-service teachers for study design and to coordinate with first-year writing courses for testing. Finally, the project asks pre-service teachers to find a workable digital medium to present their findings.

For many, this entails learning how to use a video program such as Windows Movie Maker.

However, I argue the action research model is ultimately a more efficient way to deal with several of the challenges facing writing teachers and the writing teacher educators who prepare them. For one, reading and viewing videos about specific strategies to solve writing problems introduces pre-service teachers to the theories behind these problems while also providing illustrative studies of how the theories are operating in practice. When pre-service writing teachers are directly involved with creating the links between theory, practice, and standards, they will likely have a better idea of how to apply them. This is a crucial, necessary link for pre-service teachers. Janet Alsup and Michael Bernard-Donals (2002), Mary Louise Gomez (1990), Grossman and colleagues (2000), Hesse and Sandy (2002), and Thomas McCann, Larry Johannessen, and Bernard Ricca (2005) have all argued novice writing teachers especially have trouble linking the theories and methods they have learned in teacher education programs with the realities of the writing classroom, particularly outcomes movements and other teacher accountability pressures.

If the CCSS are introduced to pre-service teachers as a starting point for research, rather than a focal point for anxiety, they will be armed with the experience of articulating how and where the CCSS fit into their teaching processes. As Gallagher (2012) argues, articulation "engages us in the necessary and difficult task of bringing educational aims—by whatever name—inside ongoing teaching and learning activities, where they will inevitably evolve as we perceive and act on the always-emerging consequences of our work with students" (56). The CCSS, then, are studied within the action research project as points for expansion of how student and teacher work might be done.

Still another concern is that WMC instructors may perceive that college courses are above concerns of the local schools and that they do not need to focus on the CCSS (Alsup et al. 2006). In fact, university teachers and librarians, like their secondary school counterparts, may feel that teaching the CCSS puts their academic freedom at risk

(Sawchuk 2012, 8). Still, as W. Douglas Baker and colleagues (2007) suggest, many WMC instructors have English education experience and have taught within secondary school contexts. WMC instructors have recognized that teaching writing theory alone will not be enough to ensure transfer of practice. My research (Tulley 2013) suggests that teacher preparation programs do recognize that pre-service teachers will have to adapt to school cultures and practices, and effective writing teacher preparation includes becoming adept at understanding, implementing, and assessing the CCSS.

Moreover, though this project is designed to be used within undergraduate writing teacher education courses, it could be extrapolated to teacher development programs with practicing writing teachers or librarians. Many practicing writing teachers could benefit from learning the action research process combined with digital publication. Research conducted on transfer problems between reading and writing by Holly Middleton (2012) and Cynthia Haller (2012) indicates the field of writing studies as a whole has grown increasingly concerned about the lack of connection between reading and writing, and this project links informational text writing and reading. Because the project specifically asks for a review of the sources that describe teaching strategies, there is direct practice with developing a response model for a nonfiction informational text (exactly the type emphasized by the CCSS), and librarians could work with writing teachers to strengthen methods for locating these types of texts and evaluating them for credibility.

Finally, the technologies pre-service teachers need to use for publication of projects don't necessarily have to pose a problem. Many easy-to-use programs exist with video tutorials, and even a program often used in college and high school classrooms such as PowerPoint can be modified to look like a video and posted on the web. In addition, when pre-service teachers invite their own students to publish digitally, the programs will constantly change and students and teachers can learn together to find the most effective (and often free) publication medium for projects. I have found that one unexpected benefit to requiring pre-service teachers to publish the project digitally is that pre-service teachers often take this as an opportunity to teach themselves new technologies.

Conclusions

Having students explicitly reframe two key Anchor Standards for Writing as digital and conduct action research projects within this framework ultimately enhances the writing methods classroom experience by offering future writing teachers rich terrain to thoughtfully consider the CCSS. Pre-service teachers have direct experience with where and how these new standards might help writing instruction—including writing instruction in digital environments with digital texts. Because findings are based on real-life investigations, debate among classmates is lively and informed, as when they uncover markedly different findings using similar remedies for fixing a specific writing problem. As an additional benefit, pre-service teachers often find that multiple standards apply to one WMC project, helping them see that it is possible to meet several CCSS at once, making the CCSS much less overwhelming. Most importantly, using a digital medium to publish the findings ensures that pre-service teachers have opportunities to collaborate and share ideas—from comments on YouTube to responses to an online journal article.

This proactive approach to the CCSS is necessary to teach to pre-service teachers because standards movements aren't going away. Today's secondary writing teachers will never know a time where they aren't held accountable to a set of standards. Gehsmann and Templeton (2012) rightly point out that "[o]ver the course of their professional careers, teachers will be expected to teach several iterations of the standards" (14). Historically, standards have often been approached reactively within the teaching of writing, rather than proactively (Hargrove et al. 2004). Yet action research projects, such as the one described in this chapter, offer "an opportunity to reflect on, identify, and operate from aims that are meaningful to them" (Gallagher 2012, 56). When faced with standards requirements such as the CCSS, novice teachers need to see how theory and practice connect.

In their study of what new English teachers need in terms of support, McCann, Johannessen, and Ricca (2005) advocate providing pre-service teachers with hands-on opportunities to develop a personal theory, and practices that support this theory, because "defining a public self as a teacher requires the teacher to have many opportunities to try out the role and shape it into a comfortable form" (97). Part of trying on the role of the teacher is finding which strategies, including those strategies for teaching writing, are workable and which are not, particularly in the moving terrain between print and digital environments. The WMC provides this testing space because students are able "to see the practical applications of what they are learning in that course, and to experiment with their own ways of understanding the theories they learn," a feature Kari Smith and Orly Sela (2005) deem essential for effective writing teacher preparation (297).

Smith and Sela (2005) describe action research as "a tool which teacher educators can use to provide help and support to novice teachers during the difficult beginning of their teaching career. They are encouraged to study their own work with the aim of improving it" (297). Using an action research project within writing teacher education can ensure novice teachers have learned flexible and replicable problem-solving strategies that will allow them to work within the CCSS but also beyond them to support writing in digital environments. Action research methodology can be applied to new writing challenges as well as shifting school cultures and variations of CCSS adoption. With practice meeting the CCSS Anchor Standards for Writing that specifically can be applied to digital literacy through an action research project, pre-service teachers are better prepared to meet the simultaneous challenges of addressing the CCSS and expanding the digital literacies their students have already begun to develop.

References

Alsup, Janet, and Michael Bernard-Donals. 2002. "The Fantasy of the Seamless Transition." In *Teaching Writing in High School and College: Conversations and*

Collaborations, edited by Thomas C. Thompson, 115–135. Urbana, IL: National Council of Teachers of English.

Alsup, Janet, Janet Emig, Gordon Pradl, Robert Tremmel, and Robert Yagelski, with Lynn Alvine, Gina DeBlase, Michael Moore, Robert Petrone, and Mary Sawyer. 2006. "The State of English Education and a Vision for Its Future: A Call to Arms." *English Education* 38 (4): 278–294.

Anson, Chris M. 2002. "Teaching Writing Creatively: A Summer Institute for Teachers." In *Teaching Writing Teachers of High School English and First-Year Composition*, edited by Robert Tremmel and William Broz, 27–39. Portsmouth, NH: Boynton/Cook.

Asher, Carla. 1987. "Developing a Pedagogy for a Teacher/Researcher Program." *English Education* 19 (4): 211–219.

Baker, W. Douglas, Elizabeth Brockman, Jonathan Bush, and Kia Jane Richmond. 2007. "Composition Studies/English Education Connections." *The Writing Instructor*, edited by Janet Alsup and Lisa Schade Eckert. Accessed February 10, 2014. www.writinginstructor.com/cseeconnections.

Bullock, Richard H. 1998. "A Quiet Revolution: The Power of Teacher Research." In *Seeing for Ourselves: Case-Study Research by Teachers of Writing*, edited by Glenda L. Bissex and Richard H. Bullock, 21–28. Portsmouth, NH: Heinemann.

Brzycki, Dolores, and Kurt Dudt. 2005. "Overcoming Barriers to Technology Use in Teacher Preparation Programs." *Journal of Technology and Teacher Education* 13 (4): 619–641.

Council of Chief State School Officers and National Governors Association. 2010. *Common Core State Standards for English Language Arts and Literacy in History/Social Studies, Science, and Technical Subjects*. Washington, DC: National Governors Association Center for Best Practices, Council of Chief State School Officers. Accessed February 10, 2014. www.corestandards.org/assets/CCSSI_ELA%20 Standards.pdf.

Drew, Sally Valentino. 2013. "Open Up the Ceiling on the Common Core State Standards: Preparing Students for 21st-Century Literacy—Now." *Journal of Adolescent and Adult Literacy* 56 (4): 321–330.

Fleischer, Cathy. 1994. "Researching Teacher-Research: A Practitioner's Retrospective." *English Education* 26 (2): 86–124.

Gallagher, Chris W. 2012. "The Trouble With Outcomes: Pragmatic Inquiry and Educational Aims." *College English* 75 (1): 42–60.

Gehsmann, Kristin M., and Shane Templeton. 2012. "Stages and Standards in Literacy: Teaching Developmentally in the Age of Accountability." *Journal of Education* 192 (1): 5–16.

Gomez, Mary Louise. 1990. *Learning to Teach Writing: Untangling the Tensions between Theory and Practice*. East Lansing, MI: Michigan State University.

Grossman, Pam, Sheila Valencia, Kate Evans, Clarissa Thompson, Susan Martin, and Nancy Place. 2000. *Transitions into Teaching: Learning to Teach Writing in Teacher Education and Beyond*. Albany, NY: National Research Center on English Learning and Achievement. Accessed February 10, 2014. www.albany.edu/cela/reports/grossmantransitions13006.pdf.

Haller, Cynthia R. 2012. "Reading Matters: Thoughts on Revising the CWPA Outcomes Statement." *Writing Program Administration* 36 (1): 195–199.

Hargrove, Tracy, Bradford L. Walker, Richard A. Huber, Stephanie Z. Corrigan, and Christopher Moore. 2004. "No Teacher Left Behind: Supporting Teachers as They Implement Standards-Based Reform in a Test-Based Education Environment." *Education* 124 (3): 567–572.

Hesse, Douglas, and Kirsti Sandy. 2002. "Teaching Teachers and the Extracurriculum." In *Teaching Writing Teachers of High School English and First-year Composition*, edited by Robert Tremmel and William Broz, 116–125. Portsmouth, NH: Boynton/Cook.

Huot, Brian. 2002. *(Re)Articulating Writing Assessment for Teaching and Learning*. Logan, UT: Utah State University Press.

Jones, Allison G., and Jacqueline E. King. 2012. "The Common Core State Standards: A Vital Tool for Higher Education." *Change* 44 (6): 37–43.

Kutz, Eleanor. 1992. "Pre-Service Teachers as Researchers: Developing Practice and Creating Theory in the English Classroom." *English Education* 24 (2): 67–76.

McCann, Thomas M., Larry R. Johannessen, and Bernard P. Ricca. 2005. *Supporting Beginning English Teachers: Research and Implications for Teacher Induction*. Urbana, IL: National Council of Teachers of English.

Middleton, Holly. 2012. "Recognizing Acts of Reading: Creating Reading Outcomes and Assessments for Writing." *Writing Program Administration* 36 (1): 11–31.

Myers, Miles. 1985. *The Teacher Researcher: How to Study Writing in the Classroom*. Urbana, IL: National Council of Teachers of English.

Ray, Ruth. 1993. *The Practice of Theory: Teacher Research in Composition*. Urbana, IL: National Council of Teachers of English.

Sawchuk, Stephen. 2012. "Higher Ed. Gauges Training of Teachers for Common Core." *Education Week* 31 (35): 8.

Smagorinsky, Peter, Leslie Susan Cook, and Tara Star Johnson. 2003. "The Twisting Path of Concept Development in Learning to Teach." *Teachers College Record* 105 (8): 1399–1436.

Smith, Kari, and Orly Sela. 2005. "Action Research as a Bridge Between Pre-Service Teacher Education and In-service Professional Development for Students and Teacher-Educators." *European Journal of Teacher Education* 28 (3): 293–310.

Tulley, Christine E. 2013. "What Are Pre-Service Teachers Taught about the Teaching of Writing?: A Survey of Ohio's Undergraduate Writing Methods Courses." *Teaching/Writing: The Journal of Writing Teacher Education* 2 (1): 38–48.

Appendix: How Phases in Action Research Project Meet the CCSS

ENGL 345 Course Project: Conducting Action Research (i.e., learning how to solve your own problems with the teaching of writing)

Action research boils down to one concept: It is a TEST of a theory (yours or someone else's) in PRACTICE.

For this project, you will complete the following phases to conduct your own action research experiment. This course project is worth 20 percent of your grade. Models of successful course projects will be shared in class.

Choose a writing problem/fear/challenge to try to explore for this project. Possible challenges 345 students have explored in the past have included teaching specific word choice, effective transition use, interpretation of quotations, revising run-on sentences, etc. Next, open the CCSS document on Blackboard to determine which standards you feel your writing challenge might meet if addressed successfully.

After determining your challenge, we will spend one or two class periods in the computer lab searching for sources about the challenge with our librarians who will help us hone our search terms. Your sources are not limited to scholarly articles as there are also effective videos, podcasts, and websites available through YouTube and Google. The librarians will help us determine if these electronic sources are credible sources. I would aim for six to seven articles and three to four digital sources to use for your initial research about your challenge. All will need to be read/viewed prior to entering the next phase of the project and you will have roughly two weeks to read them all.

Next, you will "test" three possible strategies you have determined will work best from your literature/source review for addressing this problem with a first year writing student from ENGL 104: College Writing I to determine: 1) which strategies seem to work and speculate why, 2) which strategies don't seem to work and speculate why, and 3) which strategies might work if modified (and describe the modification).

Finally, you will write up a "course project" paper describing your interest in the topic, what has been said about the challenge by others (your literature review), the three strategies you tried with your first-year composition student, your findings from your testing, and reflection.

Phases are summarized below.

Phase I: Initial Design and Start Literature Review

1. Pick a teaching of writing challenge.

2. Determine which CCSS can be met if the writing challenge is solved successfully (limit to two to three).

3. Research what has already been tried to solve the problem you want to study by looking for at least 10 articles/books/ videos/podcasts/websites/National Council of Teachers of English website position statements about this subject.

4. Begin to write up a five- to six-page literature review providing an overview of what has been tried to solve your problem (1,250 words double spaced—this will go within your final course project paper).

Phase II: Your Action Intervention With Actual Students (Testing Your Solutions/Strategies/Remedies)

Your student match from ENGL 104 is posted in Blackboard with an email address. Please email your student and arrange for three separate meetings to test your three different strategies or have the student bring three copies of the draft where each strategy can be attempted in isolation (if working in the lab, have the student make three separate copies of the essay and save them as different names such as "strategy test 1," etc.). I suggest you have the student test all three on the same paper so you can determine how much improvement happened from the strategy itself versus other strategies or other revisions the student made.

Phase III: Develop a Reflective Draft of Findings

Now that you have conducted a literature review, designed your experiment, and tested a writing strategy, it is time to compile all of this information into a cohesive report.

You may want to use the categories that follow as section headings within your paper.

Introduction (1–2 pages)

- Why did you want to try this certain writing strategy?
- What did you hope to find?
- How will/does this "test" of this solution fit into your career plans as a writer/teacher? In other words, has this been a troublesome/challenging issue for you for some time?

Literature Review (3–4 pages)

- What did you find in your articles about this strategy or the writing challenge itself?
- How do the articles differ in terms of solutions/strategies? How are they the same?
- What theories do each of these strategies seem to be grounded in? Did the articles cite any theorists? Do any cite the same theorists?
- Summarize what you found across the articles. Are there any trends? What are they? Does this particular problem seem to be one that experts disagree how to solve?

Action Intervention (1–2 pages)

- Describe the strategy you tried in great detail including who you tried it with, how you actually conducted this strategy (each step you did), and how many times you tried it. Don't forget to attach EVIDENCE that you tried this strategy in appendices.

Discussion (2–3 pages)

- What happened (each time if you did it more than once) when you tried the strategy? What did students/self do in response?

- In your opinion, did this strategy "work" to solve your writing challenge? If not, what would you modify/try next?
- Did the results surprise you? How do these results meet (or not meet) the CCSS you identified?
- What did you expect to happen? Did it?
- What didn't you expect to happen? Why not?
- How do your findings fit in with what you found in the literature review? Do they confirm the literature?

Conclusion (1–2 pages)

- Overall, sum up in at least two paragraphs if you think your strategy worked, worked with some modifications (describe), or would not work. How did you come to these conclusions? What evidence from your study led you to find these out? If your strategy did not work, what are you going to try next to solve your writing problem?
- Finally, did you learn any research skills from conducting this study? Are there any new studies you plan to try on your own based on your findings from this one? What did you learn about using the CCSS to develop a strategy?

CHAPTER **16**

From Do As We Say to Do As We (Digitally) Do
Modeling the Implementation of the Common Core State Standards

Tawnya Lubbes and Heidi Skurat Harris

Educators increasingly face classrooms of students identified as Generation D[igital], Generation-Net, or NextGen, tech-savvy students living hypermediated lives. In reality, the classroom is a space with a mixture of both the tech-savvy and the technophobic, terms that apply to students and teachers alike. The mixed nature of technology use across age groups, socioeconomic status, and gender lines poses a particular challenge in a classroom where educators are called upon to meet the media and technology components of the Common Core State Standards (CCSS).

While some believe otherwise, the use of technologies outside of the classroom does not naturally translate to the use of technologies inside the classroom. As Michael Wesch (2008) stated, "[Students] may know all about YouTube and Facebook and how to navigate these things to entertain themselves, but they know nothing about how to use these things to learn and for critical thought and more than anything, they rarely know how to use these things to create something interesting and new." While 21st-century students may have more experience with the production of digital media for entertainment and personal purposes, as Amanda Lenhart and colleagues' (2012) research reported from the Pew Research Internet Project, they frequently lack experience with critical media analysis. Similarly, teachers with critical knowledge of using digital sources and information may lack confidence in creating digital sources or materials. While a teacher may have a Facebook or LinkedIn profile that she or he updates regularly, and may even have explored the realms of blogs, online videos, and website creation, he or she may be hesitant to use these technologies to create new assignments, particularly given the high-stakes nature of standardized testing and other assessments, including those of the CCSS.

The teachers' range of experience leads us to assert that pre-service teacher training and faculty development programs can provide project-based learning (PBL) opportunities to work with Web 2.0 and cloud-based applications in designing inquiry-based projects. These projects function as a means of bringing together the critical skills of using digital technologies to *gather*, assess, and implement sources from digital sources and the functional skills required to *use* technology to produce, publish, and update products, both of which are articulated in the CCSS (Council of Chief State School Officers [CCSSO] and National Governors Association [NGA] 2010, W.9–12.6 and W.9–12.8). Jennifer Railsback (2002) defined PBL as an instructional mode that allows students to address real-world problems through planning, implementing, and evaluating their own projects. It has been found in our experience that PBL builds teachers' confidence with technology as they develop digital literacy practices through completing their own inquiry-based projects.

This chapter addresses the need for pre-service and faculty professional development that models inquiry-based projects as a means for developing both critical and functional technoliteracy. It discusses how professional development opportunities, including longer-term professional-development experiences, must focus on merging critical and functional technoliteracy skills, modeling this process for educators. The first program discussed in this chapter, a masters-level PBL class, allows pre-service educators to explore high-impact practices before bringing them to the classroom. The second program is a short-term, day-long, in-service program that supports educators through Google Summits to incorporate cloud-based applications in the K–12 setting. A third, long-term technology-rich summer institute patterned after the NWP uses free or low-cost multimedia tools (e.g., Google Apps, Educreations, screencasting) to help faculty enhance online and computer-mediated courses. Each professional development opportunity challenges faculty to learn technology skills through their own inquiry-based projects, exemplifying an inside-out approach to the integration of technology skills and digital literacy. After explaining these programs, we discuss how these professional development and pre-service experiences can serve as models for educators to facilitate similar learning communities and ask students to build on prior digital knowledge in meeting the CCSS, making them a pathway to competence in a community-oriented digital world.

Generation-D and the CCSS

The rhetoric surrounding how individuals use 21st-century technologies tends to draw clean dichotomies between the two groups Marc Prensky (2001) called "digital natives" and "digital immigrants." Digital natives, or those who are "'native speakers' of the digital language of computers, videogames, and the internet" (1), grew up in not only a media-saturated world, but a world of hypermediated and multitasked experiences. High school and college students are digital natives. The natives are cleanly separated from the "digital immigrants," or "those … not born into the digital world but have, at some later point in [their] lives, become fascinated by and adopted many or most aspects of the new technology" (1–2).

However, research in the fields of education and sociology, in addition to studies by the Pew Internet & American Life Project, demonstrated the much more complex relationship that the next digital scholar has with technology (Lenhart et al. 2010; Lenhart 2012). Sue

Bennett, Karl Maton, and Lisa Kervin's (2008) overview of research indicated that "[w]hile technology is embedded in their lives, young people's use and skills are not uniform. There is no evidence of widespread and universal disaffection or of a distinctly different learning style the like of which has never been seen before" (783). Using the frame of "moral panic" surrounding the need to change to accommodate a generation of tech-savvy learners, the authors also state that such moral panic forcing technology change can "close down debate, and in doing so allow unevidenced claims to proliferate. Not only does this limit the possibility for understanding the phenomenon, it may also alienate the very people being urged to change" (783).

While breaking large swaths of the population neatly along chronological age lines makes for a handy metaphor, the reality of the broad range of technology users in even a typical high school classroom breaks the dichotomy of *native* and *immigrant* into a spectrum of smaller groups. However, Prensky's language metaphor does provide a basis for understanding the challenges inherent in the digital aspects of the CCSS. The standards nod to the ubiquitous nature of multimedia production tools and digital media, challenging students to "gather relevant information from multiple authoritative print and digital sources" (CCSSO and NGA 2010, W.9–12.8) and to "use technology, including the internet, to produce, publish, and update individual or shared writing products" (W.9–12.6). These two standards, in fact, highlight another dichotomy: the skills required to "gather," assess, and implement digital sources and the skills required to "use" technology to "produce, publish, and update … products" (Anchor Standard for Writing 6; CCSSO and NGA 2010, 46). Educators seeking to meet these two standards are challenged to create classrooms (often with limited technology and limited time) that work for learners across the spectrum from native to immigrant while simultaneously helping all those learners gather, assess, and implement sources to produce, publish, and update digital projects (for more information, see Chapter 11 in this volume).

Issues in Implementing the CCSS

The development of the CCSS aimed to infuse literacy standards throughout all core subject areas. David Conley (2011) suggested that classroom teaching in response to the CCSS will ideally result in student-centered learning that integrates significant engagement in the curriculum and development of higher-order processing skills. In essence, the CCSS call for a transformation in instructional methods in order to better prepare learners for college and career. Thus, the standardized curriculum that once prepared students primarily for multiple-choice assessments is no longer adequate to meet the demands of the CCSS.

The infusion of technology in the CCSS requires faculty to integrate digital technologies and possibly reevaluate their teaching practices. However, as Erin Reilly (2011) maintains, faculty cannot fully reevaluate their practices "when teachers themselves are not afforded these same opportunities to grow and learn" as their students (6). Teachers who are frustrated with the constant adoption of new instructional practices and mandates do not feel adequately prepared to meet the technology demands of the CCSS. As a result, the implementation of project-based and technology-rich professional development, we believe, will best meet the needs in preparing 21st-century educators for the implementation of CCSS.

The Need for Project-Based Professional Development

Pre-service and professional development must acknowledge the complex environment and the varied users of digital technology in the 21st-century classroom. Research on professional development literature reinforces the need for professional development opportunities that mirror and model the CCSS involving digital technologies (see Chapter 15 in this volume). For example, Anchor Standard for Writing 8 emphasizes the critical tasks of understanding communicative practices in a community, including the ability to gather information from relevant digital sources in order to be able to effectively integrate that information to create well-structured documents (CCSSO and NGA 2010, 46). To capture these same outcomes in professional development, the pre-service or veteran educator should be asked to identify educational technologies that are most relevant to their classrooms within the context of their content area and community to create well-structured assignments. In addition, Writing Standard 6 for grades 11–12 asks students to practice the functional skills of technology use to "produce, publish, and update individual or shared writing products in response to ongoing feedback, including new arguments or information" (CCSSO and NGA 2010, 46). To mirror these outcomes, professional development should ask pre-service and veteran teachers to create elements in digital format, using the same tools and skills that they will be asking students to use in the classroom.

Three Models for Pre-Service and Professional Development

The three models for professional development described in this section address how teachers can develop both functional and critical technoliteracy skills that can then be practiced in the classroom to meet the needs of the CCSS. This section describes a pre-service PBL course, an in-service Google Summit offered at a middle school, and a more intensive summer institute model patterned after the National Writing Project (NWP) summer institutes.

Pre-Service Project-Based Learning in a Graduate-Level Course

Research shows that student directed learning empowers students to direct themselves and assess how they are doing (Boss 2012; Jaeger 2012; Reilly 2011; Saltman 2012). In light of the integration of the CCSS and in response to current research, PBL strategies were integrated into a secondary pre-service teacher education graduate level course. The goal was to facilitate a professional development setting in which pre-service teachers were charged with creating a project in their content area that both met the CCSS and utilized technology. The students not only had to demonstrate mastery of academic content through their project, but also had to self-monitor and assess their progress.

The following example took place in a summer PBL course designed for secondary pre-service teachers at a regional state university in the Pacific Northwest. The course met 6 hours a day over a 1-week period. Formal class meetings occurred each morning to set goals for the day and discuss progress as well as each afternoon to provide a progress report and clarify any questions they had regarding the project. The rest of the class time was used to explore, create, and implement projects, and instructors were available during this time to advise students, monitor their progress, and facilitate the development of their projects.

At the beginning of the course, instructors introduced PBL by showing video footage from an area school that uses PBL in their science and math programs as well as presenting current research and literature pertaining to PBL inquiry and its connections to the CCSS. The instructors then shared several PBL units created by previous students as well as the criteria for the course project. Each student then chose a major CCSS in their content area, selected their own project, and described how they would meet the standard through the integration of technology. Before beginning work on their projects, participants were reminded that all background knowledge and skills, including technological competencies, must be outlined and presented in a comprehensible manner to someone who may have no previous knowledge of the content, the relevant standard in the CCSS, or the technology used to accompany instruction.

After the project (see Appendices A through D at the end of the chapter) was assigned on Day 1 of the course, students were given the opportunity to explore the CCSS in order to select which project they wanted to design. The project proposal was then due by the afternoon of day two. Table 16.1 provides an outline of the daily course meetings. It should be noted that on Day 3 of the course students were assigned a partner who completed the project they constructed. One student acted as teacher/facilitator and the other as student and vice versa.

Table 16.1 PBL Course Outline

Date	Topics	Assignments Due
Monday AM: Course introduction PM: Work on proposals	• What is project-based learning? • Examples of student projects • Creating own project	---
Tuesday AM: Share ideas and review proposals PM: Turn in proposals	• Creating own project, a continuation	• Proposal
Wednesday AM: Proposals returned and partners assigned PM: Work on projects	• Becoming a student for project-based learning	---
Thursday AM: Meet with partners PM: Work on projects	• Working on a project • Looking at the rubric	---
Friday AM: Presentations PM: Grading presentations	• Presentation of projects in conjunction with the project-creator • End of course survey	• Final project presentations • Rationale for project grading

By modeling the use of PBL in secondary classrooms, pre-service educators expressed, through end-of-the-course surveys, that they were able to see the value of using this method to meet the CCSS. Further, participants were able to experience Conley's (2011) observation that "[t]he brain functions by organizing related pieces of information into databases, or schema" (18). In this instance, the pre-service teachers were able to demonstrate their ability to gain a deeper connection to content-specific concepts through real world application. In their surveys, they also expressed an understanding of how students can benefit from PBL activities where they are the center of teaching and learning. The pre-service educators were provided the opportunity to participate in a hands-on PBL approach to the CCSS and experienced a repackaging of instruction that focuses on the students' background knowledge and application of content, literacy, and technology in the same project. Dave Saltman (2012) reminds us:

> Research findings, as well as newly adopted curriculum standards, continue to send a message to educators that the work

of learning must be shifted from teachers to the ones doing the learning. That's because research and anecdotal evidence suggest that when students manage their own learning, they become more invested in their own academic success. Self-directed students also deploy critical-thinking skills more readily when confronted with challenging schoolwork. (4)

Through the PBL project, pre-service teachers were able to participate in a first-hand experience where they assumed the role of the student in self-directed learning. They invested their time in creating a project that met CCSS and were empowered to implement and assess their own progress and final outcomes.

Some of the projects created included the following:

- Health: Muscle Sculpture and Digital Demonstration
- Language Arts: Illustrated Digital Children's Book Based on a Fiction Book
- Physics: Engineered Parachute Project
- Music: Digital Musical Genres Project
- Biology: Digital "New" Species Project
- Art: Digital Graffiti Project
- History: MEanderthal Project
- English: Digital Book Jacket Project

These students were able to demonstrate the creation of phenomenal projects that represented their mastery of the CCSS in both technology and content.

An example of one exemplary project was the creation of a Shakespearean Sonnet Digital book jacket. The course participant identified the following CCSS in her project:

- Analyze how an author's choices concerning how to structure specific parts of a text (e.g., the choice of where to begin or end a story, the choice to provide a comedic or tragic resolution) contribute to its overall structure and meaning as well as its aesthetic impact. (CCSSO and NGA 2010, RL.11–12.5)

- Analyze a case in which grasping a point of view requires distinguishing what is directly stated in a text from what is really meant (e.g., satire, sarcasm, irony, or understatement). (RL.11–12.6)

- Produce clear and coherent writing in which the development, organization, and style are appropriate to task, purpose, and audience. (W.11–12.4)

- Develop and strengthen writing as needed by planning, revising, editing, rewriting, or trying a new approach, focusing on addressing what is most significant for a specific purpose and audience. (W.11–12.5)

- Use technology, including the internet, to produce, publish, and update individual or shared writing products in response to ongoing feedback, including new arguments or information. (W.11–12.6)

The project objective was to provide the student the opportunity to use their knowledge of Shakespearean sonnets to create a book jacket that would reveal their expertise of a self-selected sonnet. The student was required to create a digital book cover including the front and back covers, spine, and flaps. The illustrations and information included on the book cover had to be representative of the selected sonnet and demonstrate competency of the identified standards.

Another representative example of a project was a Facebook page project on a historical figure from the 1960s. For this project the following standards were identified:

- Determine the central ideas or information of a primary or secondary source; provide an accurate summary that makes clear the relationships among the key details and ideas. (CCSSO and NGA 2010, RH.11–12.2)

- Determine the meaning of words and phrases as they are used in a text, including analyzing how an author uses and refines the meaning of a key term over the course of a text (e.g., how Madison defines *faction* in *Federalist* No. 10). (RH.11–12.4)

- Analyze 17th-, 18th-, and 19th-century foundational U.S. documents of historical and literary significance (including The Declaration of Independence, the Preamble to the Constitution, the Bill of Rights, and Lincoln's Second Inaugural Address) for their themes, purposes, and rhetorical features. (RI.11–12.9)

- Use technology, including the internet, to produce, publish, and update individual or shared writing products in response to ongoing feedback, including new arguments or information. (W.11–12.6)

The goal of this project was to demonstrate the students' understanding of the 1960s and major historical figures of the decade. Students were required to include pertinent information that related to the individual's impact in history, such as friends, links to other historical figures, work and education information, family members, images, and interests. They were also required to include two period advertisements and relevant conversations that the historical figure would have had with other historical figures. A properly cited photo album was another requisite.

The integration of PBL in professional development models a method in which faculty and pre-service educators are able to experience a kind of learning that involves a global approach to teaching and exploring content while offering an authentic assessment of outcomes as related to the CCSS. This learning is directly transferrable to the K–12 classroom. Teachers can integrate a PBL model of teaching and assessing the CCSS in a manner that is entirely student centered, which can then be extended to mastery assessments of significant academic content along with the development of specific 21st-century skills, such as collaboration, critical thinking, and the integration of media literacy.

The incorporation of technology and media literacy into the CCSS appeals to educators to emphasize not only the delivery of content in a new manner, but also the application and assessment of content knowledge. With PBL, teachers are able to use a common assessment tool or rubric for all projects, but leave the planning and implementation of the projects in the hands of the individual learners. Students must process the CCSS that apply to their project and demonstrate how they will meet those standards. This approach allows students to customize their learning to meet their own style while analyzing texts and demonstrating comprehension in a manner that aligns with the standards.

While professional development and practice is required in order for teachers to use PBL in their classrooms, using a PBL model of professional development will greatly reduce anxiety and the need for further training. Teachers will be able to adapt more quickly to the model as they are able to experience it first hand and explore how they are able to integrate it into their teaching. Further, teachers are able to collaborate with other educators in order to troubleshoot potential pitfalls, share success, and celebrate outcomes.

In-Service Professional Development Through Google Summits

In-service professional development activities can provide teachers opportunities to focus on particular learning applications in order to integrate these applications into the classroom. While Google Summits come in a variety of shapes and sizes, the Google Summits described here are 1-day focused workshops on integrating Google Applications in the K–12 classroom.

School districts in the area surrounding most universities, along with the universities themselves, are increasingly adopting Gmail as a free, web-based email platform, which means that they have access to Google Apps for Education. To help area teachers integrate Google Apps into their classrooms, one school district along with the state virtual school district, the regional school district, and our university hosted a series of Google Summits at a local middle school. The Summits served as a professional development activity by creating learner-centered opportunities for teachers to address content-based issues through practice, including modeling, implementation, and reflection.

The Google Summits invited educators to participate in mini-workshops integrating Google technology into K–12 curricula. Summit organizers modeled the integration of technology and content by creating the registration site for the Summit in Google Sites and using a Google Forms pre-Summit survey to solicit input from participants regarding which sessions would be most useful. The schedule for presentations was then developed in Google Sites around the answers to that survey.[1]

At each Summit, facilitators encouraged participants to bring their own laptops or use laptops provided by the school for the session so that participants could create Google Apps activities for their classrooms. For example, a session on Google Forms demonstrated the basic features of Google Forms, and participants immediately designed Google Forms surveys for use as mini-quizzes or to gather student answers from small group discussions. The information gathered from the students could then be displayed at the front of the room for further class discussion. Other participants designed course webpages using Google Sites to communicate course schedules and other information to both students and parents. Some participants created Google Docs for use by small groups of students who used Docs to collaborate on analyzing and discussing class readings. Students could begin their discussion in class and then work from home in the evenings to create reading presentations. The teacher could then access those presentations, collaborate with students, and showcase the students' work in class the following day.

To further discuss the use of Google Apps in the classroom, Google Summit participants had the option to sign up for graduate credits through our university to continue practicing the use of Google Apps and reflecting on their use in the classroom. The graduate credit involved designing more extensive activities with Google Docs, Google Presentations, and/or Google Sites to implement in the classroom. Teachers were then asked to reflect on and discuss their use of Google in the classroom as a group to identify concerns and successes in their integration of technology for the classroom. The graduate credit portion of the Google Summit also integrated Google Apps into its structure, asking participants to access course materials at a Google Site, and submit answers to materials using Google Docs.[2] One participant in the graduate course, when asked what he used from his sessions, enthusiastically indicated, "I have used Google Docs, Forms, Presentations, Spreadsheets, and Sites, and I have a Google Voice account. I do everything using Google and encourage my students [to use it], too. And I want to learn more!"

Google Summits are designed to immerse teachers in a learning community structured around one particular use of technology in the classroom. Teachers learn functional uses of Google through hands-on creation of learning materials in Google Apps sessions. While each Google Summit focused on Google products in particular, which can be limiting for faculty not teaching at schools using those technologies, similar summits could focus on any number of free applications, such as Edmodo, the Khan Academy, TED Talks, or other similar educational materials that include interactive components.

The Google Summit model reflects how faculty might use Google Docs to create assignments and student-centered learning opportunities in the classroom. Teachers can send a Google Form (or a similar survey) to solicit feedback from students at the beginning of a project regarding the technology resources they are familiar with in order to design activities that take advantage of the technological skills that students bring to the classroom by creating working groups in the classroom based around those skills, pairing more techno-savvy students with less techno-savvy students so that students might be able to help their peers with the finer points of creating digital artifacts. Students can then register for Google accounts and use the applications available with those accounts to create collaborative documents and presentations in Google Docs, working either synchronously in the classroom or asynchronously from their home computers to complete group assignments, modify those assignments based on feedback from the teacher and other students, and present those projects to the class or make them available online.

The Google Summits provide professional development opportunities that encourage teachers to focus on their classroom needs, their beliefs, and their current classroom practice (Brinkerhoff 2006; Chen 2010; Ehman, Bonk, and Yamagata-Lynch 2005). The Google

Summit offers opportunities for faculty to build learning communities to discuss their technology practice with their peers, allowing them to develop proficiency in the tools while simultaneously modeling how those tools might be used to implement elements of the CCSS.

In addition to a focus on the teacher's experience, the community and environment surrounding the teacher must be addressed in effective professional development. Teachers engaged in communities of practice surrounding educational technologies were more likely to effectively implement technology practices in the classroom (Brinkerhoff 2006; Ehman, Bonk, and Yamagata-Lynch 2005; Ertmer 2005; Laferriere, Lamon, and Chan 2006). Community support for technology use and the impression that teachers had a voice as stakeholders in their communities also positively influenced the integration of technology after professional development (King 2002; Plair 2008; Schneckenberg 2010). The personal and community aspects of effective professional development mirror the very critical and functional skills the CCSS hope that students will develop in engaging in gathering and using materials that demonstrate knowledge of conversations and creation of artifacts designed to communicate within and with larger communities. The opportunity for participants to earn graduate credit for the Google Summit and continue the conversation online provides teachers with experience in online community building, a method that they can then implement in their courses.

Intensive Long-Term Professional Development Through the Summer Institute for Instructional Technology

A final model for faculty professional development, the Summer Institute for Instructional Technology (SIIT), is hosted each summer by The Center for Teaching and Learning at our regional university. The SIIT is a 2-week intensive workshop where participants create new courses or redesign old courses, leveraging a variety of technology resources to create effective learning contexts. The goals of the SIIT are to provide opportunities for faculty to develop high-quality instruction through a variety of technological means, provide resources for faculty to establish and maintain effective online and computer-enhanced courses, and to create a pool of faculty expertise that fosters the exploration and effective implementation of technology-leveraged teaching and learning. The SIIT, much like the graduate course on Google Summits, includes a mix of face-to-face workshops, technology demonstrations, and virtual sessions that place the teacher in the position of online learner as he or she works with the instructional technologies to complete projects in synchronous and asynchronous environments.

The SIIT's learner-centered approach is modeled after the NWP Summer Institute, where teachers come together to watch experienced faculty demonstrate best practices in writing. In the SIIT, experienced faculty demonstrate how they integrate technology to meet learning outcomes in their classroom using various technologies over the course of 5 days. In our most recent SIIT, faculty from the education program demonstrated how to use Google Presentations to create jigsaw assignments in their teacher education courses. Anthropology and psychology faculty demonstrated how to use self-created instructional videos to orient students with important course materials and prepare them for exams and written assignments. English faculty demonstrated the use of the free recording software Audacity to provide audio feedback on student essays. Finally, the faculty provided participants with hands-on instruction in using the different technologies, and SIIT participants discussed how the demonstrations might be implemented in their classrooms.

After viewing the demonstrations, SIIT participants were then immersed in the use of instructional technology and became "virtual students" for a 4-day period. During this time, teachers met both synchronously and asynchronously online to practice using a variety of technologies centered on facilitating communication and increasing instructor presence in online classrooms. Participants met in a small virtual group synchronously using Google Hangouts, which they were required to record and post to YouTube in order to share their discussion with other class participants. They explored the interactive components of the learning management system by participating in quizzes and assignments that were adaptive released (requiring them to achieve certain scores on quizzes and assignments before additional materials became available) and by using online discussion boards and other asynchronous features to communicate and collaborate with other participants. The SIIT's online component concluded with participants completing an online group activity using technologies their students could access, then reflecting on the use of these technologies based on their practical application in their online and computer-enhanced classrooms.

When participants returned to the face-to-face sessions in the institute, they demonstrated one way that they have designed or redesigned a unit of their course to implement instructional technologies. Business faculty created videos using Camtasia, Jing, or ScreenFlow to provide introductory materials to help online students navigate the learning management system in online classes. Math faculty created Educreations videos (short online videos that allow faculty to capture whiteboard drawings with voice-over instructions, much like the Khan Academy videos) and paired the videos with adaptive release quizzes to ensure that students reviewed the videos and understood the basic concepts before moving on to more complex conceptual material.

Participants in the SIIT leave the professional development experience with completed instructional units that incorporate technology. During the course of the following school year, the SIIT coordinator works with teachers as they implement technology in the classroom and continues to connect them with innovative technologies and provide support and encouragement as needed. Participants then serve as knowledge brokers in their content areas within their schools, modeling the teacher-consultant philosophy of the NWP.

The CCSS acknowledge that students must learn both critical and functional aspects of technoliteracy. In kind, professional development opportunities must integrate the technical aspects of educational technology as well as the pedagogy, goals, and outcomes in the class. Technology integration was demonstrated to be more effective in conjunction with content-specific concerns as well. Matching pedagogy with technological practice is a vital component of successful professional development experiences, just as teachers must meet the CCSS of both gathering authoritative digital sources (content) and creating effective digital documents (function). For those faculty and pre-service teachers who are not as experienced with technology, modeling, implementation, and reflection are keys to becoming more comfortable with technology in the classroom. In order for teachers to model the critical and functional components of technoliteracy, they must first have experiences with those components themselves.

Ertmer (2005) found that "[i]f beliefs are formed through personal experience, then changes in beliefs might also be facilitated through experience" (32). With this in mind, professional development experiences utilizing technology might be more effective through "starting with relatively simple uses" rather than expecting teachers to use technology to "achieve high-end instructional goals" (33). Vicarious experiences (i.e., modeling) also increase the tendency of students in pre-service programs to use technology because "having access to multiple models increases both the amount of information available about how to accomplish the performance and the probability that observers will perceive themselves as similar to at least one of the models, thus increasing their confidence for also performing successfully" (33). Finally, reflection on their technology practices will help pre-service and veteran faculty examine the connections between content and technology (King 2002; Laferriere, Lamon, and Chan 2006). This model reflects Anchor Writing Standard 6 as students practice the recursive process of "produc[ing], publish[ing], and updat[ing] individual or shared writing products in response to ongoing feedback, including new arguments or information" (CCSSO and NGA 2010, W.11–12.6).

This long-term intensive model of professional development addresses the elements identified by Lee Ehman, Curtis Bonk, and Lisa Yamagata-Lynch (2005) as necessary for successfully accomplishing technology integration in schools. First, the SIIT participants are nominated for the institute, but they must also complete applications that demonstrate that they are willing and desire to participate, thus avoiding the problem of working with "Shanghaied Teachers." Secondly, teachers are provided a "reasonable technology environment in which to work" (264), one that invites them to bring in their own equipment but also provides access to equipment that they would find in their classrooms. Finally, participants are provided numerous opportunities to experience what their students would experience in similar situations, including what they would experience as students using both synchronous and asynchronous technologies. While longitudinal data is still being collected regarding the levels of technology integration as a result of the SIIT, teachers who have participated in the SIIT have gone on to co-author articles with other participants (multiple chapters are currently submitted for review) and have informally reported back to their cohorts regarding their technology implementation in the classroom.

The SIIT models how teachers can take the principles of mini-lessons, or demos, followed by hands-on practice and presentation to the classroom in order to implement the CCSS involving technology. Teachers might demonstrate how they solved a problem or created an artifact using a particular tool, cloud-based (i.e., Google or similar) or otherwise. The teacher can then challenge students to identify an issue from the content of the course and create a project using similar tools (or tools with which they are familiar). Students can then come back to the classroom to demonstrate their own solutions to the challenges, incorporating technologies in the process of solving their challenges just as the teachers do in the initial demonstrations.

Conclusions and Implications for Implementation

Each of the pre-service and professional development opportunities outlined here is intended to provide participants with models that they can turn around and hopefully replicate in their classrooms to design activities to meet the CCSS related to media literacy and technology. Leu and colleagues (2011) suggest:

> To be literate today often means being able to use some combination of blogs, wikis, texting, search engines, Facebook, Foursquare, Google Docs, Skype, Chrome, iMovie, Contribute, Basecamp, or many other relatively

new technologies, including thousands of mobile applications, or "apps." To be literate tomorrow will be defined by even newer technologies that have yet to appear and even newer social practices that we will create to meet unanticipated needs. (6)

In order to facilitate literacy development and prepare both our educators and their students for the future, impactful professional development opportunities must be a priority.

Perhaps the biggest hurdle within the CCSS and implementation is the need for an incredible amount of professional development. Educators must be given ample opportunities to discuss and experience meaningful professional development that allows them to effectively implement the CCSS. This kind of professional development is transformative in 21st-century education models, as current professional development often centers on data crunching and analysis of high stakes testing. The kind of professional development that we have presented in this chapter allows teachers to be full participants in hands-on learning and application. Further, teachers must be provided ample time to explore and reflect upon their teaching as well as formulate rubrics and common performance-based assessment tools. Educators must be given the valuable time necessary to experience technologies, to "digitally do" what they ask of their students.

Endnotes

1. This Google Schedule can be found at sites.google.com/a/lagrandesd.org/summit 12/home.
2. This Google Site can be found at sites.google.com/a/eou.edu/ed510_sp12/home.

References

Bennett, Sue, Karl Maton, and Lisa Kervin. 2008. "The 'Digital Natives' Debate: A Critical Review of the Evidence." *British Journal of Educational Technology* 39 (5): 775–786.

Boss, Suzie. 2012. "The Challenge of Assessing Project-Based Learning." *District Administration* 48 (9): 46–50.

Brinkerhoff, Jonathan. 2006. "Effects of a Long-Duration, Professional Development Academy on Technology Skills, Computer Self-Efficacy, and Technology Integration Beliefs and Practices." *Journal of Research on Technology in Education* 39 (1): 22–43.

Chen, Rong-Ji. 2010. "Investigating Models for Pre-Service Teachers' Use of Technology to Support Student-Centered Learning." *Computers and Education* 55 (1): 32–42.

Conley, David T. 2011. "Building on the Common Core." *Educational Leadership* 68 (6): 16–20.

Council of Chief State School Officers and National Governors Association. 2010. *Common Core State Standards for English Language Arts and Literacy in History/Social Studies, Science, and Technical Subjects*. Washington, DC: National Governors Association Center for Best Practices, Council of Chief State School Officers. Accessed February 10, 2014. www.corestandards.org/assets/CCSSI_ELA%20Standards.pdf.

Ehman, Lee, Curtis Bonk, and Lisa Yamagata-Lynch. 2005. "A Model of Teacher Professional Development to Support Technology Integration." *AACE Journal* 13 (3): 251–270.

Ertmer, Peggy A. 2005. "Teacher Pedagogical Beliefs: The Final Frontier in Our Quest for Technology Integration?" *Educational Technology Research and Development* 53 (4): 25–39.

Jaeger, Paige. 2012. "We Don't Live in a Multiple-Choice World: Inquiry and the Common Core." *Library Media Connection* 30 (4): 10–12.

King, Kathleen P. 2002. "Educational Technology Professional Development as Transformative Learning Opportunities." *Computers and Education* 39 (3): 283–297.

Laferriere, Therese, Mary Lamon, and Carol Chan. 2006. "Emerging E-Trends and Models in Teacher Education and Professional Development." *Teaching Education* 17 (1): 75–90.

Lenhart, Amanda. 2012. "Teens and Online Video." *Pew Internet & American Life Project*. Accessed February 10, 2014. www.pewinternet.org/Reports/2012/Teens-and-online-video/Findings.aspx.

Lenhart, Amanda, Kristen Purcell, Aaron Smith, and Kathryn Zichuhr. 2010. "Social Media and Young Adults." *Pew Internet & American Life Project*. Accessed February 10, 2014. www.pewinternet.org/Reports/2010/Social-Media-and-Young-Adults/Summary-of-Findings.aspx.

Leu, Donald J., J. Gregory McVerry, W. Ian O'Byrne, Carita Killi, Lisa Zawilinski, Heidi-Everett-Cacopardo, et al. 2011. "The New Literacies of Online Reading Comprehension: Expanding the Literacy and Learning Curriculum." *Journal of Adolescent & Adult Literacy* 55 (1): 5–14.

Plair, Sandra Kay. 2008. "Revamping Professional Development for Technology Integration and Fluency. *Clearing House,* 82 (2): 70–74.

Prensky, Marc. 2001. "Digital Natives, Digital Immigrants." *On the Horizon* 9 (5): 1–6. Accessed February 10, 2014. www.marcprensky.com/writing/Prensky%20-%20Digital%20Natives,%20Digital%20Immigrants%20-%20Part1.pdf.

Railsback, Jennifer. 2002. *Project-Based Instruction: Creating Excitement for Learning*. Portland, OR: Northwest Regional Educational Laboratory. Accessed February 10, 2014. educationnorthwest.org/webfm_send/460.

Reilly, Erin B. 2011. "Participatory Learning Environments and Collective Meaning Making Practice." *Journal of Media Literacy Education* 3 (1): 6–7.

Saltman, Dave. 2012. "Student-Directed Learning Comes of Age." *Education Digest: Essential Readings Condensed For Quick Review* 77 (7): 4–8.

Schneckenberg, Dirk. 2010. "What Is e-Competence? Conceptual Framework and Implications for Faculty Engagement." In *Changing Cultures in Higher Education: Moving Ahead to Future Learning*, edited by Ulf-Daniel Ehlers and Dirk Schneckenberg, 239–256. New York: Springer International.

Wesch, Michael. 2008. "A Portal to Media Literacy." Presentation at the University of Manitoba, Winnipeg, June 17. YouTube. 10 July. Accessed February 10, 2014. www.youtube.com/watch?v=J4yApagnr0s.

Appendix A: What Is Project-Based Learning?

PBL is a method for students to use multiple abilities to create a project that is both content and standards critical. Students create projects either as an initial introduction to a unit or as a final compilation of their learning of the content of the unit. The final project may be written, electronic, performance-based, or any other process that follows best practices.

The teacher of the course must create the project that includes the following:

- Specific goals and objectives
- A clear outline of procedures and desired outcomes
- A step-by-step process
- A rubric that includes values and rationale for points
- Defined due dates and expectations for completion
- A possibility of student choice (this gives variance to the student and enables the teacher to grade multiple projects without finding the grading tedious)

The project must be organized in a sequential fashion and should enable the student to understand the requirements with minimal additional guidelines from the teacher. This provides both the student and the teacher with an understanding of what is required and when it is due.

In a project, one can also add additional points for extra inclusions (something specialized, beyond the realm of the basic requirements). However, this is up to the teacher and not required.

Projects are required to be graded with consideration of the strict rubric. The rubric should be strict enough that the grade of A is not attainable by all. This leads to grade inflation. The rubric should guide the grading. But, it also needs to be challenging to meet needs of the top students. This is one of the INTASC standards: to have each student reach academic excellence.

Students may do the following as types of projects:

- Create a website, video, or website
- Do a specific study (inquiry-based)
- Write a paper, with research as a focus

So, the rubric would have to be flexible enough to incorporate many of Gardner's multiple intelligences.

©2012 Professor Ray Brown, Eastern Oregon University. Used with permission of the author.

Appendix B: Types of Project-Based Learning

Language Arts • Create a digital children's book based on a historical text • Create a website for grammar • Create a digital Pictionary of terms in reading	**Social Studies** • Develop a digital biography of a fictional character in time • Compare today's president with platform when elected • Do an interactive slide presentation on a historical event
Math • Compare cost of one teacher vs. one sport • Consider the cost factor of building the Taj Mahal today • Use electronics to explain a mathematical theory	**Business** • Create a digital business plan • Create a business website • Create business cards, letterhead, and other promotional materials
Science • Complete an inquiry study • Research theories on medicine • Create a video on weather patterns	**Fine Arts** • Create a digital portfolio of original work • Teach, using technology, about an artist of early times • Investigate the use of fine art today
Foreign Language • Create a restaurant with menus and décor • Create a digital dictionary of proper slang • Create a digital children's book	**PE/Health** • Create a new game, combining the methods to other games • Use technology to teach about a health-related issue • Develop a design or structure of bones and muscles and explain what each part does

©2012 Professors Ray Brown and Tawnya Lubbes, Eastern Oregon University. Used with permission of the authors.

Appendix C: Project-Based Learning Checklist

- Standards listed—list the ones that are most obvious. No more than three.
- CCSS should be used as they apply to your content area.
- List of goals and objectives. Must be concrete and measurable.
- List of resources or materials student(s) will require (should include technology)
- Step-by-step process. What will student have to do to accomplish the task?
- Grading format (rubric)
- Extra component (not required)

- Checked for conventions in grammar, spelling, punctuation, and capitalization
- Due date

©2012 Professors Ray Brown and Tawnya Lubbes, Eastern Oregon University. Used with permission of the authors.

Appendix D: Project-Based Learning Rubric

	Creation of Project 50 points	Rubric of Project 10 points	Completion of Another's Project 25 Points	Grading Rationale 5 Points	Attendance/Tardiness 10 points
Superior	45–50 Project has all of the components, is clear and sequential, and ready for student usage. No errors.	9–10 Detailed and very clear on expectations. Use of proper words and phrases.	23–25 Completed the project above the level of expectation. Exceeds many of the guidelines listed in the project.	5 Clearly explained to the student with ways to improve.	10 Always present and on time.
Advanced	40–44 Project may be missing one component or is not as clear. May require some minimal explanation. Minor errors.	8 Sufficient information to grade easily. Clear on the expectations. Use of proper words/phrases.	20–22 Completed the project above the level of expectation. Meets the guidelines listed in the project.	4 Clearly explained to the student.	8–9 Missed 1 day or late once.
Proficient	35–39 Project acceptable but could be missing one or more components. May require more explanation to clarify the project. A few errors.	7 Sufficient but some areas might require interpretation. Expectations are listed, but not always clear.	17–19 Completed the project. Follows most of the guidelines listed in the project.	3 Explained to the student.	6–7 Missed 2 days or late twice.
Adequate	30–34 Project vague. Missing many components. May require rewriting. Many errors.	6 Vague and not specific in grading.	15–16 Completed most of the project. Limited in following the guidelines.	2 Explained to the student, but a little vague.	4–5 Missed 3 days or late three times.
Basic	29 or less What project?	5 or less Poorly constructed.	14 or less Missing much or created own guidelines.	0–1 Unclear explanation.	0–3 Missed 4 days or late four times.
Score/Comments					

©2012 Professors Ray Brown and Tawnya Lubbes, Eastern Oregon University. Used with permission of the authors.

CHAPTER 17

Moving Beyond Transmission to Practice
Training Teachers to Be Digital Writers

Keri Franklin and Kathy Gibson

The workshop we envisioned 5 years prior had slowly, but completely, lost its original focus. A week with kindergarten through university teachers in a digital writing institute had become a week spent learning how to create one digital story. We—Keri Franklin, a university professor and director of the local National Writing Project (NWP) site, and Kathy Gibson, a middle and high school English Language Arts (ELA) teacher—recognized that some people might have decided to attend the workshop to learn about technology. However, our goal was to provide professional development on digital literacies that focused first on the teaching of writing and second on how digital literacies develop our understanding of the teaching of writing.

As NWP teacher consultants, we privileged a more process-oriented approach that recognizes more than one way to teach writing. We feared that a focus on creating one product was leading institute participants to believe that asking students to complete one digital story as a unit during the semester would lead them to feel as if they had finished teaching digital literacies. For us, digital literacies are more than the completion of one digital composition. Therefore, the revised digital writing workshop we designed aimed to help K–12 teachers and librarians imagine the complexities and opportunities of composing with words, images, and audio, and to explore tools available—hopefully free ones—that would change how they would teach each day throughout the year, not just one week.

This chapter will help other professional development providers—K–12 ELA teachers and librarians responsible for sharing ideas for teaching digital literacies to colleagues—to have a theory of action, a toolkit of activities aligned with the Common Core State Standards (CCSS) and the Framework for Success in Postsecondary Writing (Framework), a sense of potential obstacles to consider, and recommendations for future professional development planning. First, we share the core activities and content of the digital writing institutes and how these digital writing events align with the CCSS and the Framework. Next, we describe in detail institute activities and their alignment with the CCSS, and we also offer reflections from institute participants. Finally, we provide recommendations for important elements to include in the professional development that move the workshop beyond learning how to do technology to learning how digital literacies and writing work together.

Aligning Our Institute With the CCSS and the Framework

Several documents defined our theory of action, as we planned the institute: the CCSS (Council of Chief State School Officers [CCSSO] and National Governors Association [NGA] 2010), the Framework (Council of Writing Program Administrators [CWPA], National Council of Teachers of English [NCTE], and NWP 2011), state teacher standards, and Troy Hicks's *The Digital Writing Workshop* (2009). (For more discussion of connections between the CCSS and the Framework, see Chapters 4 and 5 in this volume.)

The goals for the institute were passed out to participants in the workshop on the first day and included a description of how the "habits of mind," as articulated within the Framework, fit with the learning planned for the week:

> What's important is that we attempt to exhibit and use these habits of mind during all of our workshop. So, be curious, open, engaged, creative, persistent, responsible, flexible, and metacognitive. Use your rhetorical knowledge, critical thinking, experience writing as a process, and learn to compose in multiple environments. (Franklin and Gibson 2012, 5)

For many institute participants, writing and sharing in a collaborative environment that encourages risk-taking and reflection can be one of the most satisfying endeavors, or it can be one of the most daunting. Throw in the challenge of learning new technology, and hesitant writers often become overwhelmed. Based on this knowledge, we recommend carefully scaffolding writing in the institute to build confidence. Table 17.1 describes the alignment of the CCSS, the Framework, and activities in the institute. Table 17.2 provides a general description of the 5-day face-to-face content of the professional development institute.

Writing Prior to the Institute: The Setup

Digital writing began prior to the institute. Participants posted a digital autobiographical sketch to a class wiki, which allowed them to meet Speaking and Listening Standard 6 for grades 6–12: "Adapt speech to a variety of contexts and tasks, demonstrating command of formal English when indicated or appropriate" (CCSSO and NGA 2010, 49). This pre-institute writing helped us as institute leaders learn about participants' digital writing background and current experience while at the same time assessing their troubleshooting skills in the process of writing on a wiki—a new experience for some. We provided directions for posting to the wiki and answered questions via email. The emails

Table 17.1   CCSS and Framework Alignment

Activity	CCSS	Framework Habits of Mind	Framework Experiences	Time Frame
The Setup	W.6–12.2; W.6–12.6	Openness (4), Responsibility (5)	Rhetorical Knowledge (6), Writing Process (8)	Pre-Writing prior to the Institute
The Blog: Writer's Notebook	W.6–12.2; W.6–12.6	Persistence (4), Openness (4), Flexibility (5)	Rhetorical Knowledge (6), Writing Process (8)	Used multiple times daily for freewriting and processing
Focus on First Drafts	W.6–12.5	Curiosity (4), Creativity (4–5), Persistence (5)	Rhetorical Knowledge (6), Writing Processes (8)	Multiple times during the week
Podcast	W.6–12.4; W.6–12.7; SL.6–12.5	Creativity (4–5), Flexibility (5), Persistence (5)	Rhetorical Knowledge (6), Critical Thinking (7), Conventions (9)	30 minutes
RSS Feed (Subscribe to the blog of each participant)	W.6–12.5; W.6–12.6; SL.6–12.1	Curiosity (4), Engagement (4)	Critical Thinking (7)	60 minutes
Five Frame Story	W.6–12.7; SL.6–12.5	Creativity (4–5), Openness (4)	Critical Thinking (7)	Draft 1–1.5 hours; revised draft 1.5 hours
Ira Glass Series and Quickwrites		Engagement (4), Creativity (4–5)	Critical Thinking (7)	60 minutes with discussion and freewriting
Digital Story	W.6–12.2; W.6–12.7; SL.6–12.2	Persistence (5), Curiosity (4), Creativity (4–5)	Rhetorical Knowledge (6), Critical Thinking (7), Developing Flexible Writing Processes (8), Conventions (9)	Four hours in class over 2 days with additional work out of class
Professional Piece	W.6–12.8; L.6–12.1	Curiosity (4), Responsibility (5), Metacognition (5)	Critical Thinking (7), Composing in Multiple Environments, Conventions (9)	Final piece completed at the end of the 2-week institute
Process Writing	W.6–12.5; W.6–12.10	Flexibility (4), Metacognition (5)	Developing Flexible Writing Processes (8)	At the conclusion of each digital experience
Small Writing Groups (face-to-face and online)	W.6–12.5; W.6–12.6; SL.6–12.1	Flexibility (4), Engagement (4)	Developing Flexible Writing Processes (8)	Daily

we received from participants also provided us with additional informal assessment information on their ability to troubleshoot new digital writing experiences. Later, we used this information to create heterogeneous small writing groups.

The autobiographical sketch posted to the wiki was modeled after The Setup—an RSS feed that can be subscribed to via Flipboard or an iPad, iPhone, and Android application that allows users to aggregate news and information of their choice in a magazine format. The

Table 17.2 General Description of Main Topics

Day 1	Day 2	Day 3	Day 4	Day 5
Freewriting on the blog (What is digital writing versus traditional writing?)	Freewriting with reflection	Digital Storytelling	Group writing reflecting on progress and posting to blog	Blog post on the week
Using RSS feed to connect to class blogs	Focus on Image rather than Word	Ira Glass on Digital Storytelling (2009) videos	Crafting the digital story	Flipped classroom discussion
Begin a list of writing territories	Five Frame Story using only pictures to tell a story	Reflective writing on what makes a good digital story posted to blog	iMovie and Movie Maker	Jing, Educreations, Screenr, iShowU, ScreenToaster
Partner interview and recording	Animoto, PhotoStory, iMovie, Prezi, iPhoto	"Educational Uses of Digital Storytelling" video from University of Houston	Sharing draft of story with group	Posting digital story to blog
Audacity and GarageBand	"Days With My Father" by Philip Toledano (2012)	Create draft of digital story	Revising	Individual presentations and discussions of polished professional piece requirements
VoiceThread	Sandbox time	Collect images for story		Plan for the online writing conference next week with group
Grammar Girl example	Create second photo essay including sound, music, effects	Sandbox time		
Sandbox time	Post photo essay to blog	"Memory" by Salomeja Karaseviciute (2012)		
Create a podcast from interview and post to blog	Create questions for Troy Hicks on Google Hangout on Google Doc	Troy Hicks presentation and questions		

Setup (2012) is a short interview focused on people from a variety of disciplines, from comedians to computer engineers to musicians. The question and answer describes the "things people use to get stuff done." The "stuff" in this case refers to the digital tools respondents currently use along with their dream digital tools. Figure 17.1 shows how one institute participant used The Setup (2012) as a model and example, posting a picture and answering the following questions:[1]

- Who am I and what do I do?

- How has digital writing affected me? What do I need to learn?
- Where can you find me online?

Who I Am
I'm a small-town kid who left home in search of … another small town. Originally from Alberta, I now live in Bostwick with my wife, Karen, and our three kids. Primarily, I teach the composition courses at the high school, but I also coach football and sponsor our school's academic team. When not fulfilling professional or familial responsibilities, I enjoy:
- Buying books even if I don't know when I'll read them
- Purchasing trendy guitar gear to compensate for lack of actual talent
- Sitting in a boat with a pole (catching fish is sometimes a nice bonus)
- Laughing at my own jokes in front of my wife
- Trying to explain to others why I like *Big Trouble in Little China* so much

My Gear
I currently do most of my work on my iMac at home, but I'm starting to do more with my iPad these days. Since I've started working more on the iPad, I've been using Dropbox as my primary storage medium. This works well for me because I have a habit of losing things; I'm not sure I could even count the number of thumb drives I've misplaced.

Most of my tech gadgets are Apple products for three reasons:
- I was raised on them.
- I feel like they are superior products.
- I'm an easy target for slick marketing.

One gadget I use that isn't an Apple product is my cell phone. My wife and I had to cut some costs a few years back when she changed jobs, and a phone with a data plan became less of a priority. Thus, I'm rolling on with some Samsung phone that is essentially useless in any task beyond calling or texting.

I don't mind talking tech stuff, but I actually prefer to talk guitar gear; ask my wife and she'll back me up on that. Thus, here's a link to a quick YouTube rundown of the gear I'd rather be using than computers, tablets, or phones (the "important" gear).

Digital Writing and Me
I consume digital writing constantly through blogs and online publications; I'm an avid blogger and a Twitter addict. I've also used blogs and wikis to manage a few of my courses at BHS. However, I don't think I've truly tapped into all the possibilities that digital writing offers me in my classroom. Digital writing offers great opportunities for giving student writing an authentic purpose and authentic audience, so it's kind of sad that I haven't made it more of a focus in my classroom.

What Do I Need to Learn?
In this course, I want to learn how to:
- Incorporate digital writing as part of the writer's workshop model
- Maximize the potential digital writing has as an authentic instructional tool

Outside of this course, I want to learn:
- Patience
- How to keep my plants alive when temperatures are consistently over the century mark and rain seems like a myth

John Online
- Twitter: [deleted for confidentiality]
- Facebook: I'm a quitter. Tired of seeing former students posting pics they'll regret, tired of female friends' daily pregnancy updates, tired of game requests. If I need to reactivate it for this class, I will.
- Blogger: [deleted for confidentiality] (It's B-material, folks. I'm a work in progress.)

Figure 17.1   Example of writing assignment

This fairly low stakes writing assignment helped us as professional development providers to understand existing digital behaviors and knowledge. The same activity would be helpful working with K–12 ELA teachers and librarians or in a classroom of K–12 students. What kinds of digital backgrounds do they have? How do they use their phone? Are they on Facebook or Twitter? Answers to these questions give us a head start in understanding and then creating a digital learning community.

The Blog: A Writer's Notebook

Our first activity on the first day of the institute was to write in our digital Writer's Notebook. Each morning of the institute began with freewriting in this notebook/blog as encouraged by Anchor Standard for Writing 6: "Use technology, including the internet, to produce and publish writing and to interact and collaborate with others" (CCSSO and NGA 2010, 18). Using Peter Elbow's (1998) ground rules for freewriting, participants wrote without stopping for a period of time. We began with small amounts of time, building from 5 to 10 minutes to 20 minutes by the end of the institute. No one had to type quickly; the goal was to keep the keys clicking. Based on Hicks's (2009) suggestion, the blog became our institute portfolio. Participants saved daily freewriting, metacognitive writing, and early, middle, and late drafts of work on their blog. We asked them to save their writing as a draft, returning later to cull pieces of the freewriting for publication.

The blog helped us to meet several goals. First, institute participants experienced using a low-stakes writing and low-stakes free digital tool that allowed them (and hopefully someday the students in their classes) to collect writing over time as emphasized in Anchor Standard for Writing 7: "Conduct short as well as more sustained research projects based on focused questions, demonstrating understanding of the subject under investigation" (CCSSO and NGA 2010, 18). Daily low-stakes writing helped to generate ideas, build writing fluency, and give participants a collection to cull second drafts from later. Second, each participant subscribed to their fellow participants' blogs via an RSS feed. So, in addition to writing, participants viewed, read, and shared daily writing online. Finally, writing on the blog gave them the experience of publishing writing to the internet, albeit to a small audience. The impact of the Writer's Notebook could be seen in reflections such as this one:

> What used to be so stiff and frustrating suddenly began to flow as the week went on. Because there was no guarantee that I would publish the freewriting to my blog, I could write without a thought to judgments. I couldn't wait to write, knowing that this time I would likely reach those thoughts that had been trapped. My thinking began to flow, especially as I reaffirmed the thoughts by sharing them and building upon them at my table with like-minded learners. What I produced was unaltered, authentic reactions to the day's events. I couldn't regurgitate something that everyone else was saying, because everyone's experiences were different and unique to what they wanted to take away. We all worked at the pace we needed to set for ourselves, and we all learned what we needed to.

The blogs provided participants with the digital means to share works in progress with an authentic audience and to receive peer responses. The Writer's Notebook became a portfolio and home to all of the writing, both early and late drafts, that the participants completed.

Podcasts

After freewriting on the blog and reading each other's blogs in the first hour of the first day, we quickly moved to our next digital writing event: podcasts, or quick writes in the form of the spoken word.

The directions for the podcast activity included demonstrating briefly how to record audio using GarageBand or Audacity, partnering participants based on level of digital expertise we gleaned from The Setup, asking them to interview each other about their digital writing beliefs, and recording the interviews, using technology as encouraged by Anchor Standard for Writing 6 to produce and publish writing.

We gave the partners just minutes to edit the recordings into a short one-minute podcast which they posted to their blogs. One participant describes the process of his podcasting partnership:

> [My partner] and I came up with interview questions to guide our podcasts and break them up into more editable bits. We asked each other questions relating to the meaning of digital writing and the approach to teaching it in a writing classroom. We had completely different answers to these questions due to our different experiences with digital writing. I have taught digital writing in a college classroom for the past year, but she is preparing to teach high school English in the fall. Our students and teaching atmospheres are completely different, so our questions concerning our approach to teaching digital writing are a bit different. Once we came up with our questions, we used Garage Band to record our interviews. We recorded separate tracks for each question to make editing easier. Having the questions prepared ahead of time really cut down on the "Uhh … uhh … I don't know what to say" moments.

William and his partner discovered solutions to problems raised with the addition of an audio component to writing. Should you record one long track or several shorter ones? Should you script questions and answers ahead of time? Each team found a solution that worked to satisfy the problems they encountered without thorough directions. They problem solved as they created the podcast. After the first round of trial and error, institute participants created a second podcast that served as a second draft posted to their Writer's Notebook blog.

We envisioned and brainstormed with the group regarding many uses of podcasts. For example, ELA teachers and librarians can use this technology to assist reluctant writers through recorded speech, something encouraged by the CCSS in Anchor Standard for Speaking and Listening 2: "Integrate and evaluate information presented in diverse media and formats, including visually, quantitatively, and orally"

(CCSSO and NGA 2010, 22). An understanding of microphone use and techniques as well as public speaking can help ELA teachers and library/media specialists demonstrate to students how to create stronger recordings. In terms of writing, podcasts help teach the concept of "voice" in writing, broadening the idea with the addition of a real voice narrating a text. A podcast requires thought about text and requires thinking about tempo in spoken language. In the process, other questions often arise as well: How does a podcast require a writer to think differently about putting together written text? Should music or sound effects be included? Questions like these require writers to think more deeply about rhetorical effects for written and spoken language. Furthermore, with the opportunity to think through how the text, video, and audio come together in a digital composition, participants can begin to understand how digital writing brings together all the elements of the writing process: generating ideas, composing content, editing, and thinking critically.

RSS Feeds

Using the now defunct Google Reader as our RSS feed reader helped students to connect their blogs and allowed us to easily follow one another and offer comments, a collaboration supported by Anchor Standard for Writing 6. Alternatives to Google Reader currently include Feedly, Netvibes, Pulse, and NewsBlur. The RSS feed can become a valuable research tool when institute participants begin to seek out ideas, other blogs, and newsfeeds on topics that interest them and subscribe to these feeds as they grow their knowledge base (Hicks 2009). ELA teachers and librarians can demonstrate how to set up a reader to search for particular research topics and funnel the results into the student's chosen feed reader for a quick review. Using an RSS feed reader can save a great deal of time and effort as students conduct online research. Social bookmarking tools such as Diigo or Delicious provide another level of search and save techniques with the unique ability to share search findings with particular groups or with the world. One of our institute participants remarked that using Google Reader provided "a chance to move away from the textbook as the central way of teaching my students and using the world as a source of information for my students." The RSS feeds linked to each other's blogs and allowed participants to reflect on what others in the workshop were doing and thinking. Often, this allowed them to find solutions to problems they encountered through the week simply by reading how a classmate found a solution to an issue.

Five Frame Story

ELA teachers and librarians are experts of the written word, but standards for information/media literacy as well as the CCSS require an increased consciousness of visual and audio-based media. These expert practitioners may not respond as readily when asked to "read" a photo or pick apart the elements of a short film. Gibson used the Five Frame Story activity with her middle and high school students (for a rich discussion of this activity, see Chapter 12 in this volume). The idea originated from the photo sharing website Flickr. Hicks (2009) describes the assignment in *The Digital Writing Workshop*. Institute participants found five images and placed them in an order to tell a story without words or sound. This assignment works best with participants taking original photos, but with a shortened time frame our participants used photos already on their computers or available online to create an image-based text. One participant reflected on the process of creating a Five Frame Story this way:

> Taking unrelated objects and events, I created transitions. Creating those connections and synapses in my rusty brain forced me to examine the pictures and what they stood for. I made meaning out of a landscape or object, just as I would when analyzing literature. I created metaphors and a general theme. I had to summarize information and communicate using unexpected methods.

Using personal photos, participants avoided copyright infringement when publishing their Five Frame Stories online. However, copyright, the use of Creative Commons licensed photos, and learning to cite sources for all photos found online are significant issues that should always be discussed. Creative Commons licensing falls between the two extremes of "all rights reserved" copyright and "use it anytime you wish" public domain. Fair Use guidelines do allow students to use copyrighted materials based on four criteria, which include purpose and character of the use, the nature of the work, the amount of the work used, and the effect of the use on the value of the work. ELA teachers and librarians can work together to educate students about Fair Use and help them learn to create their own copyright licenses through Creative Commons licensing.

The Five Frame Story's focus on images took teachers out of the zone of expert practitioner and placed them squarely in the zone of learner. ELA teachers and librarians will need to guide students through the process of "reading" visual elements promoted by Anchor Standard for Writing 6 in particular. Teachers and students can learn how to read visual elements by answering the following questions:

- What does the photo convey?
- Are multiple meanings possible?
- Can the photos be rearranged to convey a different message or mood?
- How will issues of copyright be addressed?

By starting simply with a few images, participants can begin to develop ideas about visual literacy. The connections between composing a text with words and a text with images become clear as participants work through this short assignment. The next assignment can build on the first image-only project. Participants can combine visual, text, or sound to expand their thinking about digital compositions in a relatively easy way. Learning how to find the right images beyond a Google Images search and learning how to use an image while acknowledging copyright issues are critical elements of these first projects. Students can re-cut, reframe, and reuse when following guidelines of Fair Use and Creative Commons licensing, and as content creators they can make use of the protections offered by copyright laws.

Five Frame Stories do not take much time, but reflections from participants show that the short assignment resonated with them. One participant noted, "I expected the visuals to help make a more engaging story, but I was surprised by how much they deepened the audience's understanding of events." Here, the participant describes in his blog post how a story he had related many times to family and friends made a greater emotional impact after he combined photos with audio.

New literacies require a broadened ability to analyze and think critically about images and sound as well as text, and how to use digital media to present projects as encouraged by the CCSS in Anchor Standard for Speaking and Listening 5: "Make strategic use of digital media and visual displays of data to express information and enhance understanding of presentations" (CCSSO and NGA 2010, 22). Scaffolding both short and longer experiences helps participants understand how texts change when we communicate in multiple forms. After participants completed these short projects, we asked them to notice and write about how meaning is altered when we add spoken voice to the image. We also asked them to consider how the composing processes of writers, photographers, filmmakers, and musicians are similar, different, and sometimes complementary. One participant shared, "While I'm still not convinced that I could wholeheartedly say whether I begin composing in words or images first, I can say that the process of thinking about digital storytelling was revealing." While she could not at that time articulate what was revealed, we surmise that combining the visual and the audio forces writers to think differently about existing text-based composing processes.

Digital Stories

While digital storytelling had taken (too much) precedence in past institutes, we did not want to ignore it. Anchor Standard for Writing 7 asks students to "conduct short as well as more sustained research projects based on focused questions, demonstrating understanding of the subject under investigation" (CCSSO and NGA 2010, 18). Digital storytelling takes longer than a podcast, and we did not want participants to spend the bulk of the workshop working solely on one digital story.

For this reason, we let participants know that they would not leave with a final product with the time we had in the institute.

On the third day, we watched a series of videos featuring Ira Glass (from National Public Radio's *This American Life*) that described the elements of digital storytelling. His first two videos provided the next stimulus that challenged our expert teachers' learning. A good digital story, Glass says, unlike a short story, essay, or novel, must quickly and efficiently grab the listener and draw them in. We cannot write like we learned in high school with a topic sentence and then details filling in the rest. Instead of writing using this traditional model, a digital storyteller must start with an anecdote, a series of events progressing like a train to a destination. Along the way, we embed moments of reflection and questioning: What did this mean? Why did this happen? What will happen next? Institute participants watched the videos, and using Glass's questions, Franklin led the group in guided writing time for 15 to 20 minutes. This writing helped generate ideas and provided participants with a sense of a longer digital piece they wanted to compose. One participant offered the following response:

> Listening to Glass I found myself thinking something different; his "mini-story" was suspenseful and engaging because he *was reading it out loud*! Even the mild voice inflection that Glass exhibited in this case added something unique and potentially powerful to it. I then considered along these lines how it might benefit my students to read their stories out loud to themselves and hear the reading played back to them (podcast!). This could lead students to new experiments and discoveries with figurative language, tone, mood, and even "palatability" in their writing! This is an avenue that I could travel with my students even without having quick access to advanced technological resources.

Institute participants discovered what filmmakers have long known: the power of the written word grows when spoken by a real voice and combined with a compelling visual image. This combination often draws in students who are reluctant writers or readers and who may have a gift for art or music. Collaboration occurs when a student with a powerful voice is asked to speak the voiceover in a podcast for another student who fears speaking in public. The student with a strong visual eye becomes a gifted cinematographer for the class film project. Such collaborations occurred with teachers in our workshop as well.

By focusing on a compelling idea developed from the guided writing, institute participants created a draft for their first digital story, which Anchor Standard for Speaking and Listening 6 encourages with its emphasis on "adapt[ing] speech to a variety of contexts and communicative tasks" (CCSSO and NGA 2010, 22). Finding the right images, still photos, or video clips added an additional dimension to the project. A very brief tutorial (10 to 20 minutes) was then presented on how to use iMovie or Movie Maker to put words and images together. For our institute we asked the guiding question: What images would best illustrate their stories?

One of the participants wrote about the difficulty and importance of the early phases of the process: "It is so helpful to us as teachers, though, to experience both the difficulty and tremendous importance in choosing a topic and defining why it should matter to anyone at all. If no one can relate, or think about something in a new way, or take away some meaningful chunk from any portion, then it's useless." The process of tying music, narration, and image together to create a 5–8 minute digital story challenged institute participants to "gather relevant information from multiple print and digital sources" (CCSSO and NGA 2010, 18) as the CCSS emphasize in Anchor Standard for Writing 8.

Participants quickly moved from quiet corners composing print-based texts to authoring collaborative and public multimodal stories and sharing early drafts with one another:

> When I conferenced with [my partner], she gave me positive feedback but we both agreed that there were multiple stories in my story and maybe it was too broad for this assignment. Nonetheless I wrote the events down and was

> ready to make a digital story. By the time I got home, I changed my mind. I spent the evening writing the events for two more crazy experiences I have had that everyone loves to hear me tell. Of course, I act it out as well. So now I have three sets of events written! What I don't use now, I'll use in my classroom to model.

In the process of composing a digital story, which can include the filming of video, ELA teachers and librarians can teach students to set up and use video recording equipment for the best audio and video results. Concepts of camera placement, microphone use, and lighting, for example, can enhance the production quality of the work. The drafting process for the digital story also mirrors what occurs in a typical writing workshop: generating ideas, peer conferencing, responding, and revising. In our institute, participants further discussed layers of meanings uncovered by combining the visuals with words, along with the impact of using recordings of interviews with family members, friends, or experts on their chosen topics. Glass's questions can also be heard over and over as participants record and revise their stories. What's the "nugget?" What do you want your audience to leave with? Will anyone care to listen to my story? All of these questions can be used whether teaching K–12 students or leading professional development conferences.

Professional Piece

The professional piece was the final project for the course—and the one assignment that we asked participants to move beyond a first draft. We began by asking the group what their professional pieces meant to them. Because each participant was in a very different place with digital writing and teaching, several different approaches were taken. We encouraged some of the participants to create a piece for the NWP's *Digital Is* website and suggested that others could use the project to create lessons, lesson plans, or a unit plan for their upcoming courses. The goal for an assignment like this is to provide an opportunity for students to develop and refine a first draft and to apply and synthesize what they have already learned.

Small Writing Groups

Throughout the entire project, the sharing of information in both face-to-face and digital formats was essential. This exchange occurred multiple times a day through quick shares and also over extended periods of time when small writing groups worked together to share ideas and drafts of digital work. One participant's reflection describes the goals that he saw in these collaborations:

> When it comes to getting feedback on my movie, these are the questions I would like my group to answer: address, press, and bless. Did the story have momentum? Did it keep you interested? Did you learn anything? Did you feel like it was worth the 3 minutes you invested? Do you think it would be a decent icebreaker for my students? Getting feedback on these questions will help me edit my video to more effectively suit my audience.

Institute participants taught one another as they shared writing, ideas, struggles, and successes. The first week of the course was built around a face-to-face experience in a collaborative computer lab with laptops, projection capabilities, and wireless internet access. Through a mixture of whole class discussion, small group sharing, individual writing, and reflection, time and space within each day of the schedule was fully utilized and devoted to the completion of specific tasks.

This interaction was crucial to students negotiating technology problems. A K–12 student, just like an adult participant in our workshop, who struggles with a new piece of technology can seek help in the safety of the small group:

> My thinking changes when I am surrounded by such passionate, proficient, motivating learners. Everyone cares and everyone exchanges such meaningful, interesting ideas.

> When I see the work and the fun and the true growth/ enthusiasm of everyone around me, I am a different person. I will be lost when I don't have someone to share with, when conversations don't immediately turn to the process and what's the best way to facilitate learning, although I can share on the blogs of course.

During the second week of the institute, participants met online with their small writing groups using a variety of methods: Skype, Google Hangout, Blackboard, and face-to-face meetings. This type of flexibility allowed the groups to organize and choose what approach best suited their needs as learners, a type of collaboration and conversation the CCSS encourage in the Anchor Standards for Speaking and Listening 1 and 2.

Recommendations for Planning Professional Development With the CCSS and Framework in Mind

As we reviewed best practices in professional development and how the revised digital institute would be organized, several elements were non-negotiable if we were going to return the focus to digital literacies. This section describes our recommendation for planning a professional development seminar schedule.

Support Creativity in the Schedule

One habit of mind we cultivated from the Framework was creativity (CWPA, NCTE, and NWP 2011, 4–5). We suggest that workshop leaders emphasize a sense of play by including unstructured time each day for the participants to experiment with digital tools. The Sandbox was part of each day's schedule and was an hour or more that allowed participants to experiment and play with digital tools without interference or guidance. The goal of this time was to allow participants the opportunity to experience technology like their K–12 students and to provide them with the skills they need to observe the behaviors of next digital scholars. One of the attitudes we most admire in our students and want to help our participants experience is time to play, explore, and click a button without fear of making a mistake. K–12 students' openness to make a mistake and click away is a strength that is not often admired or encouraged.

Teachers, in contrast to the perceived behaviors of "fearless" digital natives, are often characterized as overly concerned with making even the smallest mistakes with digital tools. As adults and teachers, we are generally less adaptable, less willing to play, and we view troubleshooting as failure. Teachers need to experience writing and digital writing as students, and daily Sandbox time in the schedule makes this play time a priority.

Provide Skeleton Directions

Readers of this chapter may sense hesitation and concern on the part of the institute participants who have the tendency to ask, "How do we do this *right*?" In our experience, many teachers wanted to know exactly *how* to do something before beginning. We resisted providing step-by-step directions and instead encouraged participants to experiment and use their small writing groups and us—the facilitators—for assistance.

At the beginning of each new activity, we suggest leaders support participants by walking around the room and assisting with troubleshooting issues. At the same time, we suggest staying out of the way and allowing participants to figure things out—by clicking on links, making mistakes, trying something new, or working with more experienced colleagues. Scaffolding the events in class to begin with short, informal, and quick activities (like the podcast) that lead up to activities that require more time, thinking, and polishing is also encouraged.

Even with support, by the third day, it was clear some in the group would have much preferred a handout with specific directions on how to complete the task (e.g., podcast, Five Frame Story) with a high degree of competency. Teachers with less experience and those without NWP experience exhibited this tension more than experienced teachers. Professional development providers, just like the teachers they work with, should learn to read the room for this resistance. For us, a conversation about the tension was essential. Playing around with technology feels challenging and, at times, can cause feelings of anger or helplessness because a participant may not know exactly how to proceed. An open conversation about the challenges as teachers and institute participants helps to ground the group as well as allow it to reflect on how K–12 students may feel in similar learning situations.

Encourage First Draft Thinking and Writing

In a short professional development workshop, there is not enough time to polish every activity into a perfect final draft. A goal we recommend is to have as many experiences with digital writing as possible, and that means that perhaps only one will be taken beyond a first draft. The idea of not perfecting each assignment was challenging to many participants at first. For some, it helped them to think of each piece as an exercise, a practice at strengthening a skill. Asking institute participants to write many first drafts and selecting one digital piece to expand and present to the world by the end of the professional development institute seems like a more effective approach and it, in many ways, reflects the writing process. One participant describes her reaction:

> On our last break of the day, I sat outside by myself to recharge. (I am an introvert, which means that social interaction does not invigorate me, like extroverts; although I like it, it drains me dry.) I had two minor epiphanies that I probably already knew but needed to think about at that moment. I realized that it was good that I struggled, and that I am not a filmmaker. And, are you ready for this wallop of wisdom and insight? My project can have flaws—this is a draft! I kept hearing it from everyone throughout the day, but all of a sudden I just felt it. I became OK with the fact that my story was not 100%. I do not usually struggle with these types of projects. Technology is where I thrive, where I am asked for guidance. So, as we said today, it was all that much harder to bear that I wasn't getting it all the way today. But I think I'm slowly getting it through my head that I don't have to master it. When teaching, I don't

think you can master every piece of technology, and I have to be more realistic about my abilities.

The CCSS describe the importance of digital writing in literacy and also highlights language we find interesting: "The internet has accelerated the speed at which connections between speaking, listening, reading, and writing can be made, requiring that students be ready to use these modalities nearly simultaneously. Technology itself is changing quickly, creating a new urgency for students to be adaptable in response to change" (CCSSO and NGA 2010, 48). In general, teachers (that includes us) want to know, understand, and be able to articulate a subject before teaching students. This underlying belief, this sage on the stage mentality, could potentially keep teachers out of pace with digital literacies. Digital literacies change daily. If as teachers we wait to know everything before we teach our students, we lose the opportunity to allow student expertise into the classroom.

Write About the Process

Metacognition is found in both the CCSS and the Framework. Writing about the process of writing, while not a new idea, may be even more important to writing in the digital age, and it was a strategy that we felt had been lost in previous institutes. After many of our activities, we asked participants to go to their Writer's Notebook and recount the story of their writing process. We asked them to describe what they wrote, how they wrote it or produced it, what they learned, what worked, what did not, and what they would do differently.

Conclusion

Previously, our state standards had separate sections for writing, reading, math, science, social studies, and what the state called "Information and Communications Technology Literacy." The separation of technology led teachers to wonder who should teach this extra and separate section. The separation supported the idea of specialization and digital literacies as something "extra" and outside of content knowledge and expertise.

The integration of technology into the CCSS is an opportunity for professional development providers to help teachers understand how digital literacies have become everyone's responsibility.

The writing, reading, and researching habits of the next digital scholars in our classroom cannot be cultivated if we wait to know more than our students. To teach using the CCSS and Framework, we can learn from our students and experience writing in ways that mirror our students' learning. We must not wait to feel completely confident and knowledgeable with regard to digital literacies. That cannot happen. We recommend modeling for K–12 ELA teachers and librarians how to "jump in"—trying, troubleshooting, and working alongside students to learn. Through an inquiry model, we created professional development experiences for teachers to make mistakes, fail, and learn from each other. One participant shared this reflection in her final thoughts about the workshop:

> Speaking of my pieces, they are drafts; I have accepted that they are not perfect and something that can [be] built upon or something that can be discarded for another idea. One thing I know is that I can use them to show my students that even their teacher has to make a draft that may never see a final piece, but it is a process that helps me to find out what I really want to do.

And, finally, we share another participant's final thoughts:

> So what does this really have to do with the teaching of writing? Well, I've been thinking about that. Pen, paper, reading, research, all of these things have become somewhat second nature to me over the past 15 years, but for many of my students these wonderful tools are not necessarily second nature. Just as I've struggled and become frustrated over the past couple of days so do my students when we cover something in class that is simply unfamiliar to them. As a result I've come to have a rejuvenated appreciation

for the necessity for each of us writing teachers to exercise patience and understanding when introducing our students to new technology and news ways in which to communicate through the written word.

Through inquiry and play, reflection and practice, these teachers immersed themselves in the very world their students now inhabit and came a few steps closer to joining them in their classrooms.

Endnote

1. Individual citations of participant reflections do not appear in the reference list to keep participant identities anonymous. The Setup for the institute, which is cited in the references, is located on a separate wiki site that does not have corresponding entries in order to protect participant identities.

References

Council of Chief State School Officers and National Governors Association. 2010. *Common Core State Standards for English Language Arts and Literacy in History/Social Studies, Science, and Technical Subjects*. Washington, DC: National Governors Association Center for Best Practices, Council of Chief State School Officers. Accessed February 10, 2014. www.corestandards.org/assets/CCSSI_ELA%20Standards.pdf.

Council of Writing Program Administrators, National Council of Teachers of English, and National Writing Project. 2011. *Framework for Success in Postsecondary Writing*. January 2011. Accessed February 10, 2014. wpacouncil.org/files/framework-for-success-postsecondary-writing.pdf.

Elbow, Peter. 1998. *Writing Without Teachers*. New York: Oxford University Press.

Franklin, Keri, and Kathy Gibson. 2012. "A Digital Writing Workshop." Syllabus and handout, Missouri State University.

Glass, Ira. 2009. "Ira Glass on Digital Storytelling." *This American Life*. Public Radio International. YouTube. Accessed February 10, 2014. www.youtube.com/watch?v=loxJ3FtCJJA.

Hicks, Troy. 2009. *The Digital Writing Workshop*. Portsmouth, NH: Heinemann.

Karaseviciute, Salomeja. 2012. "Memory." *Center for Digital Storytelling*. Accessed February 10, 2014. www.youtube.com/watch?v=5STXZ93ZE4M.

The Setup. 2012. Accessed February 10, 2014. usesthis.com.

Toledano, Phillip. 2012. *Days With My Father*. Accessed February 10, 2014. www.dayswithmyfather.com.

University of Houston. 2014. *Educational Uses of Digital Storytelling*. Accessed February 7, 2014. digitalstorytelling.coe.uh.edu.

CONCLUSION

Teaching and Learning With the Common Core State Standards in the World of the Next Digital Scholar

James P. Purdy and Randall McClure

The Common Core State Standards (CCSS) have created quite a stir in the educational community. And they will likely continue to do so for the foreseeable future—for good reason. In addition to offering another set of standards used to measure our practices (and student performance), the CCSS cause us to reflect on what it means, at the core, to teach writing and research in a digital world (pun intended). In this conclusion, we synthesize what insights contributors to this collection offer regarding providing this instruction in response to the CCSS for the next digital scholar. Though their approaches and perspectives differ, taken together, chapters in this volume offer the following insights.

Number one: *The digital is integral.* Contributors to Part One point to trends in digital technology use for writing, researching, and reading that signal to us not just as editors, but as teachers ourselves that neither students nor teachers can treat the digital as peripheral in English Language Arts (ELA) education at any level. Not only are students coming to K–12 classrooms with literacy practices and habits of mind that are deeply embedded in and shaped by digital technologies, but the college and career worlds increasingly depend on and expect more sophisticated digital behaviors—points Troy Hicks makes in his Afterword to this volume and in his popular publications *Crafting Digital Writing* (2013) and *The Digital Writing Workshop* (2009) (see also Hicks and Turner 2013). The assignments, curricular initiatives, and teacher training programs presented by contributors in Parts Three, Four, and Five, respectively, emphasize this dependence and expectation. While, as several contributors point out, the CCSS could reflect this dependence and expectation even more—in some ways, the CCSS are still somewhat print-centric and do not embrace digital technologies as explicitly or fully as the other standards and outcomes documents discussed in Part Two—when contrasted with prior national standards documents of its kind, the CCSS represent a significant move toward defining literacy as entailing proficiency with finding, evaluating, creating, and using digital texts and technologies. Our contributors make it clear that ELA education must now involve information literacy instruction and that partnerships among ELA and writing teachers and media specialists and librarians are essential.

Number two: *Collaboration is key.* Collaboration should be foundational in meeting the CCSS. Individual teachers or librarians can feel powerless in the wake of a national standards movement like the CCSS. As this book models, however, together we—librarians, K–12 ELA teachers, university writing teachers, writing program administrators, and National Writing Project (NWP) members—can devise collective, responsive action. Contributors across all five parts of this book remind us that collaboration, among librarians, teachers, students, community members, administrators, universities, and/or secondary schools, is a productive, even necessary, response to educational imperatives like the CCSS. Indeed, the CCSS themselves stress the importance and value of collaboration for students, both in the overview of speaking and listening standards—"Students must learn to work together, express and listen carefully to ideas, integrate information from oral, visual, quantitative, and media sources, evaluate what they hear, use media and visual displays strategically to help achieve communicative purposes, and adapt speech to context and task" (Council of Chief State School Officers [CCSSO] and National Governors Association [NGA] 2010, 8)—and in Anchor Standard for Writing 6—"Use technology, including the internet, to produce and publish writing and to interact and collaborate with others" (18). Moreover, as Pamela B. Childers points out in her Foreword to this volume and elsewhere (Blumner and Childers 2011, Childers 2007, Childers and Lowry 2012), such collaborations are—and have been for decades—essential for instructors who participate in writing across the curriculum movements and who teach with technology. It is not incidental, therefore, that 11 (of 17) chapters in this collection are collaboratively authored, modeling the kinds of partnerships our contributors discuss. Even the singularly authored chapters are consciously and explicitly in dialogue with one another, listening to what other stakeholders across the educational community have to contribute to the education of the next digital scholar.

Number three: *The CCSS do not exist in isolation.* Just as teachers and librarians cannot best respond to the CCSS as isolated individuals, the CCSS themselves should not be treated in isolation. Contributors to Part Two remind us that the landscape of standards and outcomes documents is already rich and viewing the CCSS through the lens of these—including the Standards for the 21st Century Learner, from the American Association of School Librarians; the Information Literacy Competency Standards for Higher Education, from the Association of College and Research Libraries; the Framework for Success in Postsecondary Writing, collaboratively authored by the Council of Writing Program Administrators (CWPA), the National Council of Teachers of English, and the NWP; the Outcomes Statement for First-Year Composition from the CWPA; established media literacy principles; and Henry Jenkins's principles of literacy instruction—can be enormously helpful in understanding what the CCSS contribute to and require of ELA education as well as what tools are available to respond. In fact, taken as a whole, Part Two argues that the CCSS should be put into dialogue with these other documents in order to make the most informed pedagogical decisions. In other words, any changes to curricula should be grounded in a broad survey of this outcomes and standards landscape. Situating the CCSS alongside these other documents can help us better determine the affordances of the CCSS, including these:

- Increased (if still relatively small) attention to the role of digital technology

- Awareness of how communicative literacy in its multiple forms (writing, reading, speaking, information) is inherent and integral to not only ELA but all education

- Recognition of the productive place of collaboration in ELA work

This dialogue also alerts us to their limitations, including their culturally neutral stance, lack of attention to genre, privileging of a modes approach to writing, and elevation of the traditional canon.

Number four: *Rash response is unproductive.* At their best, the CCSS allow for reflectively examining our practices and considering the place of education in a changing, networked, digital world. Such reflection takes time. Contributors to this collection, in Parts Three, Four, and Five, encourage such reflection in devising individual assignments, curricular programs, and teacher training, respectively. They caution against making drastic changes before considering what practices are already in concert with the CCSS and which can be revised, what knowledge and expertise teachers and librarians possess, and what practices students have already developed and bring to the classroom. While pedagogical changes may be necessary, these contributors, together with Childers and Hicks in the Foreword and Afterword, respectively, remind us that much of what teachers, librarians, and administrators already do meets the CCSS. Applying this reflective approach can help us offer informed responses the implementation of the CCSS, such as calling for a moratorium on the high stakes testing connected to the CCSS in order to give teachers time to implement changes and procure needed resources or to give trial runs of tests to determine their usefulness (Hayes 2013; Strauss 2013; Weingarten 2013). This call for a calm, reflective response in a flurry of sometimes hasty and hysterical hand-wringing is, we feel, one of the distinguishing features of the collection.

In the Afterword that follows, Hicks offers additional concrete suggestions for productive next steps. We hope this Conclusion and the Afterword taken together offer final recommendations that readers can apply in their own local contexts moving forward. This toolkit of locally applicable strategies is an important step in taking Ken Kay and Bob Lenz's (2013) path to seeing the CCSS as more than a burden but instead as an "opportunity for our nation's teaching and learning." For us, that opportunity must necessarily be collaborative and digitally mediated to meet the needs of the next digital scholar.

References

Blumner, Jacob, and Pamela B. Childers. 2011. "Building Better Bridges: What Makes High School-College WAC Collaborations Work?" *WAC Journal* 21: 91–101. Accessed February 10, 2014. wac.colostate.edu/journal/vol22/blumner.pdf.

Childers, Pamela B. 2007. "High School-College Collaborations: Making Them Work." *Across the Disciplines* 4. Accessed February 10, 2014. wac.colostate.edu/atd/secondary/column2007.cfm.

Childers, Pamela B., and Michael J. Lowry, eds. 2012. "Introduction to Writing Across the Curriculum in Secondary Schools" [Special issue on Writing Across the Secondary School Curriculum]. *Across the Disciplines* 9 (3). Accessed February 10, 2014. wac.colostate.edu/atd/second_educ/intro.cfm.

Council of Chief State School Officers and National Governors Association. 2010. *Common Core State Standards for English Language Arts and Literacy in History/Social Studies, Science, and Technical Subjects.* Washington, DC: National Governors Association Center for Best Practices, Council of Chief State School Officers. Accessed February 10, 2014. www.corestandards.org/assets/CCSSI_ELA%20Standards.pdf.

Hayes, Sandy. 2013. "Moratorium on High Stakes Tests Is the Right Response to Common Core Implementation." National Council of Teachers of English. May 28. Accessed February 10, 2014. www.ncte.org/governance/hayes5-28-13?roi=echo4-23019295281-21272487-7acf9b79fdfa1bb11ff45c2c1666b68d&.

Hicks, Troy. 2009. *The Digital Writing Workshop*. Portsmouth, NH: Heinemann.

———. 2013. *Crafting Digital Writing: Composing Texts Across Media and Genres*. Portsmouth, NH: Heinemann.

Hicks, Troy, and Kristen Turner. 2013. "No Longer a Luxury: Digital Literacy Can't Wait." *English Journal* 102 (6): 58–65.

Kay, Ken, and Bob Lenz. 2013. "Commentary: Which Path for the Common Core?" *Education Week*. March 22. Accessed February 10, 2014. www.edweek.org/ew/articles/2013/03/22/26kay.h32.html.

Strauss, Valerie. 2013. "Common Core Supporters Back Moratorium on New Tests' High Stakes." *Washington Post*. June 6. Accessed February 10, 2014. www.washingtonpost.com/blogs/answer-sheet/wp/2013/06/06/common-core-supporters-back-moratorium-on-new-tests-high-stakes.

Weingarten, Randi. 2013. "Make the Common Core State Standards Work Before Making Them Count." American Federation of Teachers. April 30. Accessed February 10, 2014. www.youtube.com/watch?v=mUvAkm3dsH4&feature=youtu.be.

Afterword

Troy Hicks

We find ourselves at the end of this collection, one that, in the editors' words in the Introduction, would "[work] largely from students and technologies to the CCSS [Common Core State Standards], letting students' information behaviors drive the discussion rather than vice versa" (4).

Having collaborated with many of the authors in this volume through the good fortune of collegiality, whether through conference presentations, journal articles, book chapters, National Writing Project (NWP) institutes, and my own personal learning network online, I am honored to write an afterword for a collection that has, without a doubt, accomplished James P. Purdy and Randall McClure's goal.

Given the focus of this collection, and the broader educational discourse across the United States, it is clear that the CCSS have permeated every part of the conversation from classroom conversation to professional conferences to state capitols. This is, of course, the intent of a document that has become a de facto national curriculum, and it presents us with numerous challenges, many already articulated in this volume. By connecting the overarching principles that the many contributors to this collection have made, my hope is that this Afterword can, in Purdy and McClure's words, bring "the CCSS into focus, rather than using the CCSS to bring students' research-writing behaviors into line (or perhaps into submission)" (4). In order to do so, I summarize three overarching challenges ahead and the three additional principles that can guide us.

Challenge 1: While the CCSS Offer a Vision for Curriculum, We Must Recognize Where That Vision Came From

David Coleman, often considered to be the "architect" of the CCSS, has described the development of the standards and their purpose in many speeches, articles, and even with online videos. This particular quote—taken from a transcript of a speech, "Bringing the Common Core to Life," given in Albany, NY, on April 28, 2011—describes one of the "principles" that underlie the CCSS:

> The second [principle] is that these core standards had to be based on ethics. It was not enough to piously say what we believe all students need to know and be able to do. It was time to support those declarations with evidence that demonstrated that these core knowledge and skills were in fact the critical capacities predicting kids' effectiveness in college and career settings. (2011, 4, in PDF)

This is a generous vision of the CCSS, a vision that is informed by echoes of the ideals of social justice, equality, and freedom. To invoke an *ethical principle* as one on which the standards were developed is both an interesting rhetorical move—especially as it relates to the classical definition of ethos as "character"—as well as one that reminds us of the effective juxtaposition of terms such as the "soft bigotry of low expectations," a phrase used to promote No Child Left Behind (NCLB). No one, especially a politician, wants to be accused of promoting unequal, ineffective educational outcomes. So, this vision of the CCSS—promoted by the man who now directs the College Board and will, most likely, profit (literally and figuratively) from realigning the SAT to the CCSS—is a vision that we must bring into question.

Specifically, there are a number of other visions of the CCSS that are not so generous. In his insightful book, *Education Networks: Power,*

Wealth, Cyberspace, and the Digital Mind (2012), Joel Spring offers an in-depth history of the corporatized education reform movement. Spring argues "[t]oday, these networks of power tend to see technology as the panacea for world problems and the solution for classroom instruction" (2012, 25). These corporate connections have been documented quite clearly by scholars such as Spring, bloggers like Diann Woodard (2013), and advocates such as Diane Ravitch (2011) and Deborah Meier (2013). A fairly simple homemade video by Morna McDermott (2013) of United Opt Out outlines the (not-so-simple) corporate connections that underlie the CCSS.

Thus, the champions and the critics continue to promote competing visions of the CCSS as either well-researched, smart reforms or as yet another in a series of failures that began with *A Nation at Risk* (National Commission on Excellence in Education 1983) and has resulted in the standardized testing era. As we continue in our journey toward "implementation" of the standards, then, we as teachers and teacher educators are compelled to understand the origin of the CCSS. This is a critical literacy skill, and our challenge to remain vigilant.

Challenge 2: As Teachers, We Must Change Our Thinking on Literacy—and We Must Act on That Change *Now*

Speaking of literacy, as a reader of this collection, you understand the challenges that we face in our efforts to engage students in reading and writing, listening and speaking, viewing and visually representing. You live it every day in your own teaching context. There is no argument that literacy practices are constantly shifting, and the changes that we are going through now are widespread and pervasive. A number of authors in this book invoke different frameworks for understanding how reading, writing, and all literate behaviors have changed in the past two decades, including the New London Group's *Multiliteracies* (Cope and Kalantzis 2000), Colin Lankshear and Michele Knobel's *New Literacies* (2011), and many of the curricular and policy documents cited in this book such as the Framework for Success in Postsecondary Writing (Framework) (Council of Writing Program Administrators,

National Council of Teachers of English, and National Writing Project 2011) and the Connected Learning Principles (MacArthur Foundation 2011).

We know that we need to change our approach to literacy instruction. Yet, for the most part, we don't.

Despite the many calls to action in the past, and the numerous examples in this collection, it is sad to say that literacy instruction in this day and age is, well, pretty much the same as it has been for decades. For instance, see the lack of change in writing instruction documented over 30 years by Applebee (Applebee 1981; Applebee and Langer 2011).

We can't wait anymore.

Now is, indeed, a different time, and teachers must lead the charge in making the change. Along with countless studies that have documented incremental change as it relates to technology and education, Kristen Turner and I have called for an immediate overhaul to the teaching of English. Why should we? Well, we hope that the history of activism in our profession can bring us to a new place in our teaching:

> Over the years, teachers of English have rallied against censorship, fought for the inclusion of diverse voices in the canon of literature, and recognized the power of out-of-school literacies. Now English teachers must embrace a new role: We must advocate for digital literacy, not just technology, in a way that reconceptualizes our discipline. We must dump the dittos, throw out the workbooks, and remix our teaching for a digital age. (Hicks and Turner 2013, 61)

We make this plea, this demand, with good reason. In recent research with Bud Hunt, Sara Kajder, and Carl Young, we discovered that 100 years of *English Journal* have yielded an ever-present optimism that the next big change in texts would produce some substantive change in teaching practice (Hicks et al. 2012). Larry Cuban has thoroughly documented the effects of technology (or lack thereof) in a variety of educational contexts for decades (e.g., 1986; 2001). We also need to be wary of reforms that could retrench existing disparities and inequalities; Gary Stager, for instance, wonders if "bring our own device is the 'Worst Idea of the 21st Century?'" (2011).

In short, we cannot let this cycle of cautious optimism and lack of action continue. Our challenge is to change our thinking and then advocate for our students. We've always been good at this when it comes to books. Now we need to promote the kinds of internet access, instruction, and devices that will make a difference.

Challenge 3: Sustaining and Enhancing the Links Between K–12 and College Must Be Our Top Priority in an Era of Continuing "Reform"

A widely circulated "apology" letter from Kenneth Bernstein, a veteran teacher of U.S. government, ends with these sobering remarks after a decade of NCLB reforms:

> Now you are seeing the results in the students arriving at your institutions. They may be very bright. But we have not been able to prepare them for the kind of intellectual work that you have every right to expect of them. It is for this that I apologize, even as I know in my heart that there was little more I could have done. Which is one reason I am no longer in the classroom. (2013)

While Bernstein has, since publishing this letter, returned to teaching (and continues writing on Daily Kos), I have to wonder how many teachers—especially those in their first few years in the classroom—have felt the same, and indeed chose not to return. What role will the CCSS and, for that matter, digital writing technologies play in this continuing trend?

We need to maintain, strengthen, and grow anew the types of collaborative partnerships that will support teachers and kids in classrooms. We need to do this not just because students need to be "college ready," or because we need to increase our global competitiveness, but because the perspectives that university faculty and K–12 teachers share will inform conversations about massive open online courses (MOOCs), flipping the classroom, blended learning, and any number of other educational reforms that are out there. As groups such as the International Association for K–12 Online Learning (iNACOL) team with huge publishers to "deliver" online content to students, our challenge, as teachers and researchers, is that we must work together, collaboratively and often, in our efforts to keep good teaching at the forefront of the conversation.

Suffice it to say, whether we like it or not, the effects of the CCSS are already upon us, and this was just one day's worth of news. And, when the new computerized assessments arrive, what will day-to-day life in American schools look like in 18 months? 180 months? 18 years?

This then raises even more questions: What else can we do to advocate for high-quality literacy instruction? What, then, are the values from this collection that I want to see reflected in my own children's eyes? What, in the very best case, do I want them to know and experience as readers, writers, and literate citizens of our local community as well as the nation and the world? How do I want them to express themselves, interact with others, and share the planet?

There are at least three principles that I see reflected in the work of the authors in this collection as well as educators around the world who present, blog, and talk about their teaching. I thank the thousands, perhaps tens of thousands, of educators who guide their teaching, scholarship, and activism with these values. In order to continue moving forward in our efforts toward equitable access and broader participation in digital writing—both in school and in the world—I will reflect on three principles woven throughout this book, and then propose some specific, actionable ideas for us as educators.

Principle 1: Good Teaching Has the Capability of Engaging Students in Substantive Digital Writing

Elizabeth Homan and Dawn Reed remind us in Chapter 2 of this volume that "Like their students, teachers and librarians also engage with digital technologies in their lives inside and outside of school, and the span of their experiences varies as well" (38). While Christina Saidy and Mark A. Hannah argue in Chapter 9:

> The standard focusing on producing, publishing, and updating writing provides a unique opportunity for teachers and students to incorporate technology, in our case blogging, in meaningful ways to meet the CCSS, while at the same time offering opportunities for students to develop writing that engages other students and their communities. (260–261)

Writing, at the core, requires community. Writers write to be read, and the democratic ideal and community spirit that Homan, Reed, Saidy, and Hannah emphasize here can be traced back to our greatest teachers and leaders, most notably John Dewey. Authors in this volume have cited a number of critical policy documents, such as the Framework, Connected Learning Principles, and the scholarly works of Jenkins, Lankshear, and Knobel, and the NWP, all of which speak to the power of writing and the ability to affect change.

Many of the authors in this volume reiterate these egalitarian ideas in their approaches. In Chapter 7, James Cercone and David L. Bruce argue that we must remain "true to research-based, pedagogically sound practices" (223). In Chapter 11, Amanda Stearns-Pfeiffer reminds us that it is about more than tools: "Empowering students with an online voice is not complete unless they are empowered with the literacy of design" (308). Finally, in Chapter 10, R. Spencer Atkinson aims "both to address the CCSS and to stay true to the spirit of meaningful work that [he] believe[s] is implied by them" (295). Each holds tightly to the idea that teachers and students are at the core, not the standards themselves.

When we value principles, and not just standards, we focus on good teaching and learning—not just neat new devices, the latest app, or a fancy website. Teaching writing well is a principled activity, an activity that technology can enhance; yet, it can never fully replace the role of a good teacher.

Principle 2: Balancing the Norms of the Internet With the Policies and Expectations of School Remains a Delicate, Yet Necessary, Act

To produce and publish writing, especially for the internet, changes our expectations for purpose, audience, and context. In Chapter 6, Clancy Ratliff suggests that we often reduce "writing to nothing but a classroom exercise done for a grade, with no real transferability to other classes or writing situations outside of school" (187). Our understanding of literacy practices—as scholars like David Barton and Mary Hamilton (1998), Anne Haas Dyson (2003), Shirley Brice Heath (1983), and numerous others have shown over the past few decades—are culturally influenced in some obvious and not-so-obvious ways. School, as one of those cultures, remains notoriously resistant to change, especially in regards to technology.

Yet, as Rachel Bear, Heidi Estrem, James E. Fredricksen, and Dawn Shepherd demonstrate in Chapter 5, "the classroom can, in fact, embody and promote many aspects of participatory culture" and change can happen with smart instruction and, as noted, principled practice (143). Antero Garcia and Cindy O'Donnell-Allen in Chapter 12 reiterate another powerful idea from Paulo Freire, in the sense "that students are likely to have more powerful literacy learning experiences when their cultural identities and linguistic diversity are viewed as valuable resources" (331).

At risk of sounding clichéd, context matters. In Chapter 15, Christine Tulley reminds us that "[t]oday's secondary writing teachers will never know a time where they aren't held accountable to a set of standards" (432), and in Chapter 8, Laura J. Davies points out that students may "lack the skills and strategies of an inquiry research process" (230). As Stephanie West-Puckett and William P. Banks in Chapter 13 remind us in the starkest terms, sometimes digital simply is *not* a part of school and community cultures. It is our challenge to teach students how to participate both in school and in the world. Being held accountable should be about doing a good job for one's self and community, not just for a grade.

Principle 3: Our Work as Teacher-Scholars Has Become Inherently Interdisciplinary and the Need for Us to Cross Boundaries Has Become Imperative

Boundary crossing is both a disciplinary act, moving from one subject to another, and it is also an act that encourages us to break existing norms. Many people want boundaries, directions, and order. Because "many teachers wanted to know exactly how to do something before beginning," in Chapter 17 Keri Franklin and Kathy Gibson remind us that we may need to actively resist our own impulses to provide such step-by-step instruction (485). We, too, need to step into a constant state of remixing, rethinking, and reimagining. This requires us to take on new models of teaching and learning, such as the "increasingly virtual, and thereby increasingly personal" learning environments described by Amanda Nichols Hess and Katie Greer in Chapter 3 (99). In Chapter 14, Lisa Litterio reminds us of the necessity of experimentation and play, so students can explore "forms of digital writing as well as consider how research practices are subject to significant changes within digital environments" (404).

Finally, we must bring seemingly contradictory curriculum and policy documents into conversation. In Chapter 4, Angela Clark-Oates, Allyson Boggess, and Duane Roen argue that:

> When we bring the CCSS into a dialogue with the Framework around this issue of technology, we open up possibilities for students to reflect on their use of technology, asking how digital technology enhances rhetorical choices. (120)

These tensions between competing visions can lead to dialogue, and to action. In addition, Tawnya Lubbes and Heidi Skurat Harris in Chapter 16 show us that we must cross boundaries of instructional design, too, especially when we move to a model of student-centered "assessments of significant academic content along with the development of specific 21st century skills" (451), which is quite different than a typical standardized test. When we reach out and are intentional in our willingness to learn from others, to put various perspectives together, we become better teachers in our own right, and we also have the opportunity to create professional learning experiences for our colleagues.

From Here Forward

In an online addition to his aptly titled book, *Holding On to Good Ideas in a Time of Bad Ones: Six Literacy Principles Worth Fighting For*, Thomas Newkirk (2013) provides a new postscript, "Speaking Back to the Common Core." In it, he outlines a number of points about how the standards have been marketed to states as bait in the Race to the Top program. Near the end of this postscript, he asks:

> Another way in which they [the CCSS] walk a fine line is the claim that they are not dictating curriculum or teaching methods; promoters claim these decisions should be made at the local level, by teachers and curriculum directors. The mantra is that the standards indicate where students are going but not how they are to get there.

But can this line hold?

Newkirk asks a smart question, one that invokes a principled understanding about where the CCSS have come from and, more importantly, where we as educators need to go. We must hold our own line, too. This is the line between best practices in writing instruction and creating the next generation of digital scholars, and, on the other side, selling out our students and colleagues to corporate education reform. This is the line between indicating where students should go and *how we choose to get them there*.

When we invite our students to sit down in front of the computer or pull out their smart phone or tablet, we need to hold on to the principles evident throughout this collection: good teaching, blending norms of the internet with those of school, and embracing interdisciplinarity. In our efforts to move across these boundaries, we must engage students, parents, colleagues, and our communities through action. I respectfully propose three concrete steps that you can take here.

First, as busy as we already are, we must be more involved. I know that your job already asks enough of you to fill up more than 24 hours each day. Still, outreach is our best opportunity. Organize a digital literacy program for families and youth to engage in substantive learning outside of school contexts, even if you bring them to the school computer lab to do so. Here are a few models on which you might frame your own outreach:

- The Digital Youth Network (digitalyouthnetwork.org), based in Chicago, describes itself as "a hybrid digital literacy program that creates opportunities for youth to engage in learning environments that span both in-school and out-of-school contexts" ("Overview" n.d.).

- Tech Goes Home (techgoeshome.org), based in Boston, "focuses on serving the U.S.'s most vulnerable populations, including children/youth, adults, seniors, and people with disabilities who are predominantly low-income and/or from challenged neighborhoods" ("What Is TGH" n.d.).

- Global Kids (globalkids.org), based in New York, "works to ensure that urban youth have the knowledge, skills, experiences and values they need to succeed in school, participate effectively in the democratic process, and achieve leadership in their communities and on the global stage" ("About Global Kids" n.d.).

Take some time to explore these sites, each rich with resources that can help you think about how successful, nonprofit digital literacy ventures can be brought to scale with parents, educators, and community volunteers. Then, with your colleagues and students, start one of your own.

Second, the ways in which we use technology must be conscious, critical, and creative. As the authors in this collection have shown, we simply cannot use technology for its own sake or as an enhancement to a writing curriculum. Instead, we must rethink how we are teaching. Because I did not see their work mentioned much in the book, I will suggest the work of two educators who bring us a different perspective on technology, as well as a modest suggestion for the reader to further explore some of my work as well.

One is Renee Hobbs, currently professor and founding director of the Harrington School of Communication and Media at the University of Rhode Island, and a long-time scholar of media literacy. Her work spans all grade levels, from elementary (Hobbs and Moore 2013) to high school (Hobbs 2006) and teacher professional development (Hobbs 2011). She has also done extensive work with copyright and fair use, exemplified by the *Code of Best Practices in Fair Use for Media Literacy Education* (Center for Social Media, School of Communication, American University 2009) and her book, *Copyright Clarity: How Fair Use Supports Digital Learning* (Hobbs 2010). Her work can be found in a variety of online spaces including the Media Education Lab (mediaeducationlab.com) and Copyright Clarity Wiki (copyrightconfusion.wikispaces.com) and via her Twitter feed (twitter.com/reneehobbs).

The other is Joyce Valenza, a former teacher-librarian at Springfield Township (PA) High School and current faculty member of Rutgers University School of Communication and Information. She writes the blog Never Ending Search (blogs.slj.com/neverendingsearch), which is hosted by the *School Library Journal*, and won a lifetime achievement award from Edublogs. She also curates a number of wikis including Copyright Friendly (copyrightfriendly.wikispaces.com), which covers resources available under public domain and Creative Commons licensing), and can be followed on Twitter (twitter.com/joycevalenza).

I offer a variety of resources as well. My work is targeted at the intersection of smart writing instruction and effective technology integration. Helping students think about how and why to compose digital texts will help them grow as readers, writers, researchers, and thinkers. Resources I offer include My Digital Writing, Digital Teaching Blog (hickstro.org), my wiki with workshop agendas and resources (hickstro.wikispaces.com), my books' companion wiki page (digitalwritingworkshop.wikispaces.com), and my Twitter feed (twitter.com/hickstro).

There are, of course, hundreds, perhaps thousands, of educators who are also blogging, tweeting, curating materials, and otherwise making their teaching practice public. My hope is that you will find some rich resources for you and your students by starting with Hobbs, Valenza, and me, and then continue to explore the rich variety of resources available online. More importantly, please contribute your own great ideas by blogging, tweeting, and participating.

Third, as we reach out and engage our writers in these conscious, critical, and creative ways, we must also teach them how to join the participatory culture referenced in this book. I, like many others, have often made the claim that digital writing invites us to imagine audiences, both intended and incidental, that reach beyond the classroom walls. Our writers have the potential to reach a global audience. Yet, if the audience fails to engage the writer, then the recursive nature of the writing process stops. Or, if the response is strictly a criticism, then the writer could become discouraged. In other words, we need to teach our students to be both good writers as well as good responders. Here are a few tools and resources for equipping them with the types of response skills that they will need. The following three spaces offer the technological infrastructure to help writers create compositions while also supporting peers in the response process.

Eli Review (elireview.com) is for high school and college. It describes itself as a "social writing" platform. Students go through a three-step cycle of writing, reviewing, and planning for revision: "Writing tasks can be completed by composing in Eli or uploading a file. Reviews are done in Eli, guided by criteria provided by teachers. Students use the feedback they receive to make revision plans, and then revise and resubmit their drafts" ("How Eli Works" n.d.). In the interest of full disclosure, I am currently working with one of Eli's inventors, Jeff

Grabill, on a research project measuring its effectiveness in classrooms across Michigan, but the application has received numerous positive reviews from other writing teachers and students besides me.

Youth Voices (youthvoices.net) is for middle school and high school. It is "a site for conversations. We invite youth of all ages to voice their thoughts about their passions, to explain things they understand well, to wonder about things they have just begun to understand, and to share discussion posts with other young people using as many different genres and media as they can imagine" ("What's Youth Voices All About?" n.d.). Paul Allison and his colleagues have been facilitating student writers on Youth Voices for over 10 years, teaching them intentionally how to write as well as respond to the writing of their peers. He welcomes new contributors and responders at any time.

Kidblog (kidblog.org) is for elementary school and provides teachers with control over the blogging activity created in their classroom community. According to their website, "Kidblog allows students to exercise digital citizenship within a secure, private classroom blogging space" ("Why Kidblog?" n.d.) without ads, widgets, and the clutter that accompanies other blogging tools. It is easy for students to write their own posts and respond to the work of others. Of the few teachers with whom I have worked who use Kidblog so far, all of them report a positive experience, noting that the technology itself contributes to a sense of online community for writers.

Across these three online spaces where writers can do their work, the consistent theme of writing coupled with response shows how the two processes are reciprocal—and entirely necessary—in order to grow successful writers.

My final suggestion is simple. Move forward from here by engaging, participating, advocating, and teaching. The value we place in our own ideas, our collaborations with colleagues, and our relationships with students will carry us forward. Purdy and McClure have guided many contributors to create a timely, useful, and principled collection that will encourage us to move forward, and I hope that I have provided just a few more ideas to help you along in that journey.

References

"About Global Kids." n.d. Global Kids. Accessed February 10, 2014. www.globalkids.org/#/about-global-kids.

Applebee, Arthur N. 1981. *Writing in the Secondary School: English and the Content Areas*. Report No. 21. Urbana, IL: National Council of Teachers of English.

Applebee, Arthur N., and Judith A. Langer. 2011. "A Snapshot of Writing Instruction in Middle Schools and High Schools." *English Journal* 100 (6): 14.

Barton, David, and Mary Hamilton. 1998. *Local Literacies: Reading and Writing in One Community*. New York: Routledge.

Bernstein, Kenneth. 2013. "Warnings From the Trenches." *American Association of University Professors*. January–February. Accessed February 10, 2014. www.aaup.org/article/warnings-trenches#.UiiwG2SAdqp.

Center for Social Media, School of Communication, American University. 2009. *Code of Best Practices in Fair Use for Media Literacy Education*. Accessed February 10, 2014. mediaeducationlab.com/sites/mediaeducationlab.com/files/CodeofBestPracticesinFairUse.pdf.

Coleman, David. 2011. "Bringing the Common Core to Life." Speech given in Albany, NY, on April 28. Accessed February 10, 2014. usny.nysed.gov/rttt/docs/bringingthecommoncoretolife/fulltranscript.pdf.

Cope, Bill, and Mary Kalantzis, eds. 2000. *Multiliteracies: Literacy Learning and the Design of Social Futures*. New York: Routledge.

Council of Writing Program Administrators, National Council of Teachers of English, and National Writing Project. 2011. *Framework for Success in Postsecondary Writing*. Accessed February 10, 2014. wpacouncil.org/files/framework-for-success-postsecondary-writing.pdf.

Cuban, Larry. 1986. *Teachers and Machines: The Classroom Use of Technology Since 1920*. New York: Teachers College Press.

———. 2001. *Oversold and Underused: Computers in the Classroom*. Cambridge, MA: Harvard University Press.

Dyson, Anne Haas. 2003. *The Brothers and Sisters Learn to Write: Popular Literacies in Childhood and School Cultures*. New York: Teachers College Press.

Heath, Shirley Brice. 1983. *Ways With Words: Language, Life, and Work in Communities and Classrooms*. New York: Cambridge University Press.

Hicks, Troy, Carl A. Young, Sara B. Kajder, and Bud Hunt. 2012. "Same As It Ever Was: Enacting the Promise of Teaching, Writing, and New Media." *English Journal* 101 (3): 68–74.

Hicks, Troy, and Kristen Turner. 2013. "No Longer a Luxury: Digital Literacy Can't Wait." *English Journal* 102 (6): 58–65.

Hobbs, Renee. 2006. *Reading the Media in High School: Media Literacy in High School English*. Illustrated edition. New York: Teachers College Press.

———. 2010. *Copyright Clarity: How Fair Use Supports Digital Learning*. Thousand Oaks, CA: Corwin Press.

———. 2011. *Digital and Media Literacy: Connecting Culture and Classroom.* Thousand Oaks, CA: Corwin Press.

Hobbs, Renee, and David Cooper Moore. 2013. *Discovering Media Literacy: Teaching Digital Media and Popular Culture in Elementary School.* Thousand Oaks, CA: Corwin Press.

"How Eli Works." n.d. Eli Review. Accessed February 10, 2014. www.elireview.com/how-eli-works.

Lankshear, Colin, and Michele Knobel. 2011. *New Literacies: Everyday Practices and Classroom Learning.* New York: Open University Press.

MacArthur Foundation. 2011. "Connected Learning Principles." Accessed on February 10, 2014. connectedlearning.tv/connected-learning-principles.

Meier, Deborah. 2013. *In Schools We Trust: Creating Communities of Learning in an Era of Testing and Standardization.* Ypsilanti, MI: Beacon Press.

McDermott, Morna. 2013. *Walking the Labyrinth of the Corporate-Owned-Common Core.* July 23. YouTube. Accessed February 10, 2014. www.youtube.com/watch?v=vvUMk1ro27E&feature=youtube_gdata_player.

National Commission on Excellence in Education. 1983. *A Nation at Risk: The Imperative for Educational Reform.* Accessed February 10, 2014. datacenter.spps.org/uploads/SOTW_A_Nation_at_Risk_1983.pdf.

Newkirk, Thomas. 2013. "Postscript: Speaking Back to the Common Core." Accessed February 10, 2014. www.hcincmann.com/shared/onlineresources/E02123/Newkirk_Speaking_Back_to_the_Common_Core.pdf.

"Overview." n.d. Digital Youth Network. Accessed February 10, 2014. www.digitalyouthnetwork.org/1-about/pages/1-overview.

Ravitch, Diane. 2011. *The Death and Life of the Great American School System: How Testing and Choice Are Undermining Education.* New York: Basic Books.

Spring, Joel. 2012. *Education Networks: Power, Wealth, Cyberspace, and the Digital Mind.* New York: Routledge.

Stager, Gary. 2011. "BYOD—Worst Idea of the 21st Century?" *Stager-to-Go.* November 8. Accessed February 10, 2014. stager.tv/blog/?p=2397.

Woodard, Diann. 2013. "The Corporate Takeover of Public Education." *Huffington Post.* June 6. Accessed February 10, 2014. www.huffingtonpost.com/diann-woodard/the-corporate-takeover_b_3397091.html.

"What's Youth Voices All About?" n.d. Youth Voices. Accessed February 10, 2014. youthvoices.net/about.

"What Is TGH?" n.d. Tech Goes Home. Accessed February 10, 2014. www.techgoeshome.org/whatistgh.

"Why Kidblog?" n.d. Kidblog. Accessed February 10, 2014. kidblog.org/why-kidblog.

About the Contributors

R. Spencer Atkinson has taught high school English Language Arts (ELA) and social studies in California and Wisconsin. He completed his MEd in teacher leadership at the High Tech High Graduate School of Education, the U.S.'s only graduate school of education housed entirely in a K–12 institution. In 2011, he participated in the inaugural cohort of the Greater Madison Writing Project, from which the project discussed in this volume emerged. He completed his MS in educational leadership and policy analysis at the University of Wisconsin–Madison, where his research examined the role of hip-hop pedagogy in supporting identity development of historically underserved students.

William P. Banks is director of the university writing program at East Carolina University (ECU) and of the Tar River Writing Project. He is associate professor of rhetoric and writing at ECU, where he teaches graduate and undergraduate courses in writing, research, and pedagogy. He has published articles on history, rhetoric, pedagogy, writing program administration, and sexuality in several recent books, as well as in *College Composition and Communication*, *English Journal*, *College English*, *Computer and Composition*, *Dialogue*, and *Teaching English in the Two-Year College*. His current book project, *Queer Literacies*, explores the ways in which gay men and lesbians articulate literacies of queer(ed) identities.

Rachel Bear has taught high school English for 8 years. Her teaching experience includes ninth- through 12th-grade ELA, including sheltered English language learners and advanced placement (AP). She has served on the leadership team for the Literacy in the Common Core State Standards (CCSS) initiative through the National Writing Project (NWP) and is the CCSS implementation team leader for the Boise State Writing Project. She has designed and developed work around digital literacy for her students and for professional development for teachers. She is also currently working on an i3 grant through the NWP that will focus on improving the teaching of writing in high needs, rural schools.

Allyson Boggess is the course coordinator of the ENG 101 program in the Writers' Studio at Arizona State University and adjunct faculty at the Harvard University Extension School where she teaches expository writing. She completed her Master of Fine Arts degree in creative writing at Arizona State University in 2011. Her professional interests include contemporary poetry and writing anxiety.

David L. Bruce is a research associate professor of English Education at the University of Buffalo (UB). Prior to working in higher education, he taught secondary ELA classes for 11 years. His research and teaching interests deal with students composing with digital video (DV) technology in classroom contexts, incorporating multimodal literacies into teacher education, and exploring uses of DV as a research tool. He is currently working with several initiatives with colleagues at UB, such as the Writing With Video (WWV) project, a Teacher Leadership Quality Partnership Grant, and the new literacies group. He has served as president of the Ohio Council of Teachers of English and as the director of the commission on media through the National Council of Teachers of English (NCTE).

James Cercone is an assistant professor of English secondary education and English education program coordinator at Buffalo State.

Before joining Buffalo State, Cercone was a clinical professor of English education at the University at Buffalo and a former high school English teacher. Cercone's research focuses on the role English education programs play in the development of English teacher professional social networks and the impact such networks have on teacher identity development, classroom instruction, and student learning. Cercone also studies inquiry-based models of ELA instruction and the integration of 21st-century literacies in English classrooms. He has presented and published on the subjects of digital video composing, diversity, high-stakes testing, curriculum development, and clinically rich models of teacher education. He is a co-founder and director of the Western New York Network of English Teachers, a professional social network linking English teachers across the Buffalo-Niagara region.

Pamela B. Childers, executive editor of *The Clearing House*, serves on the International Writing Across the Curriculum (IWAC) board of consultants and as series editor of the *Excellence in K–12 WAC Series* (wac.colostate.edu). As Caldwell Chair of Composition Emerita at the McCallie School, she directed the writing center and WAC program. An AP language and composition table leader, Childers has written more than 100 professional columns, articles, and chapters, and presented keynotes and workshops at national and international conferences, including the Conference on College Composition and Communication (CCCC), International Writing Center Association (IWCA), IWAC, National Science Teachers Association (NSTA), National Council of Teachers of English (NCTE), and European Writing Centers Association. Former president of IWCA, she received the IWCA Outstanding Service Award. Her books include *ARTiculating: Teaching Writing in a Visual World* (with Hobson and Mullin), *Programs and Practices: Writing Across the Secondary School Curriculum* (with Gere and Young), *The High School Writing Center,* and *WAC Partnerships Among Secondary and Post-Secondary Institutions* (with Jacob Blumner), which is forthcoming.

Angela Clark-Oates is the course manager for the Writers' Studio in the School of Letters and Sciences at Arizona State University. In this role, she also teaches first-year composition and supervises a writing fellow program. She is the former coordinator of the ASU Writing Center—Downtown Phoenix campus, where she also designed and implemented ASU's first online writing tutoring program and co-designed a university/K–12 school partnership. Her research is focused on how writing identities are shaped by discourses and ideologies of peers, teachers, and institutions. She completed her doctorate at Arizona State University in May 2013.

Laura J. Davies is an assistant professor of rhetoric and composition at the United States Air Force Academy, where she directs the first-year writing program. As a New York State certified social studies teacher, she has always been interested in the intersection between university and K–12 writing instruction. Her other scholarship has focused on writing program administration and systems of teacher evaluation and professional development. She is currently working on a project that investigates how the concepts of leadership, followership, and command could be useful tropes for designing writing curriculum. She is a graduate of Syracuse University's composition and cultural rhetoric PhD program.

Heidi Estrem is an associate professor of English and the director of the first-year writing program at Boise State University. Her research interests in first-year writing pedagogy, writing program administration, assessment, and instructor development and support have led to publications in *Writing Program Administration*, *Rhetoric Review*, *Composition Studies*, *Pedagogy*, and several edited collections. She regularly teaches both first-year writing and graduate seminars focused on writing pedagogy, theory, and research.

Keri Franklin is an associate professor of English at Missouri State University and founding director of the Ozarks Writing Project, a site of the NWP. Her work is focused on English education, writing, and professional development. Franklin frequently conducts professional development related to writing. As the university's Provost Fellow for Writing, Franklin developed faculty writing retreats and a university writing fellows program. Currently, she is the director of assessment at Missouri State University and studying the impact of NWP professional development on student writing and teacher beliefs and practices. The next digital scholars in her life are her 5-year old daughter, Josie Rae, and her 1-year-old son, Kelly.

James E. Fredricksen is an associate professor of English at Boise State University and the co-director of the Boise State Writing Project as well as a leadership team member of the Literacy in the Common Core initiative through the NWP. He is co-author of three books (published by Heinemann in 2012) on teaching to exceed the CCSS (*So, What's the Story: Teaching Narrative to Understand Ourselves, Others, and the World*; *Oh Yeah?!: Putting Argument to Work Both in School and Out*; *Get It Done!: Writing and Analyzing Informational Texts to Make Things Happen*).

Antero Garcia is an assistant professor in the English department at Colorado State University in Fort Collins. His recent research focuses on critical literacies, technology, and youth civic engagement. For 8 years, he was a teacher at a public high school in South Central Los Angeles. In 2008, Garcia co-developed the Black Cloud Game. A Digital Media and Learning Competition award recipient, the Black Cloud provoked students to take real time assessment of air quality in their community. Using custom-developed sensors that measure and send data about air quality, students critically analyzed the role pollution played in their daily lives and presented recommendations to their community. He is a 2012–2014 Cultivating New Voices Among Scholars of Color fellow with the NCTE and a 2010–2011 U.S. Department of Education Teaching Ambassador Fellow. Garcia's numerous publications and conference presentations address technology, educational equity, youth participatory action research, and critical media literacy.

Kathy Gibson has an MST in composition studies from the University of New Hampshire and an EdM in curriculum and instruction from the University of Missouri. She is an assistant professor teaching ELA and media at Greenwood Laboratory School on the campus of Missouri State University where she also teaches university middle school methods. She edits the journal *The Transescent* for the Missouri Middle School Association and recently co-authored an article on digital storytelling for *School Library Monthly*. She has presented locally and nationally on using iPads and one-to-one technology in middle and high school classrooms. An avid Mac enthusiast, she follows tech news for tips teachers can adapt for classroom use. Her interests include media literacy, photography, film study, reading, and animation.

Katie Greer is an assistant professor and the first-year experience librarian at Oakland University in Rochester, Michigan. She holds an MA in art history from the University of Notre Dame and an MS in library and information sciences from Drexel University. Greer contributes to *CHOICE Reviews* and has also been published in the *Journal of Academic Librarianship*.

Mark A. Hannah is an assistant professor of rhetoric and professional writing at Arizona State University. His research focuses on rhetorics of cross-disciplinarity, in particular the development of rhetorical practices and mechanisms for working through the communication challenges that arise in complex, collaborative work environments. Hannah's interest in secondary school writing stems from the new emphasis on professional writing in the CCSS. His current work investigates the ways science and engineering post-secondary students learn to write for professional contexts.

Heidi Skurat Harris is an assistant professor of rhetoric and writing at the University of Arkansas at Little Rock (UALR) and a member of the CCCC committee for Effective Practices in Online Writing Instruction. Prior to her position at UALR, she designed and coordinated the Summer Institute for Instructional Technology at Eastern Oregon University, where she was also the coordinator of innovative teaching initiatives. Her current research focuses on the implementation of the Position Statement of Principles and Example Effective Practices for Online Writing Instruction from CCCC.

Amanda Nichols Hess is an assistant professor and eLearning/instructional technology librarian at Oakland University in Rochester, MI. She earned her MSI from the University of Michigan and an EdS in instructional technology from Wayne State University, and previously worked as a school library media specialist and K–12 technology integration specialist. Hess has been published in *School Library Monthly*, *Journal of Library and Information Services in Distance Learning*, *New Library World*, and in the anthology *Library Youth Outreach*.

Troy Hicks is an associate professor of English at Central Michigan University (CMU) and focuses his work on the teaching of writing, literacy, and technology, and teacher education and professional development. Hicks is author of the Heinemann titles *Crafting Digital Writing* (2013) and *The Digital Writing Workshop* (2009) as well as a co-author of *Because Digital Writing Matters* (Jossey-Bass, 2010) in addition to numerous journal articles and book chapters. In March 2011, Hicks was honored with CMU's Provost's Award for junior faculty who have demonstrated outstanding achievement in research and creative activity.

Elizabeth Homan is a doctoral candidate in the Joint Program in English and Education at the University of Michigan in Ann Arbor, Michigan. Before returning to graduate school to earn her PhD, she was a high school and middle school ELA and communications teacher in Indiana, where she earned her MS in Curriculum and Instruction at Purdue University. She has written for the *Journal of Technology and Teacher Education*, *CLAS Statement*, and *NCTE Press*, and is currently a blogger for Inside Higher Ed's GradHacker and the Sweetland Digital Rhetoric Collaborative. Her dissertation examines how teachers' professional learning networks shape their development of digital literacies and pedagogies.

Lisa Litterio is an assistant professor of English at Bridgewater State University and received her PhD in rhetoric and communication from Rensselaer Polytechnic Institute in Troy, NY. She has an MA in English with a concentration in composition and rhetoric from the University of New Hampshire/Cambridge University, England, and a BA in classics (Magna Cum Laude, Phi Beta Kappa) from the College of the Holy Cross. Her work appears in journals such as the *Journal of Business and Technical Communication* and *Rhetoric Review*. She has presented her research on multimodal compositions, professional and technical communication, and integrating digital technologies in the classroom and writing centers at numerous national and international conferences, including Columbia University's Teacher's College Educational Technology Conference, National Communication Association Conference (NCA), CCCC, and IWCA. Litterio has received numerous awards for her scholarship and research, including an RPI graduate fellowship, a Pearson Emerging Pedagogies Travel and Research Grant, a Summer Institute Scholarship from Rhetoric Society of America, and the Robert J. Connors Memorial Scholarship from the Northeast Writing Centers Association for her contributions to writing centers.

Tawnya Lubbes is an assistant professor of education, advisor, and English as a Second Language (ESOL) program coordinator in the College of Education at Eastern Oregon University in La Grande, Oregon. She specializes in ESOL, Spanish, diversity, and online pedagogy. She holds a BA from Pacific University and an MTE from Eastern Oregon University, and she is currently completing her PhD in education with an emphasis in ESOL and multicultural education from Walden University (anticipated completion summer 2014). Lubbes actively contributes to field research on the topics of culturally responsive pedagogy, teacher identity development, ESOL best practices, and online pedagogy through various presentations and publications at the local, national, and international levels. Her current research is in regard to the stages of rural pre-service teacher identity development and how teacher identity influences the integration of culturally responsive pedagogy in K–12 classrooms.

Cindy O'Donnell-Allen is a full professor in the English Department at Colorado State University (CSU), where she directs the CSU Writing Project. She was a secondary English teacher in Oklahoma for 11 years and became a member of the Oklahoma Writing Project in 1991. She serves on the NWP board of directors and co-chaired the NWP Teacher Inquiry Communities Network for several years. O'Donnell-Allen is the author of numerous articles and two books, *Tough Talk, Tough Texts: Teaching English to Change the World* and *The Book Companion: Fostering Strategic Readers in the Secondary Classroom*. Winner of several research awards, she has been a member of the editorial board for *Research in the Teaching of English*, an NCTE Promising Researcher, and a Spencer Dissertation Fellow. She currently co-chairs the NCTE Research Forum with Antero Garcia and serves as an NWP Connected Learning Ambassador.

Clancy Ratliff is the director of first-year writing at the University of Louisiana (UL) at Lafayette, a position she has held for 7 years. She has published articles on feminist rhetorics, writing program administration, and computers and composition. Her administrative work, particularly her work with high schools on dual enrollment writing course offerings, and her work with UL Lafayette's College of Education, led to her research interest in the CCSS.

Dawn Reed is an English teacher at Okemos High School in Okemos, Michigan, and a co-director of the Red Cedar Writing Project at

Michigan State University. She earned her MA in rhetoric and writing from Michigan State University, and she continues to engage in teacher inquiry and research. Her research interests include the writing process, the teaching of writing, and digital literacies. She has published in various journals and books, including *English Journal* and *Teaching the New Writing: Technology, Change, and Assessment* (Teachers College Press, 2009).

Duane Roen is a professor of English at Arizona State University, where he serves as head of interdisciplinary and liberal studies in the School of Letters and Sciences and as assistant vice provost for University Academic Success Programs. He is past-president of the Council of Writing Program Administrators. He formerly served as secretary of the CCCC. Roen has written extensively about writing curriculum, pedagogy, and assessment; writing program administration; writing across the curriculum; gender; writing family history; and collaboration. He has authored/co-authored and edited/co-edited nine books, and has authored or co-authored more than 250 chapters, articles, and conference presentations. His most recent books include the third edition of *The McGraw-Hill Guide: Writing for College, Writing for Life* (with Greg Glau and Barry Maid) and *The WPA Outcomes Statement: A Decade Later* (co-edited with Nick Behm, Greg Glau, Deborah Holdstein, and Edward White).

Christina Saidy is an assistant professor of English education and rhetoric at Arizona State University. Her research focuses on teacher preparation, the rhetoric of educational policy, effective writing in secondary schools, and transitions between secondary and university writing. Saidy taught secondary ELA for 8 years in the greater Los Angeles area, and she remains committed to working with teachers to implement innovative and effective writing instruction in urban schools. Currently, she is working on a teacher action project in an urban high school and on a NWP Intersections grant to foster science writing and literacy in greater Phoenix.

Dawn Shepherd is an assistant professor of English and associate director of the first-year writing program at Boise State University. She is the co-author, with Carolyn R. Miller, of two book chapters on genre and weblog, and her work on matching technologies and algorithmic culture has been featured in local and international media, including BBC World and *The Times of London*. She teaches upper-division and graduate courses in rhetoric and writing with a new media emphasis and regularly facilitates workshops on integrating mobile strategies into the classroom and teaching with technology.

Amanda Stearns-Pfeiffer recently accepted a position as assistant professor of English at Oakland University. Her doctoral degree in English Education was awarded in 2012 from Western Michigan University, where she defended her dissertation titled "Interpreting and Implementing ELA Standards/Expectations in Secondary Classrooms." Upon completion of her doctorate at WMU, she served one year as assistant professor of English Education at the University of Wisconsin-Eau Claire. Her current research interests include the CCSS (their implementation, consequences, and challenges), effective professional development models for teachers, and preparing pre-service English teachers for successful internship experiences. For further information about Stearns-Pfeiffer, visit her website at stearnspfeiffer.weebly.com.

Christine Tulley is the director of writing and former director of English education at The University of Findlay. She is the author of several articles in journals such as *Pedagogy*, *Computers and Composition*, *Journal of Writing Teacher Education*, and *Journal of Faculty Development*. In addition, she is the Praxis section editor for *Kairos: A Journal of Rhetoric, Technology, and Pedagogy*.

Stephanie West-Puckett is a digital rhetorician, compositionist, and activist scholar engaging digital writing, new media, critical web literacies, and professional communication in K–12, university, and community learning environments. She is passionate about innovative, research-based writing pedagogy and writes and manages grants to build university/school/community collaborations, leveraging digital media for student, teacher, and community empowerment. She is currently a doctoral student, writing teacher, and associate director of the Tar River Writing Project at East Carolina University as well as conference director for the North Carolina English Teachers Association.

About the Editors

James P. Purdy is associate professor of English and director of the University Writing Center at Duquesne University. He teaches courses from first-year writing to graduate seminars in composition theory and digital writing. With McClure, he edited *The New Digital Scholar: Exploring and Enriching the Research and Writing Practices of NextGen Students,* also published in the Information Today ASIS&T Monograph Series. His scholarship has appeared in *College Composition and Communication, Computers and Composition, Computers and Composition Online, Journal of Literacy and Technology, Kairos, Pedagogy,* and *Profession* as well as in several edited collections. With co-author Joyce R. Walker, he won the 2011 Ellen Nold Award for the Best Article in Computers and Composition Studies and the 2008 *Kairos* Best Webtext Award.

Randall McClure has taught writing at several universities, including Miami University, Georgia Southern University, Cleveland State University, and Minnesota State University, Mankato. He researches in the areas of information behavior and academic writing, teaching and learning online, and academic policy. He has published articles recently in *The Department Chair, Inside Higher Ed, portal: Libraries and the Academy, Computers and Composition Online, Academic Exchange Quarterly, Computers and Composition, Writing Spaces, WPA: Writing Program Administration, Writing & Pedagogy,* and *Journal of*

Literacy and Technology. He is co-editor with James P. Purdy of *The New Digital Scholar: Exploring and Enriching the Research and Writing Practices of NextGen Students*.

Index

Note: Page numbers in *italics* indicate figures and tables.

A

AASL. *See* American Association of School Librarians
academic argument, conflating with civic argument, 191, *192*
academic writing, public writing compared to, 264
accessibility of technology, 305–307
accessing information stage of information literacy cycle, 80–84, *81*
ACRL. *See* Association of College and Research Libraries
ACT, writing assessment for, 41
action research projects
    caveats, 429–432
    CCSS and, 420–421, *422,* 436–439
    design, 421–427, *437*
    developing reflective draft of findings, 425–426, 437–439
    outcomes, 427–429
    publishing findings, 426–427
    researching problems, 422–424
    testing three strategies, 424–425, *437*
ACT-style prompts, 51–52
"Adaptive Testing Evolves to Assess Common-Core Skills" (Davis), 316–317
Adobe Captivate, 97
advertisements, reading, 211–212
American Association of School Librarians (AASL). *See also* information literacy
    history of standards of, 73–74
    Standards for the 21st Century Learner, 71
    teaching and assessment of standards of, 99
American Library Association, 298
American Literature case examples
    digital composition, 47–51
    reflections on, 57–59
    standardized writing, 51–57, 66–67
Amusing Ourselves to Death (Postman), 297
anchor standards. *See also* College and Career Readiness Anchor (CCRA) standards
    production and distribution of texts, 116–121
    range of writing, 122–123
    research to build and present knowledge, 121–122
    text types and purposes anchor, 114–116
Anchor Standards for Language, 312–313
Anchor Standards for Reading, *320,* 417
Anchor Standards for Speaking and Listening, *320,* 469, 475, 479, 481, 493
Anchor Standards for Writing
    connection to digital, 24
    digital storytelling and, 479
    digital writing institutes and, 473
    impact and role of digital technologies and, 26
    literature class websites and, 311
    Standard 4, 310
    Standard 6, 309, 354, 362, 426, 446, 458, 473, 478, 493
    Standard 8, 445–446, 481
    Storify-based assignments and, *320*

527

annotated bibliography projects,
    318–320
Applebee, Arthur N., 199, 500
argumentation
    academic, conflating with civic, 191,
        192
    Toulmin model of, 360
Arola, Kristin L., 308–309
Ashby, David, 286
assessment. *See also* formative assessment;
        writing assessment
    automated essay assessment
        technologies, 45–46, 55–57,
        62–63
    collaborative writing in, 40–46, *43*
    digital portfolios as tool for, 126, 127
    large-scale, standards and, 44
    standardized, skills measured by, 63
    summative, 64
Association of College and Research
        Libraries (ACRL). *See also*
        information literacy
    history of standards of, 73–74
    Information Literacy Competency
        Standards for Higher
        Education, 71
    teaching and assessment of standards
        of, 99
Audacity, 120, 216
audience
    for blogs, 267, 272, 274
    Framework and, 377
audience analysis, 118–119, 183–184
automated essay assessment technologies,
    45–46, 55–57, 62–63

B

backward design, 289
Baker, W. Douglas, 431
balancing norms of Internet with
        school policies and expectations,
        504–505
Ballenger, Bruce, 184
Ballentine, Brian, 236
Barton, David, 357, 504
Barton, Matt, 287–288
Baru, Chaitanya, 26

Beach, Richard, 262, 263
Bean, John, 184
Bear, Rachel, 149–150, 155–156, 159,
        161
Because Digital Writing Matters (National
        Writing Project), 43–44
Bellavance, Sam, 402–403, *403*
Bennett, Sue, 443–444
Bernstein, Kenneth, 501
big idea questions, 289
Blogger, 281
blogging. *See also* blogging curriculum
    in classrooms, 86, 261–263, 279
    in digital writing institutes, 473–474
    overview of, 259–261
    public writing, CCSS, and, 263–264
    by teachers, 38–39
blogging curriculum
    choosing platform, 280–281
    decisions about use, 279–280
    implementing, 278–279
    overview of, 266
    producing, 267–271, *270*
    publishing, 271–274
    secondary-university partnership for,
        264–266
    seeing students as experts, 281
    teacher preparation and, 263
    updating, 274–278, *276*
blogging sites, 59, 281–282
blogrolls, 273
Bohn, Roger E., 26
Boise State University, 150–152
Bonk, Curtis, 458
Boolean searches, 249
Borsheim, Carlin, 262
boundary crossing, 505–506
brainstorming, think-pair-share, 79
browsing
    as distant reading, 238–243, 255–256
    search engine and database results
        pages, 240–250, *241, 243,
        246, 247, 248*
    suggestions for classroom, 251–255
Brzycki, Dolores, 417
Buchanan, Judy, 30, 31
Buckingham, David, 237–238
Bursiek, Paul, 39
BYOD (Bring Your Own Device)
        strategy, 307

C

Camtasia Studio, 97
canonical texts
   analysis of characters in, 214
   CCSS and, 199–200
   film adaptations of, 208–209
Carr, Nicholas, 236
case examples
   automated assessment system and, 55–57
   digital composition, 47–51
   reflections on, 57–59
   standardized writing, 51–57, 66–67
Castells, Manuel, 375
CCRA. *See* College and Career Readiness Anchor (CCRA) standards
CCSS. *See* Common Core State Standards
CCSSO (Council of Chief State School Officers), 112
Center for Research and Writing in Digital Environments, 23
Center for Social Media, "Code of Best Practices in Fair Use for Online Video," 394–395
Childers, Pamela B., 493
citation management tools, 96–97
Citation Project, 232–233
CiteULike, 97
civic argument, conflating with academic argument, 191, *192*
civic literacies, 342–345, 348
Clark, Christina, 25, 26, 27
class blogs, 86, 261–263, 279
classroom extensions of media literacy
   reading, 208–209, 215, 217–218, 221
   writing, 206–207, 210–211, 213–214, 216–217, 219–220, 222–223
classrooms. *See also* classroom extensions of media literacy; high school English classroom context; participatory culture and literacy classrooms
   blogging in, 86, 261–263, 279
   browsing in, 251–255

digital literacy in, 35–40
virtual, peer review in, 134
close reading, 232–233
"Code of Best Practices in Fair Use for Online Video" (Center for Social Media), 394–395
Coleman, David, 498
collaboration. *See also* digital spaces, participation and collaboration in
   on critique of CCSS, 359–362
   in digital writing institutes, 483–484
   as form of collective intelligence, 147–149
   importance of, 492–493
   in response to demands of CCSS, 2
collaborative tools and information literacy, 91–92
collaborative writing
   in assessment, 40–46, *43*
   in digital composition, 49
collective intelligence
   in first-year writing context, 150–152
   in high school English classroom context, 149–150
   overview of, 147–149, *148*
college, links between K–12 and, 501–502
college and career readiness
   concept of discipline and, 376–377
   connecting to, 79–80, 84, 89–90, 94–95, 98–99
   described, 294
   technology and, 304–305
College and Career Readiness Anchor (CCRA) standards
   overview of, 113–114
   production and distribution of texts, 116–121
   range of writing, 122–123
   research to build and present knowledge anchors, 121–122
   text types and purposes, 114–116
college-level writing. *See* Digital Expository Writing Program; first-year writing context; Writing Program Administrators (WPA) Outcomes Statement for First-Year Composition

College of Saint Rose, 385. *See also*
    Digital Expository Writing
    Program
college writing classrooms, students
    entering, 21–22
Colorado State University Writing
    Project (CSUWP), 331–332,
    337–338. *See also* Saving Our
    Stories (SOS) Project
Comic Life, 218–219
Common Core State Standards (CCSS).
    See also College and Career
    Readiness Anchor (CCRA)
    standards; *specific Anchor
    Standards*
  access to by teachers, 359–360
  adoption of, 1, 4–5, 71, 416
  aligning with WPA OS, 176, 178–
    180, *180–182*
  on argumentative writing, 267
  canonical literature and, 199–200
  collaboration in response to demands
    of, 2
  on collaborative writing, 41–42, 44,
    61
  collective intelligence and, *148*
  college and career readiness and,
    79–80, 84, 89–90, 94–95,
    98–99, 100
  connecting with digital, 23–24,
    27–28
  as counterbalance to STEM push,
    6–7
  digital literacy and, 37, 327–328,
    329–331, 354
  digital writing institutes and, 468–
    469, *470*
  introduction to, 293–294
  issues in implementing, 445, 459–
    460
  "Key Design Considerations,"
    383–384
  limitations of, 5, 327–331, 345–346,
    349–350, 354, 360–362,
    375–378, 417
  media literacy and, *203,* 223
  on multimedia projects, 397
  NCTE and, 325–326
  negotiation and, *158*

  networking and, *153*
  overview of, 1
  positive aspects of, 5–6, 24–25,
    416–417
  principles underlying, 498
  Ratliff on experience with, 177–178
  in relation to other standards and
    outcomes documents, 493–
    494
  on research, 231–232
  responses to, 5, 494–495
  on school librarian role, 74
  SOS Project and, 334, *335–336,* 336
  sources for lesson plans, 4
  teaching and learning with, 491–495
  on technology, 444, 487
  technology as skill in, 72
  WPA OS and, 183–186
communication in digital spaces, 37
community college, level of literacy and
    success in, 28–29
community-focused writing, 260–261,
    277–278. *See also* blogging;
    blogging curriculum
community support for technology use,
    455
competition and standardized writing,
    53
composition, digital vs. standard, *43*
computers
  as information "epicenters" for
    students, 23
  student to computer ratio, 306
concept mapping, 77–78, *78*
Confederation of British Industry, 28
*Confronting the Challenges of
    Participatory Culture* (Jenkins),
    143, 144, 354
Conley, David, 445, 448
Connors, Robert, 186–187
constructedness of media messages,
    203–211
contexts for writing, 40–46, *43*
conversational void and standardized
    writing, 54–55
Cook, Leslie, 420
Cope, Bill, 60
Council of Chief State School Officers
    (CCSSO), 112

Council of Writing Program
Administrators (CWPA), 42, 107
Creative Commons licensing, 477–478
creativity, 131, 484–485
Criterion (Educational Testing Service),
46
Critical Elements Framework, 367
critical thinking
close reading and, 232
Framework and, 114–115
in WPA OS and CCSS, 189–190
CSUWP (Colorado State University
Writing Project), 331–332, 337–
338. *See also* Saving Our Stories
(SOS) Project
Cuban, Larry, 500
cultural diversity and CCSS, 329–331,
345, 347–349
curators, researchers as, 396–404
curiosity, 115–116, 128–129
curricular shifts and technology
demands, 303–307, 321
curriculum. *See also* blogging
curriculum; Digital Expository
Writing (DEW) Program; Project
Connect; Saving Our Stories
(SOS) Project
decisions about, documents affecting,
141–143
future discussions of, 404–405
teacher agency in construction of,
355
vision for, 498–499
CWPA (Council of Writing Program
Administrators), 42, 107
cyberbullying, 292

D

Dadonna, Patricia, 6
datacloud, 236
Davis, Michelle, 316–317
DebateGraph, 77
democratic processes and media
messages, 220–223
design-based teaching, 338–341,
347–348
design thinking, 339–340

DeSimone, Laura, 367
determining information needs stage
of information literacy cycle,
75–80, *76*
Dewey, John, 111, 294, 299
DEW Program. *See* Digital Expository
Writing (DEW) Program
digital book jacket project, 449–450
digital composition case examples,
47–51
digital devices and interaction with
information, 27
Digital Expository Writing (DEW)
Program
overview of, 384–387, 404–405
remix video assignment, 387–389
teaching with technology, and issues
of fair use, 389–391
technical proficiency and, 391–393
digital immigrants, 444
digital information, CCSS through lens
of, 23–24, 27–28
digital information literacy, 5–6, 235–
239. *See also* information literacy
Digital Is website, 63, 128, 333, 482
digital literacy
CCSS and, 37, 327–328, 354
in classrooms, 35–40
as "culturally neutral" in CCSS,
329–331
definition of, 22
focus on, as curricular shift, 304–305
overview of, 307–308
teaching, 467–468, 486–487
digitally aided writing assessment,
45–46, 62–63
digital natives, 296, 443
digital portfolios
as assessment tool, 126, 127
habits of mind reflected in, 127–136
self-evaluation and, 125–126
uses of, 125
digital portfolio tools, 92–94, *94*
digital research, 229–235
digital spaces, participation and
collaboration in
collective intelligence, 147–152, *148*
Google Presentations lesson, 165,
166

digital spaces (*cont.*)
   How Do Stories Matter? lesson, 163–165
   multimodal essay assignment, 166–168
   negotiation, 157–161, *158*
   networking, 152–157
   overview of, 141–144
   participatory culture and literacy classrooms, 144–146, 161–162
   rhetorical problem-solving assignment, 168–173, *173*
digital storytelling, 479–482
digital technology
   CCSS and, 345–346
   Framework and, 119–120
   as integral, 491–492
   librarian engagement with, 38
   research and, 29–30
   teacher engagement with, 38–39
   Writers' Studio and, 120–121
   writing behavior and, 30–31
digital writing. *See also* digital writing institutes
   engaging students in, 502–504
   open-source tools, 368–369
   reframing, 362–363
"Digital Writing" (Sibberson), 2–3
digital writing institutes
   aligning with CCSS and Framework, 468–469, *470*
   blogs, 473–474
   digital storytelling, 479–482
   Five Frame Story activity, 477–479
   overview of, 487–488
   planning, 484–487
   podcasts, 474–476
   professional pieces, 482–483
   RSS feeds, 476–477
   small groups in, 483–484
   topics of, *471*
   writing prior to, 469–473, *472*
Digital Writing Workshop, The (Hicks), 468, 477
Digital Youth Network, 507
Diigo, 97
directions, skeleton, tension over, 485–486
disciplines, 376–377
discourse communities, 377
distant reading
   browsing as, 238–243, 255–256
   clouds, links, tags, and, 250–251
   digital information literacy and, 235–239
   overview of, 232–235
   of search engine and database results pages, 243–250, *246*, *247*, *248*
Dobrin, Sidney, 238
doctoral students, research attitudes and habits of, 229–230
Doering, Aaron, 263
Dreamer, The (Ryan), 332
Drew, Sally Valentino, 416–417
Dropbox, 86
Dudt, Kurt, 417
Dyson, Anne Haas, 504

E

ebooks, 27
economic issues and technology accessibility, 305–307
Economics of Attention, The (Lanham), 236
editorials, newspaper, 220
Educational Testing Service, 45–46, 370
EduCorps, 363, 370
Ehman, Lee, 458
Eisenberg, Michael, 318, 399
ejournals, 230
ELA. *See* English Language Arts
Elbow, Peter, 473
Eli Review, 509–510
ELLs. *See* English Language Learners
employers, dissatisfaction with skills of graduates, 28
engagement. *See also* professional development and engagement model
   civic, 342–345
   with digital technology, 38–39
   fostering, 122–123
   as habit of mind, 130–131
   social networking as medium of, 287–288

in substantive digital writing, 502–504
English Language Arts (ELA). *See also* high school English classroom context
　Anchor Standards in, 24
　civics and, 342–345
　class websites, creating, 310–312, *311*
　close reading and, 232
　curricular shifts and technology demands in, 303–307, 321
　historical tensions within, 199–201
　types of texts for, 197
English Language Learners (ELLs)
　CCSS and, 331
　Saving Our Stories Project for, 331–334, *335–336*, 336, 338–347
EPUB format, 222
E-Rater technology (Educational Testing Service), 46
essential questions (EQs), 289, 295
Estrem, Heidi, 150–151, 156, 159–160
ethically considering information access and use stage of information literacy cycle, *95*, 95–99
ethics challenge and media literacy, 144
Eubanks, Philip, 114
evaluating information stage of information literacy cycle, *85*, 85–90
everyday life research, 318–319
Ewing, Jessica, 151–152, 156–157
expertise of students, and blogging, 281

F

Facebook
　CCSS and, 293–297
　context for using, 285–290
　historical figure project, 450–451
　implications for future practice, 297–299
　PowerPoint template for, 286–287, *287*
　results of project using, 290–293, *291*, *293*

fair use
　defined, 223n.1
　Five Frame Story activity and, 478
　nonprint texts and, 393–396
　teaching with technology and, 389–391
Faith in the Five Boroughs website, 400–402, *401*
Ferguson, Kirby, 387
first draft thinking and writing, 486–487
"first mindset" literacies, 327–328
first-year writing context. *See also* Digital Expository Writing Program
　collective intelligence in, 150–152
　Google Presentations lesson, 165, *166*
　negotiation in, 159–161
　networking in, 156–157
　rhetorical problem-solving assignment, 168–173, *173*
Five Frame Story activity, 477–479
five-paragraph essays, 360
flexibility, 134–135
flexible writing processes, 42–43, *43*
Florida Virtual School program, 3
formative assessment
　citation management, 96–97
　concept mapping, 77–78, *78*
　digital portfolios, 93–94
　future of, 60
　information pathfinders, 82–83, *83*
　online quizzes, 84
　online tutorials, 97–98
　research process journals, 87
　resource and website evaluation skills, 89
　social and collaborative tools, 92
　think-pair-share brainstorming, 79
Formby, Susie, 25, 26, 27
Fox, Tom, 363
Framework for Success in Postsecondary Writing. *See also* habits of mind
　audience and, 377
　benefits of, 363
　collective intelligence and, *148*
　development of, 107–108
　digital writing and, 63
　digital writing institutes and, 468–469, *470*

Framework for Success in Postsecondary Writing (*cont.*)
    implementation of CCSS and, 111–113
    large-scale assessments and, 44
    as lens for understanding and integrating CCSS, 109–111
    negotiation and, *158*
    networking and, *153*
    overview of, 6, 142
    using to engage with CCSS to foster habits of mind, 113–123
    in Writers' Studio, 123–127
    on writing practices, 42–43
Frankenstein (Shelley), 329–330
Franklin, Keri, 467
free browses, 252–253
freewriting, 473
Freire, Paulo, 345
Friedrich, Linda, 30, 31
Fulwiler, Megan, 385

G

Gallagher, Chris, 416
Gallas, Karen, 218
Garage Band (Apple), 216
Garcia, Antero, 329
Gay, Geneva, 328–329
Gehsmann, Kristin, 416
Generation-D, 441, 443–444
genre
    disconnect between reading and writing in, 191–193
    organization of digital portfolios by, 127–128
    in WPA OS and CCSS, 186–189
Gettysburg Address (Lincoln), 217–218
Gibson, Kathy, 467, 477
Gillis, Gregg, 387
Gioia, Dennis, 122
Glass, Ira, 480
Global Information Industry Center, 23, 26
Global Kids, 507
glogs, 206
Goodman, Yetta, 137
Google. *See also* Google Docs
    apps, 151
    as information source, 230
    search engine, 240–245, *241, 243,* 399
    search results page, 243–245
    Wikipedia and, 254
Google Apps for Education, 452, 453–454
Google Books, 237
Google Docs
    editing on screen, 39
    negotiation skills and, 160
    for project-based learning, 454
    research process journals and, 86
    shared file interface, 92
Google Drive, 59
Google Forms, 83
Google Knowledge Graph, 242
Google Reader, 476–477
Google Sites, 93, *93,* 120, 124
Google Summits, 452–455
Grabill, Jeff, 509–510
Graduation Project in Pitt County, NC, 356–357, 364, 365, 366, 375–376
Graphs, Maps, Trees (Moretti), 234

H

habits of mind
    creativity, 131, 484–485
    curiosity, 128–129
    Dewey and, 294, 299
    in digital portfolios, 127–128
    engagement, 130–131
    in Facebook project, 292–293
    flexibility, 134–135
    fostering, 113
    Framework and, 108–109, 358
    metacognition, 135–136, 487
    openness, 129–130
    persistence, 131–133
    responsibility, 133–134
    universality of, 111
    in Writers' Studio, 124–125
Hain, Bonnie, 6
Haller, Cynthia, 431
Hamilton, Mary, 357, 504
Hamlet (Shakespeare), 208

Hargittai, Eszter, 237
Hargrove, Tracy, 419
hashtagging, 209–211
Hawkes, Lory, 393
Hayles, N. Katherine, 232, 233–234
Head, Alison, 318, 399
Heath, Shirley Brice, 504
Herrington, Anne, 44–45
Hicks, Troy, 45, 468, 477, 492, 508–509
high school English classroom context. *See also* English Language Arts
 collective intelligence in, 149–150
 How Do Stories Matter? lesson, 163–165
 multimedia projects in, 396–398
 multimodal essay assignment, 166–168
 negotiation in, 158–159
 networking in, 155–156
historical speeches, reading, 211–212, 217
Hobbs, Renee, 508
Hodgson, Kevin, 44–45
Holding On to Good Ideas in a Time of Bad Ones (Newkirk), 506
Homan, Elizabeth, 36
Howard, Rebecca Moore, 232–233
How We Think (Dewey), 111
Hunt, Bud, 500
hyperlinks, 250, 317
hyperreading, 233, 234

I

iBook Author, 222
I Have a Dream speech (King), 211
iMovie, 120, 390, 392
information
 quality of, 29–30
 quantity of, 236, 297
information literacy. *See also* digital information literacy
 accessing information stage of, 80–84, *81*
 defined, 298
 determining information needs stage of, 75–80, *76*
 digital tools for stages of, *100–101*
 ethically considered access and use stage, *95*, 95–99
 evaluating information stage of, *85*, 85–90
 importance of, 298–299
 stages of, 74–75, *75*
 using information stage of, 90–95, *91*
information load, management of, 26–27
information pathfinders, 81–83, *83*
Inoue, Asao, 110
Inspiration software, 77
intellectual conversations and digital composition, 50
Intelligent Essay Assessor (Pearson Education), 46
interactivity in digital composition, 48–49
International Reading Association (IRA)/NCTE standards, 330
internet. *See also* web; websites
 balancing norms of with school policies and expectations, 504–505
 "cell-mostly" users of, 27
 Youth Internet Safety Survey, 292
invention work, 118
iPhoto, 334
isolation in standardized writing, 52

J

Jamieson, Sandra, 232–233
J.C. Penney website, 256n.2
Jenkins, Henry, 143, 144, *148, 153, 158,* 346, 354. *See also* digital spaces, participation and collaboration in
J. H. Rose High School (JHR), 355–356, 358, 359, 378. *See also* Project Connect
Jing, 97
Johnson, June, 184
Johnson, Kristine, 188–189
Johnson, Tara, 420
Johnson-Eilola, Johndan, 236, 399, 400
Jones, Allison, 417

Julius Caesar (Shakespeare), 207
justice-oriented model of civic education, 342–343

K

Kabodian, Aram, 128
Kahne, Joseph, 342
Kajder, Sara, 37, 500
Kay, Ken, 5, 495
Kervin, Lisa, 444
Kidblog, 510
King, Jacqueline, 417
King, Martin Luther, Jr., 211
Knobel, Michele, 327, 365, 499
knowledge production, process of, 154

L

Lanham, Richard, 236
Lankshear, Colin, 327, 365, 499
large-scale assessments, standards and, 44
Learnist, 79
Lenhart, Amanda, 442
Lenz, Bob, 5, 495
Lessig, Lawrence, 388–389
Levy, Pierre, 147
librarians. *See also* media specialists
 CCSS and, 110
 engagement with digital technologies, 38
 evaluation of online information and, 221
 media literacy and, 213
 role of, 184, 193
library standards. *See also* information literacy
 history of, 73–74
 overview of, 71–72
Light, Richard, 129
linear texts, 44–46
literacy. *See also* digital literacy; information literacy; media literacy
 changing thinking on, 499–501
 civic, 342–345, 348

"first mindset," 327–328
integrated model of, 6, 7
level of, and success in community college, 28–29
out-of-school, 200
"second mindset," 327–328
as tool for success and empowerment, 357–358
in workplace, student views of, 25
literacy narratives, 218–219
Livefyre, 321n.1. *See also* Storify
Louisiana
 CCSS in, 175, 177
 PARCC in, 177–178, 194n.1
Lunsford, Andrea, 298

M

MacArthur Foundation Connected Learning Principles, 358, 363–364
Macedo, Donaldo, 345
machine reading, 233–234
Mancabelli, Rob, 316
map project, online, 156–157
Maranto, Gina, 287–288
Marlow, Jennifer, 385, 399
massive online open courses (MOOCs), 99
Maton, Karl, 444
McClure, Randall, 254, 288, 497
McComiskey, Bruce, 112
McDermott, Mona, 499
McTighe, Jay, 289, 338–339
meaning construction, 217–220, 395
media literacy (ML)
 aligning with CCSS, *203,* 223
 all messages as constructed principle of, 203–207
 approaches to, 202–203
 competencies for, 146
 construction of meaning from messages principle of, 217–220
 core concepts of, 201
 each medium as unique principle of, 207–211
 ecological approach to, 145

historical tensions within ELA and, 199–201
incorporation into CCSS, 451–452
"laissez faire approach" to, 144
messages as containing values and points of view principle of, 214–217
messages as produced for purpose principle of, 211–214
next digital scholar (NDS) approach to media literacy principle of, 220–223
overview of, 198–199
media specialists. *See also* librarians
Project Connect and, 369, 371
role of, 206–207, 209, 219
Meier, Deborah, 292, 499
Merritt, Kelly, 262
metacognition, 116–118, 121, 135–136, 487
metalanguage, 238
Michigan State University, Red Cedar Writing Project, 36–37
Microsoft Access databases, 83
Microsoft Office 365, 86
Middaugh, Ellen, 342
Middleton, Holly, 431
Middleton, Kim, 385
Mindomo, 77
ML. *See* media literacy
mobile connectivity, teens as leading edge of, 27–28
modes of discourse, 186–187, 188–189
Moffett, James, 125
Monroe, Barbara, 371
MOOCs (massive online open courses), 99
Moodle, 83, 84
moral panic facing technology, 444
Moran, Charles, 44–45
Moretti, Franco, 234–235
Mueller, Derek, 235
multigenre writing, 221–223
multiliteracies approach, 261–262
multimedia projects, 396–398, 402–403
multimodality
assignment example, 166–168
in digital composition, 49–50
in digital storytelling, 479–482
in high school English classroom context, 155–156
NDS approach to writing and, 205–206
technologies for, 59–60
Murphy, Christina, 393
Murrow, Edward R., 216
music videos, analysis of, 214–215
MY Access! (Vantage Learning), 45–46

N

National Association for Media Literacy, 201
National Center for Education Statistics, 305
National Center on Education and the Economy report, 25, 28–29
National Council of Teachers of English (NCTE), 107, 175–176, 197, 325–327, 330
National Governors Association (NGA), 112
National Literacy Trust (U.K.), 25
National Writing Project (NWP). *See also* Digital Is website
Because Digital Writing Matters, 43–44
digital writing and, 63, 362
Framework and, 107
models of, 367, 370
partnership method of, 374
philosophy of, 368, 457
Summer Institute, 456
natural language processing techniques, 55
NCTE (National Council of Teachers of English), 107, 175–176, 197, 325–327, 330
NDS approach. *See* next digital scholar (NDS) approach to media literacy
negotiation of diverse contexts and situations
in first-year writing context, 159–161
in high school English classroom context, 158–159
overview of, 157–158, *158*

networking
    in first-year writing context, 156–157
    in high school English classroom context, 155–156
    overview of, 152, *153,* 154–155
New Digital Scholar, The (McClure and Purdy), 21–22, 23, 30
Newkirk, Thomas, 506
New London Group, 499
next digital scholar (NDS) approach to media literacy
    all messages as constructed principle, 203–207
    construction of meaning from messages principle, 217–220
    each medium as unique principle, 207–211
    influence of media and messages principle, 220–223
    messages as containing values and points of view, 214–217
    messages as produced for purpose principle, 211–214
    overview of, 202–203
NextGen students, 22
NGA (National Governors Association), 112
Nickoson, Lee, 374
nonprint texts. *See also* Digital Expository Writing Program
    access to new forms of, 384
    criteria for evaluation of, 400–402
    fair use practices with, 393–396
    professional examples of, 402–403
    remix video, 387–391
North Carolina. *See* Project Connect
NWP. *See* National Writing Project

O

Oakland University, Plagiarism Tutorial, 97–98, *98*
O'Brien, David, 262, 263
O'Donnell-Allen, Cindy, 332–334, 336, 337, 341
Of Mice and Men (Steinbeck), 214
O'Hanlon, Leslie Harris, 304–305
O'Neill, Peggy, 109

online distant reading skills
    clouds, links, and tags, 250–251
    defined, 232
    search engine and database results pages, 243–250, *246, 247, 248*
online map project, 156–157
online quizzes, 83–84
online tutorials, 97–98, *98*
openness, as habit of mind, 117–118, 129–130
Opposing Viewpoints in Context, 239, 241, 245–250, *246, 247, 248*
outcomes. *See also* Writing Program Administrators (WPA) Outcomes Statement for First-Year Composition
    of action research projects, 427–429
    standards compared to, 179
outcomes assessment movements, 415–416, 432
outreach, 507

P

Padlet, 79
Paper Graders, The (blog), 39
Paper Rater, 55–57
PARCC. *See* Partnership for Assessment of Readiness for College and Careers
participation gap and media literacy, 144
participatory culture. *See also* participatory culture and literacy classrooms
    Connected Learning Principles and, 358
    defined, 346, 354
    joining, 509–510
participatory culture and literacy classrooms
    collective intelligence, 147–152
    Google Presentations lesson, 165, *166*
    How Do Stories Matter? lesson, 163–165
    multimodal essay assignment, 166–168
    negotiation, 157–161

networking, 152–157
overview of, 143, 144–146, 161–162
rhetorical problem-solving assignment, 168–173, *173*
Partnership for Assessment of Readiness for College and Careers (PARCC)
  Automated Scoring Technical Working Group, 46
  CCSS and, 6
  digital texts and, 61
  governing states, 194n.1
  in Louisiana, 177–178
  writing assessment and, 40, 41
partnership method of NWP, 374
partnerships
  building capacity through, 336–338, 341–342, 348
  Project Connect and, 355–356, 358, 359, 377–379
pathfinders, 81–83, *83*
PBL. *See* project-based learning
Pearson Education, 45, 46, 370
pedagogy, matching with technological practice, 457–458
peer review in virtual classrooms, 134
persistence
  fostering, 118, 120, 122–123
  as habit of mind, 131–133
persuasive writing, 215–217
Pew Internet & American Life Project reports
  How Teens Do Research in the Digital World, 29
  on search engines, 399
  Teens and Technology 2013, 27
Pinterest, 79
podcasts, 215–217, 474–476
political advertisements, reading, 211–212
positive peer effects, 295
Postman, Neil, 297
power and discourse, issues of, 189–190
pre-determined texts and topics in standardized writing, 55–57
Prensky, Marc, 296, 443
pre-service teachers. *See also* project-based learning; writing methods course

preparation programs for, 417–418
service-learning projects for, 336–338
Prezi, 77, 78, *78*
Principles. *See* MacArthur Foundation Connected Learning Principles
print-centric, Anchor Standards as, 24
producing, in blogging curriculum, 267–271, *270*
production and distribution of texts anchor standards, 116–121
professional development. *See* digital writing institutes; project-based learning
professional development and engagement model, 367–372, 373, 378–379
project-based learning (PBL)
  checklist for, 464–465
  in-service, 452–455
  intensive, long-term, 455–459
  as model for classroom activities, 459–460
  need for, 445–446
  overview of, 442–443, 462–463
  pre-service, 446–452, *448*
  rubric for, *465*
  types of, *464*
Project Connect
  building, 365–367
  impact of, 372–373
  partnerships and, 355–356, 358, 359, 377–379
  professional development and engagement model for, 367–372, 373, 378–379
  professionalizing teachers around standards, 359–362
  reframing standards, 362–365, 375–378
Project Information Literacy Research Report, 90
Project New Media Literacies, 362
public rhetoric, 376–377
public service announcement videos, 212–214
public writing. *See also* blogging; blogging curriculum
  as actionable, 267–268
  benefits of, 308

public writing (*cont.*)
  CCSS and, 263–264
  defined, 260
  secondary-university partnership for, 264–266
"Publishers' Criteria," 3
publishing
  in action research project, 426–427, 431–432
  in blogging curriculum, 271–274
Purcell, Kristen, 29, 30, 31
Purdy, James P., 249, 298, 399, 497
purpose-driven navigation and digital composition, 50–51
purposes of media messages, 211–214

Q

quizzes, online, 83–84

R

Railsback, Jennifer, 442
Raising Arizona (film), 204
Ramage, John, 184
range of writing anchor standards, 122–123
Rankins-Robertson, Sherry, 108
Ratliff, Clancy, 111
Ravitch, Diane, 499
Ray, Katie Wood, 126
reader response, role of, 185
reading. *See also* distant reading
  on cell phones, 27
  close reading, 232–233
  connecting with writing, 431
  genre, disconnect between reading and writing in, 191–193
  hyperreading, 233, 234
  long or complicated texts, 31
  machine reading, 233–234
  media literacy and, 203–205, 207–208, 211–212, 214–215, 217, 220–221
Red Cedar Writing Project, 36–37
"Red Wheelbarrow, The" (Williams), 206
Reed, Dawn, 36, 63, 262

reflective thinking, 136
reframing CCSS, 362–365
RefWorks, 96–97
Reid, Alex, 262–263
Reid, Louann, 326
Reilly, Erin, 445
remix video assignment
  Events Library, 408
  fair use and, 393–396
  Projects Library, 408–409
  rationale for inclusion in writing classroom, 387–389, *394*
  teaching with technology, fair use, and, 389–391
  technical proficiency and, 391–393
  texts and transitions, 409
  transition slides, *394*
research. *See also* action research projects; sources for research
  analysis of search engines and results, 410–411
  attitudes and habits of, 229–230
  to build and present knowledge anchor standards, 121–122
  community-focused writing and, 277–278
  cultivating digital information literacy and, 235–239
  as curation, 396–404
  distant and close reading and, 231–235
  as inquiry, 184–185
  as narrative, 315–317
  navigating information through, 152, 154–157
  nonlinear nature of, 272
  prompts for group work, 409–410
  search engine and database results pages and, 243–250, *246, 247, 248*
  Storify and, 314–320
  suggestions for classroom, 251–255
  teacher-research, 374, 426, 505–506
  "usefulness" in, 253–254
research papers, 221–222
research process journals, 86–87, *88*
research simulation task in PARCC assessment, 41
research-writing problem, responses to, 30–32

resource evaluation skills, 87–89
resourceful student, defined, 152
resources, 508–510
respect in digital platforms, 158–159
responsibility, as habit of mind, 122, 133–134
revision in digital composition, 49
rhetorical digital education. *See* digital spaces, participation and collaboration in
rhetorical knowledge, 116–117
Richardson, Will, 262
Rogerian rhetoric, 137n.1
Romano, Tom, 221–222
Romeo and Juliet (Shakespeare)
    Facebook project about, 288, 290–293, *291, 293*
    traditional support for understanding of, 209–210
"Root, The" (video), 402–403, *403*
RSS feeds, 476–477
Rush, Leslie, 113
Ruth, Deborah Dashow, 201–202
Ryan, Pam Munoz, 332

S

Saltman, David, 448–449
SAT, writing assessment for, 41
Sauer, Laura, 38, 39, 59, 63
Saving Our Stories (SOS) Project
    as framework for addressing needs of ELLs, 338–347, 349
    overview of, 326, 331–334, *335–336*, 336
    questions for, 347–349
    service-learning project and, 336–338
SBAC (Smarter Balanced Assessment Consortium), 40, 41, 46, 61
Scherff, Lisa, 113
school librarians. *See* librarians
school library standards. *See* library standards
"Schools Must Help Educators Transform 'PD' into Personal Discovery" (Mancabelli), 316
Schramm, Richard R., 3
Screencastle, 97

Screencast-o-matic, 97
Screenr, 97
search engines
    analysis of results from, 410–411
    construction of, 237, 253
    exercises on, 399–400
    J.C. Penney, 256n.2
    results pages of, 240–250, *241, 243, 246, 247, 248*
"second mindset" literacies, 327–328
Sela, Orly, 433
Selber, Stuart, 369
self-evaluation and digital portfolios, 125–126
Self-Paced Online Tutorial (SPOT), 110–111
sentence-level writing issues, 185–186
service-learning projects for pre-service teachers, 336–338, 341
Setup, The, 470–473
Severino, Carol, 113
Shepherd, Dawn, 150–151, 156, 159–160
Short, James E., 26
Short, Kathy, 137
Sibberson, Franki, "Digital Writing," 2–3
SIIT (Summer Institute for Instructional Technology), 455–459
Silva, Mary Lourdes, 252
Silver, Nate, 297
skills and experiences in Framework, 142
Smagorinsky, Peter, 420
Smarter Balanced Assessment Consortium (SBAC), 40, 41, 46, 61
Smith, Kari, 433
social bookmarking tools, 476
social learning, 375–376
social networking, as medium of engagement, 287–288. *See also* Facebook
social tools and information literacy, 91–92
SOS Project. *See* Saving Our Stories (SOS) Project
sources for lesson plans for CCSS, 4
sources for research
    credibility of, 237–238
    relevancy of, 249, 250

sources for research (*cont.*)
  suggestions for, 251–255
  triangulating, 398
SPOT (Self-Paced Online Tutorial), 110–111
Spring, Joel, 498–499
Spruz, 47
Stager, Gary, 307, 501
Standard English, transformative definitions of, 345–347, 349
standardized assessment, skills measured by, 63
standardized writing case example, 51–57, 66–67
standards. *See also* Common Core State Standards
  AASL, 71, 73–74, 99
  IRA/NCTE, 330
  landscape of documents, 493–494
  large-scale assessments and, 44
  linking theories and methods with, 420
  outcomes compared to, 179
Stanford University
  Institute of Design, 339–340
  Literary Lab, 235, 237
STEM push, 6–7
Storify, 303, 314–320, *317*
Stott, Jay, 39
Student-Centered Language Arts and Reading, K-13 (Moffett and Wagner), 125
students
  computer as information "epicenter" for, 23
  doctoral, research attitudes and habits of, 229–230
  entering college writing classrooms, 21–22
  as experts in blogging, 281
  resourceful, defined, 152
  views of workplace literacy, 25
  views of writing, 25–26
student to computer ratio, 306
summative assessment, 64
Summer Institute for Instructional Technology (SIIT), 455–459
Survey Monkey, 83
synergy, 377–378
synthesis, process of, 154

T

tags, 250
Tar River Writing Project (TRWP), 355–356, 358, 359, 378. *See also* Project Connect
teacher blogs, use of in classrooms, 279
teacher preparation programs. *See also* project-based learning; writing methods course
  characteristics of effective, 427
  for pre-service writing teachers, 417–418
teacher-research, 374, 426, 505–506
teachers
  access to CCSS by, 359–360
  blogging curriculum and, 263
  conflicting imperatives of, 356–357, 416
  engagement with digital technologies, 38–39
  pre-service, service-learning projects for, 336–338, 341
  technological proficiency of, 442
teaching
  AASL and ACRL standards, 99
  with CCSS, 491–495
  design-based, 338–341, 347–348
  digital literacy, 467–468, 486–487
  with technology, and issues of fair use, 389–391
  of writing, and outcomes assessment movements, 415–416
Teaching with Technology workshop, 337, 340, 341
Tech Goes Home, 507
technology. *See also* digital technology
  accessibility of, 305–307
  automated essay assessments, 45–46, 55–57, 62–63
  CCSS on, 444, 487
  college and career readiness and, 304–305
  as concept, 238
  curricular shifts and demands of, 303–304, 321
  integration of, 488
  for multimodality, 59–60
  of power, writing as, 189–190
  proficiency with, 26, 391–393, 441–442, 443–444

Index   543

as skill in CCSS, 72
Storify, 314–320, *317*
teaching with, and fair use, 389–391
use of, 508
Web 2.0, 259–260, 288, 296
Weebly, 93, 303, 308–314, *314*
Writers' Studio and, 120–121
Templeton, Shane, 416
testing movement, companies capitalizing on, 45
Text2MindMap, 77
texts. *See also* nonprint texts
concept of within ELA, 200–201
production and distribution of, 116–121
types and purposes of, 114–116
THINK mnemonic, 271
think-pair-share brainstorming, 79
This I Believe essays, 47, 216–217
time constraints and standardized writing, 52–53
"To an Athlete Dying Young" (Housman), 203–204
To Kill a Mockingbird, character analyses for, 286
Toulmin model of argumentation, 360
"train the trainer" model, 373
transition slides, *394*
transparency problem and media literacy, 144
Trimbur, John, 357
TRWP. *See* Tar River Writing Project
Turner, Kristen, 500
tutorials, online, 97–98, *98*
Twitter as NDS approach, 209–211

U

Understanding by Design (Wiggins and McTighe), 289, 338–339
unimodality and standardized writing, 54
University of California, Irvine, Digital Media and Learning Research Hub, 364
updating, in blogging curriculum, 274–278, *276*
using information stage of information literacy cycle, 90–95, *91*

V

Valenza, Joyce, 508
Vantage Learning, MY Access! program, 45–46
video. *See* remix video assignment
virtual learning commons, 99
visions of CCSS, 498–499
voice and podcasts, 216–217
VoiceThread, 87, 92
Vojak, Colleen, 59

W

Wagner, Betty Jane, 125
Walcott, Dennis M., 3
Wardle, Elizabeth, 191–192
web. *See also* browsing; Internet
as primary information interface for students, 23
safety on, policies for, 36
sources, credibility of, 220–221, 237–238
Web 2.0 technologies, 259–260, 288, 296. *See also* blogging
websites. *See also specific websites*
design projects, 307–310
evaluation skills for, 87–89
for literature classes, 310–312, *311*
moving from class project to independent website, 312–314
Webspiration, 77
Weebly, 93, 303, 308–314, *314*
Weiler, Greg, 261
Wesch, Michael, 441–442
West, Kathleen C., 262
Westheimer, Joel, 342
White, Edward, 108
Wiggins, Grant, 289, 338–339
Wikipedia, 147, 240, 254
wikis, 91–92, 149–150, 155, 217–218
Wix, 93
WMC. *See* writing methods course
Woodard, Diann, 499
WordPress, 93, 281
workplace, literacy in, student views of, 25
Writer's Notebook blog, 473–474

Writers' Studio, Arizona State University
  audience analysis and, 118–119
  curiosity, developing in, 115–116
  curriculum in, 110
  described, 109
  digital portfolios, habits of mind, and, 127–136
  engagement in writing process and, 118
  Framework in, 123–127
  research experiences in, 121–122
  rhetorical knowledge and, 117
  technology and, 120–121
writing. *See also* blogging; digital writing; digital writing institutes; first-year writing context; Framework for Success in Postsecondary Writing; National Writing Project; public writing; Tar River Writing Project; writing assessment; writing methods course
  about process of writing, 487
  across curriculum, 6
  argumentative, 267
  collaborative, 41–42, 61, rr
  community-focused, 260–261, 277–278
  connecting with reading, 431
  contexts for, 40–46, *43*
  digital technologies and, 30–31
  first draft thinking and, 486–487
  foundational understandings of, 59
  freewriting, 473
  future of, 404–405
  media literacy and, 205–206, 209–210, 212–213, 215–216, 218–219, 221–222
  multigenre, 221–223
  persuasive, 215–217
  remix video assignment and, 387–389
  sentence-level writing issues, 185–186
  standardized, 51–57, 66–67
  student views of, 25–26
  teaching, and outcomes assessment movements, 415–416
  as technological and situated, 5–6
  as technology of power, 189–190
writing assessment
  competitive and collaborative in, 40–46, *43*
  concerns about, 62–64
  promise of, 61–62
  reflections on, 59–64
writing center consultants, 393
writing centers, 137n.3
writing curriculum, building, 113, 114
writing methods course (WMC)
  assignment used within, 418–420
  caveats, 429–432
  outcomes, 427–429
  overview of, 418
  project design, 421–427
  using action research to meet CCSS, 420–421, *422,* 436–439
Writing Program Administrators (WPA) Outcomes Statement for First-Year Composition
  adoption of, 178
  aligning with CCSS, 176, 178–180, *180–182*
  audience and, 377
  college-level writing and, 190–194
  critical thinking in, 189–190
  development of, 111
  Framework and, 107–108
  genre in, 186–189
  similarities between CCSS and, 183–186
  in Writers' Studio, 123–124
Wysocki, Anne Frances, 308

Y

Yagelski, Robert, 112
Yamagata-Lynch, Lisa, 458
Yancey, Kathleen Blake, 127, 308, 358
Year of Reading, A (blog), 2
Young, Carl, 500
Youth Internet Safety Survey, 292
Youth Voices, 510

Z

Zerwin, Sarah, 38, 39, 63